THE WORLD OF 1  ΛRSH

∀ ∀ ∀

THE WORLD OF THE SALT MARSH

Appreciating and Protecting the

Tidal Marshes of the

Southeastern Atlantic Coast

CHARLES SEABROOK

THE UNIVERSITY OF GEORGIA PRESS

ATHENS AND LONDON

A Wormsloe
FOUNDATION
nature book

Paperback edition, 2013
© 2012 by the University of Georgia Press
Athens, Georgia 30602
www.ugapress.org
All rights reserved
Designed by April Leidig
Set in Arno Pro by Graphic Composition, Inc., Bogart, Georgia

Most University of Georgia Press titles
are available from popular e-book vendors.

Printed digitally

The Library of Congress has cataloged the hardcover
edition of this book as follows:
Seabrook, Charles.
The world of the salt marsh : appreciating and protecting the tidal marshes
of the southeastern Atlantic coast / Charles Seabrook.
367 p. ill., maps ; 24 cm. — (A Wormsloe foundation nature book)
Includes bibliographical references and index.
ISBN-13: 978-0-8203-2706-8 (hardcover : alk. paper)
ISBN-10: 0-8203-2706-9 (hardcover : alk. paper)
1. Salt marshes—Atlantic Coast (U.S.) 2. Salt marshes—Southern States.
3. Salt marsh conservation—Atlantic Coast (U.S.) 4. Salt marsh conservation—
Southern States. 5. Salt marsh ecology—Atlantic Coast (U.S.)
6. Salt marsh ecology—Southern States. 7. Salt marsh restoration—Atlantic Coast (U.S.)
8. Salt marsh restoration—Southern States. I. Title.
QH76.5.A85S43 2012
577.60975—dc23
2011038256

Paperback ISBN-13: 978-0-8203-4533-8

British Library Cataloging-in-Publication Data available

To my brothers, Jim, Carl, and Wilson

In respectful memory of
Eugene Odum
Edgar "Sonny" Timmons Sr.
Peter Verity
Richard Wiegert
Sam Hamilton
Ogden Doremus
Charles Wharton
Vernon "Jim" Henry
Jimmy Chandler
Nick Williams
Reid Harris

CONTENTS

ACKNOWLEDGMENTS

EVERY PERSON WHOSE NAME appears on these pages deserves my considerable thanks for their guidance and kind advice during the research for this book. To name everyone who graciously helped me, though, would require the equivalent of another chapter. I am grateful to them all. I must, however, express my special gratitude to some very helpful individuals: Ron Kneib, Merryl Alber, and Lawrence Pomeroy at the University of Georgia; Fred Holland at the Hollings Marine Laboratory in Charleston; Charlie Phillips, fishmonger and airboat pilot supreme; library director John Cruickshank and public information director Mike Sullivan at the Skidaway Institute of Oceanography; James Holland of the Altamaha Riverkeeper; Larry and Tina Toomer, co-owners of the Bluffton Oyster Company; and my fellow board members of the Center for a Sustainable Coast—Dave Kyler, Charlie Belin, Steve Willis, Peter Krull, Mindy Egan, Les Davenport, and Ellen Schoolar.

Many thanks to Christa Frangiamore, Judy Purdy, and Laura Sutton, who as editors at the University of Georgia Press encouraged me to pursue the book when it seemed a daunting task. Thanks to Mindy Conner for her skilled editing. And thanks to the entire UGA Press staff for their talent and professional ability.

Finally, thanks to my wife, Laura. Without her, I would be an aimless wanderer.

THE WORLD OF THE SALT MARSH

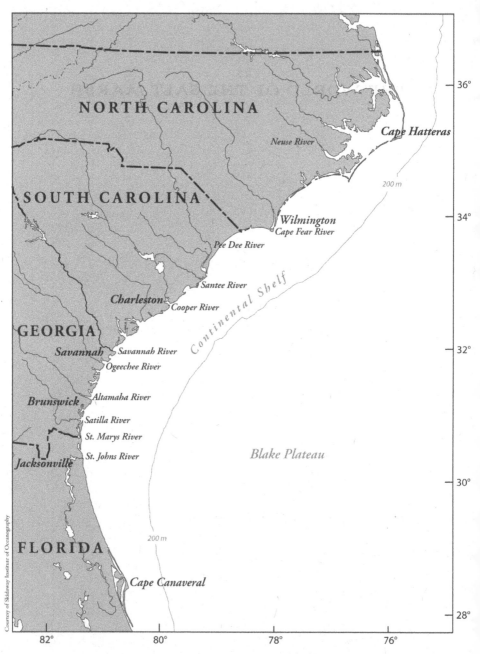

The South Atlantic Bight is an indentation in the coastline stretching roughly
from Cape Hatteras, North Carolina, to Cape Canaveral, Florida, and
encompassing the continental shelf offshore.
Map by Anna Boyette at the Skidaway Institute of Oceanography.

I SPENT HALF MY childhood trying to get off an island. I have spent half my adulthood trying to get back.

The island is John's Island, one of the sleepy, semitropical sea islands nuzzling the South Carolina coast that are surrounded by vast salt marshes, broad sounds, and winding tidal rivers. It was home to my ancestors for two hundred years, a haven where everyone knew my name. My daddy once warned me how it would be when I left: "When you leave this island, nobody will give a damn whether your name is Seabrook," he said.

But I could not wait to leave. There were soaring mountains with snow-capped peaks and tropical rainforests with wild, howling monkeys to see. I wanted to ride a camel across the Sahara and descend into deep caverns to gaze upon stupendous geological wonders. I wanted to see Paris, London, New York, Rio, Rome, Istanbul, and the thousands of other places I read about in *National Geographic.*

So, three days after graduating from high school in 1962, I left my island. Since then I have seen many of those places. As a science reporter for thirty-three years with the *Atlanta Journal-Constitution* I wrote stories from such far-flung places as the Arctic National Wildlife Refuge in Alaska and the rainforests of Guatemala. I walked on the Great Wall of China, paddled a dugout canoe down an Amazon tributary in Brazil, and rode through the Panama Canal in an outboard skiff. I saw Paris, Rome, London, Rio, Berlin, Beijing, Hong Kong, Prague, Budapest, and other marvels.

But I know now that the most wondrous, magical place of all was the place I left as soon as I got the chance—my island. I remember the moment when I finally realized that. I had been living for many years in Atlanta, and I was crossing the bridge to the island on a glorious autumn afternoon to see my mother. It was high tide, and the golden marsh with the tidal creeks twisting through it glowed softly in the afternoon sun. The beauty took my breath away.

An unnamed salt marsh creek in late summer on John's Island, South Carolina.

The creeks, of course, have always wound through the marsh; the sun has always set over it. I just hadn't appreciated the splendor of the view before. I was too busy plotting to get away. Now, after years of being away, I long for what I once took for granted.

In my boyhood, John's Island—a twenty-minute drive from downtown Charleston—was a place of magnificent spreading live oaks dripping with Spanish moss that formed cathedral-like canopies over the sandy roads and pathways; of stately palmettos that rustled when nudged by the soft air; of the broad Stono River, now placid blue, now roiling green in mood with the sky. Dolphins frolicked in the water and rolled up on mud banks and then back into the water again. You could spend all day sailing the river or searching its high bluffs for arrowheads, rusting Civil War cannonballs, and long-lost pirate booty.

Anyone who flung a cast net into the tidal creeks pulled out bountiful shrimp, blue crabs, and mullet. Oysters crowded the creek banks and were there for the taking. At oyster roasts, we tossed the mollusks onto a red-hot sheet of tin, threw wet croaker sacks soaked in salt water over them, let them steam several minutes, then shucked them open to get at the succulent meat.

On certain Sunday afternoons in summer, church members gathered at the river's edge to witness as the preacher in hip boots dipped the white-robed baptismal candidates into the ebb tide, the best tide for washing away sins.

At church suppers, tables sagged with platters of juicy tomatoes and corn on the cob and steaming bowls of beans, peppers, peas, and collards. The island's fertile black loam yielded a cornucopia of vegetables for anyone with the energy to drop a few seeds into the ground and do a little weeding.

There was something else, too: John's Island was a stronghold of "cunjuh," a brand of voodoo practiced on the sea islands. I believed in it as a child, and to this day I don't challenge it. I lay in bed many a night and heard the cunjuh drums thumping on Whaley Hill, just across the salt marsh from my home. Nighttime was when the hags and the boodaddies and the plat-eye and the cunjuh world's other sinister denizens came out.

Boodaddies were the spirits of dead people who had returned to Earth to take somebody back with them. If you saw a boodaddy, you were supposed to stand stock-still and say, "I ain't ready to go yet." The plat-eye, the all-seeing spirit, could appear as a pig, a calf, a yellow cat, or some other form, but all were distinguished by one formidable trait—a big, ugly eye hanging out the center of the face. Hags were invisible and could ride you and sap the strength from your body. They could come through a keyhole and sit on your chest and stop your breathing. Nearly every sound of the night was a hag omen. The soft creaking of a porch swing nudged by a light breeze was really a hag scratching around, trying to get in. A barking dog was being harassed by a hag. Even daytime sounds were signs that hags would be up and about that night.

"Hag gon' come 'round tonight," warned one of our neighbors, Sis' Mamie, when a rooster crowed or an Air Force jet broke the sound barrier. Sis' Mamie spoke in Gullah, the lilting patois that is unique to the sea islands and incomprehensible to outsiders.

As much as I long for my island, I can never return to the place I knew as a child. Its verdant maritime forests have given way to subdivisions and shopping centers and horse farms. Because of pollution, oysters no longer can be taken from many of the creeks. The beautiful Gullah dialect is dying out, victim of television's pervasiveness and pompous educators who believe everybody should talk the same way.

Gone is John Isabull, who nearly every day—except Sunday—drove his wobbly, mule-drawn wagon down the road to a little field, where he unhitched the weary animal from the cart and hooked him up to a plow to cultivate sweet watermelons and other produce. John's "gees" and "haws" at the stubborn old mule could be heard a mile away across the salt marsh.

Gone, too, is Mr. John Limehouse's store, a wondrous place redolent of tobacco, smoked sausage, herring, and bananas. On sultry summer days it was pure pleasure to stick your hand in the drink box and feel around in the icy water for a Nehi grape soda or Coca-Cola. The old store was torn down to make way for a fancy convenience mart with self-serve gas pumps.

Long gone are the gypsies who came in the summer, three or four families in dilapidated cars pulling rickety wooden trailers. They set up a "carnival" and a tent in Mr. Limehouse's pasture on the edge of the salt marsh and showed movies Monday through Friday nights. On Saturdays they staged a "rodeo" with a half-starved bull and some broken-down horses that were candidates for the glue factory. To a child who had never wandered far from the island, it was a glorious spectacle.

Our parents told us not to go to the camp by ourselves because the gypsies stole children. I believed that back then, just as I believed in the hags and the boodaddies. And now I long for my island. In my heart, I never really left it.

THE BEAUTY OF my island was undeniable even to a child. But I didn't realize back then that the tidal marsh surrounding the island and backing up to our backyard is one of the most remarkable natural systems on Earth. The salt marsh has been described as a biological factory without equal—far more fertile than the fields in which we raised our tomatoes and soybeans, more productive than the great fields of wheat and corn in the Midwest called America's breadbasket.

Twice a day, the tides ferry in a perpetual supply of nutrients, which the plants and microorganisms of the marsh break down and use with amazing quickness. The unfailing cycle nourishes the vast meadows of salt-tolerant *Spartina alterniflora*, or smooth cordgrass, by far the most important plant of the salt marsh. It is the canelike spartina that makes the marsh a great productive sanctuary, nourishing and protecting the young of blue crabs, shrimp, flounder, menhaden, mullet, oysters, and dozens of other species of ecological and gastronomic importance.

You can see this great fecundity with the naked eye. I do not exaggerate when I say that I have had shrimp and mullet in a tidal creek literally leap out of the water and land in my boat, as if begging to be caught.

During spring and summer, especially at night on a rising tide, enormous populations of juvenile shrimp graze on microscopic algae and on organic detritus, the end product of the huge swaths of spartina. These teeming multitudes can make swimming in a tidal creek slightly unpleasant. Scores of shrimp constantly run into you, their sharp tails and spines pricking your skin like so many little stickpins. If you swim at night, their little red eyes surround you, thousands of tiny points of light darting about like tiny little spooks. Many times, creek shrimp got inside my swimsuit— if I was wearing one—and their flipping and jabbing required quick action to protect certain parts of my anatomy.

LEGIONS OF SCIENTISTS and their students have come to the tidal marshes, the sea islands, the creeks, and the rivers to understand this remarkable fertility and to quantify it. One of the most venerated of those scientists was Eugene Odum, the father of modern ecology, whose patient scrutiny of natural marsh processes helped him formulate some of his bedrock tenets of ecology.

What the scientists learned is this: A single acre of marsh produces ten tons or more of dry organic matter, while the most fertile farm acre produces less than half as much. Their enormous fertility aside, the marshes also help filter and purify water. They dissipate the fury of howling storms blowing in from the sea. They shelter enormous numbers of creatures from predators. A healthy marsh is a prime example of the "silent economy of nature," a truly wondrous thing.

Another great man came to the marsh seeking revelation of another kind: the poet Sidney Lanier. In the 1870s, sitting under a spreading live oak at the edge of a great salt marsh in Georgia's Glynn County, he pondered how we all yearn for the beauty of the woods, the sea, and the marshes amidst the grit and grind of modern life. "Ye marshes, how candid and simple and nothing-withholding and free; / ye publish yourselves to the sky and offer yourselves to the sea," he wrote in his famous poem "The Marshes of Glynn."

But despite the magnificent fertility that amazed the scientist, despite the serenity that inspired the poet, there are those who destroy the marsh. They use it as a place to dump the caustic wastes of their industry; they drain it, dike it, dry it out, and turn it into factory sites and suburbs surrounded by asphalt and concrete. They mine the marsh for its minerals, leaving behind a landscape stripped of its ability to produce.

In many places the ecologist, the poet, the conservationist, the politician, and the lawyer have risen up together to save and protect the marsh from destruction. To them now belong our grateful thanks that vast stretches of this vital natural resource remain intact. But the battles continue; we must be vigilant.

SALT MARSHES, brackish marshes, and freshwater marshes, all influenced by the rise and fall of the tides, hug the coastlines of the United States—the Gulf Coast, the Pacific Coast, and the Atlantic Seaboard. The marshes of all these regions are in many ways similar, but they are also different in so many ways that each region deserves separate treatment in a book.

This book is devoted to the tidal marshes of the southeast Atlantic Coast, a broad, flat coastal plain bordered by lush barrier islands and sandy beaches interspersed with scenic tidal inlets and broad rivers. Its magnificent salt and brackish marshes stretch like vast, manicured lawns—sometimes nearly eight miles wide—between the mainland and the barrier islands from Cape Hatteras, North Carolina, to Cape Canaveral, Florida.

This book is also about the places vitally connected to the southeastern marshes—the estuaries, the sea islands, the broad rivers, the maritime forests, the tidal creeks, all of which hum and interact like the pulsating organs of a great benevolent being. They are all unceasingly shaped and altered by tidal currents, winds, and storms that spin, blow, and throb where the sea meets the land.

One cannot talk about the marshes of the Southeast, however, without talking about the people intimately linked to them. Therefore, this book is also about the scientists who study the marsh and the poets who celebrate it—and the ordinary people who make a living from it and are fed by it, entire cultures that turn on its daily rhythms. Most notable are the Gullah-Geechee people, whose lilting dialect and unique arts, crafts, and traditions are disappearing under the onslaught of unbridled development on the coast.

This book is for everyone, though, for all of us whose spirits are uplifted and whose weary minds are refreshed when we gaze upon a vast marsh stretching to the far horizon.

CHAPTER ONE

The Poetry of the Marsh

RIDDEN WITH tuberculosis, his strength ebbing away, the man who was to become Georgia's most revered poet came to Brunswick on the Georgia coast in the 1870s, seeking respite from his affliction. The clean ocean breezes and the deep pine fragrance suffusing Brunswick's air were thought to be excellent elixirs for those plagued by the then-incurable lung disease.[1]

Sidney Lanier had contracted "consumption" during the Civil War at Camp Point Lookout, Maryland, a crowded Union Army prison where he was locked up in 1864 after being captured by Union forces. After the war, to support his young wife, Mary, and growing family, he became a lawyer in his native Macon. He was not cut out to be a lawyer, and the law practice broke down his health. He was, however, an accomplished musician, self-taught on the flute, piano, organ, violin, banjo, and guitar. He had made his first flute from a reed cut on the banks of Georgia's Ocmulgee River and imitated the sounds of birds.

Eventually Lanier moved his family to Baltimore, where he became first flutist for the Peabody Symphony Orchestra and taught English literature at Johns Hopkins University.[2] His restless, creative mind yearned for more. His true passion, he came to realize, was poetry. He spent long hours writing verse and studying it while his malady continued its relentless assault on his body. Sometimes he was confined to his room for weeks on end. His doctors advised him to seek a place more suitable to his frail condition, where the air was gentler and the climate warmer, where his sickly lungs stood less chance of further damage.[3]

That advice brought him to Brunswick. His wife's family owned land there, and his brother-in-law had a rambling home on the south side of town. Lanier was struck by the natural beauty surrounding Brunswick— especially the vast expanse of salt marsh with its sparkling creeks and rivers that seemed to twist and turn just for the pure joy of it. He reveled in the region's splendor. It touched something deep inside him, and he longed to understand the mysterious forces at work in the marsh.[4]

Sitting beneath a shady live oak, he gazed on the "world of marsh that borders a world of sea" and was inspired to write some of his finest poems. The most cherished of these is "The Marshes of Glynn," named for the county in which Brunswick is located. Generations of Georgia and South Carolina schoolchildren have committed passages of it to memory.

As Lanier's biographer Edwin Mims explained, the poet represents himself in the poem as having spent the day in the forest and coming at sunset into full view of "the length and the breadth and the sweep of the marshes of Glynn."[5] The glooms of the live oaks and the emerald twilights of the "dim sweet woods, of the dear dark woods," had been a refuge from the blazing noonday sun. Within the deep recesses of the forest he had felt the passionate pleasure of prayer. But at the same time, the forest had constrained him. When he looks out upon the marsh, his spirit soars to a "lordly great compass within"—a sense of limitless space, of freedom. According to Mims, Lanier is ready for what English poet William Wordsworth called a "god-like hour":

> But now when the noon is no more, and riot is rest,
> And the sun is a-wait at the ponderous gate of the West,
> And the slant yellow beam down the wood-aisle doth seem
> Like a lane into heaven that leads from a dream,—
> Ay, now, when my soul all day hath drunken the soul of the oak
> And my heart is at ease from men,
> and the wearisome sound of the stroke
> > Of the scythe of time and the trowel of trade is low,
> > And belief overmasters doubt, and I know that I know,
> > And my spirit is grown to a lordly great compass within,
> That the length and the breadth
> and the sweep of the marshes of Glynn
> Will work me no fear like the fear they have wrought me of yore

When length was fatigue, and when breadth was but bitterness sore,
And when terror and shrinking and dreary unnamable pain
Drew over me out of the merciless miles of the plain, —

Oh, now, unafraid, I am fain to face
    The vast sweet visage of space.
To the edge of the wood I am drawn, I am drawn,
Where the gray beach glimmering runs, as a belt of the dawn,
    For a mete and a mark
        To the forest-dark: —
            So:
Affable live-oak, leaning low, —
Thus—with your favor—soft, with a reverent hand
(Not lightly your person, Lord of the land!)
Bending your beauty aside, with a step I stand
On the firm-packed sand,
            Free
By a world of marsh that borders a world of sea. (lines 21–48)

Lanier penned several other grand poems of the salt marsh. In "Sunset," composed on his deathbed, he professed deep reverence for the marsh, symbolic of his profound love of nature: "Reverend Marsh, low-couched along the sea, Old chemist, rapt in alchemy, Distilling silence . . ." Mims called him "the poet of the marshes as surely as Bryant is of the forests, or Wordsworth of the mountains."[6]

Lanier could not know that his name would become revered throughout Georgia, with schools, bridges, a county, and a huge artificial lake north of Atlanta named after him. The tuberculosis wracking his body took its final toll in 1881; he died at age thirty-nine.

In the Marshes of Glynn

I am one of those schoolchildren whose teacher made sure that her pupils could recite from memory at least a few lines of "The Marshes of Glynn." "Miss Ruby" Glover, an unabashed Lanier fan, opined that since we lived on an island surrounded by a salt marsh, it behooved us to become familiar with the most famous poem about the marsh.

On a sizzling day in June I am going one step further: I am becoming

Georgia's best-known poet, Sidney Lanier (1842–1881), author of "The Marshes of Glynn." Photo courtesy of the Library of Congress.

intimately familiar with Lanier's marsh itself. Miss Ruby would be proud. I am tromping around in the marshes of Glynn, going boldly where few have gone before. I am desirous of seeing firsthand what so enraptured Lanier, wondering if I will have an epiphany of my own.

It's dead low tide. To the east, green and brown spartina stretches like a suburban lawn for unbroken miles to the horizon. To the west, the mainland begins only a few hundred feet away. In plain view, aptly named, is the spanking new Sidney Lanier Bridge accommodating a roar of traffic over the Brunswick River. The live oak under which Lanier sat and marveled at the natural beauty spread before him is a mile away. The venerable old tree, wispy Spanish moss dangling from its boughs, now stands in the grassy median of U.S. Highway 17, once the main artery for northerners heading to and from Florida. A state historical marker tells passersby of the tree's significance. Few can read it at highway speeds.

I am trying to keep up with Todd Schneider, an ornithologist with the Georgia Department of Natural Resources. He has let me come along as he looks for bird nests as part of a breeding bird survey. He has spent many a day in the marsh and moves with amazing agility through the dense spartina and sucking mud. He says he understands why the marsh so inspired

Lanier. The waving acres of grass, he says, can bring on a deep sense of isolation that is strangely satisfying to the soul.

"We're only a few hundred feet from shore where we can see several buildings and an asphalt parking lot," he says, nodding toward the mainland. "But I feel content in this marsh; it seems as if we're in a different world. It's so peaceful."

He and I wonder, though, if Lanier himself actually ever strode through the marsh. Most people, Todd says, probably would not think of slogging laboriously through this place as we are doing. Striding would be out of the question.

"They see the marsh only from their boat or car or from a bank or a dock," he notes. "They never actually walk in the marsh itself. The idea of that would be foreign to them. Those people speeding over that bridge over there probably don't have a clue as to what's in this marsh."

The mud where the spartina grows thickly is firmer than I expected. But the "pluff mud" at a small drainage creek that we must cross is much, much softer—near the consistency of mayonnaise—and I am quickly bogged nearly to my hips. I struggle to extricate myself. The mud is gripping my legs, and my old sneakers are about to slip off my feet. For a fleeting instant I panic, fearful that I might sink deeper and become irretrievably stuck. But I have been in this predicament before. I bend over and lie on my stomach in the mud. This somehow gives me leverage enough to wiggle my legs free, and I belly-crawl in the mud to the edge of the creek, where the mud is firmer. Thank goodness it's low tide and no water is in the creek.

I am not sure why the technique works. Maybe it's because crawling on your stomach distributes your weight more evenly across the mud and you are less apt to sink into it. In any case, I am free but covered with thick black muck, which is already starting to dry in the hot sun and turn powdery gray. It leaves me smelling like the marsh. But that bothers me not a whit. The odor of a healthy salt marsh is sweet balm to my nostrils. Pat Conroy, the great novelist, called it the smell of the South in heat, "a smell like new milk, semen and spilled wine, all perfumed with seawater."[7] In their book *Life and Death of the Salt Marsh*, John and Mildred Teal explained that the smell is that of spartina and the sea and salt water, of decayed life and traces of iodine and hydrogen sulfide from the mud. "These are clean, fresh smells that are pleasing to one who lives by the sea but strange and not altogether pleasant to one who has always lived inland," they wrote.[8]

To me, it is the smell of home, a smell I have never forgotten. My big brother Jim, who lived near the salt marsh around John's Island all his life, once told me how he loved the pungent aroma wafting from the marsh: "When we had been gone from the island for a day or two, we would be headed back, and just before we got to the bridge you got a whiff of the marsh. It was a welcome smell. Mama would always say, 'Smell that mud? We're home.' When I've been gone from the island for a long time, I'm so glad to be home I could scoop up that mud and throw it all over me. Just as sweet as magnolia blossoms in spring."

I catch up with Todd, who is plodding along more slowly now, scrutinizing the spartina for the nests of seaside sparrows, marsh wrens, and clapper rails—about the only birds that exclusively raise their babies in the marsh. Most of the marsh grass is a robust mint green. The rest is brown and decaying, which is also good. Dead or alive, spartina is crucial to the ecological health of the marsh.

Clad in a red baseball cap, yellow T-shirt, and blue jeans, Todd is keeping track of the nesting birds in this marsh to see if their populations are rising, falling, or holding steady. Just as Sidney Lanier found spiritual uplifting in the beauty and spaciousness of the marsh, Todd says he never fails to be awed by the marvels he finds here, like the bird nests.

"A lot of the nests are so well camouflaged that you could walk right by them and never see them," he explains as he peers into the dense clumps of dead and living spartina.

He's right. As familiar as I was with salt marshes as a boy, and as many times as I slogged through them, I remember seeing few bird nests. They were that well concealed. Todd points to something about fifty feet away; a little male seaside sparrow is clinging to a spartina stalk. In quick succession we see another male on another stalk, and then a juvenile and a female. After diligent search we find a few of their nests—simple, open cups constructed deep in the spartina but above the high-tide line. Some sport a canopy of living marsh grass pulled down from above. Todd says that seaside sparrows are so consistent in their choice of habitat that it would be useless to look for them anywhere else but a marsh. They spend much of their time on the marsh floor, scurrying mouselike through the spartina, searching for grasshoppers and other insects, snails, small crabs, marine worms, and seeds.

In chest-high spartina next to a tidal creek we find some marsh wren nests. The secretive little marsh wren forages for insects and spiders in the spartina canopy but tends to stay well hidden, even when defending its territory. "They'll come at you and fuss at you, but they won't show themselves," Todd says as we listen to a scolding marsh wren somewhere nearby. "He's telling us to get the hell out of here. He weighs only ten grams, but he's saying he's going to kick our butts. All wrens have attitudes." A male marsh wren, Todd explains, takes several mates, each of which lays three to six eggs in an oblong nest made of reeds and grasses secured to the spartina. Most often the female completes an unfinished nest started by the male, fashioning a central cavity in it to hold her eggs. The male usually builds more than a dozen flimsy nests, most probably never meant for use. We find several of them the size of cantaloupes in the tall spartina. Todd says the dummy nests may be decoys to fool would-be predators, such as the red-winged blackbirds and boat-tailed grackles that we also see flitting about.

We have no luck finding a finished clapper rail nest, although we come across what appears to be the beginning of one. Todd says that as many times as he has been in the marsh looking for clapper rail nests, he has found only a few because they are even better hidden than those of the seaside sparrows.

Pairs of clapper rails build their platform-like nests of spartina and other material low in the marsh. They usually construct a dome over the nest from the surrounding vegetation. Because their nests often are only a foot or so above the mud, their biggest worry is high tide, although the eight or so eggs the female lays in the nest can withstand immersion in salt water, and the downy chicks are able to swim from the time of hatching.

Clapper rails—or "marsh hens" as we called them because they look, strut, and bob like skinny chickens—tread easily through the grass and soft mud on their wide-spreading toes, three on each foot. They are surprisingly good swimmers, even though their toes are not webbed like a duck's.

Like the wrens and sparrows, the rails are super-secretive birds. But I very much would like to see one, or at least hear one. I regard them as old friends. Their wild, cackling call is the sound I most identify with my

The marshes of Glynn County made famous by Sidney Lanier's poem.

childhood—a *yenk, yenk, yenk, yenk, yenk* that sounds like hands clapping. It regularly emanated from the salt marsh next to my island home. Once you hear that harsh sound, you're unlikely to forget it.

Sidney Lanier must have had a similarly hard time finding a clapper rail nest. In his "Marshes of Glynn," he used the bird's hidden nest as a simile for his faith in God and the mysteriousness of the sacred:

> As the marsh-hen secretly builds on the watery sod,
> Behold I will build me a nest on the greatness of God:
> I will fly in the greatness of God as the marsh-hen flies
> In the freedom that fills all the space 'twixt the marsh and the skies:
> By so many roots as the marsh-grass sends in the sod
> I will heartily lay me a-hold on the greatness of God:
> Oh, like to the greatness of God is the greatness within
> The range of the marshes, the liberal marshes of Glynn. (lines 71–78)

Then, standing there in the marsh, I hear it—a clapper rail cackling in the distance, and I, too, am content.

The next day I stop at the city of Brunswick's Marshes of Glynn Overlook Park, just off U.S. 17. Across two lanes of the busy thoroughfare, in the median, is the Lanier Oak. The state historical marker says that Lanier "frequently sat beneath this live oak" and looked out over the marsh. "Here he received the inspiration which resulted in some of his finest poems."

My eyes also are drawn almost instinctively toward the marsh. As the small park's name suggests, I still can get a far-as-the-eye-can-see view of the gleaming green fields Lanier made famous. On the distant horizon I see the faint outlines of Saint Simons Island and Jekyll Island, both part of the low-lying barrier island chain known as Georgia's Golden Isles. Beyond is the sea that generates the life-giving tides.

Nevertheless, if Lanier were looking out—and breathing—from here today, he would be mighty disappointed. Certainly he would not be enraptured. On the edge of the marsh, within plain view of the park and Lanier's venerable old oak, is a McDonald's golden arches sign. The most visible thing from here, however, is a big chemical plant. Its tall smokestack, etched starkly against the blue sky, belches out a thick, white plume that drifts out over the marsh. The emissions hardly ever cease. Sometimes they mingle with those from a giant paper mill on the edge of a marsh four miles across town. Seven public schools and a public hospital stand between them.[9] Just a few years ago the stench from the plants was literally nauseating. A writer once likened the odor to what mustard gas must have smelled like as it billowed across the trenches of the Marne in World War I.[10] Sometimes, Brunswick's factories seemed to be competing for the title of smelliest. Even now, on certain days, industrial odors are still offensive in Brunswick. If visitors complain, local boosters laugh and say that the fumes "smell like money."

Perched on a peninsula flanked by tidal rivers and the great salt marsh, Brunswick, population sixteen thousand, is Glynn County's seat and industrial center. Georgia's founder, James Oglethorpe, laid out its streets and squares in 1771. In 1789 George Washington proclaimed Brunswick one of the five original ports of entry for the colonies. The city boasts another original: it is the birthplace of a tangy stew. A plaque on an iron pot at the city's visitors center states that the first Brunswick stew was cooked on July 2, 1898, on nearby Saint Simons Island. The pot supposedly held the first stew. At one time the city also billed itself as "the Shrimp Capital of the World," for the many shrimp harvested in local waters. During World War II, at a sprawling shipyard on the edge of the marshes of Glynn, thousands of workers labored around the clock to build liberty ships that ferried troops and supplies to the war theater in Europe.[11]

Today, Brunswick is one of the most productive ports on the Atlantic Coast. Besides handling wood pulp, paper products, wheat, soybeans, and heavy machinery, it is a primary U.S. port for numerous automobile manufacturers, including Jaguar, Land Rover, Porsche, Mitsubishi, Volvo, Ford, GM, and Mercedes. Another Brunswick landmark is the Federal Law Enforcement Training Center (FLETC), a former Navy installation and World War II blimp base, which brings in thousands of students each month from various federal agencies that have law enforcement programs.[12] The bustling city proudly supports its industries, which employ many people, pay good wages, and contribute generously to local causes.

But if Sidney Lanier were alive today, Brunswick might be the last place doctors would send him to take the cure. Its polluting industries still make it one of the most contaminated places in the South. In addition to its stinky factories, the city is home to sixteen hazardous waste sites, including four so contaminated they were designated to receive federal funds for cleanup under the national Superfund priority program. Superfund sites are the most polluted spots in the United States.

The most notorious of the Superfund sites is the old LCP Chemicals plant, which dumped staggering amounts of mercury into the marshes of Glynn between around 1980 and the early 1990s.[13] It has been called the worst Superfund site in the South and one of the worst in the entire nation.[14] The mercury was used in the manufacture of chlorine bleach, most of which was sold to local paper mills to make whiter paper. Mercury is a potent neurotoxin; even small amounts can cause developmental problems in fetuses and young children. It makes its way into the human bloodstream when people eat contaminated fish.[15] Georgia environmental officials once banned fishing altogether in several local creeks and estuaries—and still post fish consumption warnings—because of the mercury dumped by LCP. Seven of its officers and managers went to prison after being convicted of crimes against the environment.[16]

Another of Brunwick's Superfund sites is Terry Creek, a placid tidal stream that winds through the marsh that so enraptured Lanier. A few years ago the creek was so polluted with the pesticide toxaphene—once widely used to kill boll weevils but now banned—that shrimpers docked their trawlers in the stream so that the tainted water could kill barnacles and other undesirable organisms fouling the boat hulls. The toxaphene, a suspected carcinogen, came from Hercules, Inc., a Brunswick chemical plant that manufactured great quantities of it until 1980. In the 1990s scientists found serious genetic damage and reproduction problems in toxaphene-contaminated grass shrimp from Terry Creek.[17] The tiny shrimp is a "sentinel species"; that is, a species that researchers use to determine if pollution is causing possible widespread harm to other creatures in its environment.[18]

Because of lingering contamination from toxaphene and other closely related compounds, Georgia environmental authorities still recommend that anglers limit eating certain fish—and avoid consuming some fish altogether—from certain stretches of Terry Creek and a connecting waterway known as Dupree Creek.[19]

Toxaphene has been detected in fish caught as far away as Jekyll Island, a state park several miles away from Brunswick, across the wide salt marsh and Saint Simons Sound. Presumably, the fish fed on contaminated grass shrimp, mummichogs, and other creatures in the tidal creeks and then migrated into the rivers and sounds.[20]

Hercules' activities were also responsible for still another of Brunswick's Superfund sites—an old landfill next to the salt marsh containing toxaphene and all manner of other nasty chemicals. The landfill's contents have been solidified, and the groundwater is now monitored to make sure no contamination leaches off the site. The U.S. Environmental Protection Agency says that further cleanup may be necessary.[21]

Brunswick's fourth Superfund site is a former wood-preserving factory that used creosote, copper-chromated arsenate, and other toxic chemicals to render telephone poles and fence posts rot-proof.[22] EPA officials told me in 2010 that the cleanup was at least two years away, depending on whether or not Congress appropriates twenty-eight million dollars for the project.

Ecologists and environmental activists tell me that wide expanses of the marshes of Glynn will be blighted for years to come because of the damage from these noxious sites. "Millions of pounds of toxaphene were released into neighborhoods, school yards, and our salt marshes and estuaries, contaminating our seafood," Daniel Parshley, the feisty head of the Glynn Environmental Coalition, told me. Parshley contends that state and federal environmental authorities have been far too easy on polluters. "It is the circumventing of environmental laws, that continues to this day, that has left us with four Superfund sites and more than a dozen other hazardous waste sites," Parshley said.

Brunswick, though, is not an isolated example. Salt marshes almost everywhere are facing a multitude of threats. The biggest threat by far is unbridled land development and the choking pollution it brings. "The most important factor in the decline of environmental conditions within the coastal zone has been the unprecedented increase in human population growth, particularly in the southeastern United States," Dr. Fred Holland, retired director of the Hollings Marine Laboratory in Charleston, explained.

In Georgia alone, growth projections for the coast predict a 20 percent population increase each decade.[23] Development will breed more development. More people will want to use the coast for recreation, homes, commerce, industry, and waste disposal. Golf courses that require tons of herbicides and fertilizer will be must-have components of the new developments. But new residents also will want drugstores and supermarkets and hair salons and gas stations and shops of all kinds.

All of this growth will engender more pollution. And the splendor that so enthralled Sidney Lanier will be diminished, perhaps lost altogether. The marshes will lose their great capacity to produce. Time and again, too much use of coastal resources has ruined the very beauty and environment that drew people there in the first place.

Will this be the fate of the glorious wetlands immortalized by Lanier well over a century ago when he wrote in "The Marshes of Glynn":

> And what if behind me to westward the wall of the woods stands high?
> The world lies east: how ample, the marsh and the sea and the sky!
> A league and a league of marsh-grass, waist-high, broad in the blade,
> Green, and all of a height, and unflecked with a light or a shade,
> Stretch leisurely off, in a pleasant plain,
> To the terminal blue of the main. (lines 55–60)

If we are to really appreciate this great ecosystem and understand what will be lost if we destroy it, we also must understand its crucial role as a cleanser of precious water, a recycler of nutrients, a protector of the shore when fierce storms blow in from the sea, and a vast nursery that succors untold numbers of marine creatures great and small.

CHAPTER TWO

A Walk across the Marsh

O N AN APPLE-CRISP October morning, a couple of hours after daybreak, I'm at the edge of another Georgia salt marsh—off Skidaway, a half-wild, half-resort sea island near Savannah, seventy miles north of Brunswick. I'm about to follow a muddy path that winds a few hundred yards across the marsh and then across a hammock, a small island. The path ends at my destination, a tidal creek on the other side of the hammock.

Raccoons and marsh rabbits probably carved the path. The creatures often build networks of narrow, muddy trails through the spartina on their nightly feeding forays. Local hikers and fishermen probably widened the track to access the hammock and the creek beyond.

The salt marsh is typical of those along the U.S. coastline south of Cape Hatteras. I have come here to reacquaint myself with the hardy plants and creatures of the marsh that were so familiar in my childhood. I don't have to remember much: Despite its great productivity, the salt marsh doesn't harbor the incredible array of species that Earth's other great ecosystems, such as rainforests, do.

A salt marsh is a harsh, stressful place for its residents. The plants and animals that live here must be super-hardy, able to tolerate drastic changes every few hours as tides advance and retreat. A crab covered with cool, soothing water in the morning may be exposed to blazing, drying heat in the afternoon when the tide recedes. If one thing defines this taxing world and dictates who survives here, it is salt, mostly common sodium chloride.[1] Salt marsh organisms, both plants and animals, must adapt to varying degrees of salinity. On a daily basis, water entering a marsh may be as salty as seawater in the morning but nearly as fresh as tap water at night if heavy thunderstorms drench the area and storm water rushes off the land. Many marine marsh creatures also need particular salinity levels at various stages of their lives, and salinity may dictate when and where they reproduce.

The species that do thrive here occupy nearly every available niche— testimony to the toughness and vitality of life in general. As with other great ecosystems, the salt marsh encompasses several biological zones in which certain species do well and others do not.[2] To the uninitiated, the marsh may look like a monotonous, table-flat expanse of grass shaped to the same height, as if neatly trimmed by a giant mower. But ecologists delineate biological zones depending on, among other things, how long and how deeply each swath is submerged in salt water. I expect to go through most of these zones this morning, pausing in each—smelling the fragrant mud and savoring the ambiance as I trudge across the marshland.

At the Edge

My starting place, logically, is at the marsh's upland edge, an abrupt transition zone between dry land and wetland—between the dark, shadowy maritime forest at my back and the sun-spangled marsh in front of me. I pause here to admire a picturesque scene found only along a southern salt marsh: a ponderous live oak, laden with Spanish moss, jutting a parasol of dark evergreen leaves out over the marsh—Lanier's "Affable live-oak, leaning low."

Surrounding me at the marsh's upland border are wild plants once as familiar to me as the flowers in my garden. The plants here are tough, able to survive hurricane-force winds, scorching sun, and sandy soil that does not store water well. They provide stability and prevent erosion along the shore. They must have high salt tolerance to withstand salt spray and storm surges and the extra high tides of new moons and full moons that push salt water up to their roots at least a few hours each month. No wonder they are close cousins of the strong, resilient plants of western salt deserts. When not beset by salt, they are under the sway of fresh water draining from the uplands.

I spy clusters of one of the most common shrubs here, marsh elder, also called high-tide bush because it grows just out of the reach of regular high water. Its shallow roots quickly capture rainwater trickling into the

A salt marsh on Skidaway Island, Georgia, typical of the Southeast coast.

sand; its thick, stiff, wax-coated leaves conserve water; its pliant branches easily bend before a stiff wind, even a hurricane. The horizontally growing branches form dense thickets—further protection against strong breezes. For all of that, however, marsh elder gets little respect. It sports small, non-descript, greenish-white flowers in late summer, but, overall, it's one of the homeliest plants in this maritime shrub community between land and marsh.

Not so, though, with another evergreen shrub growing in a nearby thicket—the groundsel tree, also known as silverling, sea myrtle, or saltbush. It is dioecious, meaning that male and female flowers occur on separate plants. The showstopper is the female, whose snowy white flowers with silky, hairy tufts completely cover the shrub like a billowing cumulus cloud. Several female shrubs in full bloom make a stunning sight here by the marsh. Their seed-bearing tufts will float away on the wind in December. Male flowers are pale yellow and smaller, but their abundant nectar lures swarms of honeybees, bumblebees, gulf fritillary butterflies, and other nectar-sipping insects that pollinate the shrubs. From groundsel nectar the honeybees will concoct a strong, wild-tasting honey that is often sold as "myrtle honey." Coastal residents found groundsel useful for other reasons. Its springy branches were the "yard brooms" with which my mother swept bare the ground around our home—an old Lowcountry custom; not even a blade of grass grew in that yard. Medicinal herbalists brewed a tea from groundsel roots and leaves, which contain glycosidal saponin, a compound supposedly good for treating colds, stomachaches, and fever. Hence the shrub's other name, "consumption weed."[3]

Closer to the marsh are dense clumps of sea ox-eye daisies that put forth big, yellow, sunflower-like blooms in spring and summer. Now, in early October, only their brown seed heads remain. Clusters of sweetgrass, or muhley grass, just starting to bloom, have a pinkish glow. Sea island Gullah people harvest muhley grass to weave their famous sweetgrass baskets, a craft passed down from their African slave forebears.

The High Marsh

Leaving the upland edge, I step onto the path and enter the marsh itself. This "high marsh" zone has a mixture of plants. The purplish haze from the mistlike blooms of sea lavender adds a dash of color. Dense colonies of saltgrass, or spikegrass, grow here, still close to land. Like many other marsh plants, the green, wiry saltgrass, whose spiky leaves curiously branch off at a forty-five-degree angle from the main stem, forms thick mats of roots and underground stems called rhizomes.

But black needlerush is the dominant plant where I walk now. It often covers large swaths of the high marsh where fresh water still exerts a major influence. I move through waist-high clusters of this plant, whose rounded, hollow stems resemble giant needles. Their wickedly sharp tips can puncture skin and do serious damage to an eye. Indeed, they inflict mini–stab wounds now on my bare arms. Slaves on southern rice plantations once fashioned "fanner baskets" from needlerush to toss rice grains into the air and let the breeze blow away the husks.[4]

A few steps farther along the sudden scurrying of countless little creatures startles me—I've entered the realm of inch-long fiddler crabs, which regard me as a potential enemy. They rustle helter-skelter as they scoot away and dive into the innumerable crab holes that punctuate the mud. I stand stock-still, and soon they cautiously sidle back out. Like grazing herds of wildebeest on Africa's Serengeti Plains, they recongregate to feed

Spartina and black needlerush in a Georgia salt marsh. Pure stands of spartina dominate more than 80 percent of southeastern salt marshes; needlerush often dominates in the higher marsh elevations.

on algae, bacteria, and microscopic food particles in and on the mud. With a slight crackling sound like millions of tiny lips smacking, they shovel soupy muck into their mouths with their claws and sieve out the edible pieces. Indigestible material is ejected onto the marsh floor as tiny mud balls. The females use both of their tiny claws to eat, but the males have only one claw suitable for that purpose. The other claw is huge, much too large for dining. Instead, the male rhythmically waves it back and forth to attract females to his burrow or to warn other males to back off—a routine that resembles fiddle playing, hence the crab's name.

Scientists estimate that a million fiddler crabs or more inhabit just one acre of healthy salt marsh—another measure of its amazing productivity. The fiddlers' burrows help aerate and drain the mud and stimulate marsh plant growth. The holes also are fiddlers' refuges at high tide. The crabs reemerge at low tide to resume feeding.[5]

I once had a little pup that loved to taunt fiddlers at the marsh edge— and paid dearly for it. Many times he came scooting up from the marsh with a big male fiddler clasping his nose. His yelps sounded something like *ike, ike, ike,* so I named him Ike.

Past the needlerush, my path winds mostly through spartina about a foot tall. I am now well into the high marsh zone. Simply put, the high marsh is higher than the low marsh—the stretch of marsh closest to tidal creeks. The change in elevation between the zones is only a matter of inches, but it is enough to make each distinctly different.[6]

Some of the differences: the low marsh may be covered for hours each day with a foot or more of seawater; the high marsh, where I now stand, is lucky if it gets a few inches of seawater for an hour each day. The low marsh soil generally is soft, pluffy, and silty; high marsh soil is sandy and firmer. In the low marsh spartina rules, growing three to four feet tall and sometimes topping nine feet along the highly fertile creek banks. In the high marsh spartina is runty—only a foot or so tall, perhaps because fewer nutrients reach the high-tide zone and because it must compete with other plants such as black needlerush. A biologist once told me that as soon as you encounter another plant species besides spartina, you're in the high marsh.

A curious thing about the high marsh: Even though it's barely covered with seawater for only a short time each day, it is usually the saltiest part of the entire marsh. That's because after the seawater recedes, the high marsh soil is exposed to air for the rest of the day. Much of the surface water evaporates, which causes water below the surface to be drawn upward by capillary action, like a paper towel absorbing spilled liquid. This water, too, evaporates. Continued evaporation leaves behind a higher salt level in the soil.[7]

All plants in the high marsh must have a high degree of salt tolerance. In addition to salt grass and needlerush, spartina's rivals in the high marsh include certain succulents, notably saltworts and glassworts. I'm happy to see the "worts," with their pale green stems and leaves and virtually microscopic flowers, for they are some of my favorite salt marsh plants. Saltworts favor the marsh's outer fringes, where they grow in dense masses. To survive in the highly saline environment, the saltwort's leaves are covered with fine hairs to reduce the amount of water lost to the air. As I walk across a clump of saltworts, they crunch under my shoes like frozen grass in winter. I pick a stem and nibble it—salty but tasty, like a moist potato chip. Great in stuffed crab.

A similar plant is the glasswort, also edible and good in salad. On my boyhood island, glasswort was called "pickle weed" because it tastes like little dill pickles. At one time glasswort was harvested and then burned, and the ashes were used to make soap and glass, hence the name glasswort. A single glasswort plant looks like several long green pipe cleaners attached to a long stem. When a stem tip becomes heavily encrusted with salt, it dies and falls off. Actually, two very similar looking glasswort species grow here: perennial glasswort and the more common annual glasswort. The latter turns brilliant red in autumn, adding a welcome dash of bright color to the marsh.

In some high marsh areas, however, the salt concentration is so great— more than three times saltier than seawater—that nothing grows.[8] I see one of these "salt pans" in the near distance, a patch of starkly bare sand devoid of vegetation. Without doubt, the salt pans, often covered with a crystalline saline whiteness, are the harshest areas in a salt marsh. Nevertheless, salt pans are wonderful places for spotting bird and animal tracks. On many mornings on a salt pan in a South Carolina marsh I could count footprints of more than a dozen bird species and of raccoons, white-tailed deer, and bobcats, all crisscrossing in a splendid montage.

The Lower Marsh

As I walk further down the path, the vegetation becomes exclusively spartina. I'm in what some scientists call the mid-marsh area, between high marsh and low marsh. Here and there, ribbed mussels poke out of the mud. Thousands of pale white periwinkle snails cling to spartina stems, gleaning algae and other tiny organisms from the plant surfaces. When the tide rises, the snails will inch up the reeds on their single foot to escape predators such as blue crabs brought in by the tide.

As I slog along, spartina's tough, spreading roots and rootlike rhizomes provide a somewhat firm base—"so many roots as the marsh-grass sends in the sod," as Lanier said. But my "mud shoes," an old pair of Reebok running shoes that I use only for marsh walking, are starting to sink a little deeper into the muck. It's not genuine pluff mud, so I won't worry about sinking nearly to my hips as I did in the marshes of Glynn.

I do know that wherever I step now, I am treading on organisms too small for me to see—bacteria, algae, fungi, protozoa, nematodes, copepods, and other microscopic life living in the billions per square inch in and on the mud.

In short order, though, I approach the outer edge of the hammock, where needlerush, glasswort, and marsh-edge shrubs greet me once again. The path will lead me across the little marsh island, which is about a couple of acres in size, and then to the tidal creek.

On a Hammock

Thousands of nameless hammocks like this one dot the vast marshes of coastal Georgia, Florida, and the Carolinas. Ranging in size from less than an acre to hundreds of acres, they are eye-catching as they rise abruptly on the horizon from long, flat stretches of marsh. Most of them are remote, uninhabited, and unnamed. Only wind-twisted cedars and scraggly live oaks top many of the smaller ones. Larger ones might contain the East Coast's last vestiges of virgin maritime forest—canopies of oak, palmetto, and sweetgum; thickets of wax myrtle, holly, and saw palmetto; and jungle-like tangles of woody vines and evergreens. Regardless of size, nearly all of the hammocks are minihavens for wildlife and form a crucial link with the surrounding salt marsh.

As I step onto the hammock, a torrent of memories of the small hammock that rose from the marsh in back of my boyhood home on John's Island floods my mind. Many a time I poled an old dinghy across the marsh or simply trudged by foot through the spartina to get to the hammock. It was only a five-acre lump of sand with a few rugged trees, mostly cedars, but it was my magical island. I was lord of the land; my imagination ran wild there. One day I might be a hermit, tired of civilization, reduced to a simple existence; another day I was a river pirate lying in ambush for passing boats. Sometimes I was a Robinson Crusoe, shipwrecked, living off the land. I had all kinds of hiding places there in case bad people were after me.

The best time to visit the little marsh islet was after a big storm. Blustery winds and surging tides washed up all manner of wondrous things that became entrapped in the groundsel bushes—grotesquely shaped driftwood, paddles, old chairs, broken tables, nets, and, once, an old boat; the treasure was endless. I found half an airplane propeller and wondered if a plane had gone down offshore. I found an octagonal red-and-white highway stop sign, which I set up in the middle of the hammock, marveling that I had my own road sign on my own island. Once I found a fifth of Seagram's 7 with the seal intact. I opened it and took a swig. The strong whiskey burned my throat and I wondered how people could drink such stuff. I delayed returning home because I feared my teetotaler mother would smell it on my breath.

As I walk onto the hammock off Skidaway in Georgia, greeting me first is a thicket of wax myrtles. Where I grew up, the wax myrtle was regarded as a trash tree because it seemed always to spring up where it wasn't wanted. Some people, like me, found beauty in its open natural shape and shiny evergreen leaves, which give off a sweet aroma. I rank wax myrtle, live oak, magnolia, and longleaf pine as my favorite southern trees. Bird lovers covet the myrtle because its bluish berries nourish well over thirty-five bird species. Sea island Gullah folk made fragrant candles from the waxy berries and boiled the leaves to make a tea to treat colds and chest congestion. We crushed the leaves and rubbed them on our arms to ward off biting deerflies.

A few more steps across the hammock I brush aside yaupon holly leaves. Yaupon's leaves and twigs have an especially intriguing trait—they hold copious amounts of caffeine; it is the only North American plant that does so. Early coastal Indians such as the Timucua, who inhabited several Georgia islands and much of north Florida, brewed a caffeine-laced potion called "black drink" from the leaves. The accounts of early Spanish explorers say that Timucua men met each morning to discuss tribal matters over sips of black drink just as people meet today in coffee shops. Black drink also served another purpose: gulped in liberal amounts, it induced vomiting; hence, yaupon's scientific name, *Ilex vomitoria*. Indian men supposedly believed that retching their guts out before heading into battle or on an important hunt purged their bodies of bad spirits.[9]

Further up the path, saw palmetto grows in seemingly impenetrable thickets beneath the taller trees on each side of the trail. The thickets are favorite haunts of the dangerous eastern diamondback rattlesnake, so I watch my step. A member of the palm family, the saw palmetto is common in these parts. Its dense growth comes from hairy rhizomes, which, like those of spartina, spread laterally underground, sending up fresh green fronds every few inches or so. So strong are they that they push up asphalt in parking lots and highways. The fronds, fanning out like a tom turkey's tail, are equipped with sawlike spikes sharp enough to slice through leather.

On a more pleasing note, bees make honey from the saw palmetto's tiny, fragrant white flowers. In fall, many coastal residents reap the saw palmetto's black, olive-like berries and sell them to small pharmaceutical concerns that concoct folk medicines from them. The formula may have originated with the Seminole Indians and other tribes, who used extracts from the berries to treat a variety of symptoms, including those from an enlarged prostate gland. The Indians might have been onto something. A paper published in the *Journal of the American Medical Association* in 1998 reported that saw palmetto extract provided relief similar to that from finastride, a prostate-shrinking drug marketed as Proscar—and with fewer side effects, including impotence.[10] The researchers were not recommending that men give up prescription drugs for the extract, but it makes you wonder how many treatments for all manner of human ills are awaiting discovery in the wild.

I spy many other familiar plants. A prickly pear, Georgia's only native cactus, sports reddish purple fruits that people harvest to make jellies and sometimes wine. Some people eat the fruit raw after peeling off the tiny, sharp bristles. The burrlike seed balls of a tall sweetgum tree—important food for birds—carpet the path. In a sunny spot near the sweetgum, a large Cherokee rose vine grows. Come spring, it will sport beautiful white-and-yellow flowers. The plant is not native to the region, having been imported either directly from China or through England from China in the late 1700s, but it is nevertheless Georgia's official state flower.

A soaring specimen of another coastal native grabs my eye. Well over fifty feet, the palmetto is much taller than the other trees growing here. Arrow-straight and rot resistant, palmetto tree trunks once were used widely for wharf pilings, poles, and seawalls. Nothing gives me the sense of being on a coastal isle like the tropical-looking palmetto, also known as cabbage palm and sabal palm. The palmetto is the official state tree of South Carolina, the "Palmetto State," and a palmetto graces the state's flag.

My alma mater, Saint John's High School on John's Island, named its yearbook *The Palmetto*. Most years the image of a palmetto graced the yearbook's cover. But one year, when seniors picked up their copies, they quickly noticed that the tree had a curved trunk—and a distinct cluster of coconuts dangling from its canopy. An outraged Miss Ruby, the yearbook adviser, made the publishing company replace the coconut tree with a palmetto. It cost the company a pretty penny.

Saw palmettos grow in dense clusters in the understory of maritime forests along the Southeast coast.

The palmetto may not be as world famous as the coconut, but in the coastal ecology of the Southeast it is of great importance. A multitude of raccoons, gulls, mockingbirds, crows, and other creatures feed on palmetto fruit. Woodpeckers drill nest cavities in the trunks of dead trees. Snakes, lizards, and insects live in the piles of dead fronds on the ground around the trees. The decaying fronds build up humus in the sandy soil of hammocks and sand dunes, providing fertilizer and helping to protect against erosion. The fronds fall off as the palmetto ages, leaving the trunk with a crisscross pattern like a thatched skirt or a woven basket. When the tree is full grown, the trunk's outer layer decays and animals peel off the basket-weave pattern, leaving a smooth, fibrous gray trunk. A century ago, however, countless young palmettos weren't allowed to grow old—they were sacrificed early on for a highly sought-after delicacy, palmetto heart, or heart of palm. Chopped up and mixed in salads, palmetto heart was a gourmet's delight. Indians boiled it with bear fat to make porridge. Cutting out the heart, however, kills the young tree.

Just as important as palmettos are the red cedars that also grow profusely on hammocks in spots where lime from old oyster shells sweetens the soil. Birds and squirrels use red cedar's stringy bark for nests; white-tailed deer savor its evergreen foliage. Songbirds get excellent nutrition from cedar berries in the fall. Coastal people once used the fragrant, rot-resistant cedar wood to make fence posts, chests, and cabinets. It also was good for pencils: the Eagle Pencil Company in 1908 bought Little Saint Simons Island—the entire eighty-eight hundred acres—for its abundant cedars. Numerous cedars were cut and shipped to the pencil factory.[11] The wood of many of them, however, was found to be stressed by wind and salt spray, and unsuitable for pencils. I equate red cedar with Christmas. In December, my older brothers would take me with them in our old family bateau to the hammock near our home to cut a cedar for our holiday tree. Even today, when I smell a cedar's sweet fragrance, I recall those happy times.

As expected, my path ends abruptly at the edge of a bend in a placid tidal creek some twenty feet wide. I've been following the path for more than half an hour. Extra tall spartina, the low marsh, borders the creek. A dense cluster of greenish-gray shells—an oyster reef—lines the bank. The tide is coming in, and I realize that I must head back soon to shore, lest I have to splash through foot-deep water on the return.

Still, I linger to drink in the peacefulness. Songbirds chirp, tweet, and sing from the woods. A stunning hooded warbler, still sporting its bright yellow plumage, hops around in a shrub. Across the languid creek, amid the spartina, a statuesque great egret—long S-shaped neck, brilliant white feathers, long yellow bill—stands rigidly in a pose straight out of an Audubon painting. Nearby, just as motionless, a great blue heron is standing on a toppled, sun-bleached tree trunk. Then, to my delight, one of the loveliest creatures in North America flashes by in front of me. The dazzling red, green, blue, and yellow plumage of the male painted bunting looks like a parrot's. The bird disappears into the spartina, presumably in search of insects or seeds. I am amazed that such a colorful creature can blend so well into the marsh grass. I also am a little surprised that it is still here, because these buntings migrate in early fall to their winter grounds in Central America.

I wait a few minutes for it to reappear, but it doesn't. A mullet plops in the creek. Seconds later, I hear heavy splashing from around a bend downstream. I can't see what's going on, but I suspect a bottle-nosed dolphin is chasing mullet upstream, trying to trap them on the creek bank, as is the habit of dolphins.

A Roar in the Marsh

Suddenly, from somewhere nearby to my left, a bulldozer roars to life. Seconds later, a dull, heavy *thump, thump, thump* joins the 'dozer's raucous roar. I quickly make my way through saw palmetto and wax myrtle to the other side of the hammock. Looking across a three-hundred-yard-wide expanse of marsh toward Skidaway, I see a pile driver steadily pounding a stout pole into the island's black soil. The bulldozer, puffing thick exhaust, is scraping away dense, shrubby vegetation. A bonfire billowing clouds of gray smoke devours a pile of dead trees. A strip of garishly orange plastic netting stretches along the marsh edge, apparently to prevent dirt from going into the marsh.

Another subdivision with fancy houses and views of the marsh is being born. It is next to a marsh cove area, out of view from the path I just followed to the hammock. Had I not heard the bulldozer and the pile driver, I probably would not have seen this site. Now it's in plain view. Anxious to check it out, I hurry back across the hammock and the marsh to the shore of Skidaway, where my car is parked. I drive along a sandy dirt road toward the construction.

Soon I am staring at a big sign announcing the Marshes at Skidaway, "a continuing care retirement community." A free brochure that I take from a box hanging from the sign says that if I buy a place here, it will be my "private residence . . . thoughtfully designed to blend smoothly and gracefully into the natural beauty of the coastal marshes."

Another development. Scores of subdivisions and retirement communities like this one are sprouting up all along the coasts of Georgia and the Carolinas—like the proverbial mushrooms springing up on a lawn overnight. Numerous other developments are planned. A ranger at nearby Skidaway Island State Park tells me that the Marshes at Skidaway is the reason the park pulled up one of its boardwalks across the marsh and tore down an observation tower. The huge houses sitting on the marsh edge will spoil visitors' grand views of the marsh, the ranger says.

Land Boom

The Southeast coast is under siege. So rapidly is real estate development exploding along the coasts of Georgia, Florida, and the Carolinas that you have to wonder if the land will sink under all the extra weight. Developers are rolling out plans for gated subdivisions, condo complexes, golf courses, and shopping centers on any piece of land that appears dry—or that can be drained and made that way.

"Poorly planned development—like what we see in Florida—is the single largest threat to the Southeast coast," warns David Pope, a lawyer and director of the Southern Environmental Law Center's Atlanta office. "Large tracts of previously undeveloped land are being sold for development that is not environmentally sensitive. Lax enforcement of environmental laws is making matters worse. If these trends continue, the marshes and the coast will be unrecognizable within a decade."

The steep plunge in the nation's economy, Pope tells me, will provide only a brief respite from the frenzied pace. The economy will bounce back—and with it a resumption of the coast's torrid growth, he predicts. "It's tough to picture during our current economic downturn, but there is a tidal wave of growth headed straight for Georgia's coast." The population of the ten-county coastal region jumped by 62 percent between 1970 and 2000, he notes, and conservative estimates call for a whopping 51 percent increase by 2030.[12] The estimate has remained unaltered despite the weak economy.

Pope, one of some forty savvy environmental lawyers with the SELC, says the organization's priority is to protect the coast from willy-nilly development. That is not at odds, he says, with appropriate and lawful use of private property. "But current development trends on the Southeast coast are highly disturbing."

Even the hammocks in the middle of salt marshes are not immune. As available mainland property is snatched up, hundreds of marsh hammocks like the one I was just on—considered unbuildable on only a few years ago—are being targeted for McMansions. Developers up and down the coast are besieging state authorities for permits to build bridges across the marsh to the fragile islands. The impending threats prompted Scenic America, a Washington-based group that recognizes places of exceptional beauty, to place Georgia's hammocks on its list of America's ten most endangered landscapes.[13] Coastal ecologists say the unfettered development of hammocks could be the tipping point—we could look back some day and say, "That's where we lost our marshes."

Where will the rush to build on the coast end? No one knows. What is known is that the environmental health of salt marshes is inextricably tied to the well-being of the land. Protection of the marshes must begin with protection of the land.

Tide Watching

O N A GLORIOUS June morning on the South Carolina coast, the tide is out and a salty tang suffuses the air. I'm tarrying on my brother Wilson's splintery, barnacle-encrusted dock, which juts into a tidal creek. The little stream twists and curves through the salt marsh in back of my old home on John's Island. The spartina is lush, mint green, and summertime beautiful. Red-winged blackbirds questing for insects wheel and swoop through the cloudless blue sky and light among the spartina stalks.

With the tide out, the creek is little more than a trickle. Its exposed bottom is mostly a glistening mudflat—black muck stewing in the sun. The mud exudes the sulfide aroma that reminds me I'm home. Like a mass of olive pits, hordes of little black mud snails patrol the mud's surface in search of algae and anything dead. Along the bare lower creek banks, countless creeping fiddler crabs forage.

The little unnamed tributary is typical of thousands of small streams that dissect southeastern tidal marshes. I am here to watch the tide come in. Honest. The tides' rising and falling always have been magical for me— like witnessing the inner workings of a great circulatory system whose systolic and diastolic forces pump lifeblood through pulsating tissues.

Above all else, salt marshes are ruled by the tides. Coastal marshes are among only a handful of Earth's natural ecosystems—the others being mangrove forests, beaches, and rocky seashores—subjected to these predictable daily inundations. Animals that live in the marsh or regularly come to it for food and shelter must move to the tidal beat. Here in South Carolina, the tides twice daily sweep into the rivers and sounds and then into smaller and smaller creeks—and then cover the entire marsh with

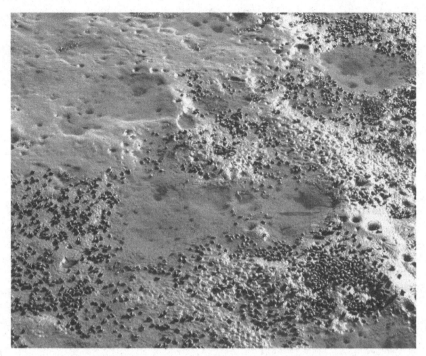

Mud snails (*Ilynassa obsoleta*) congregate by the thousands in tidal creeks at low tide and feed in the film on top of the bare mud.

a mixture of salt water from the sea and fresh water off the land. It's a remarkable transformation that amazes those who witness it for the first time—and even those who have seen it countless times. A professor once explained the process to me: "Tidal creeks and rivers," she said, "assume dendritic patterns of smaller and smaller channels, which act both as tributaries during ebb tides and distributaries during flood tides."

Sidney Lanier had the same idea but expressed it differently:

Look how the grace of the sea doth go
About and about through the intricate channels that flow
Here and there,
Everywhere.
Till his waters have flooded the uttermost creeks and the low-lying lanes,
And the marsh is meshed with a million veins. ("Marshes of Glynn," lines
81–86)

Like the blood coursing through my arteries, the brownish-green tidewater that soon will fill my creek will bring in life-giving oxygen and the daily supply of nutrients and sediments that help spartina flourish. The incoming water will be engorged with life—young fish seeking food and shelter, free-floating microscopic plants and animals collectively known as plankton, and an assortment of other creatures too numerous to mention. Later, the outgoing tide will flush from the marsh a literal bouillabaisse of decayed spartina and energy-rich algae, fungi, bacteria, and other microorganisms that will help sustain masses of other organisms in the creeks and estuaries, and perhaps in the sea beyond.

My little creek is fed by the broad Stono River, which connects directly to the Atlantic Ocean some fifteen sinuous miles downstream from where I loll on the dock. Across the marsh I see the river's open, shimmering blue water. A one-masted sailboat, white jib and mainsail hoisted, plods down the river. Named for an ancient Indian tribe, the Stono wraps around John's Island and separates it from James Island and the Charleston County mainland. In all, the Stono meanders inland for some twenty miles through wide expanses of salt marsh. At its mouth, a large sandbar harbors one of the largest brown pelican rookeries on the East Coast. In its upper reaches, where I sit, the Stono is part of the Atlantic Intracoastal Waterway—an artery of commerce and small-boat thoroughfare that extends two thousand miles from Massachusetts to the Florida Keys. Boats plying the Stono reach Charleston Harbor via a short stretch of water called Wappoo Cut.

Like nearly everything else around Charleston, the Stono is redolent of history. Its banks once abounded with antebellum plantations of rice and indigo—and later, of sea island cotton—where teams of sweating African slaves labored. Fierce Revolutionary and Civil War battles were fought along its banks.

A few miles upriver from me, on the Sunday morning of September 9, 1739, slaves rose up against their masters in what became known as the Stono Rebellion—the largest slave uprising in the American colonies prior to the Revolution. The band of twenty slaves, some newly arrived from Angola, marched down the dusty road that they believed would take them to Florida. Bearing banners proclaiming "Liberty," they broke into a store and snatched guns and ammunition. Marching south, they recruited more slaves, and their number swelled to as many as a hundred. They killed several whites along the way. By nightfall, the authorities had caught up with them. All but one of the freedom seekers were eventually captured and put to death.[1]

As I watch the tide come in, I wonder if any of those enslaved people ever gazed upon this same salt marsh and pondered what lay beyond the horizon—beyond the dark green band of trees across the river where busy U.S. Highway 17 now runs down to Florida. Surely they would have been in tune with the tides—life on the sea islands revolved around the rising and receding waters. The coastal plantations depended on the tidal rivers for travel, hauling supplies, and shipping cotton. My ancestors' John's Island Presbyterian Church, erected in 1719 and still used today, once scheduled its services in accordance with the tides to accommodate families on far-flung plantations. The tides would have dictated when fish, shrimp, oysters, and other seafood could be taken from the waterways.

Tidewater also was power. Rice plantations carved from brackish and freshwater marshes along the river's upper reaches utilized tide-run threshing mills, which threshed and ground the rice grown in fields flooded by the tides. Controlling water flow in the fields was a system of gates, valves, and sluices operated by slaves.

I wonder if they knew what powered the tides.

The Tides

The energy for these daily water movements comes primarily from the gravitational tugging between Earth and its moon—and, at certain times of the month, the sun. Like magnets, the Earth and moon attract each other. As the moon passes over any given area, it pulls at the Earth and everything on it. The pulling causes the ocean directly facing the moon to bulge out toward it, creating a high tide on that side of the Earth. Another high tide is occurring on the planet's other side at the same time because the entire solid Earth is being drawn slightly toward the moon, leaving the ocean waters behind.

Meanwhile, the sides of Earth between the tidal bulges experience low tide. It all works amazingly like clockwork because the moon circles the Earth every twenty-four hours and fifty minutes. The heaping ridges of seawater follow the moon in its rotation. Thus, a high tide occurs on shorelines every twelve hours and twenty-five minutes, with a low tide happening midway between the highs.

About every two weeks, when the moon is new or full, we get extra high tides. At these times the Earth, sun, and moon are in a straight line, and the gravitational pull of the latter two bodies combines, causing tides to be exceptionally high and strong. These higher tides are known as "spring tides," although they don't have anything to do with the season of that name. Rather, they seem to "spring" from the Earth.

During the moon's quarter phases, the sun and moon work at right angles, causing the bulges almost to cancel each other out. The result is a smaller difference between high and low tides; the resulting "neap tides" are especially weak tides.

The difference between the water levels at low tide and high tide here on my brother's dock can be eight feet or more; it is one of the greatest tidal changes along the Southeast coast. But it is not *the* greatest. That distinction belongs to an area south of me, near Brunswick, Georgia, where the tidal range is as much as ten feet.[2] That is because Georgia's shore is the westernmost coastline on the Atlantic Seaboard, putting it at the center of a giant coastal arc between Cape Hatteras, North Carolina, and Cape Canaveral, Florida, called the South Atlantic Bight. At high tide, the inward-curving coastline forces water along the entire Southeast coast to "pile up," creating a ten-foot tidal change at the arc's center near Brunswick. The arc's sides, essentially the coasts of Florida and North Carolina, have tides of only two or three feet.[3]

The higher tides on the Georgia and South Carolina coasts are the main reason why the tidal sounds, rivers, bays, and marshes indenting those shorelines are places of tremendous water exchange. In general, the higher the tidal range, the greater the salt marsh's productivity. It follows, then, that the salt marshes of Georgia and South Carolina produce more food energy than any other stretch of marsh on the Eastern Seaboard. The marshes attain their greatest width—nearly eight miles—at the apex of the South Atlantic Bight between Brunswick and Beaufort, South Carolina. The two states together harbor in excess of eight hundred thousand acres of salt marsh, more than half of all the marsh along the entire U.S. East Coast. Nearly every acre of the endless wetlands is drained and refilled during each tidal cycle—some 1.3 trillion gallons each cycle.[4]

Loaded with silt, sand, and clay from land and sea, the incoming high tide ripples swiftly into the tidal creeks, gouging out the channels and deepening them. Mud scoured from the bottoms and banks also becomes suspended in the water. But once the fast-moving water leaves the narrow creeks and spills into the marsh, the resistance of the countless spartina stalks and the sudden increase in area decelerate its flow. The slower-moving water is no longer able to hold onto its suspended sediments, which settle out along the creek banks and into the marsh itself.

This deposition often forms one of the most remarkable features of southeastern salt marshes—natural levees along creek banks. Rising like gentle speed bumps on a street, the mud humps build up until they are higher than all but the highest spring tides. The levees wield a strong influence over water movement in the marsh—dictating, for instance, how much water reaches various marsh areas. Well-developed levees on older creeks can funnel water, organisms, and nutrients farther into a marsh's nooks and crannies, thus increasing productivity there.[5]

Water coursing into a creek moves along until it either finds breaks in the levees or reaches "distributaries," smaller streams that branch off from the head of the creek into the marsh. From there, the water flows over the marsh in a sheet and slowly engulfs the entire wetland. At the peak of the six-hour tidal cycle, the marsh is at its highest inundation.[6]

During the outgoing tide, the water exits the marsh in reverse fashion. Most small streams are left nearly empty, their oozy, black-mud bottoms exposed once again to sun and air. In the smaller creeks, not even a lone shrimp can find water enough to stay alive. Only the larger, deeper creeks and some shallow depressions still hold enough water at low tide to sustain shrimp and other swimming creatures.

Low tide also exposes mudflats—wide swaths of bare, mushy mud on the edges of creeks, rivers, and bays that are similar to floodplains along inland rivers but too low in elevation to support vegetation even as hardy as spartina. Ecologically, mudflats are closely related to the marshes, but they are also valuable ecosystems in their own right for an array of marine life.

Not all tidal floodwater exits the marsh and mudflats at low tide. A considerable portion seeps into the mud's countless tiny pores—the air spaces between the tightly packed mud particles. Enough of this "pore water" remains in the mud to render it squishy and waterlogged. Most of it eventually will move by gravity and other forces as groundwater toward the creek beds and will enter the creeks at low tide. As it slowly moves, the pore water deposits nutrients in the marsh for spartina and other living things and helps flush out wastes.

A fraction of an inch into the mud, however, the water circulation and diffusion are insufficient to supply oxygen readily to the microscopic spaces between mud particles—and thus to meet the oxygen demand of aerobic microbes in the mud. It is a major reason why marsh mud is anaerobic, or without air, except for the thin layer at the surface. Only anaerobic bacteria can live in the airless mud.[7] Rather than using oxygen for their metabolic needs, these bacteria remove sulfates from the water and release hydrogen sulfide gas as a waste product. The "rotten egg" odor of the gas contributes to the marsh's characteristic smell.

The countless fiddler crabs, worms, and other creatures that burrow into the marsh mud have their own special adaptations for getting oxygen. Their burrows help diffuse oxygen to deeper sediment layers and to plant roots.

Marsh Origins

The origin of the great marshes of the Southeast can be traced back about eighteen thousand years to the time when the Earth started warming its way out of the Pleistocene Ice Age and the stupendously thick glacial ice sheets that smothered much of North America, Europe, and Asia began to melt and recede. A prevailing theory is that the ice melt raised sea levels and flooded the coast and the mainland. High coastal dunes and ridges kicked up over the millennia by winds, waves, and tides became barrier islands as the rising seas surrounded them.[8]

The quiet ocean waters in the islands' lee formed extensive shallow lagoons, which began filling with sand brought in from the sea by the tides and with eroded clay, silt, and minerals ferried in by rivers originating inland in distant foothills. As the lagoons became clogged, they built up in altitude to a point where they were no longer under water at low tide. They became fertile ground for fast-growing *Spartina alterniflora*, which took root and thrived. The densely growing marsh grass slowed wind and currents, causing even more sediment deposition. In time, spartina-dominated salt marshes spread far and wide between the islands and followed tidal estuaries and rivers, such as the Stono, for several miles inland.

Amazing Spartina

Spartina thrives in tidal marshes because it is one of the most remarkable plants on Earth. Few plants can live where land meets sea. Most other plants would quickly perish when confronted with so much salt. Spartina throws it off—literally. Its root cells bar most of the salt in seawater from entering the plant. Specialized glands in the tough, narrow blades pump out any salt that does get in. Examine a blade of living spartina and you'll see flecks of ejected salt crystals sparkling in the sunlight—a remarkable example of an organism evolving and adapting to harsh surroundings.[9]

Spartina endures another adversity that would spell doom for most other plants—the near absence of oxygen in marsh soil. The pore water blocks oxygen from penetrating more than half an inch into the mud, and the soil's surface is crowded with trillions of microorganisms that consume most of the oxygen that is present; very little is left to percolate into the mud.[10]

The shortage of oxygen presents a problem for spartina's roots, which extend into the anaerobic mud. Roots need oxygen. Spartina meets this need through another adaptation: a system of hollow tubes like giant soda straws that run lengthwise through its leaves and stems to its roots. The leaves take in air from the outside through tiny openings called stomata, which slam shut if necessary to keep water out—an important trait at high tide. The tubes conduct the oxygen down to the roots, where cells use the gas to produce energy for growth.[11] (The air ducts also provide ants and spiders with a refuge both from predators and from water at high tide.)

Most of the time, the tubes are so efficient that the root cells have more oxygen than they need. The extra gas diffuses out into a small area around the roots where aerobic (oxygen-using) bacteria process vital nutrients such as nitrates, phosphates, sulfates, and potassium that nourish spartina.

The escaped oxygen helps spartina in another way as well. Spartina has an unusually high appetite for iron, which is crucial for its growth. Most of the iron in the mud is locked up in iron sulfide, which is not soluble in water and is thus unavailable to spartina. But the oxygen released by the roots oxidizes iron sulfide to form water-soluble ferrous sulfate, which spartina can absorb to get the iron it needs.[12]

Spartina is well anchored in the mud by its extensive tangles of roots and rootlike rhizomes—underground stems growing horizontally in the mud. The rhizomes promote rapid colonization by giving rise to new growth. As the rhizomes grow outward from a plant, they push new spartina shoots to the surface.

Spartina's belowground mass is substantial, as much as two and a half times that of the visible aboveground parts. The underground growth helps spartina recover from freezing, fire, and other hazards. Of utmost importance to the environment, this growth also helps keep the marsh intact. Without the dense network of roots and rhizomes binding the soil, the muddy banks of rivers and creeks would wash away. By holding creek banks together, spartina also helps buffer the mainland and mitigate damage from storm surges and waves. Just a ten-foot-wide stretch of spartina can absorb most of a wave's energy, easing the pounding from storms and boat wakes.

The Marsh Zones

Although the marsh looks flat from above, spartina's height and density vary considerably depending on its location in the marsh. No one knows exactly why this is so, but it probably has something to do with the tides' waste-flushing actions and the amount of nutrients they ferry into the various marsh reaches. It also apparently has something to do with the amount of time spartina stands in water. The marsh grass is one of nature's hardiest plants, but there's a limit to how long even spartina can stay submerged—probably six hours.[13]

Spartina doesn't grow at all on the lowest parts of creek banks, where tidal flow is greatest and the mud is inundated for hours on end. The mud surface there is bare except for simple organisms such as single-celled algae, which often are so abundant that they create a golden sheen. Lacking spartina's roots and rhizomes to give it structure, the mud here is the mushiest of the whole marsh. This is where you're most likely to sink hip-deep in sucking muck.[14]

The upper creek bank, though only a few feet higher, is an ideal environment for spartina. The marsh grass is at its most luxuriant here, grow-

Salt marsh on Sapelo Island, Georgia.

ing as tall as nine feet and producing more than seventeen tons of biomass per acre annually—as productive as a well-fertilized field of sugar cane. Although the tides regularly swab the boggy upper creek bank soil, it is not flooded for as long a time as the lower creek bank. The tide efficiently brings in loads of nutrients and sediments to the upper bank and washes away salt, dead matter, and other wastes. Changes in temperature and water salinity are minimal here. The mud also is better aerated, which keeps the marshy sulfide odor at bay.

The spartina atop the levees and in the expansive lower marsh area directly behind them is shorter, about three to four feet tall. Though the tides also flood this marsh zone for several hours a day, it doesn't get as many nutrients and sediments as the upper creek bank does. Still, the lower marsh appears rich, like a waving, grassy meadow. This zone also happens to be one of the liveliest places in the entire marsh. Fungi, bacteria, algae, and other microscopic life-forms cover nearly every square inch of its mud. Feeding on them are masses of slightly larger, but still ultratiny, creatures collectively known as "meiofauna"—nematodes, protozoa, copepods, amphipods, and annelids that live on or just below the mud's surface. Foraging for the meiofauna and for algae and bits of dead spartina on the mud are the more conspicuous "macrofauna" such as mud fiddlers, purple marsh crabs, snails, and several mud-burrowing marine worm species known as polychaetes. Oyster beds line the creek banks. Clumps of another mollusk, the ribbed mussel, are especially dense in the lower marsh.[15]

Closer to land and only a few inches higher in elevation is the high marsh zone. Flooding here is less frequent and of shorter duration. The soil is sandier and the spartina is only a foot or two tall. Its productivity is only about one-half to one-fourth of that in the taller stands, and it must compete with other plants such as needlerush and saltbush for nutrients and space. Meiofauna abundance is lower in the high marsh zone, and the mud fiddlers and purple marsh crabs give way to sand fiddlers, red-jointed fiddlers, and wharf crabs. Periwinkle snails, though, are abundant, perhaps because two of their larger predators, blue crabs and diamondback terrapins, are not as populous here.[16]

But the most remarkable thing about spartina marshes is not readily apparent: the incredible array of valuable services they render to the environment. Not only do they buffer the land from surging storm waters, they also filter out pollutants, recycle immense quantities of nutrients, and help prevent upland flooding. As green plants, they also absorb carbon dioxide and produce oxygen. And all the while the marshes serve as vast nurseries — vital shelters and feeding grounds for young shrimp, blue crabs, menhaden, oysters, anchovies, red drum, and on and on. They can do all of this because they form intimate, intricate relationships with some of the planet's most remarkable bodies of water, the estuaries. For every acre of permanently submerged estuary there are one to three acres of marsh fringing it. Together, the marshes and estuaries form an extraordinary ecosystem.

The Estuaries

Estuaries are transition zones between land and sea — mixing bowls, in essence, where ocean-strength salt water pumped in by the tides blends with fresh water that washes directly off the land or is delivered by rivers flowing down from uplands. Oceanside bays, inlets, sounds, and lower stretches of rivers: all are estuaries, sheltered on two or three sides by land and connected on one side to the open sea.

The clashes between salty ocean water and fresh river water in the estuaries kick out rich loads of nutrients and sediments. These ultimately make their way into the marshes at high tide via the connecting tidal creeks, providing nutrients for spartina and sediments that build up the marsh and keep it above rising sea levels.

The fertilized spartina grows abundantly. When the plant dies and decays, the ebb tide transports a substantial portion of its nutritious remains, called detritus, out of the marsh and into the creeks, and from there into the estuaries, where it becomes food for still another wide array of creatures.

The creeks also are the essential pathways by which swarms of larvae and juveniles of shrimp, crabs, finfish, and other marine creatures come into the marsh from the estuary to feed and dodge predators. Born in nearshore ocean spawning grounds, the teeming masses are carried into the creeks by the tides and water currents. They stay until late summer or early fall, growing rapidly until they reach early adulthood, then head back to nearshore ocean waters to spawn and complete their life cycles.[17]

In general, the more creeks a marsh has, the greater the exchange of nutrients, sediments, and animals between the marsh and estuary.[18]

The major estuaries of the Southeast extend inland as much as thirty miles or more, to the point where river water becomes fresh and tides have negligible effect. For all of their importance, however, estuaries aren't outlined on maps. They have no well-defined borders and, unlike sounds, bays, rivers, and creeks, are not generally accorded proper names.

Most of the eighteen major estuaries on the Southeast coast connect to the Atlantic through bays and wide sounds that lie between the barrier islands. The lower stretches of the Altamaha River in Georgia, the Pee Dee in South Carolina, the Cape Fear in North Carolina, and the Saint Johns in Florida are among our largest estuaries. Though they all have common features and functions—high productivity and nutrient trapping—each is unique in its biology, geology, and water characteristics.

In between the larger estuaries are smaller constricted inlets—in essence, smaller estuaries—that also allow the passage of seawater into tidal creeks and marshes but are seldom connected to sizable freshwater streams.[19] Most of the fresh water in these smaller estuaries comes directly from local storm runoff—as is the case, for example, in the Stono River. But in the major estuaries, most of the fresh water is delivered by rivers originating far inland and meandering for hundreds of miles through swamps, farms, cities, and forests. Along the way the water loads up with nutrients and sediments—and pollutants—from the land.[20]

The extent of freshwater-seawater mixing dictates an estuary's most important characteristic: its salinity, the amount of salt in the water. Scientists now have new ways for reporting salinity, but in this book I use the older measurement, parts per thousand (ppt). In a typical southeastern estuary, salinity decreases steadily from ocean to river. At the seaward edge of the estuary, the water is still near ocean strength—about thirty-five parts salt per thousand parts water, corresponding roughly to a tablespoon of salt in a glass of water. Away from the sea, salinity levels drop as fresh water (zero salinity) pushes into the estuary. The salt tang in the air diminishes, as does the presence of marine life in the water. Saltwater-loving creatures such as starfish, present at an estuary's salty mouth, are absent from the upper estuary.[21]

Scientists have special names for the zones of varying salinity levels in estuaries. The high-salinity area (18–35 ppt) adjacent to the sea is called "polyhaline." The middle-salinity area (5–18 ppt) constitutes the "mesohaline" zone. The low-salinity area (0.5–5 ppt) is the "oligohaline" zone. Marshes flooded by polyhaline water are overwhelmingly dominated by the salt-tolerant *Spartina alterniflora*. Brackish marshes, having both salt- and freshwater characteristics, occur in the mesohaline and oligohaline areas and are usually dominated by black needlerush.[22] Also growing thickly there is another spartina species, *Spartina cynosuroides*, or big cordgrass, which is better suited to lower-salinity waters than its relative. In the least salty parts of the marsh, wild rice—good food for birds—often dominates. Many large expanses of tidal brackish and freshwater marshes were impounded and transformed into rice fields during the great rice-growing era before the Civil War.

Several factors, especially daily and seasonal cycles, drive estuarine water mixing. Storms at sea, for instance, can push seawater high up a river and render it saltier. Seasonally, salinity goes up during summer when river flow and stream flow are lower as a result of higher evaporation rates.

Salinity declines in March, the month of maximum freshwater runoff. After heavy rains the salinity may drop so much that freshwater fish come poking around in an estuary.[23] Physical factors also influence salinity. Salt water, for instance, is heavier than fresh water; thus, water at the bottom of an estuary may be saltier than that at the top.

The biggest influence on water mixing, though, is the daily tides. Strong high tides, especially spring tides, can shove salt water further upstream, thereby raising an estuary's overall salinity. At low tide, when the force of the tide eases, rivers may gain the upper hand and deliver fresh water further downstream — thus lowering the salinity. In general, the greater the river's flow, the more influence it has on water mixing in the estuary.[24]

Of all the attributes that determine whether an estuary will be a sanctuary for marine creatures, salinity is by far the most crucial. Marine animals are generally adapted to living in water of high salinity, although some can tolerate much lower salt levels. Oysters, for instance, can survive for a while in water with salts as low as five parts per thousand, whereas their predator, the oyster drill, can stand no less than nine parts per thousand. The difference results in an oyster "line" that marks a safe zone for oysters.[25]

For the many fish, shrimp, crabs, and other creatures that spend at least part of their lives in estuaries and marshes, salinity ups and downs are of utmost significance for other reasons. These creatures use salinity, along with other environmental cues, as ecological clocks to time reproduction so that it coincides with the best environment for their young. The young usually have broad salinity tolerances and tend to do well in upper estuaries and headwaters of tidal creeks, which generally have the widest salinity fluctuations of any areas of marsh and estuary. The variable salinities work in the young creatures' favor because potential predators and competitors from the ocean are less tolerant of the ever-changing conditions.[26]

It should come as no surprise that when humans manipulate freshwater flows, as by building dams, the intricate life cycles of estuarine creatures can be upset. Understanding salinity's daily and seasonal fluctuations is vital in managing and maintaining the health of estuaries and salt marshes. Upset the daily salinity rhythms of a marsh, and many organisms will perish.[27]

The marshes also are vital dining areas for the teeming masses. Without them, untold numbers of marine creatures in the estuaries and nearshore ocean waters would starve. The food web begins with the green plants, as it does in nearly every other ecosystem on Earth.

The Marsh Food Web

Whether it is an ocean, rainforest, freshwater lake—or salt marsh—an ecosystem's "primary producers" are the green plants and algae that capture the sun's energy through the process of photosynthesis and provide the basic nourishment, directly or indirectly, for all other organisms. Scientists once used the term "food chain" to describe how energy is passed from one living thing to another, from primary producers to consumers. More popular now is the more encompassing term "food web."

In salt marshes and estuaries, spartina and microscopic algae (though not necessarily green) floating in the water and living on the mud are the primary producers. Myriad "consumers" such as zooplankton, fish, and crabs rely on the food they produce.

When scientists began studying food webs in salt marshes and estuaries in Georgia during the 1950s, they focused primarily on the most visibly dominant species—*Spartina alterniflora*—and considered production by algae and other microorganisms insignificant. The scientists postulated that snails, worms, nibbling and sucking insects, and other lowly invertebrates were chewing up vast amounts of marsh grass and were in turn being eaten by higher-level consumers. To their surprise, they discovered that insects, snails, and other herbivores eat only about 5 percent of the living spartina. One reason is that spartina is made mostly of indigestible cellulose, the extratough substance from which most green plants make their cell walls and derive their strength.[28] Most of the spartina, then, was going down some other food pathway. But which one?

Scientists found the answer while puzzling over another phenomenon: although huge expanses of spartina wither and die every year in late fall and winter, most of the marsh floor remains remarkably bare of the dead material. The scientists postulated that the marsh's teeming microscopic life, a massive invisible bulk in the ecosystem, had something to do with it. And they were right—the marsh is a veritable microbial food factory.[29]

When spartina succumbs to old age or to freezing temperatures or to other causes of death, fungi and other microbes living on its stems and leaves immediately attack it. Even so, the dead plant may remain upright for weeks. Tides and winds and waves tug at it and further weaken it. When it does topple over, an immense multitude of bacteria and other microbes join the feast. With amazing efficiency they shred, break, and grind the dead stalks and leaves into tiny pieces called detritus—a basic staple of the salt marsh—while deriving energy for their own growth.[30]

Much of the disintegrated spartina remains on the marsh surface, but the tides also transport large amounts of it to mudflats and other locations around the marsh and estuary. Other microorganisms and ultratiny invertebrates latch onto the flecks and break them down into even more minute bits, in effect transforming the indigestible spartina into a highly nutritious mass of microbial protoplasm that numerous creatures can readily digest.

In the marsh itself, the decomposition occurs mostly in or on the mud. Bottom-dwelling consumers such as worms, amphipods, fish, shrimp, and crabs gorge on the tiny bits of enriched matter. At high tide, filter feeders such as oysters, clams, and mussels filter the detritus from the water. The detritus eaters digest the material and excrete the undigested, nutrient-rich remains in feces, which are colonized by more microorganisms and provide food for still others—a process that goes on and on until only traces of detritus are left. The remainder helps fertilize the next spartina crop, and the whole food web cycle is repeated—a remarkable example of nature's highly efficient recycling.[31]

A substantial portion of the detritus, however, may not be consumed in the marsh at all. A large percentage may be carried out by the tides to form a nutritious broth—a veritable "sea soup" that ultimately provides at least some nourishment for marine life in marshes, estuaries, and nearshore ocean waters. The detritus consumers themselves become food for bigger fish and other creatures—birds, raccoons, otters, minks, and humans.[32]

Detritus and Algae

The overall importance of detritus in sustaining life in the salt marsh, estuary, and nearshore ocean has been the subject of considerable debate. Scientists now believe that very few organisms of the marsh and estuary rely solely on detritus.

In particular, scientists have gained great respect for the single-celled photosynthetic algae that occupy the lowest levels of the salt marsh food web. As late as the 1980s, algae's contribution to the food web was thought to be small, less than one-tenth of spartina's. We now know that algae generate nutrients equal to at least one-third of spartina's net production. In some cases algae actually equal spartina as a food resource in marsh and estuary.[33] Marsh consumers probably eat a combination of detritus, algae, and other items, depending on their life stage. The larvae of bottom-feeding white shrimp, for example, eat algae and tiny invertebrates such as copepods, while juvenile and adult white shrimp feed on detritus, microorganisms, tiny marine worms, and other ultrasmall organisms.

Two general types of one-celled algae are primary producers in the creeks, marshes, and estuaries of the Southeast—phytoplankton, which float freely in the water; and benthic algae, which live on mudflats, creek bottoms, and in the marsh itself. For their growth, both types absorb phosphates and nitrates derived from decomposed spartina or brought in by the tides and rivers.[34]

The floating algae, however, may not be abundant throughout the year. In the Southeast—especially in Georgia and South Carolina—tidal water made cloudy by detritus, suspended sediments, and dissolved organic material washing down from uplands and upriver swamps may limit algal growth by blocking sunlight. During those times, detritus might have to take up the slack. Fortunately, as already noted, numerous creatures of marsh and estuary can thrive on either.[35]

Free-floating phytoplankton provides nutrition for swarms of microscopic animals known as zooplankton, a name that covers a wide assortment of living creatures that includes larvae of oysters, clams, crabs, shrimp, snails, worms, fish; and tiny tintinnids, ciliates, amoebae, rotifers, arthropods, and copepods. All are found in the water in varying numbers and composition according to the season. Zooplankton feed on phytoplankton like deer grazing on a meadow and, in turn, become prey for other creatures, such as juvenile fish, which in turn are eaten by adult fish and wading birds.[36]

The microscopic benthic algae, or mud algae—diatoms, flagellates, dinoflagellates, and the like—may cover the mud of creek bottoms, mudflats, and the marsh itself by the billions per square foot. Like spartina, the algae are vital for the health of the marsh. The thin mats they form trap fine sediments, help stabilize mud particles against resuspension in the water, and provide homes to numerous tiny invertebrates. Diatoms, each encased in a filigreed skeleton of silica, are by far the most numerous—so dense are they, in fact, that they form a characteristic greenish-gold film on the mud surface of creek banks and levees. At low tide, herds of hungry mud snails and fiddlers forage for them on the mud.

Winter is peak mud algae production time. Winter sunlight is weak and not likely to dry them out, as summer's heat does. At low tide in summer, diatoms glide into the mud to escape the heat and reemerge at high tide, when the water filters out the sunlight. But then they are exposed to ravenous juvenile shrimp and to filter feeders such as mussels, oysters, and worms.[37]

Lawrence R. Pomeroy, a retired University of Georgia researcher and renowned salt marsh expert, is among those who maintain that the benthic algae and phytoplankton equal detritus in importance as food sources in creeks and estuaries. After years of research he arrived at a provocative conclusion: Rather than feeding the animals in the estuary, the marsh's primary role may be in providing structure and stability for them. It stabilizes the sediments and provides good habitat in which they can hide from predators and feed on the microalgae.

While some other scientists still believe that spartina is the marsh's most important nutrient provider, newer research supports Pomeroy's view. Studies by Wei-jun Cai and colleagues at the University of Georgia suggest that the primary role of the microbes eating dead spartina in marshes and estuaries is carbon dioxide fixation—helping to regulate the gas in the atmosphere, and thus playing a huge role in the planet's carbon cycle. Such intense microbial activity also might explain why the water leaving the marsh at high tide is low in dissolved oxygen: the microbes use vast amounts of it in digesting the spartina.[38]

But whatever the marsh's main function may be, one thing is starkly clear: without spartina there would be no salt marsh. Spartina protects flora and fauna with the roots and stems and food-rich nooks and crannies that make the marsh the ocean's nursery. If something happened to remove spartina from the marsh, the consequences would be catastrophic. Populations of our crabs, shrimp, and fish would plummet to drastically low levels, perhaps leading to extinction in many areas.

Studies confirm this prediction. The nearby offshore waters yield much more seafood in places with extensive salt marshes along the shore. Catches of shrimp, for example, greatly increase with the amount of salt marsh directly inshore of the shrimping areas.[39]

Nonetheless, were spartina the only basic food source in marshes and estuaries, these ecosystems would not be the highly productive places that they are. It is the combined input from spartina, phytoplankton, and benthic algae that makes the marshes and estuaries such vastly important feeding grounds and nurseries for marine creatures. Tinker with this well-tuned ecosystem, and you risk ecological chaos.

The Tide Comes In

As I tarry on my brother's dock, watching the tide rise, I am pondering these facts. The little creek flowing below me is becoming a broad, unde-fined waterway as it and the surrounding marsh fill with tidewater. The incoming water is saturated with life-giving oxygen, a result of churning by waves, winds, and currents in the estuary. It also is laden with dissolved ni-trogen, phosphorus, and other nutrients that will be delivered to all parts of the marsh.

As the tide rises, sharp encounters between producer and consumer, prey and predator, small fish and big fish, will take place in nearly every niche of the marsh. Already the rising water is bestirring smaller creatures to swim, wiggle, or scurry for cover to escape the hungry predators that will come in with the tide.

Sidney Lanier, looking out over the marshes in Georgia, wondered what was in the incoming water: "And I would I could know what swim-meth below when the tide comes in / On the length and the breadth of the marvelous marshes of Glynn" (lines 104–5).

I can't see everything in the murky water, but past experience helps me guess what is in the waterborne parade entering the creek. Each splash holds bits of detritus and a riot of tiny life—diatoms, coiled filaments of cyanobacteria, and numerous other phytoplankton species. Frenziedly consuming the phytoplankton and the detritus are the swarms of free-floating zooplankton. The zooplankton will become food for fingerlings such as menhaden, which will in turn be eaten by larger fish.

More than fifty species of fish, shrimp, and crabs of all ages and sizes are present. Riding the crest of the incoming tide are schools of tiny fish collectively known as "baitfish"—mummichogs (mud minnows), killifish, and sheepshead minnows—and the young of species such as menhaden, croaker, striped mullet, flounder, bluefish, brown shrimp, white shrimp, and blue crab. Most of them head directly into the marsh as it floods and try to hide in the spartina while feeding on detritus, algae, tiny round-worms, nematodes, amphipods, and other minute organisms.

They must stay inconspicuous to avoid the predators that follow them into the creeks. Among the latter are adult blue crabs and larger fish such as red drum, flounder, bluefish, striped bass, Atlantic croaker, trout, and even squid. If the tide is high enough, these larger animals—particularly red drum—may leave the creek and enter the salt marsh to hunt among the spartina, making a meal of any fiddler, snail, shrimp, or minnow that doesn't find a refuge.

The filter feeders—oysters, mussels, and annelid worms—also perk up as the tidewater comes in. Unlike the fish and other mobile marine creatures, the filter feeders stay put—in the mud of creek banks and bottoms—as the tide rises. They strain the water for their food. Earthworm-like an-nelids in the mud, having rested safe in their tubes during low tide, project their feathery filters to strain phytoplankton and detritus from the rushing water. At the creek's edge, oysters open their hinged shells to strain out mi-croscopic food particles as the water washes over them. Their filtering will make the filmy water clearer. An adult oyster three to four inches long can sieve as much as twenty-five to fifty gallons a day! Working no less hard for their dinner are the ubiquitous ribbed mussels also lodged in the marsh mud. Though the same size as an oyster, a single adult mussel strains only about a gallon of water per hour.

On the mud, the marsh's more visible residents have built-in clocks that warn them—like a vibrating cell phone signaling a call—of the approach-ing flood. Coinciding with the rising water, their alarms go off every twelve hours or so. Before the water reaches them they take protective action ac-cording to their kind.

Some spider and ant species take refuge in spartina's hollow air tubes. A few individual ants perform the ultimate sacrifice: with their bodies they plug holes in the air tubes to keep the water out, thus protecting their sis-ters. Other creatures, such as the salt marsh grasshopper, simply climb to the tips of spartina blades to escape the advancing water and predators in it. Most conspicuous of the spartina climbers are the pale white periwinkle snails. When the tide is out, they graze contentedly on the fungi and algae coating spartina stalks just above the mud. As the tide rises, they ascend higher up the stalks to escape waterborne predators, eventually clinging to the stem tops like a field of ripening cotton. It's a scene you'll see only in a salt marsh at high tide—terrestrial organisms such as grasshoppers and ants coexisting with marine creatures such as periwinkle snails on a single spartina stem.[40]

Elsewhere on the marsh mud, fiddler crabs must be especially wary because the big predators, particularly red drum and blue crabs, consider them delectable. Woe to any fiddler that doesn't hide at high tide. To protect themselves, mud fiddlers in the muddiest areas of the marsh crawl into their chimney-like burrows and wait until the water recedes before coming out again. Amazingly, their burrows in the stiff, compact mud do not collapse when flooded. Not so the burrows of their cousins and neighbors the sand fiddlers, which dig their holes in the sandier areas of the marsh. The tide destroys their holes at every flooding—twice daily. To survive, a sand fiddler must plug its burrow with sand before the inundation. The plug entraps an air bubble, forming, in essence, a tiny air-filled cavern where the sand fiddler waits out the high tide.

Other small crabs of the marsh are trying just as diligently to avoid being someone else's lunch. Small brown square-backed crabs, or wharf crabs, climb spartina as the grasshoppers do. But being heavier and not as agile, they are more apt to fall or be knocked off. This unfortunate circumstance is offset by where they choose to live—either in the streamside marsh where the grass is thick and tall, or so close to land that they can scoot out of the marsh entirely.

Purple square-backed crabs, or marsh crabs, hole up in burrows in the streamside marsh during both high *and* low tides. They venture out to munch on spartina only when the tide is starting to flood and predators are still scarce, and return to their burrows before the water is deep enough for larger predators to swim in.

One of the smaller crabs' greatest enemies is also a relative, the adult blue crab, which regularly comes into the creeks and marsh at high tide to forage. I can see their dark, menacing forms now in the greenish-brown water below me. Opportunistic feeders, they snatch whatever comes their way—fiddlers, shrimp, worms, young fish, dead animals, detritus, even their own young. Their highly developed olfactory receptors help them smell potential food, and they will dig into the mud to grab it if they must. They can crush the shells of mussels and snails to get to the soft body inside, and they swim into the marsh and pluck the unfortunate snails right off the spartina. Sometimes blue crabs burrow into the bottom with only their eyestalks visible and lie in wait for unsuspecting fish or other creatures to happen by.

Another marauding crab is also lurking about—the white-clawed mud crab, which lives in the dense marsh near the creek. It cautiously emerges from the hole in which it waited out low tide and goes out in search of small fish, worms, tiny crustaceans, and just about anything else it can get its claws on.

As the tide rises, marsh-foraging land animals such as raccoons, rice rats, and minks retreat to high ground. If a raccoon does get stranded in the marsh at high water, it may quickly build a flimsy platform out of the marsh grass and stay on it until the tide recedes. Minks and their young may ride out the tide on marsh wrack—dense floating mats of dead spartina.

Marsh hens, silent now as the tide comes in, congregate on the edges of hammocks or seek refuge on marsh wrack along creek edges. If nesting, the birds will tend their globular nests, which are anchored firmly on spartina stems.

The inundation of the marsh will continue until nothing shows except an expanse of waving grass amid the dark water. The tide-swollen marsh will appear peaceful and serene to observers above, belying the frenzied interactions of predators and prey going on below. Depending on where a creature ranks in the food web, high tide is a time of great feasting or sheer terror.

All of this, of course, goes on for a definite period. After six hours, the tide will reverse itself and drain the marsh and the shallow creeks.

The Tide Goes Out

"Steady and free / Is the ebb-tide flowing from marsh to sea," Sidney Lanier wrote in "Sunrise" (lines 112–13).

The outgoing tide will cleanse the marsh of wastes. The receding tidal water is low in oxygen; most of it was removed during high tide by the marsh organisms and by chemical reactions within the anaerobic mud.

The ebbing water may be laden, though, with rich detritus and algae that will be delivered to the estuary. Also in the water are intact pieces of marsh grass pulled away from the banks—so much, sometimes, especially after a storm, that it forms large mats of marsh wrack. The wrack also benefits the environment because much of it ends up on barrier island beaches where it helps to stabilize sand dunes.

Fish and shrimp sense the dropping tide and move back into the deeper creeks, rivers, and estuaries, wherever there is enough water to allow them to survive at low tide. The very shallow creeks, like the one I'm watching from my brother's dock, retain only a tiny trickle of water, not enough to support even a few hardy minnows. But in creeks holding just a few inches, young shrimp, fish, and other smaller animals may congregate. They can, in fact, become quite abundant there, sometimes as many as a thousand individuals per square yard. The smallest shrimp remain near the creek banks while larger juveniles head into the deeper areas to avoid predators. No matter where they go, though, once they leave the protection of the marsh they are at the mercy of creatures bigger than themselves.

Some hardy organisms may stay in the marsh, finding refuge in potholes and other standing puddles of water on the marsh surface. Killifish, grass shrimp, mummichogs, sailfin mollies, and mosquito fish are among those that can endure pothole living for a few hours. Obviously, those that remain in the small puddles are safe from the larger swimming predators. They might, however, be easy targets for wading birds.

As the water drops along the creek banks, gray-green oyster bars dripping with algae become visible again. Juvenile crabs that hid among the oyster clusters at high tide reemerge and scurry about looking for food. The marsh clicks and pops as oysters and mussels close their shells to await the next flood tide and as water bubbles collapse with a pop on the bare mud. Some of the loud pops are made by snapping shrimp, which live in mud banks and can snap their claws shut with considerable force.

Fiddler crabs excavate themselves from their burrows and forage in ever-widening circles. Periwinkle snails slowly descend the spartina stalks and return to feeding low on the stems and marsh surface, now reglazed with fresh layers of fungi, algae, and detritus. On the mudflats and bare creek bottoms, hordes of mud snails regroup to patrol for dead organisms and other food.

Low tide, however, also brings another round of famished predators into the marsh. The raccoons, otters, minks, and rice rats that sought high ground when the tide came in now spread out over the exposed marsh floor and creek banks, diligently looking for oysters, fish, mussels, and other food. The diamondback terrapin, the salt marsh's only resident reptile, joins the mammals in their hunt for fish and crustaceans. Herons, egrets, ibises, and marsh hens station themselves along creek banks and in the shallow water to feast on fiddlers, marsh crabs, snails, shrimp, and small fish. Marsh hens probe the mud with their bills looking for worms. Red-winged blackbirds and seaside sparrows forage for insects among the spartina stems.

With the tide out, the bare creek banks once again take on soft gold and green tints from the diatoms and other microorganisms abounding on the mud surface. The marsh once again appears as a broad plain interwoven with tidal creeks.

Unending Cycles

These are the eternal rhythms of the great salt marshes and estuaries of the Southeast; life, death, and rebirth. The rising and falling of the tides go on, unending. But a growing number of people—scientists, environmentalists, government regulators, lawyers, and everyday folk—worry that if human assaults on coastal areas continue, as surely they will, the marshes and estuaries will no longer be able to carry out their intricate workings as nature intended. How long, then, will the marsh exist as Sidney Lanier rejoiced over it at high tide?

> The creeks overflow: a thousand rivulets run
> 'Twixt the roots of the sod; the blades of the marsh-grass stir;
> Passeth a hurrying sound of wings that westward whirr;
> Passeth, and all is still; and the currents cease to run;
> And the sea and the marsh are one.
>
> How still the plains of the waters be!
> The tide is in his ecstasy.
> The tide is at his highest height . . . ("The Marshes of Glynn," lines 90–97)

CHAPTER FOUR

Too Big for Its Britches

AFTER A SPELL of tide watching, I'm hot and thirsty. I stroll over to the nearby home of my brother Carl and his wife, Mildred, and plop down in their breakfast nook for a glass of iced tea. Through a lace-curtained window we can see the Stono's calm blue waters and glimmering salt marsh. In the short spartina a great egret stands still as a statue, waiting to snatch a fish or unwary fiddler. A fisherman in a bateau putt-putts down the river.

Mildred, seventy-four, wonders how much longer she'll have this tranquil scene to enjoy. She worries that John's Island is getting too big for its britches. "I just wish growth would stop," she says. "We have enough." Her bright blue eyes glance at the cars and trucks zipping by on two-lane River Road, a hundred yards from where we sit. Few of the motorists obey the forty-five-mile-per-hour speed limit. "Growth is inevitable, I guess, but I do wish it weren't so."

Mildred was born on neighboring Wadmalaw Island but has lived on John's Island ever since she and Carl were wed fifty-four years ago. She fiercely loves the land, a fidelity that newcomers don't seem to grasp. For the right price, most of them would walk away from their property without looking back.

Mildred can't understand that mentality. She is born and bred to the islands, as much a part of them as their sturdy oaks and resilient spartina. Perhaps it is in her genes, passed down from her English forebears. Those who settled the Carolina Lowcountry developed a sense of place that meant strong ties to the land. As Gerald O'Hara said passionately to his daughter Katie Scarlett in *Gone with the Wind*: "Why, land's . . . the only thing that lasts."

Other islanders whose families have lived and farmed on John's Island and have fished, crabbed, and swum in the Stono and its tidal creeks for generations echo Mildred's concerns.

John's Island, population fourteen thousand and growing, is the second largest island in size on the East Coast. Only New York's Long Island is larger. It's also the closest area to the city of Charleston that is still agricultural in nature. It has long been known for its prized tomatoes, antebellum plantations, and picturesque groves of moss-draped live oaks—the most famous of which is the Angel Oak, a fourteen-hundred-year-old stalwart whose massive limbs shade more than a third of an acre.

People who want to get to the affluent communities of Kiawah and Seabrook islands must drive across John's Island, passing small family compounds that make the island a stronghold of the African American Gullah culture. Several of the one-story homes, built mostly of clapboard or cinder blocks, are still trimmed in blue to ward off the evil spirits of the voodoo world.

John's island also is home to Fenwick Hall, an early eighteenth-century plantation replete with a castle-like manor house and an enduring legend. According to the story, the plantation owner, Edward Fenwick, Lord Ripon, had a comely daughter named Anne. At age seventeen Anne fell in love with Tony, the stable boy who tended Lord Ripon's Thoroughbreds. Anne wanted to marry Tony, but her outraged father would not hear of it. So they eloped. When His Lordship learned of it, he and his men gave chase, catching up with the couple as they tried to cross the Stono. Tony was brought back to the plantation and mounted on a horse. A noose was looped around the trembling youth's neck, and the rope was secured over an oak limb. Ripon whipped the horse, which sped off, leaving Tony dangling from the tree. When Anne saw her lover's lifeless body swaying there, she collapsed. To this day, one version of the legend goes, you can still hear Anne crying for Tony at Fenwick.[1]

Some say that you also can hear Tony calling for Anne from the jungle-like woods, or what's left of them, that surround the house. While Fenwick Hall and sixty acres surrounding it have been spared at least so far from development, much of the old plantation's original two thousand acres of maritime forest have been carved up for progress in the form of banks, drugstores, doctors' offices, and subdivisions with cookie-cutter houses. If ghosts still haunt Fenwick, they do it beneath bright neon signs and streetlights.

Elsewhere on the island, fields once lush with tomatoes and pastures once bucolic with grazing milk cows also are being buried under urban creep. Construction crews hammer and saw, putting up hundreds of new houses and townhouses. Several farmers who sold out to make way for these developments were, like Carl and Mildred, longtime residents whose families had called John's Island home for generations.

"I see other people selling, people I grew up with on these islands. It's their decision, and I hope they're happy with it. But I'm not going to give up my property," Mildred declares. "All the developers see in a piece of land is how much money they can make off it. But we love this land because it's a part of us; it's our heritage."

Passion for the Marsh

Carl and Mildred live on five acres bordering the salt marsh—Carl's share of the old farm where we grew up, land that has been in the Seabrook family for generations. It's called Ferry Field because a ferry once plied the Stono near here. Carl, seventy-eight, says he remembers when you could hardly give away land next to the salt marsh. No one wanted to live next to a smelly old marsh.

Now, land with a marsh view commands premium dollar. Developers drool over it; they pester landowners to sell. Carl and Mildred's property taxes have shot up along with property values, nearly doubling in one year. "I have no interest in selling," Mildred says. "This is home; this is where I'm happy."

Carl reminds her that the island is going to get much more crowded, and she had better get used to more cars and perfect strangers and more farmland and forest being buried under new rooftops and asphalt. The downturn in the economy is temporary, he predicts; growth will return with a vengeance.

"River Road used to be very safe," Carl says. "It was a dirt road when I was growing up. I watched them pave it when I was a teenager. It was still safe years later for our kids to ride their bikes on. They couldn't do that now. It's not safe anymore. You're taking a great risk now if you walk on that road or ride a bike on it. Somebody gets killed or maimed on that road all the time, it seems."

Carl's passion is the salt marsh. "When we were growing up, Wilson and I spent almost every day of the summer there," he says. "We swam in the creek. The shrimp would stick us all over. Sometimes on nights with a full moon, we'd go out in the river in our little boat and paddle around and sing as loud as we could. We just felt like singing. Mama sat on shore and listened to us. Mullet in the creeks would literally jump into our boat. We were always flinging a cast net into the creek. We caught so many fish and shrimp and crabs that Mama didn't know what to do with them all. We stretched seine nets across the creeks to catch fish coming out of the marsh with the tide." ·

Looking back, those were idyllic days, he says.

Our late daddy, after he retired, went out onto the rickety old dock almost every morning in summer, before the sun was too hot, with a drop net to harvest the creek's bounty. The simple drop net was no more than woven mesh attached to a large metal ring similar to a Hula Hoop. Smelly chicken heads or herrings tied to the middle were his bait. Heavy metal sinkers made the net sink quickly into the brownish-green water. Daddy let it stay there a minute or so, then quickly pulled it up. As it rose, it held flipping shrimp, blue crabs, flopping mullet, and occasionally a stingray or other marine creature. The shrimp, crabs, and mullet went into a foot-tub, and he tossed the rest back into the creek. In less than half an hour Daddy would have enough to feed the family for a couple of days.

We ate the shrimp for breakfast, and most of the time for dinner, too. Mama had almost as many ways of cooking them as Bubba Blue, who reeled off an endless list of shrimp dishes to his army buddy Forrest Gump. He didn't mention shrimp gravy, though. Mama concocted hers from little creek shrimp, bits of bacon, onions, and other ingredients. We poured it over white rice or grits, and to this day it is one of the best dishes I have ever tasted.

Now, as Carl looks wistfully through his window at the salt marsh, he wonders what changes are in store for it as development soars. A looming battle shaping up on the island is Charleston County's plan to extend a spur of I-526 across the island despite the county's professed goal to keep it rural.

Environmentalists staunchly oppose the highway, which they say will spawn more development. "If you zone something as rural and then connect a highway to it, it won't stay rural for long," explained Megan Desrosiers of the prominent Coastal Carolina Conservation League in a letter to the U.S. Army Corps of Engineers, the permitting agency for the road. The National Marine Fisheries Service is against the project, too. White and brown shrimp, gray snapper, blue crab, southern flounder, black drum, and red drum use the estuarine marsh and tidal creeks in the highway's path for spawning, foraging, and nursery habitat.[2]

Carl says he's not a scientist, but it doesn't take a slew of research to know that the marsh will suffer—and no doubt already is hurting—as the land is covered with more hard surfaces and more noxious chemicals run off into the marsh. "I seldom hear a marsh hen now; it was one of the most familiar sounds of my boyhood," Carl says. He has read that marsh hens are indicators of a marsh's health, so he wonders if what he can't hear portends trouble.

Carl's observations are not far off the mark. A few years ago some scientist friends told me that marsh hens indeed are a measure of a salt marsh's health because of the birds' strong fidelity to certain marshes and their predictable diet of fiddlers and other invertebrates. They noted that marsh hens are in serious decline in salt marshes along the West Coast, but no one has documented a similar problem in the East. At the same time, though, they acknowledged that no one is carrying out detailed marsh hen surveys in the Southeast, and they couldn't say for certain what the bird's status is in the region.

Marsh hens aside, scientists have other evidence that estuaries and marshes are on shaky ground as development soars. Some friends suggested that I go to Skidaway Island near Savannah and pay a visit to Dr. Peter Verity, a respected marine scientist.

Estuary Woes

Verity was at the Skidaway Institute of Oceanography when I went to see him in 2009. The institute is a complex of laboratories, office buildings, dormitories, a library, an aquarium, and other units run by the university system of Georgia that was set up in the late 1960s to conduct research in oceanography and marine sciences. It's located about three miles as the crow flies from where I had walked across the marsh several months ago with Todd Schneider. Sadly, Verity died at age fifty-six in January 2010 after an accidental fall at his home in Savannah.

On the sunny June day when I paid the lean, bookish scientist a visit, we walked to Skidaway's well-maintained dock. I had asked to see it because it was where he had carried out his long-term research—work that had revealed convincing evidence that unbridled human population growth can do serious harm to estuaries and salt marshes. The dock stretched to the edge of the Skidaway River, which runs past Savannah and twists through wide expanses of salt marsh. In essence, the Skidaway is a small estuary like the Stono in South Carolina. Unlike major estuaries, the Skidaway has no freshwater river running into it. Its seawater is diluted mostly by rainfall and storm water running off the land.

A soft, briny breeze blew off the river that day. A flock of white shorebirds flapped across the mirror-smooth water. From the dock I could see McMansions probably worth a million dollars or more lining each side of the river. One even loomed up on a small hammock in the middle of the marsh.

When Verity came to Skidaway in 1986, after getting his doctorate in biological oceanography from the University of Rhode Island, he decided to keep doing what he'd learned to do in Rhode Island—sampling water regularly for dissolved oxygen and other qualities. He made water sampling a weekly routine. It's a labor-intensive process, but he figured it would be a good technique for his students to learn.

So, one day each week, for twenty years, Verity and his colleagues stood on this dock and filled plastic bottles and buckets with the Skidaway's briny water. Each sample was analyzed in the laboratory for dissolved oxygen, nutrients, chlorophyll, bacteria, and several other variable characters. The frequent sampling made the Skidaway research unique in the United States, Verity said. "In most parts of the country, this kind of data wasn't collected until a problem was recognized. The fact that we have data collected weekly is highly unusual."

What the researchers saw from the long-term analyses troubled them. Pieced together, the data showed that the Skidaway's health over the years had slipped gradually from relatively pristine to seriously impaired.

The main problem, Verity said, was nutrient overload—excess tons of phosphorus, nitrogen, and silicates discharged from sewage treatment plants, leached from septic tanks, or washed off the land from farms, suburban lawns, and golf courses dosed heavily with fertilizer and pesticides. Scientists use the term "eutrophication" in referring to an oversupply of nutrients in water. "When you fertilize your lawn, pay for golf fees, or flush your toilet, ultimately you are responsible for the injection of nutrients into local rivers and estuaries like this," Verity explained.

In limited amounts, these nutrients are crucial for the normal growth of phytoplankton. A nutrient overload, however, can promote runaway algae growth. "Think of what happens to your body if you regularly consume more food than you burn off in your daily activities—you get bigger," Verity said. "Well, so does the amount of algae in water bodies that receive extra nutrients."

That growth in turn boosts the growth and metabolism of the bacteria that decompose and consume algae and its by-products. To digest the algae, the bacteria must use the oxygen dissolved in water—the same oxygen that other marine organisms also need for survival. Ultimately, greater numbers of the bacteria mean less dissolved oxygen for the other creatures—leading to an oxygen deficiency known as "hypoxia," a particularly dangerous condition for marine life.[3]

Water is considered hypoxic when dissolved oxygen levels drop below two to three milligrams per liter. Healthy water has an oxygen level of five or more milligrams per liter of water. Shrimp, crabs, and fish either avoid hypoxic water by moving away or, if they stay, face being stressed and becoming more vulnerable to predation and disease. For oysters, mussels, and others that cannot swim away, hypoxia can be lethal.[4]

It was this scenario that Verity and his colleagues were seeing in the Skidaway—increasing amounts of nutrients from skyrocketing growth that taxed the estuary's capacity to assimilate them. Some nutrient levels had tripled since the water-sampling program began in 1986. With the higher levels, algae and bacteria numbers also had shot up. "It's remarkable how each summer the highest concentrations of algae are greater than the summer before," Verity said. Dissolved oxygen levels, in turn, had dwindled by 15–30 percent in the estuary's surface and bottom waters; during the hottest part of summer, the Skidaway estuary was becoming hypoxic. Summer is an especially critical time because warm water holds less oxygen.[5]

If the downhill trend were to continue, Verity feared that the shrimp, crabs, fish, and other denizens of a healthy Southeast estuary and salt marsh would be replaced largely by gelatinous organisms such as jellyfish that are typically better suited to low oxygen. In a double whammy, the "jellies" also feast on baby fish and shellfish.[6] Verity told me that he was already witnessing such changes in the Skidaway. His sampling showed a

70 percent jump in jellyfish between 1987 and 2000, but he did not publish the data before he died. Since then, other scientists have started new studies to measure jellyfish presence in the estuary.[7]

In the worst possible case, Verity said, the bacteria could consume all of the oxygen needed by other marine organisms, creating a dead zone like the gigantic one in the Gulf of Mexico off the Louisiana coast, which has been linked to nutrients carried by the Mississippi River.

∀ ∀ ∀

LOW OXYGEN WAS not supposed to be a problem in the Southeast's estuaries, especially those of Georgia and South Carolina. Scientists assumed that the region's vigorous twice-a-day tides efficiently churned the water, mixing in enough oxygen from the atmosphere to supply marine life—from aerobic bacteria to fish—with all they needed. "At the time this study was initiated," Verity told me, "estuarine waters of Georgia and South Carolina were considered relatively pristine with respect to eutrophication."

Other scientists have cautioned against extrapolating Verity's findings to other coastal water bodies. Spud Woodward, director of Georgia's Coastal Resources Division, which regulates marine fisheries, agreed with Verity that tainted water harms marine life. But there isn't enough information to know the degree to which shrimp, blue crabs, oysters, and fish are suffering from human pressure on coastal waters. "The multimillion-dollar question is what are those effects going to mean for the life support for species that we place great value on? That's what we would like to know," Woodward told me. "A lot of that change we want to blame on man, but a lot of that is due to natural fluctuations, I think. It's like the debate on global warming—how much of that is man and how much of it is the natural variation that you're going to see out there?"

Verity had also noted, however, that land-use impacts on an estuary may begin without obvious warning and be difficult to reverse by the time they are documented. "We should all be working collaboratively on the problem while it's relatively easy to fix. We need to start taking steps now," Verity warned.

In 2011, a year after Verity died, new data showed that conditions in the Skidaway estuary seemed to be getting better. Nutrient loads entering the water body had lessened, and dissolved oxygen levels appeared to be improving, probably because development on Skidaway Island had come to a near standstill in recent years and also because efforts had been made to reduce storm-water runoff. Marc Frischer, the Skidaway scientist who took over Verity's studies, is not sure whether the estuary will ever make a complete turnaround. It is possible that the years of environmental assaults pushed it past a "tipping point," beyond which it will never achieve full recovery. And if the frenzied development pace of the 1980s and 1990s resumes when the economy bounces back, as many predict it will, the estuary could quickly go downhill again. Definitive answers probably will come only after years, even decades, of research, which is why the long-term studies that Verity began must continue.[8]

The Tidal Creeks Project

Other researchers also have solid scientific data showing that too many houses, roads, and other development in fragile coastal areas endanger life in the tidal marshes and streams. What's more, the studies suggest that coastal sprawl is jeopardizing the health and well-being of people who eat the fish or swim, water ski, or even wade in the tainted waters.

The impairment actually begins in the uppermost reaches of tidal creeks where they're little wider than a home hallway, well before they flow into their connecting rivers and estuaries. Even minimal development—just 10 percent of a watershed—may do measurable harm to the streams.[9] That unsettling fact comes from studies that began in 1992 of twenty-three tidal creeks along the South Carolina coast, including nineteen draining into the Charleston Harbor estuary and others to the north and south of the harbor. Marine scientists Fred Holland and Denise Sanger and their colleagues at the Hollings Marine Laboratory in Charleston commenced the studies to learn how land development and population growth are affecting the area's creeks and life therein. The results garnered front-page headlines. As more rooftops, pavement, and other "impervious surfaces" cover a creek's drainage area, or watershed, the stream and its denizens suffer proportionately. Once a creek is impaired, it's a sure bet that the salt marshes, coastal rivers, and estuaries connected to it will face the same fate.[10]

"Tidal creeks are the zones of first impact, the proverbial 'canaries in the mine,' for coastal ecosystems," Holland told me. "They are, in effect, the 'first responders' to impacts of pollution."

Most of the foul stuff entering the creeks comes from so-called non-point-source pollution—pesticides, fertilizers, oils, metals, bacteria, viruses, eroded dirt, and so on—washed off parking lots, streets, rooftops, lawns, and golf courses when it rains. As development increases and more hard surfaces are laid down—and there is less soil and vegetation to soak up storm water—runoff becomes more torrential, more voluminous. A one-acre paved parking lot produces sixteen times more runoff than a one-acre meadow. More runoff means more pollution dumped into the creeks, where it poisons life.[11]

Holland had suspected as much from his boyhood days in the early 1950s, when he and his brother were growing up on a tobacco farm near Florence, South Carolina, and spent summer vacations at Myrtle Beach. "We could gather enough fish, crabs, and oysters from the tidal creeks around Myrtle Beach to feed us for the week," said Holland, a stocky, intense man with a shaved head. Then, almost overnight, Myrtle Beach grew from a sleepy vacation retreat to a world-famous resort buried under layers of asphalt and concrete and jammed with fancy hotels, amusement parks, and shops. "Today, eating the shellfish from most of those creeks is too unsafe; but, then, too few fish occur in them anyway to make fishing worthwhile," Holland said.

In their creek studies, Holland and his associates used the amount of impervious cover as a measure of the degree of development within each stream's watershed. Watersheds ranged in size from about thirty to more than a thousand acres and represented various degrees of development. Forested tracts were defined as areas with less than 10 percent impervious cover; suburban watersheds had 11–50 percent; urban and industrial watersheds had more than 50 percent.

Growth, however, did not stand still while the studies were under way. During the study period, thousands of people bought or built houses in subdivisions along the creeks, primarily to enjoy sweeping views of water and tidal marsh. The subdivisions—often cul-de-sac'ed, gated affairs—spun off "secondary" development such as new streets, shopping centers, and country clubs.

To the researchers' amazement, the secondary buildup engulfed the land at a rate six times faster than the rate of population growth. Almost as fast as the researchers could amass field data, several watersheds had to be reclassified at higher development levels. The watershed of Horlbeck Creek, a gentle, twisting tidal stream east of Charleston, had to be reclassified from forested to suburban as impervious cover in its drainage area jumped from 2 percent to more than 16 percent in less than seven years. Shem Creek, lined with seafood restaurants and picturesque shrimp boat docks, went from suburban to urban after impervious surfaces in its watershed leaped from 35 percent to 55 percent.[12]

The pace continues today, and far too many watersheds have passed the 10 percent threshold of development. What does 10 percent look like on the ground? "The ten-percent threshold of imperviousness translates into housing densities in the range of one unit per two to three acres," Dana Beach, executive director of the South Carolina Coastal Conservation League, said in his report on coastal sprawl.[13]

Even at that low density, nutrients and noxious chemicals—motor oil, gasoline, chlordane, DDT, chromium, mercury, copper, and so on—start accumulating in creek-bottom mud at levels potentially harmful to marine life. Copper, for instance, is a big concern because it is toxic to marine organisms in very low concentrations. More than half the copper contamination in storm water comes from automobile brake-pad wear. Copper-based pesticides are also heavily used to prevent algae growth in golf course ponds, which have been popping up almost as fast as new Burger Kings on the Southeast coast.[14] In the water itself, higher-than-normal levels of fecal coliform bacteria—indicators of disease-causing germs from human and animal wastes—show up at the 10 percent development level. Salinity levels start getting thrown out of kilter.

When a watershed's impervious surfaces surpass 20 percent, creek conditions really start getting out of whack. Nasty chemicals start accumulating in the mud at potentially toxic levels. The contaminants take a marked toll on pollution-sensitive organisms, especially some marine worms and tiny crustaceans that are vital food for juvenile shrimp, finfish, and shellfish. The young animals start disappearing as their food sources grow scarce. The shrimp get special attention because their decline indicates the degree to which a marine nursery area has been harmed.[15]

As more asphalt and concrete smother the ground, the situation worsens. When shrimp and other pollution-sensitive species abandon a tainted creek, hordes of pollution-tolerant worms begin to dominate it. When fecal coliform bacteria foul the stream, health authorities ban oyster and clam harvesting. Being filter feeders, the shellfish concentrate the bacteria in their entire bodies. Shellfish pose an increased threat to humans because we consume the whole body, guts and all. Nearly a third of South Carolina's shellfish grounds — including large swaths of Charleston Harbor — are now closed to harvesting because the tainted oysters and clams might sicken or even kill anyone who ate them.

Especially vulnerable to development, Holland, Sanger, and others found, are the headwaters of tidal creeks — vital places for the maturation of young marine creatures. "The upper reaches of marshes and tidal creeks are prime nursery areas for shellfish and finfish," Holland noted in his report on tidal creeks. Usually less than twelve feet wide, the headwaters are often low in salinity and dissolved oxygen, especially during summer. That so many young marine organisms would want to congregate and feed here might seem counterintuitive, but their predators shy away from the headwaters for those very reasons. Young organisms can survive here because their metabolism is much lower and they don't need as much oxygen.[16]

When polluted runoff piles on additional stress, though, it may be enough to tip the balance and push the creek's creatures beyond even their highest levels of endurance. In particular, the warm water running off hot pavements and roofs may cause dissolved oxygen levels to plunge to zero, forcing even the hardiest animals to abandon their headwaters haven.

Unfortunately for young marine life, people are lining up to build along the upper stretches of tidal creeks. "Land adjacent to headwaters is highly desirable real estate," Holland told me. "Most of the land along bays, lagoons, and deeper portions of tidal creeks was developed in the seventies, eighties, and nineties. So the shallower headwaters are apt to be the next areas to feel the impacts of development." Damage to those areas "provides early warning of ensuing harm to larger tidal creeks, tidal rivers, and estuaries."

Since the Tidal Creeks Project was initiated in the early 1990s, Holland and his group have expanded their studies to include more than thirty other creeks in South Carolina, North Carolina, and Georgia. The additional work has confirmed their initial findings.

The Charleston Harbor Project

The Tidal Creeks Project initially was part of an even bigger endeavor, the Charleston Harbor Project, which evolved from a grassroots effort by local civic, business, and environmental leaders in the early 1990s into a full-tilt campaign. The five-year project eventually involved dozens of scientists, environmentalists, government regulators, prominent citizens, and others and encompassed nineteen hundred square miles of open water, marsh, swampland, and upland draining into Charleston Harbor.[17] According to its management plan, the project's primary aim was to protect the Charleston area "from the inadvertent natural resources degradation experienced by many urban coastal communities as they have grown." In short, Charleston's leaders said they wanted to head off the type of situation that turned Boston Harbor, New York Harbor, and Chesapeake Bay into foul stinkpots.

"Charleston citizens want to avoid a future where only strangers would think of swimming in the harbor," a project brochure touted. The project aimed to "identify and promote land-use management practices which reduce adverse impacts on the Charleston Harbor estuary." Another goal was to "protect and re-open shellfish harvesting areas of tidal creeks draining into the harbor or its tributaries."

Home to one of the nation's busiest container ship ports, busy Charleston Harbor surrounds the peninsula on which the storied city sits. At every turn, Charleston and its harbor are cloaked in history. In February 1770, when the Revolutionary War was raging, British general George Clinton's troops encircled and laid siege to the city. And as any student of American history knows, Charleston Harbor is where the Civil War started. Cadets at the Citadel military college on the Ashley River discharged the war's first salvo on January 9, 1861, when they took aim at the Union ship *Star of the West* steaming into the harbor. Four months later, on April 12, 1861, shore batteries commanded by General Pierre G. T. Beauregard opened fire on Union-held Fort Sumter in the middle of the harbor. After thirty-four hours of bombardment, Major Robert Anderson surrendered the battered fort.

No less steeped in history are the sea islands and the mainland surrounding the harbor. Rice, indigo, and cotton cultivation; commercial trade; phosphate mining; shipbuilding; and manufacturing in the outlying areas helped shape Charleston's physical structure and its future. The city and its adjacent landscape boast architectural styles reaching back into the seventeenth century. That so many early structures still stand and are still in use is testimony to long-term, persistent efforts by a proud local citizenry to preserve and restore them.

Charleston, however, was not always as protective of its scenic harbor, estuary, and salt marshes. Over the decades, thousands of acres of marsh were filled in with garbage and other rank material to expand the city. About half of downtown Charleston today sits atop such "reclaimed marsh." Moreover, decades of dumping raw sewage and industrial wastes directly into area rivers—so-called point-source pollution because it comes from pipes—had turned much of the harbor into a fetid, malodorous lake. The abuse culminated in massive fish kills that left people outraged. In response, the South Carolina legislature in 1963 passed the "Charleston Harbor pollution law" requiring municipalities to implement wastewater treatment by 1970. Charleston began construction in 1968 on its plant to curtail pipe-spewing pollution by the state's deadline. In 1972 Congress passed the federal Clean Water Act, which set an even stricter goal: that the nation's waterways should be clean enough for swimming and fishing. The federal law kindled strong enforcement of water quality rules and doled out billions of dollars to help states and cities like Charleston become even more diligent in cleaning up their messes. By the time the Charleston Harbor Project kicked off in the early 1990s, the harbor was deemed "in relatively good shape" by the project's initiators.

In their "Charleston Harbor Special Area Management Plan," released in 2000, the project's diverse members came up with twenty recommendations for keeping the harbor in good shape, including curtailing golf course runoff, limiting the amount of impervious surfaces, and controlling storm-water pulses into tidal creeks.

But maintaining even the status quo in Charleston Harbor—much less making it cleaner, as the project intended—has been a daunting task in the face of overwhelming population growth and development and the higher pollution loads so many more people, buildings, and streets entail. Pollution threatens once again to overwhelm the harbor, as a front-page headline proclaimed in an October 2007 edition of the *Charleston Post and Courier.* "A generation after tougher industrial pollution laws cleaned up the nearly fetid water of Charleston Harbor, storm-water runoff has begun to threaten it," environmental reporter Bo Petersen noted in the article. "Monitoring in the harbor has found spots where the water quality is considered 'fair to poor' for supporting marine life, in contrast to the overall good shape of coastal water across the state." Petersen identified the trouble spots as—surprise!—the headwaters of tidal creeks in developed areas. "The big problem appears to be impervious surfaces: roofs, streets, parking lots that drain instead of absorbing rain," he continued.[18]

Bob Van Dolah, director of South Carolina's Marine Resources Research Institute, sees "real problems" in the harbor. "The concern is that we get to a point where we really can't fix the problem," he told me.

And what is that point of no return? No one knows, but more pollution is almost certainly headed into the harbor. Hard surfaces in 2010 already covered 14 percent of Charleston County's 917 square miles, up from 10 percent in 2000. In locations close to the water, such as the city peninsula, the percentage was much higher. And developers were planning to build tens of thousands more homes over the next two decades in the metropolitan area surrounding Charleston. Land was still being developed five to six times faster than the population was growing.[19]

Not even the unprecedented meltdown in the economy has put a major crimp in the growth projections. Most of the newcomers are well-heeled retirees and others able to afford private golf courses, marinas, yacht clubs, and other amenities. "We're under an awful lot of pressure. Everybody wants to live next to the water," said Charles Newell, shellfish program manager in South Carolina's Department of Health and Environmental Control. "Every time someone puts up a house or a parking lot, that's just less permeable surface for drainage."[20]

Horlbeck Creek

Horlbeck Creek, whose watershed converted from a forested to a suburban category as Fred Holland and his group conducted their studies, is a twisting, picturesque waterway winding more than two miles through a wide salt marsh in the Mount Pleasant area, east of Charleston across the wide Cooper River. Its banks offer spectacular views of the creek and marsh—and that may be its undoing.

On its east side is Parker Island, named after the family that owned it in the early eighteenth century and sold it in the early nineteenth century to the Horlbeck family. The Horlbecks converted a small portion of Parker Island into a brickyard. The bricks made there and in other brickyards along the Wando River helped fuel the movement from wood to brick construction in downtown Charleston. Horlbeck Creek's watershed, though, remained mostly forested, and the stream flowed pristine and clean.

Upstream, along the creek's upper reaches, across from Parker Island, a community of black freedmen sprang up in the 1870s. Called the Phillips Community after one of the plantations in the area, it offered ten-acre parcels of land from the former plantation to the freedmen for sixty-three dollars—a princely sum at that time. Later, a wooden bridge connected the community to Parker Island, where the people hunted for food and visited the graves of their ancestors buried on the old plantations. The bridge also became a neighborhood gathering place where people swam, fished, caught blue crabs, netted shrimp, and socialized. For more than a century the Phillips Community remained a tight-knit Gullah enclave where women sat on front porches and chatted while sewing colorful quilts and stitching sweetgrass baskets. They swept their yards bare and tended their gardens. The men brought home venison and tubs full of shrimp and crabs. And the land passed down from generation to generation.

"It was close-knit. One family always looked after the next," Richard Habersham, a community leader, told me. "I could walk around this community and tell you who lived in each house and who had lived there before. If we saw a dog running around, we knew who it belonged to."

In the 1980s the developers came, envisioning immense profits from the upscale subdivisions with marvelous views of the tidal creek that they planned to build. They began carving subdivisions from the maritime forest and the old farms along the creek. The big tone-setter came in 1999 when the Ginn Company, based in Celebration, Florida, bought Parker Island and built a premier eighteen-hole golf complex fringed by hundreds of luxury homes. Before long the RiverTowne Golf Club, with most of its links overlooking Horlbeck Creek, dominated the area.

Soon after the golf course and clubhouse were completed, contractors bulldozed the old bridge to Parker Island—thus obliterating the cultural link that had existed for generations between the island and the Phillips Community. Other problems surfaced. African American graves on the island were vandalized; gravestones were stolen. Phillips Community elders remember when there were many stones, several dating back to the nineteenth century. Few now remain.

Like a doughnut hole in the center of relentless, high-toned sprawl, the Phillips Community is fighting to have a future, to hold on to its very soul. Habersham and his neighbors have fought every project that threatens their peace—a proposed road widening, say, or a potential commercial development at the community's edge. "It never ends," he said. "Just when you end one battle, you have to turn around and start fighting another."

The residents worry that developers are waiting for the right moment to pounce on their properties. Indeed, developers are already paying top dollar for land within the community when owners are willing—or forced—to sell. But many of the remaining five hundred or so residents feel that their roots are being ripped out of the ground and that they're being unmercifully squeezed out.

"This is our home," Habersham said. "Some people see it as an investment to make big bucks; we see it as home."

Phillips Community resident Jonathan Ford explained to a researcher with the South Carolina Sea Grant Consortium: "People tell us we can just sell out and go somewhere else. For the people in RiverTowne, mainly northerners, property is an investment. For us, property is home. You live, you grow up, you die, and you pass it on. We're just trying to preserve what was passed on to us. Our grandfathers and great-grandfathers had to work and buy property that they handed down to us."[21]

The sentiments are the same as those I heard from my sister-in-law on John's Island, across the harbor.

The biggest blow to the Phillips Community, however, may be what happened to its beloved Horlbeck Creek. National Park Service researchers found that chemical runoff from the golf course and surrounding subdivisions has had a deleterious impact on the marshes and waters.[22] The creek's fish and crabs are no longer abundant. Fiddler crabs, though plentiful on the Phillips side, decline in number and disappear entirely as one approaches the golf links.

Dana Beach, founder and leader of the influential South Carolina Coastal Conservation League, based in Charleston, is not too surprised by any of this. Beach wrote the widely distributed, often-cited Pew Oceans Commission's 2002 report, *Coastal Sprawl: The Effects of Urban Design on Aquatic Ecosystems in the United States.*[23] The report claims that if today's land consumption trends continue, more than 25 percent of the coast's acreage will be developed by 2025, up from 14 percent in 1997—"a prescription for severe ecological damage."

The effects of this decline will be felt in our economy, our recreational pursuits, and our quality of life, Beach said. He noted that what Fred Holland's group found backs up what dozens of other researchers around the nation have realized. "When more than 10 percent of the acreage of a watershed is covered in roads, parking lots, roof tops, and other impervious surfaces, the rivers and streams within those watersheds become seriously degraded."

Testifying in Washington before the federal Commission on Ocean Policy in January 2002, Beach warned that in general, population growth spawns land development and makes protection of ecosystems a huge challenge. But growth and development are not directly proportional—especially in coastal areas. "The situation is considerably more difficult because, in almost every coastal area, land consumption is occurring at rates of up to 10 times the rate of population growth—particularly bad news for coastal ecosystems," Beach said.

Unfortunately, Beach pointed out to the commission, the present prevailing system of coastal management, with its emphasis on site-specific measures such as detention ponds, swales, and filters, won't turn the situation around. If we are to have healthy estuaries, we must change the patterns of coastal development. This will not be easy, he noted, but it can be done. "Fortunately, new technology for mapping and analysis provides tools we have never had before. And we know what development patterns will sustain coastal ecosystems. In other words, we've identified the disease and we know the cure. The question is whether we will exert the energy and the leadership to apply it."

In 2011 the answer to that question was still pending.

CHAPTER FIVE

Farms in the River

ON A RADIANT DAY in October I'm hunkered down on the pas-
senger bench of Charlie Phillips's airboat, which is skittering
over the mirror-smooth water of the Sapelo River in McIntosh
County, Georgia. I wear industrial-strength earmuffs to guard my hearing
from the piercing whine of the five-hundred-horsepower GM engine that
spins two huge counter-rotating propellers and hurtles us down the river.
The airboat's aluminum frame barely skims the water.

Lean, bearded, and tanned, Charlie, fifty-six, occupies the pilot's seat
directly behind me. Proudly calling himself a fishmonger, he buys fish,
shrimp, crabs, and oysters from local fishermen and processes them at his
seafood packinghouse in the nearby village of Bellville, perched on a picturesque bend of the Sapelo. The seafood is sold fresh to stores and restaurants up and down the Southeast coast and as far away as Canada. Charlie
owns a shrimp trawler and a grouper boat, whose crews haul in their own
catches.

But today we're headed to another of Charlie's enterprises—his clam
farm. On a large mudflat at the edge of a salt marsh in the Julienton River, a
tributary of the Sapelo, Charlie raises the tasty clams known as littlenecks.
They are the same shellfish that grow wild from the Gulf of Mexico to
Canada and grace sauces, pasta dishes, and chowders across the nation.

Charlie prefers his noisy, gas-guzzling airboat to an outboard Carolina
skiff—the usual craft of local fishermen—because the airboat can get him
to places the conventional boats cannot, namely onto the mudflat.

It's low tide, and the ten acres of bare mud glisten directly in front of us.
The whizzing airboat is rapidly approaching it, but Charlie slows down
nary a bit. I shudder and brace myself for a hard impact. But the airboat

Clam grower Charlie Phillips inspects his "clam
farm" in the Julienton River in Georgia.

glides smoothly onto the mud with barely a bump. Even over the whining
engine and the earmuffs I hear Charlie's whoop. The airboat zigzags and
pirouettes across the mud, around and around. Charlie is having fun. I'm
impressed by his craft's maneuverability, even as I hold on tight to keep
from being slung out. Suddenly, the boat stops. Charlie kills the engine.
"You like that?" he asks with a wide grin.

He dismounts from the pilot's seat, walks to the bow, and, arms akimbo,
surveys the dark mud spread before him. "This is it—my farm," he says
with obvious pride. But all I can see is a large patch of bare muck where innumerable mud snails serenely graze. A dark green, meshlike material covers the mud; a white great egret stands at the edge of it. In the distance, a
white-painted shrimp trawler steams down the river, heading to the docks.
Charlie tells me to keep an eye out for a bald eagle that flaps daily over the
marsh.

White PVC pipes poking up here and there mark the extent of the farm
where Charlie and his workers "plant" thousands of BB-size seed clams in
the healthy muck and raise them to maturity. Though we can't see the bur-

ied clams, Charlie knows exactly where they're planted and their stage of growth—including whether they're ready for harvesting—based on a grid map he maintains. Charlie and his crew come here several times a month at low tide to tend the "crop" and harvest full-grown clams—laborious work.

Today, though, we will gather only half a bushel for tonight's dinner. Charlie will bake them and serve them piping hot. We'll pry them open, dip their meat in a tangy sauce, and pop them into our craws. My mouth waters in anticipation.

Charlie dons gloves and knee-high rubber boots, slips gently over the side, and stands ankle-deep in the thick mud. He slogs to a spot several feet away, bends over, and plunges his arms halfway to his elbows into the squishy mud, feeling around for the prized shellfish. He comes up with several at a time. In short order the sack is full. Charlie says he can't wait to taste one, so he opens a clam right there in the marsh and savors its rich, raw flesh.

I ask about the plastic mesh covering the mud. Charlie explains that it holds the tiny seed clams planted there. It also protects maturing clams from predators such as crabs, birds, and raccoons—and from human thieves bent on stealing some of the crop.

Back in the airboat Charlie pulls off his boots and gloves and chats about the future. "I see these clams being as recognizable and as desirable as sweet Vidalia onions one day," he says. "People won't want just regular clams—they'll ask specifically for Sapelo clams, what we raise here." He pauses and looks across the marsh at the far shore. He frowns. As many pains as he takes to protect his clams and keep them healthy, he says, there's a growing threat that leaves him feeling nearly helpless: the relentless growth and development pushing right up to the marsh and the estuary.

He is keenly aware that of all the factors that make a mudflat, a creek, or a marsh suitable for growing and harvesting shellfish, none is more vital than clean water. "It wouldn't take a lot of pollution to ruin the clams and oysters in these marshes," Charlie says. If that happens, his investments—some five hundred thousand dollars in the clam farm alone—would go swirling down the drain.

THAT THREAT IS the reason Charlie has kept a wary eye on a low peninsula jutting out from Harris Neck Island, across the river and marsh

Woody Pond at Harris Neck National Wildlife Refuge, Georgia, is an
important rookery for herons, egrets, and endangered wood storks

from his clam beds. Surrounded by salt marshes, rivers, and deep tidal
creeks, semiremote Harris Neck is still covered mostly by maritime forest
abounding with giant live oaks. But it is prime real estate in real danger of
being carved up for house lots, marinas, golf courses, clubhouses, and boat
docks. It would make a developer a pile of money.

That is exactly what real estate companies keep pitching for large swaths
of Harris Neck and surrounding areas. It causes Charlie to lose sleep. Pollution and tainted storm runoff from such projects could ruin his way of
life. "If they put a lot of houses over there, it could be only a matter of time
before my clam beds are shut down," he says. He emphasizes that he is not
against limited growth compatible with the land. But he fears Harris Neck
is in line for substantial development, much more than is healthy for the
adjacent marshes and estuaries. He knows about Fred Holland's tidal creek
studies in South Carolina and understands that it wouldn't take much development to jeopardize his clam farm.

The first big scare came in June 2007. Builders asked McIntosh County
authorities to rezone a thirteen-hundred-acre parcel on Harris Neck from

a highly protective agriculture-forestry classification to a less-restrictive single-family residential zone. The less-stringent category would accommodate many more homesites, roads, docks, and the like. Charlie and several other like-minded people pleaded with the county authorities to resist pressure from realtors and developers pushing for rezoning. The officials, however, citing their county's rules and guidelines, granted the rezoning request.

For Charlie, it became an agonizing wait-and-see situation. He remained fearful for his clams, and his fears were justified. The developers escalated their attack. Their initial plan for a low-impact, "environmentally protective" development changed into a plan to build a high-density resort with golf courses, extensive boat facilities, and more than a thousand residential and resort units.

"I guess they suckered me in," Charlie says.

The developers' plans were put on hold when the economy soured. That brought Charlie some relief, but not much. More battles, he knows, are coming.

Garish billboards along the rural oak-shaded roads on and around Harris Neck tout other huge land tracts for sale—some eleven thousand acres altogether. Much of the "for sale" property surrounds the twenty-seven-hundred-acre Harris Neck National Wildlife Refuge, home to endangered nesting wood storks, among other things. Conservationists are already envisioning the day when the refuge will be an island of greenery in a sea of subdivisions, strip malls, and fast-food joints.

Several of the parcels to be developed also border headwaters of tidal creeks that flow into the Sapelo River and its peaceful tributary, the Julienton. Bulldozers have already wrecked some marshes and other wetlands in the area. The ruination left environmentalists fuming and vowing to take legal action. "We can't depend on the state and federal governments to protect our natural resources from the ravages of bad development," said Altamaha Riverkeeper, a powerful McIntosh County–based environmental group and a staunch ally of Charlie Phillips.

The destruction belied the developers' sugar-sweet fliers. Touted one: "The marshes along the headwaters of the Sapelo River offer a rare opportunity for investors to purchase some of the most pristine coastal pine and hardwood hammocks on the East Coast." Said another: "One owner has the chance to own the last open water run of the Sapelo River. A tidal

Signs reflecting the land boom in coastal Georgia.

daily flow brings the marsh alive with saltwater and freshwater fish, along with crabs and lots of ducks."

The Mother Lode of Real Estate

Until developers started drooling over Georgia's coast and envisioning stacks of money to be made from land sales, McIntosh County and Harris Neck were regarded mostly as somnolent, snake-infested, poverty-ridden enclaves. If the area was famous for anything, it was for corrupt politics, shady businesses, and racial injustice.

Until a few decades ago, most of the people living on and around Harris Neck were black families descended from slaves who once worked the area's big cotton plantations. After the Civil War, much of Harris Neck, named for one of the old plantations, was sold in small plots to the former slaves, who practiced subsistence farming and raised just about all the food they needed—fruits, vegetables, hogs, chickens, and cows. The salt marsh and tidal creeks yielded bountiful shrimp, crabs, oysters, and fish.[1]

The only outsider with big bucks attracted to the area after the war was tobacco magnate Pierre Lorillard. He first spied lush Harris Neck in 1890 from the deck of his luxury yacht and decided to build a winter retreat there. On a tract near the South Newport River, he built a palatial home replete with gushing outdoor fountains and shimmering pools. He didn't have much time to use the estate, for he died within a decade of building it.[2]

Later, most of the estate became federal property. In the mid-1930s the federal government built an emergency landing strip at Harris Neck for planes flying the Jacksonville–Richmond air route. After Pearl Harbor was bombed on December 7, 1941, the government announced that the Harris Neck property would become an airfield to base planes patrolling the shoreline for German U-boats and to train fighter-bomber pilots.

In addition to what it already had at Harris Neck, the government needed another twelve hundred acres for the air base. Most of that extra acreage was owned by black families. To get it, the government condemned their land and served eviction notices. Several refused to move and were physically ejected. By July 1942 all the families were gone; a complex of eleven prefabricated buildings and concrete runways sprang up almost overnight.[3]

When the war ended in 1945, the government turned the airfield over to McIntosh County. The black families who had been forcibly removed pressed claims to get their land back, but their petitions fell on deaf ears.

What did get attention was a quickly erupting scandal among the county's leaders. While under their management, the airfield and the nearby former Lorillard estate were looted and stripped. Two county commissioners were charged with stealing, but a local judge dropped the charges. The federal government, however, had had enough of McIntosh and its peculiar brand of politics and management. In 1962 the feds reclaimed the property, most of which became the Harris Neck National Wildlife Refuge.[4]

McIntosh County's scandals did not end there. Up through the 1970s the county was notorious along the Eastern Seaboard for its corruption. Author Melissa Fay Greene focused a national spotlight on it in her best-selling book *Praying for Sheetrock*. The book vividly describes a poverty-stricken county ruled by an iron-fisted sheriff, Tom Poppell, who

Marsh in McIntosh County, Georgia.

wielded his scandal-tainted power to keep African Americans in check, even though they made up at least half the population.

"Most of the blacks inhabited the semi-tamed land between the shoreline of salt marsh and the fringes of the great southern pine forests," Greene wrote. "They still lived in slave or sharecropper shacks . . . or in trailers on dirt roads. . . . They lived without plumbing, telephones, hot water, paved roads, electricity, gas heat, or air conditioning into the 1970s."

One of the county's biggest industries was fleecing northern tourists driving through on U.S. 17 on their way to Florida. "The northern end of McIntosh County was the Kingdom of the Clip Joint, and the only way the Yankees could be sure of traversing it safely was to roll up their windows, lock their doors, stare straight ahead, not stop for strangers or gas, and keep on driving."[5]

Nevertheless, many did stop and play the games. No one knows, said Greene, how much vacation and retirement cash the Yankee tourists dropped in McIntosh County. When duped tourists threatened to call the

Shellman Bluff, Georgia, is one of several quaint, scenic fishing villages that attract people to the Southeast coast.

sheriff, the clip joint owner would inform them that gambling was a felony in Georgia and the tourists themselves might be locked up.

But despite the poverty, the abuse of power, and the tainted politics, McIntosh has always had something immensely desirable: its superb coastal beauty. The never-ending salt marshes, shimmering tidal rivers, and giant live oaks veiled in Spanish moss are the same kind of unspoiled beauty that so inspired Sidney Lanier in Glynn County, just south of McIntosh—the "semi-tamed" land that Melissa Fay Greene described so eloquently. That beauty today draws travel writers who describe McIntosh's quaint, off-the-beaten-path old fishing villages—Shellman Bluff, Contentment Bluff, and Pleasure Bluff, all so-named for their high bluffs offering stunning views of the salt marshes and the rivers cutting through them.

McIntosh also encompasses most of the great Altamaha River estuary, one of the most productive bodies of water on the Atlantic Coast. The estuary is arguably the largest intact and relatively clean estuary system in the East. It's the main reason McIntosh bills itself a "Fisherman's Paradise." The Altamaha flows into the Atlantic near the historic town of Darien, the county seat about midway down Georgia's coastline. Each day the river delivers hundreds of millions of gallons of fresh water, nutrients, and sediments to the estuary and the nearshore ocean waters.

And this in turn has drawn droves of land dealers, real estate investors, and wealthy homebuyers to McIntosh in recent years, setting the stage for raging new conflicts—and posing new headaches for Charlie Phillips and others like him.

Shrimping Fever

Some forty-two years ago Charlie's father, Mike Phillips, sold a feed and seed supply store in Jesup, a city some forty miles upstream on the Altamaha in southwest Georgia, and moved his family to a cottage on the Sapelo River near the sleepy fishing village of Crescent. One day he went out on a shrimp boat with a friend. He had a marvelous time; the catch was excellent and the work exhilarating. Before the boat returned to the dock, Mike had come down with shrimping fever. His day on the water marked the beginning of a multifaceted, family-owned aquatic and aquaculture business on the Georgia coast.

Mike started Phillips Seafood, a wholesale seafood distributor that provided dockage and supplies for area shrimpers and fishermen and purchased their catches. Adjacent to the dock in 1986 he opened Pelican Point Restaurant, now famous for its fresh seafood straight from the dock. He later sold the seafood company to his son Charlie and continued to operate the restaurant.

Charlie quickly learned that running a seafood supply business is essentially a round-the-clock, seven-day-a-week venture. Delivery truck engines blow up on the interstate; underwater hazards shear off costly boat propellers; storms at sea upset supply and delivery schedules for days on end. Finally, government rules and regulations to protect human health, fisheries, employees, and the environment are numerous, stringent, and onerous.

"In essence, I have to be a jack-of-all-trades," Charlie says. At his wood-and-concrete 1970s-era boat docks behind his dad's restaurant, it is not uncommon to see him in a wetsuit, diving under his boat to fix a problem or under another docked vessel to tell a boat captain what's wrong with his craft—and then fixing the problem if he can.

Mature clams
harvested from Charlie
Phillips's clam farm
in the Julienton River
in Georgia.

In 1996 Charlie and his then–business partner Roger DeWitt started
Sapelo Sea Farms to raise clams. Together, they also purchased the four
thousand acres of mostly salt marsh known as Four Mile Island. (Although
almost all of Georgia's salt marsh is owned by the state, portions of it are
still held in fee simple by private owners who cite legal rights dating back
to late-1700s king's grants.) A few years later Charlie bought out DeWitt's
interest in the clam business, although both men retained half interests in
Four Mile Island.

Eventually, most of Charlie's business began coming from his clams; he
is one of nine clam farmers on Georgia's coast. He credits his clam-growing
start in part to University of Georgia marine extension agents who came
to him and DeWitt one day and asked if they wanted to try growing clams.
A bonus, the agents noted, was that shellfish farmers don't use fertilizers,
herbicides, drugs, or chemicals. They don't even have to feed the clams,
which filter algae and nutrients from the water. The main thing needed is
clean water, and that was in good supply in the nearby rivers.

Charlie and DeWitt took the bait, and the agents taught them how to
grow littleneck clams in Georgia's warm waters.

Now, Charlie buys grit-size seed clams from hatcheries in Florida and
brings them to his clam "nursery" next to his dad's restaurant. Under Charlie's careful tending the tiny clams grow until they're slightly larger than
BBs. At that point they won't fall through the special mesh bags used to
"plant" them in the river beds. The clams mature to golf ball size in about
two years.

By early 2007 Charlie had about five million clams in his beds—worth some five hundred thousand dollars at maturity, a nice return on his investment. But as sprawling new subdivisions, shopping centers, and highways laid the seeds for urban sprawl all around him, Charlie Phillips's once rosy future seemed to pale. "We are so blessed to live in such a pristine place, but if we're not careful, we're going to lose it," he says.

It is a feeling shared by others elsewhere along the Southeast coast.

Wall-to-Wall Housing

In 1994, when Jim and Bonnie Swartzenberg began farming clams and oysters in Stump Sound on the southeastern coast of North Carolina, not a single house spoiled their view across the marsh-fringed waters. "Now it's wall-to-wall housing," said Jim, a retired Marine, when I spoke to him in March 2008. Now the view is of tall gray condominiums in the resort community of North Topsail Beach in Onslow County. The complex is one of three such incorporated resorts on twenty-six-mile-long Topsail Island, which stretches northward into neighboring Pender County. Stump Sound, a long, narrow body of water famous for its meaty oysters, separates part of the island from the mainland.

Topsail Island's year-round population of thirty-five hundred leaps to more than thirty-five thousand in summer. To accommodate the massive influx, scores of beach houses, condominiums, motels, strip shopping malls, restaurants, and other structures have been erected over the years— despite ferocious hurricanes that periodically lay waste to the island. The lure of the coastal lifestyle apparently overrides people's fears of the powerful storms. Of particular note, Hurricane Fran in 1996 obliterated or severely damaged hundreds of island buildings. Most of them were replaced or rebuilt almost immediately, often with federal subsidies.[6]

In his book *Echoes of Topsail*, author David A. Stallman explained why people find such places so enticing: "It's salt marsh, sea tides, and unrelenting surf, sea breezes and shifting sand, echoing life's never ending change. If we pay attention, we can learn from Topsail how to enjoy life's journey."[7]

Jim and Bonnie Swartzenberg, however, feared that Topsail will teach a lesson of a harsher kind: that too many people, roads, and rooftops can destroy a site's great natural beauty, charm, and fecundity—the very attributes that drew people there in the first place. The Swartzenbergs, understandably, were especially worried about impacts of the unceasing growth on Stump Sound, which yielded their livelihood.

Owners of the seafood-packing company J & B AquaFood, Inc., near the community of Holly Ridge, the Swartzenbergs have long known that a healthy Stump Sound is crucial to their way of life. On their state shellfish leases in the sound, they plant fifty thousand to sixty thousand clams per year and harvest about 80–90 percent of them. They also raise eighteen hundred to two thousand bushels of oysters annually. The oysters grow in rectangular, flat mesh baskets designed to float just below the water's surface. They are sold as half-shell oysters packaged in half-bushel boxes of 200, or as steamers packaged in full-bushel boxes of 185 to 200. Jim tends the shellfish almost daily—from hatching through delivery—to ensure freshness and to meet the stringent standards set by North Carolina's Shellfish Sanitation Commission and the U.S. FDA.

For decades before Jim and Bonnie started their business, Bonnie's family had gathered clams and oysters from the sound and adjacent waters, combining that business with more traditional agricultural pursuits at the family's ninety-two-acre farm overlooking the sound. After he married Bonnie, Jim, now sixty-six, taught high school English. But he eventually decided he wanted another job. With assistance from North Carolina Sea Grant, he and Bonnie began growing and harvesting clams and oysters on her family's one hundred acres of state shellfish leases. Fifteen of those acres are adjacent to the farm.

It hasn't been an easy life; nor has it made them a lot of money. Still, it's a business that Jim and Bonnie enjoy, one they said they hoped to continue for a few more years.

But each new house that has sprouted around Stump Sound has made making a living from shellfish harvesting more difficult. The huge prices for beachfront property on Topsail have been pushing prospective buyers to build on the mainland instead, near tidal rivers and creeks that drain into the shellfishing areas. Jim noted that eleven hundred new homes were slated to rise at the edge of his and Bonnie's shellfish farm. Also, some forty to fifty houses were being built near Turkey Creek, three-quarters of a mile east of J & B AquaFood. A half-mile west of the farm, a seventy-five-home development was planned for Kings Creek.

"That used to be wild," Jim said of the adjacent property. "But now it's nearly in my backyard." He said that plans for some four thousand other homes within five miles inland of the family farm are also on the books. "I don't know if there are many pluses with that," he added.

The minuses, though, are clear. The new subdivisions, whose waterfront lots sell in the high six figures, spell almost certain problems for the waters in which Jim and Bonnie grow their shellfish. The new homes and people will require roads and driveways, impervious surfaces that do not allow storm water to percolate into the ground.

"The more chemicals and unnatural things in the water, the harder it is for shellfish to grow," Jim said. And the chancier the shellfish could be for humans to eat. He and his wife already had to close their shellfish beds temporarily after even moderate rainfall because it produced too much dirty runoff.

Indeed, after about one and a half inches of rain or more, most of coastal North Carolina's "conditionally approved" shellfish harvest areas are shut down. Before they can reopen, shellfish sanitation officials must take samples to determine if fecal coliform bacteria levels are within safe limits. Water sample tests must have a fecal coliform bacteria count of no more than 14 MPN (most probable number) per 100 milliliters.

Only a few years ago it took a two-inch rainfall to shut down the beds. But now that development has almost surrounded him, Jim said it's probably only a matter of time until a one-inch storm will trigger a closure. And every time there's a shutdown, it can take several days for the waters to reopen. Closing their shellfish beds for a few days out of the year is usually not a major financial blow for him and Bonnie. But if several days of heavy rain close the beds at the height of shellfish season, say in November or December, it leaves the restaurants that Jim supplies "begging for oysters."

Despite all this, Jim remained surprisingly philosophical about the looming problems. He said he understands why people want to live on the coast. Like Charlie Phillips in Georgia, Jim isn't against development— just development that sells out the environment for a quick buck. "A man's got a right to do with his land what he wants, if he does it within the law," he explained. "It's progress. You can't stop progress. I understand that."

What does eat at him, he said, is that the rampant coastal growth comes at his and others' expense. "We know how to protect our water quality," he said. "It's difficult, but not impossible."

But why fight it? Why don't Jim and Bonnie and her family simply follow the trend and sell their farm and shellfish operations to developers, which probably would set them up for life? It's not that they haven't had lucrative offers: Jim said that developers and speculators in droves have phoned, mailed, or stopped by, wanting to know if he and Bonnie and her family wanted to make a deal.

But the family gave all of them the same answer—not interested in selling, at least not yet. They love the land. Period. Developers slackened their inquiries after that but have not ceased entirely. Jim said he believed that a deal with the developers would be a short-term, Faustian bargain. "In the long run," he said, "we'd all be better off holding on to the land."

$$\psi \quad \psi \quad \psi$$

IN THE MID-1980s North Carolina legislators adopted new rules that officials said were sufficient to protect coastal waters from pollutant-laden runoff. The rules were a miserable failure. For more than twenty-five years they allowed sprawling subdivisions and businesses to be built ever more densely in North Carolina's coastal areas. Brunswick County's population has grown by 60 percent since 1990, and New Hanover County's has jumped by more than 40 percent, according to the U.S. Census Bureau. The phenomenal growth spurt simply overwhelmed the land's capacity to filter out oil, mud, fertilizer, bacteria, and other undesirable substances carried by storm runoff during heavy rains.

As a result, the list of North Carolina coastal areas closed to shellfishing grew longer. Since 1984 the amount of coastal waters off-limits to shellfish harvesting has grown by more than 13 percent. Of the state's some 2 million acres of coastal waters, about 365,000 are closed to shellfishing. Another 56,000—up by 12,000 acres since 1984—are closed temporarily after periods of moderately drenching rains.[8]

Nearly all the clams and half the oysters harvested in North Carolina are from south of Cedar Island, or within Carteret, Onslow, Pender, New Hanover, and Brunswick counties.[9] In New Hanover, however, North Carolina's second most densely populated county, nearly all the tidal creeks and sounds are closed to shellfish harvesting. Fast-growing Brunswick County may be about to challenge New Hanover for that dubious distinction.

"The overall impacts of growth on shellfishing grounds have been huge," Larry Cahoon, a biologist at the University of North Carolina at Wilmington, told me. He explained why it was necessary to close such wide expanses: "We can't let people get sick from eating shellfish. A lot of North Carolina shellfish are exported out of state, and that can create legal and economic concerns."

Faced with such a possibility, North Carolina's Environmental Management Commission, a government-appointed regulatory panel, proposed—after much wrangling—stricter rules in early 2008 to reduce storm runoff pollution in tidal waters of the state's twenty coastal counties. It was a frank acknowledgment that the old rules simply had ceased being effective.

Tom Reeder, chief of the wetlands and storm-water unit of the state's Division of Water Quality, noted in a newspaper interview that "the pollution associated with stormwater runoff is the No. 1 water-quality problem in North Carolina. The existing rules aren't really protecting the water quality of coastal North Carolina." Ernest Larkin, a member of North Carolina's Environmental Management Commission, said in the same article that "coastal stormwater is the biggest contributor to the degradation of water quality, and our rules have been inadequate."[10]

The commission's new regulations were designed to rectify the gaping deficiencies of the old rules, its members said. Under the new rules, new development in coastal areas had to have fifty-foot-wide vegetative buffers—an increase from thirty feet. Developers of projects that paved or roofed over more than 12 percent of a tract of land within a half-mile of shellfishing waters had to add engineer-designed storm-water controls—such as storm-water detention ponds—to slow runoff and allow seepage into the ground. Developers now had to get a storm-water permit for a project that disturbed a quarter acre or more. The old rules required a permit for only one or more acres.

But other forces were at work here—in particular the politically well-connected North Carolina Home Builders Association. The group estimated that the stricter storm-water control requirements would tack an extra three thousand dollars onto the cost of building a house—a hefty increase for a homebuyer. Larry Sneeden of ESP Associates, a land-planning and engineering design consultant firm in Wilmington, contended that storm-water control expenses would unintentionally promote higher-density development near sensitive waters as developers tried to reduce the amount of land they disturbed. "I hate to see the trend we're going to see—everything going high density," he said. Builders such as Hiram Williams of Pender County questioned the need for the fifty-foot buffer, insisting that a well-designed thirty-foot zone would be adequate for filtering out pollution. "They're just taking away the right to use a lot of people's property," he said. Lisa Martin of the Home Builders Association insisted that home construction and real estate are vital parts of the coastal economy. "This is going to affect affordability on the coast," she said.[11]

The developers and other opponents of the new regulations took their complaints to the 2008 session of the North Carolina General Assembly, whose representatives had the legal right to review the new regulations and deny them, let them stand, or even—though hard to imagine— strengthen them. Hundreds of private citizens rallied at the state capitol in Raleigh in support of the proposed regulations.

In the end, the legislators scrapped the new rules and set about writing their own. In what they billed as a compromise among local governments, homebuilders, and environmentalists, the lawmakers voted in mid-July 2008 to considerably weaken the proposed storm-water control measures.

Developers would now have to contain a much smaller amount of runoff than the Environmental Management Commission rules had de-manded. They would be required to control runoff only from the first 1.5 inches of rain rather than the first 3.5 inches. The "compromise rules" allowed some exemptions from buffer requirements and excluded proj-ects that had already received state and local permits. In addition, existing homes and businesses could be replaced without having to comply with the new rules. Such replacements would not have been permitted under the rules adopted by the Environmental Management Commission. The legislature's measure did retain the commission's original proposal that de-velopers who have impervious surfaces exceeding 12 percent of the prop-erty must install runoff controls such as cisterns, ponds, rain gardens, and rainwater collectors. But developers won a concession on that, too: most wetlands, where construction cannot occur, could be included in the cal-culations that determine those percentages. In sum, the measure permit-ted more development than the commission's rules had allowed.

Environmentalists resigned themselves to a partial victory rather than a major win: "Storm-water pollution is the biggest threat to water quality in North Carolina," said Elizabeth Ouzts of Environment North Carolina. "We felt the bill provided some really basic and important protections for our coastal marshes and wetlands and creeks."[12]

The developers also looked at the new law as a partial win for their side: "It's certainly better than what the [commission] did," said Martin of the Home Builders Association.[13]

$$\downarrow \quad \downarrow \quad \downarrow$$

THE FUTURE HAD just become bleaker for the oysters, clams, and other inhabitants of North Carolina's estuaries, tidal creeks, and marshes. Cahoon and others predicted that coastal water quality will continue its downward slide as growth continues. "There has been some relief in development because of the downturn in the economy," Cahoon told me in late 2010. "But the development pressure likely will return, and it is unlikely that any of the closed shellfishing beds can ever be reopened."

Cahoon and others also predicted that as North Carolina's more populated coastal counties become saturated with even more transplants and retirees, nearby coastal counties—some with more rural land—will absorb the overflow. Indeed, Pender County's population in 2008 was more than 50 percent larger than it had been in 1990; Carteret County's population was up more than 17 percent. In Onslow County, where Jim and Bonnie Swartzenberg run their clam and oyster farm, population growth surged from less than 0.5 percent between 1990 and 2000 to more than 2.5 percent during the next four years, and the pace is still accelerating.

That means that the list of shellfishery closings is likely to get even longer.

The Multiplier Effect

A tall, shaggy, sandy-haired man with a sunburned face, Mike Mallin was exposed to environmental horrors early in life. Growing up in Cleveland, Ohio, he witnessed the gross pollution of the Cuyahoga River, famous for being "the river that caught on fire." Actually, it burned more than once, helping to spur the environmental movement in the late 1960s. Also ap-

The traditional fishing village of Sneads Ferry, North Carolina.

palling were the massive algal blooms along the shores of Lake Erie, stark sights Mallin remembers to this day. The grim memories spurred his desire to become an aquatic ecologist.

As a scientist at UNC-Wilmington, Mallin focused on sources of nonpoint coastal pollution (pollution caused by storm runoff) and its link to population growth. He scrutinized population trends and shellfish bed closures in Carteret, Onslow, Pender, New Hanover, and Brunswick counties from 1984 to 1997. It should be no surprise that his analysis showed a strong correlation between increases in the number of people and increases in shellfish bed shutdowns due to high fecal coliform bacteria counts. In 1984, when 352,000 people lived in the five counties, a little more than thirty-five thousand acres of shellfish waters were closed; by 2003, when the combined population had soared to 502,000, the closures had bulged to more than forty-two thousand acres.

Clearly, more people—and the secondary development that followed—meant more pollution, which meant more shellfish beds off-limits to harvesting. But Mallin's scrutiny revealed an even stronger connection: Although wild animal droppings, livestock manure, and other contaminants contribute to fecal coliform levels in water, the human population increase alone could explain 70 percent of the annual shellfish area closures in North Carolina's tidal waters. No matter which way Mallin analyzed the results, the correlation was strong—the more people living in a watershed, the higher the fecal coliform bacteria levels in the water.

The revelations were similar to what Fred Holland and Denise Sanger had found in South Carolina—the more impervious surface that is present in a watershed, the greater the volume of bacteria-laden storm water going into its streams. In essence, by the time 20 percent of an area is covered with hard surfaces, waterways have become too polluted for shellfishing. Mallin concluded that shellfishing bans increase concomitantly with increases in impervious cover.

As if this were not enough, Mallin found what he called the "multiplier effect," which he explained in the June 2006 issue of *Scientific American*. He pointed out that the abnormally high flows of storm water rushing from parking lots and streets often erode drainage ditches, stream banks, and construction sites—and thus carry suspended dirt, especially clay, and other sediments into a receiving stream. The suspended material turns the stream cloudy. Once in the stream, the sediments chemically bind with other pollutants such as ammonium, phosphate, metals, and fecal bacteria, and the binding and the water turbidity protect the bacteria from ultraviolet radiation that normally would kill them. What's more, the microbes can obtain nourishment—carbon, nitrogen, and phosphorus—from the soil particles. The microbes can remain viable for a long time and travel far downstream hitched to the sediments. Mallin "found a highly significant correlation between turbidity and the abundance of fecal coliform bacteria" in New Hanover County and noted that "other studies performed in the Chesapeake Bay, western Florida, the Mediterranean coast, and Australia have yielded similar findings."[14]

Does rapid population growth on the coast ultimately mean the end of shellfish harvesting, or can the two coexist? Mallin, for one, thinks the two can be reconciled—with considerable effort, of course. It can be done, he said, by planning ahead to minimize the amount of impervious surfaces and maximize swards of green space. "To protect America's coastal waters, developers and builders clearly need to move away from their current destructive practices—including clear-cutting, wetlands drainage and extensive use of pavement—and switch to smart-growth strategies.

When planning new resorts, shopping centers, office complexes and residential subdivisions, the designers must minimize the use of impervious surfaces and maximize the amount of vegetated areas. A site with plenty of green spaces among the paved areas will have less runoff, and percolation through the soil will remove many of the contaminants swept from the asphalt and concrete."[15]

Easily said; probably very hard to do.

Deborah Shepherd, head of Altamaha Riverkeeper and a close ally of clam grower Charlie Phillips, told me that the problem is quite clear in Georgia: "Developers want to cover about 80 percent of the land and leave only 20 percent of green space open."

THE BATTLES IN Georgia and North Carolina described above are examples of seething conflicts up and down the Southeast coast. More—and bigger—issues are looming. Demands from angry homeowners, fishermen, environmentalists, and others for stricter coastal water protection likely will get louder. The big problem, though, is that the development train has long left the station, and no one seems to have a blueprint for how to deal with the full scope of the problems unrestricted growth has created. Clearly, new coastal protection strategies are called for.

"By emphasizing 'end-of-pipe' controls such as stormwater detention ponds, the best-management practices outlined in [state and federal regulations] create a false sense that they alone will solve the runoff problem," noted Dana Beach in his Pew Commission report. In fact, he said, most suburban developments are now 30–35 percent impervious, so far above the 10 percent threshold of damage to streams that even the best management practices cannot substantially reduce runoff to safe levels. Cities, of course, are even more impervious.[16]

CHAPTER SIX

Gone with the Flow

SO MUCH FRESH WATER comes down the Altamaha River that some people liken it to the Nile. In a normal rainfall year the Altamaha pumps more than three trillion gallons of fresh water—a hundred thousand gallons per second—into the Atlantic Ocean, one-sixth of the South Atlantic Bight's entire freshwater complement.[1] The great outpouring makes the river the third-largest supplier of fresh water on the Eastern Seaboard.

With a watershed basin encompassing fourteen thousand square miles, the Altamaha is also the largest intact, free-flowing river system on the East Coast. Its headwaters rise some 250 miles from the sea, near the bustling cities of Atlanta and Athens in the red clay hills of northern Georgia's Piedmont region. The headwaters mingle and form the Altamaha's two main tributaries, the Ocmulgee and the Oconee. Major rivers in their own right, the two form the Altamaha when they run together in Wheeler County in the heart of southern Georgia. The Altamaha then winds 137 miles across the flat Coastal Plain, unfettered and unobstructed, to the sea. Together, the Altamaha and its tributaries drain all or part of fifty-three Georgia counties, one-fourth of the entire state. Midway down the Georgia coast, in Altamaha Sound, the river's fresh water blends with the ocean's salt water to create one of the most expansive and highest-quality estuaries in the world. The Altamaha's fresh water also flows north into a neighboring estuary, Doboy Sound, through connecting creeks and from the river's "plume," which extends several miles into the Atlantic.

Conservationists call the Altamaha "the perfect image of a true southern river" as it meanders through rich bottomland hardwood swamps,

Huge bald cypress trees still stand along Georgia's Altamaha River.

cypress-tupelo sloughs, former rice fields, endless salt marshes, a broad multichannel delta, and finally into the estuary occupying much of McIntosh and Glynn counties. The huge freshwater flow links the region's natural environments into one magnificent, interdependent system. The Nature Conservancy calls it one of "75 Last Great Places" on Earth.[2]

Upstream, the vast, alligator-inhabited swamps export immense amounts of organic matter such as decaying leaves, twigs, and other detritus into the river. Natural weathering and voracious microbes break much of it down into key nutrients and tiny bits and pieces of organic carbon. Spring and winter floods flush this mother lode downstream, where it is trapped by the estuary and tidal marshes. The nutrients, especially nitrogen and phosphorus, are natural fertilizers that nourish spartina and phytoplankton, which in turn feed zooplankton and the other creatures that make up the estuary's food web.

The sediments the river carries help build, maintain, and stabilize the marshes, two major barrier islands (Sapelo and Saint Simons), and the wide river delta that is a crucial winter feeding ground for thousands of migratory shorebirds.

The Altamaha's delta, woods, swamps, marshes, and estuary are refuges for at least 130 species of rare or endangered plants and animals. Migratory fish such as American shad, herring, and the endangered shortnose sturgeon spawn in the river. Just offshore, a vibrant shrimp population is the bedrock of a commercial fishery valued at twenty million dollars a year. Farther out to sea, nearly eighteen miles due east of Sapelo Island, nutrients and fresh water pumped into the ocean by the river help support a subtropical paradise—Gray's Reef National Marine Sanctuary, one of the largest nearshore live-bottom reefs in the Southeast.[3]

But there's trouble afoot in this munificent provider. Even though much of the Altamaha watershed remains relatively unsullied, human development and the subsequent demands for more water to drink, flush toilets, and irrigate suburban lawns are quickly increasing in the basin. In 2002 the growing demands prompted an alarmed American Rivers organization to place the Altamaha seventh on its list of the nation's ten most endangered rivers. "A seemingly insatiable demand for services such as drinking water and electricity threatens to overwhelm the Altamaha," explained the group. "One of the healthiest rivers on the eastern seaboard [now] faces a future of perpetual drought."[4]

A major cause for worry is the big gorilla upstream, Metro Atlanta, the third-fastest-growing urban area in America. Atlanta, in short, is running out of water. Its suburban communities are in a hell-bent race to snatch a share of water from the Altamaha and its tributaries before their neighbors beat them to it. Without more water they can't add on new subdivisions and shopping centers and sewer lines. In 2010 more than half a dozen proposals were on the table to build new drinking water reservoirs in the Altamaha's headwaters.

Metro Atlanta's communities themselves face strong competition from other quarters—especially from big corporations wanting more water for their own needs. In 2010 six power producers in the Altamaha basin intended to install new combustion turbines in their plants; one wanted to build a new coal-fired plant. The new and upgraded plants would suck millions of gallons of water each day from the streams for cooling. Most of it would evaporate away as steam. Only about one-third to one-half of it would ever see the Altamaha. If urban and industrial users continue to up their usage, the myriad creatures that seek sustenance, shelter, and support in the Altamaha's estuary and vast salt marshes are bound to suffer the consequences.

In essence, nothing is more fundamental to a healthy estuary than the quantity and timing of freshwater delivery. That's why any major proposal to tamper with a river's regular flow sends shudders down the spines of scientists and environmentalists. Their spines really rattled in the early 1970s when the Georgia legislature created the Altamaha River Commission "for the purpose of encouraging and promoting the expansion and development of the full economic, industrial and recreation potential of the Altamaha River Basin." For several reasons that ill-begotten idea petered out. But in late 1997 the river protectors' hackles rose again. A coastal company known as the Savannah Group (TSG) announced that it had officially asked the Georgia Environmental Protection Division (EPD) for a permit to withdraw eight and a half million gallons of water per day from the Altamaha to sell to yet-to-be-named customers. The company also wanted to pump, treat, and sell water from two other Georgia rivers, the Savannah and the Ogeechee. The EPD informed the company by letter that the state intended to grant the permits if certain environmental requirements were met.[5]

By then, however, TSG's proposals had kindled a near rebellion among coastal seafood producers, environmentalists, and even local politicians. They roundly condemned the planned water withdrawals, which they said would seriously damage the Altamaha and its estuary. "This is an outrageous violation of the law and the public trust," a protester said.

The river's allies sought advice from experts such as Dr. Merryl Alber, a University of Georgia marine scientist who has devoted her career to understanding the importance of fresh water in estuaries. "Freshwater delivery defines almost all of the physical, biological and chemical properties of an estuary," Alber warned. "Decreases in freshwater inflow can have far-reaching, sometimes disastrous, consequences downstream."[6]

TSG's proposals were placed on indefinite hold, but the Altamaha's protectors now fear that it's only a matter of time before other powerful and well-connected groups make new demands for the precious water. And if it can happen to the Altamaha, they warn, it can happen to other rivers.

While they fret about the water in the rivers they also should be nervous about the water beneath their feet—the groundwater in underground aquifers, especially the Upper Floridan, the coastal region's main water supplier. An extremely generous water provider, the aquifer was first developed in the 1880s and has been used extensively since then. But that may be coming to an end. The U.S. Geological Survey has warned that rapid population growth, more tourists, and prolonged industrial activity in coastal Georgia have reduced the area's groundwater levels and limited the available water supply. Heavy pumping from the aquifer already has had serious repercussions, including saltwater tainting of wells in Brunswick, Georgia, and Hilton Head Island, South Carolina. In addition, decreased groundwater inflow to springs, freshwater ponds, marshes, and wetlands may be upsetting the delicate balance between fresh water and salt water in tidal rivers and estuaries.[7]

The Role of Fresh Water

Scientists such as Alber have identified more than a dozen functions for fresh water in estuaries and salt marshes. Foremost is its role in maintaining salinity levels. Such levels, of course, depend largely on the amount of water coming down the river and the degree of mixing between fresh water and seawater. Most of the organisms inhabiting coastal ecosystems occur within specific salinity ranges. Many of them have specific salinity needs at certain life stages.

A prime example is the prized blue crab, which needs both inshore brackish waters and salty ocean waters to complete its life cycle. In the Southeast, blue crabs mate in low-salinity estuarine areas from February to November. After mating, females migrate to saltier water in the lower reaches of estuaries or the nearshore area of the ocean. Each female carries some two million fertilized eggs in an orange "sponge" that remains attached to her abdomen until the eggs hatch and the larvae emerge. The tiny organisms undergo several larval stages until they reach the "megalopal stage" when they are about a tenth of an inch wide. They then migrate into the low-salinity, nutrient-rich waters of upper estuaries and tidal creeks, where they settle onto the bottom and begin transforming into juvenile blue crabs. The lower salinity levels discourage saltwater predators from swimming into the crabs' nursery areas, so the little creatures can forage and develop in relative security. In general, small crabs survive best during years of relatively high freshwater runoff, which increases nutrient input and decreases salinity—although too much fresh water can flush them from the marsh.[8]

Fresh water also performs impressive janitorial services. As river water moves through an estuary, it helps wash out wastes, pollutants, spilled oil, and even microbial pathogens. The time it takes for fresh water to "flush out" the estuary—from the point upstream where tides begin to influence the river to the river's mouth at the ocean—is known simply as the "flushing time." The flushing time may vary a lot, from a week on a large river to a couple of months on a smaller one. Usually, the shorter the flushing time, the quicker the estuary is rid of contaminants. A prolonged flushing time can allow wastes and other unwanted materials to accumulate in an estuary and in the tissues of its fish and shellfish. Aside from damaging the ecosystem, that can lead to a shutdown of shellfishing grounds and a ban on fishing and swimming. On the other hand, a longer flushing time can allow more time for the system to process minerals, nutrients, and other substances. Flushing time, Alber said, is so important that it and salinity levels "set the context for all of the biological and chemical processes that occur in the estuary."[9]

Fresh water has another vastly important role. In many estuaries it sets up a conveyor belt of sorts to transport assorted marine creatures—such as the larvae of crabs and shrimp—from their ocean hatching grounds into the nursery areas of the estuary and salt marsh. The unique manner in which water circulates in an estuary makes the system work. Less-dense fresh water floats on top of denser seawater. The low-salinity liquid at the surface wants to flow seaward, but the denser seawater beneath it wants to flow into the estuary. If the larvae position themselves in the lower stratum of salty water moving inland, eventually it delivers them to their nurseries. Once there, they sink to the bottom and are kept there by the inflowing bottom currents instead of being swept back out to sea by the surface currents.

Fresh water does not come down a river such as the Altamaha in a steady stream all year long. The flow's volume and timing depend on rainfall, temperature, and other variables. In the Southeast, freshwater flow is heaviest in spring and winter; thus, river flow into the coastal systems is usually greatest during those seasons. The life histories of many fish and crustaceans such as the blue crab have evolved in accord with these seasonal variations—for at least ten thousand years in the Altamaha, about the same amount of time that the region's salt marshes have been evolving. The organisms' life stages, then, are cued to spring and winter runoff. Changes in timing could seriously disrupt their intricate spawning and nursery cycles.

Rivers and Estuaries

Scientists know surprisingly little about the complex relationships between rivers and their estuaries. But what scientists do know, and greatly appreciate, is that rivers like the Altamaha have a tremendous impact on coastal ecology. "For a long time, we thought the rivers came down and dumped water into the ocean, and that was the end of it," wrote the late University of Georgia marine scientist Richard Wiegert, who died in 2003. "Here is this huge ocean. What impact do these rivers have? Through their delivery of nutrients, through their delivery of pollutants if they are polluted, and through their change in salinity, they really do have an impact. We recognize that now."[10]

Ordinary people also are getting the message—particularly about fresh water's key importance to coastal ecosystems. Less water coming down the rivers means saltier estuaries and wider swings in seasonal salinity patterns, which could do significant harm to the natural nurseries of shrimp, blue crabs, and other marine life. Studies of Georgia's rivers show worrisome trends toward higher salinity levels.[11] Already, oyster distribution along the Georgia coast has shifted, quite possibly for that reason.

"People are starting to think about how changes in the rivers and taking water out of them might affect the estuaries," Merryl Alber said. "There are some fishermen on the Georgia coast who swear that things have changed in their lifetime. They say, for instance, that wild rice, which requires fresh water, used to grow farther down the coast than it does now."[12] Some say that they now have to scrape saltwater-loving barnacles off their boat hulls at docks in stretches of tidal rivers where they never had to do so before. "That suggests, of course, that the water has gotten saltier in those stretches," Alber said.

Crabbers say there's less "sweet water"—their name for fresh water—

in the Altamaha and other rivers than there used to be. That adversely affects blue crabs, which need a certain amount of sweet water to complete their life cycles.

One of these crabbers took keen notice of the waning amounts of fresh water and became angry, very angry. He made up his mind to do something about it. In the process he became a piercing thorn in the sides of coastal regulators and developers and anyone else he perceived as threatening his beloved coast and rivers.

↓ ↓ ↓

BEEFY, ROUGH-HEWN, and outspoken, James Holland grew up in the 1950s in the somnolent town of Cochran in middle Georgia, where hunting and fishing seemed as natural as life itself. He loved to roam the shady woods and wetlands abounding with wildlife. When he was thirsty, he sipped cool water from one of the many branches and creeks running clean and clear. He began spending more time in the outdoors than in the classroom, a factor that led to his dropping out of school in the ninth grade.

When he turned seventeen Holland enlisted in the Marines. After his service he moved to Brunswick for a civilian job—a food-service worker—at the Navy's Glynco Naval Air Station. In his spare time he fished in the local creeks and rivers, especially the Altamaha and Satilla rivers, which teemed with seafood. Along the rivers' banks he hunted all manner of game inhabiting the wide stretches of woods, fields, and wetlands.

In the early 1970s the Navy announced that it was shutting down its Brunswick operations. Holland, by now the father of three children, had to find another line of work. He already had in mind what he wanted to do—he would become a crabber. He had watched other people make a decent living from crabbing and shrimping, and it appealed to his spirit of independence. It gave him a buoyant outlook that reminded him of his childhood, when he freely roamed the woods and fields.

In 1977 Holland bought a Carolina skiff, crab traps, and tackle and started working for himself. In the beginning he ran most of his traps in the Satilla River, which forms one of Georgia's five great estuaries. Then he began working his traps in the nearby Altamaha estuary.

Former crabber James Holland helped found the Altamaha Riverkeeper and became a fierce protector of the river and the entire Georgia coast.

"No one will tell you crabbing is easy," says Holland, now seventy, his blue eyes focusing sharply as if to make sure I catch his drift. "I wasn't going to get rich off it, but the money was OK. I really did love it. I was my own boss. There was plenty of crabs, and I was in the outdoors every day in one of the most beautiful places on Earth."

For more than twenty-five years he trapped and sold blue crabs. When he was out on the water, he often found himself pausing just to drink in the great splendor of the salt marshes and to watch the migratory shorebirds that congregated by the thousands along the shore to rest and feed. "I sat in awe of it all," he says. "I still do."

He recalls with nostalgia tending his traps in the Altamaha and the Satilla. The rivers' currents can be swift, so he had to rig his two-foot-square metal crab pots with eleven-pound weights to keep them stable. Attached to the weights were specially marked floats to let him know which traps were his. Many of his fellow crabbers used motor-driven winches to haul up their traps, but Holland raised and lowered his by hand, even though the current might be strong. The weights on the traps were an added burden, but in those days some of the extra heft was likely to include a goodly number of crabs.

The daily routine was fast and simple: Grab the pot as it comes out of the water, shake the crabs into plastic containers, separate the smaller males and females from the more valuable large males, bait the pot with fresh-cut pogeys, then toss it back into the swirling water. If there are no crabs, just replace the bait, lower the trap back into the water, and head for the next float.

In his heyday in the 1980s Holland owned three boats and more than a hundred crab pots. He harvested fifteen hundred pounds of crabs a day from the Altamaha and Satilla rivers and sold most of the catch from a backyard shed that he built of scrap lumber and tin. He invested in a shiny industrial freezer to hold his crab harvests. He also went into the soft-shell crab business, building a twenty-foot-by-fifty-foot cinderblock building to house the tanks and pumps necessary to sustain the molting crabs.

In all, Holland figures he put close to $150,000 into his crabbing business. And the investment was paying off; he was making a decent living—until the early 1990s, when he and other crabbers started noticing that their crab and fish catches seemed to be steadily declining. Fewer crabs were coming up in his traps. The crabbers—there were hundreds of them along Georgia's coast at that time—talked among themselves, sharing figures and ideas. The dwindling crab numbers posed a direct threat to their livelihood. If the situation weren't turned around, their very way of life would come to an inglorious end.

In 1994 they banded together to try to figure out why the catches were shrinking. They approached state biologists, who concluded that crabs simply were being overharvested. So the crabbers went to lawmakers at the statehouse in Atlanta and asked for legislation to limit the number of crabs that could be legally caught. The result was the Georgia Blue Crab Management Program, which greatly limited the number of crabbers and the number of crab traps allowed by law in state waters at any given time. In effect, only 159 people at a time were allowed to catch crabs commercially. The state also forced crabbers to use traps with holes of a certain size so that juvenile crabs could escape—and perhaps grow old enough to mate and produce annual crops for the future.

But the smaller crab catches persisted. "Kept getting worse and worse," Holland laments. He began seeing other troubling changes. Crabs started to show nasty-looking lesions and other ailments. And the crabs and other fish were starting to turn up in places where they were not supposed to be.

In the Altamaha, for instance, hermit crabs, spadefish, and angelfish—primarily saltwater creatures—were surviving well upstream from the point where the Altamaha traditionally was brackish or fresh. One day on the Satilla, Holland saw a "sponge crab"—a female crab bearing eggs—more than ten miles upstream from the open sea. Usually egg-laden females are found only in salty ocean water.

"I had been crabbing in the river for years, so it was obvious something was going on," Holland says. Then it dawned on him—saltwater creatures higher up the river meant that salt water was creeping inland. The most likely explanation was that the rivers weren't pushing enough fresh water downstream into the estuaries to keep salt water from coming upstream. Holland suspected a reason, too—intensive logging, ditching, and draining of land for agriculture and pine plantations upstream were disrupting the flow of fresh water to the coast. If that were true, Holland realized, the blue crab population was headed for trouble. He knew that too much salt water at certain stages in a crab's life cycle—especially at the larval stage—can doom the animal.

The worst, however, was still to come. Around 1998, a searing, tenacious drought took hold of Georgia and the rest of the South, further reducing freshwater flow into the Altamaha and other rivers and causing even higher salinity levels. Crab harvests sank even lower.

But the problems did not stop there. The relentless drought was blamed for still another catastrophe. The higher salinity levels allowed a saltwater-loving, crab-infecting parasite, a dinoflagellate named *Hematodinium perezi*, to thrive in coastal waters. The parasite prevented the crabs' blood cells from carrying oxygen, and they died of oxygen starvation. There was a massive outbreak among the blue crabs, killing untold numbers.

"I saw mudflats just covered with dead crabs," Holland says. "I pulled up crab traps and every one of the crabs in them was dead. Not only does the parasite kill them outright, but crabs also are cannibalistic. If one crab dies from the parasite, it's passed along to others."

By 1999 crabbers were very lucky if they got two hundred pounds of crabs per day—less than a fifth of the fifteen hundred pounds they were taking in the 1980s.

For Holland, it was the final insult. That year he sadly pulled up his pots for the last time and walked away from the life he loved. He closed his store and sold the industrial freezer and the soft-shell crab tanks. The shed in which he had kept the tanks became a storage room for his lawn mowers and other household equipment. "To operate my little store without having to work seven days a week, I needed to catch about five, six boxes of crabs a day. When you're only catching two boxes a day, working seven days a week—I couldn't do it. I knew right then it was time for a change."

Dozens of other Georgia crabbers chose the same route—gut-wrenching decisions for many of them. Those who stayed in the business saw crab harvests continue to plummet. In a last-ditch effort to halt the downward spiral, the Georgia Department of Natural Resources banned the harvest of "sponge crabs." Even that was not enough: Georgia's 2003 commercial blue crab harvest of 1.8 million pounds was the lowest ever reported in nearly a half century of recordkeeping—95 percent below the long-term average. Between 1976 and 2001 a crab trap yielded nine crabs per day on average. In 2003 the average was less than one per day. Those figures prompted the National Marine Fisheries Service to declare Georgia's blue crab fishery a "failure" and a "disaster." The next year, the harvest was still 55 percent below the twenty-year average.

Biologists and state regulators said the foremost reason for the blue crab nosedive was the four-year drought that began in 1998, curtailing freshwater flow and helping trigger the *Hematodinium* epidemic. But another possible cause, the agency acknowledged, was "an unquantified but suspected" impairment of the crabs' essential habitat due to coastal development and upstream "land-use changes" that upset normal freshwater and nutrient-supply rhythms and made the drought even more onerous.[13]

In 2009 the agency's fisheries biologists announced that blue crab numbers had never fully returned to long-term historic averages and the sponge-crab harvest ban would remain in effect indefinitely.

MEANWHILE, THE WORLD had not heard the last of ex-crabber James Holland, his hair now gray and his skin bronzed and wrinkled from years on a crab boat. Although he had given up the crabbing business, his passion for the great salt marshes, estuaries, and rivers of Georgia's coast had not cooled. If anything, he was more zealous than ever to protect them from would-be spoilers; he would not forsake the place he loved.

"So I became an activist," he says. A few months after bowing out of crabbing in 1999, he joined forces with several other angry crabbers and environmentalists also worried about the health and future of Georgia's coast. Many of them had worked together to stop TSG from drawing water from the Altamaha. With surprisingly little disagreement, they organized themselves into the Altamaha Riverkeeper, a grassroots organization based in the historic old port of Darien on a tributary of the river. They chose the Altamaha because it is Georgia's largest river. The new organization was modeled after the Hudson Riverkeeper, a group founded in 1966 by commercial fishermen determined to revive the nearly dead Hudson River in New York.

Among the Altamaha Riverkeeper's stated goals was educating the public about the importance of healthy rivers. More confrontational, though, was the members' vow to be watchdogs for the river: to monitor its water quality, ferret out polluters, and stop projects that posed a threat to it dead in their tracks.

Holland was an unabashed ringleader. He knew, though, that activism by itself would not necessarily save the day. To fight despoilers of the river, estuary, and marshes, the organization had to be armed with solid scientific data and legal evidence of violations.

Undeterred by his lack of a high school diploma, Holland began reading through piles of data and statistics and scientific publications on water quality and on the life cycles of shrimp, crabs, and fish. If he didn't understand something, he asked questions, lots of them.

"I began grilling a lot of scientists, and I began to understand why we need clean, fresh water in our estuaries, and why things can go to hell if you mess with the system," he says. Fresh water, he learned, is of utmost importance for maintaining fragile salinity levels and for delivering nutrients and sediments to sustain the integrity, health, and productivity of estuaries and tidal marshes. What's more, the timing of the river flow is critical—too much fresh water or too little at certain times of the year can wreak havoc on coastal ecosystems. He learned another valuable lesson: The upstream riverine swamps and bottomland forests where he so often fished and hunted as a child are an integral part of the estuarine system.

In the course of his research he began to develop a clearer picture of what had happened to the crabs. He had never bought into the notion that the drought was the single overwhelming cause of the crab population's decline. The four-year dry spell, he surmised, would account for why there wasn't enough fresh water to push saltwater out of estuaries, marshes, and rivers, but the crab losses that drove him and others out of business began well before the drought started and appeared to continue once the drought was declared over.

Holland became convinced that the basic problem confronting Georgia's coast was a steady degradation of water quality in the Altamaha and other rivers as they meandered to the sea. He placed much of the blame on the thousands of new houses, golf courses, and shopping centers built to the very edge of the marshes and estuaries that were causing huge volumes of pollutant-laden storm water to gush into the fragile ecosystems. Also to blame, he says, was the wholesale conversion of swamps and wetlands upstream into croplands and sprawling pine plantations by farming interests and timber growers. Even Metro Atlanta, some 250 miles inland, was partly to blame because of its unquenchable thirst and its pollution that washed downstream.

Until he witnessed the massive crab losses, Holland had never given much thought to how all of these interlocking factors might affect his livelihood. "I realized that what was going on had gotten to my pocketbook, impacted my way of life and my family's life and the recreation I enjoyed," Holland says. "The health of those upstream wetlands was directly tied to the health of the blue crab."

First and foremost for the new Riverkeeper, then, was to protect the quantity and quality of fresh water coming down the Altamaha. Holland did that with a vengeance. As the organization's field director, he became the river's fiercest, staunchest defender, patrolling the waterway almost on a daily basis by foot or boat, taking water samples, snapping pictures, keeping a keen eye out for even the slightest hint of abuse—then staying on the backs of federal, state, and local regulators to force corrective action when violations were found. Sometimes the government itself was the scofflaw.

Holland is legendary on the Georgia coast today, a folk hero to some, a burr under the saddle to others. His fellow environmental activists say he might be the best thing that ever happened to the Georgia coast. In the Altamaha Riverkeeper's first decade of existence, Holland responded personally to more than six hundred citizen tips and complaints about alleged violations. He became an accomplished photographer, recording in thousands of photographs the river's beauty—and also documenting the ugliness of polluted sites. He learned how to use the Georgia Open Records Act, wielding it like a fine-edged sword to ferret out critical information; wage war on polluters; and make industries, developers, and the government itself toe the line.

Holland claims that his vigilance landed him in jail twice and that he was the target of death threats. "But I was just too dumb or too stubborn to let it bother me."

His dogged determination produced results. In 2003, for example, when word leaked out that coastal Glynn County was going to redig some old mosquito-control ditches in the salt marsh, the Altamaha Riverkeeper filed an open records request to find out exactly what the county planned to do and whether it had an up-to-date federal permit to do it.

"We didn't want Glynn County turned loose in the salt marsh with a ditch-digging machine without a permit," Holland says. "We can't afford to lose any of our salt marshes."

The information Riverkeeper obtained showed that the county's permit was out of date. The county then was forced to get a new permit limiting how much it could dig.

"Georgia has some good laws, and they could be very effective if they were enforced," says Holland, who has blamed the lack of enforcement on a lack of funding for Georgia's lead environmental agency, the Environmental Protection Division of the state Department of Natural Resources.

The Altamaha Riverkeeper now has more than one thousand members. "The crabbers finally learned we need clean, fresh water," Holland says. "They got a lesson that the environment does matter. It took a long time to teach 'em."

The Swamp

On a balmy day in February I'm tramping along a moldy, moss-shrouded path in a muffled bottomland hardwood swamp in the floodplain of the mighty Altamaha—sixty miles from the sea. I'm walking with Christi Lambert, who has studied and watched over the river and its wetlands for years on behalf of her employer, the Nature Conservancy of Georgia. Few people know the slow-flowing Altamaha and its prominent swamps better than Christi.

Some people regard swamps as dark, shadowy, mysterious places. But not Christi. Here in the swamp, she says, there is peace, serenity, and an otherworldly beauty. It is a place redolent of fertile earth. Its seasonal ebbs and flows have sculpted rich wildlife habitats, including deep sloughs and the floodplain itself.

As we tramp amid towering cypresses and tupelos and a dense understory of red mulberries and swamp dogwoods, Christi tells me to stay alert for yellow-bellied sliders and perhaps an early-arriving Mississippi kite. The graceful raptor starts showing up here about this time of year after spending the winter in South Florida or even as far away as South America.

Christi and I have come here to see what a healthy, intact riverine bottomland swamp looks like. This is the type of wetland that James Holland, Christi's friend, says is vital to the well-being of blue crabs and other marine life in the estuary far downstream. It is a big part of what the Altamaha Riverkeeper is urgently trying to protect. Without mature, fully functional riverine swamps like this one, the high productivity of many southeastern estuaries and salt marshes would plummet.[14]

Bottomland hardwood swamps are among the most productive and biologically diverse ecosystems in the Southeast. They contain some of the region's best remaining habitats for bats. Nearly two hundred species of birds have been documented in them—including the beautiful bright yellow prothonotary warbler, found virtually nowhere other than hardwood swamps. The famed ivory-billed woodpecker—once called the "Lord God" bird (as in "Lord God, what a bird!")—can no longer be found here. If it still exists, as some naturalists believe it does, it is in an intact riverine swamp.

By the usual definition, bottomland hardwood swamps hold standing water for a few days to several months during rainy spells—especially in winter and spring, when river flow is heaviest and the rivers overflow onto their floodplains. Even after the standing water dissipates, the soil remains moist and soggy for most of the year. Bottomland swamps support numerous oaks, maples, hickories, ashes, and sweet gums, as well as bald cypresses and tupelo gums. The cypress–tupelo gum swamps are so close to the river that they hold water nearly all year and are completely dominated by the water-loving cypresses and tupelos. As you walk through a southeastern bottomland forest toward its river, the forest usually gives way to a cypress-gum swamp along the stream.

The bottomland swamp where Christi and I walk is part of the forty-five-hundred-acre Moody Forest Natural Area. The magnificent bald cypresses in this protected swamp are some of the largest (ten feet wide at the base) and oldest (more than six hundred years old) in the region. The preserve also includes uplands harboring some of the purest remaining stands of longleaf pines in the Southeast.

The Moody Forest lies in Appling County, girlhood home of naturalist Janisse Ray, author of the award-winning book *Ecology of a Cracker Childhood* and cofounder of the Altamaha Riverkeeper with James Holland. She speaks eloquently of growing up in Appling and hearing about Moody's "mythical swamp." Working with Christi and others, she helped win permanent protection for Moody Forest.

"This is a special place, one of the last large areas of habitats along the Altamaha undisturbed by development or timber cutting," Christi says as we walk the swamp path. "Just look at those cypresses. Anywhere else, they would have been logged long ago." The main reason they weren't, she notes, is that the Moody family who owned the tract practiced good stewardship.

OTHER TRACTS WEREN'T so fortunate. Bottomland hardwood and cypress-gum swamps once dominated the broad floodplains—often many miles wide—that flank the Altamaha and other so-called alluvial rivers, which begin in the mountains or the hilly Piedmont and meander across the flat Coastal Plain. About two hundred years ago, old-growth bottomland hardwood forests covered nearly thirty million acres across the Southeast. Then came farmers and big timber companies who ditched, drained, channelized, and cleared vast swaths of swamps to plant rice, row crops, and commercial pines in the nutrient-rich soil. When famed naturalist John Bartram traveled through the Southeast in 1765, he observed African slaves frenziedly clearing swamps along the Altamaha and the Satilla.

Today, only a fraction of the bottomland swamps remains. The huge loss contributed to the extinction of the ivory-billed woodpecker and other species. And the destruction continues. In the Altamaha's lower basin alone, more than thirty thousand acres of wetlands have been converted to pine plantations since 1985.[15]

The loss of swamplands has taken a toll on the freshwater flow downstream. Bottomland hardwood swamps regulate river flow by storing and detaining floodwaters during the heavy flows of spring and winter, when the rivers surge out of their channels and inundate the floodplains. Ecologists call these episodes "pulses." In addition to the floodwater retained by a swamp on its surface, a large portion of the water seeps into the soil and recharges groundwater tables—vital in helping maintain river flow during droughts and traditionally dry months.

"The wetlands essentially buffer freshwater flow," said Ron Carroll, co-director of the River Basin Science and Policy Center in the University of Georgia's School of Ecology, in a talk on Saint Simons Island in 2004. "They act like hydrological control valves on the rivers, and that's the main connection to the estuarine animals."

Periodic inundations are as natural to bottomland hardwood swamps as the tides are to estuaries. "Some people think the floods—the pulses—need to be controlled," explained Darold Batzer, a University of Georgia entomologist who has extensively studied the Altamaha. "But in many ways, they are what make southeastern rivers tick."[16]

Take away this storage and flow-regulation capacity, as people do when they ditch and drain the swamps, and downstream estuaries begin to brim with excess fresh water—much more than is good for blue crabs, oysters, and the other marine life that rely on certain salinity levels at certain times of their lives. If there is too little fresh water, the harm to estuarine creatures can be equally devastating, of course.

THE CURTAILED RIVER flow has another serious consequence: downstream salt marshes and estuaries may be cut off from the sediment, organic matter, and essential nutrients they must have to survive. "The importance of freshwater delivery from the Piedmont and Coastal Plain via floodplain rivers cannot be overestimated," the late Charles Wharton, one of the Southeast's most revered ecologists, noted in 1982. "Rivers directly or indirectly provide sands for the construction of coastal features . . . silts from upstream may be deposited on downstream salt marshes."[17]

The dead leaves, twigs, flowers, nuts, fruits, and other bits of vegetation of the swamp, collectively known as organic litter, pile up in layers on the floodplain floor during times of low water, such as in summer and fall. Weather, natural leaching, bacteria, fungi, mites, nematodes, earthworms, and hordes of other organisms immediately start working on the material, breaking it down into ever smaller and simpler pieces. Eventually, only basic constituents of the debris remain—including organic carbon and compounds of nitrogen and phosphorus. Most of the carbon is so fine that it dissolves in water as dissolved organic carbon. Some carbon, though, remains as particulate organic carbon. Whatever its form, the organic carbon is vital to life in the ecosystem.[18]

When heavy flows come and the engorged river overflows and forms a shallow layer throughout the swamp, a substantial portion of the nutrients, organic carbon, and other products in the debris are pulled into the swamp water and flow into the river—and then are carried down the river to coastal wetlands. Complex chemical and physical interactions cause the swamp-derived material to settle out of the water. Much of it may end up on mudflats and tidal creek bottoms where bacteria and other microbes derive nourishment from it and convert it into biomass—good food for many creatures, especially for filter feeders such as oysters and mussels.

Scientists do not agree on how essential these river-derived nutrients are for estuarine productivity. Each estuary is unique in that regard; the river-borne nutrients are crucial for some and may be only supplemental for others. But there is no dispute over the necessity of freshwater flow into estuaries. It's a complex pattern evolved over eons, and the entire system suffers greatly when the rivers are tampered with.

That's what happened to another Georgia river, the Savannah, which became a poster child for how a river can suffer immeasurably from constant ecological meddling. A cadre of scientists and environmentalists now want to make it a poster child of another kind—an example of how a seriously degraded river can be returned to ecological health.

CHAPTER SEVEN

A Tale of Two Rivers

SOME SEVENTY MILES north of the Altamaha, the Savannah River threads its way to the sea between Georgia and South Carolina, forming the boundary between the two states. The Savannah and the Altamaha are alike in many ways. Both are alluvial rivers that rise in the mountains and Piedmont and meander across the Coastal Plain to the ocean. Their waters transport tons of nutrient-laden sediments that help maintain coastal islands and salt marshes. Their broad floodplains harbor rich bottomland hardwood forests of haunting beauty and amazing wildlife diversity. Both form wide deltas and empty into extensive estuaries fringed by expansive freshwater, brackish, and saltwater marshes. Both support endangered species, most notably the shortnose sturgeon, which lives in salty water but swims upriver, past the reach of the tides, to spawn in fresh water. Both rivers support major wildlife refuges. The Savannah is the lifeblood of the twenty-nine-thousand-acre Savannah National Wildlife Refuge, one of the last great sanctuaries of tidal freshwater marshes in the eastern United States.

But in some respects the two rivers are vastly different. Whereas the Altamaha is still mostly an intact, natural river system unimpeded by dams and other obstructions, the three-hundred-mile-long Savannah is constrained by three huge earth-and-concrete barricades holding back 156,000 acres of reservoirs—all built by the U.S. Army Corps of Engineers. In essence, the Savannah's freshwater flow is at the mercy of federal dam operators. The river begins in the middle of the most inland reservoir, Lake Hartwell.

The Corps over the decades has also transformed the Savannah's once-winding route to the sea. To give the inland city of Augusta a faster ship-

The New Savannah Lock and Dam near Augusta, Georgia.

ping route to the seaport of Savannah some 180 miles downstream, the agency in the 1950s gouged out a navigation channel nine feet deep and ninety feet wide. Forty arrow-straight cuts were slashed across the bends in the river to straighten the channel, shortening the flow of the lower Savannah by twenty-six miles. Thousands of old dead trees and limbs, or snags, that provided valuable fish habitat were removed to clear a way for freight barges. To get the boats around shoal areas in a scenic and biologically diverse stretch of river just downstream of Augusta the Corps maintained a massive structure called the New Savannah Bluff Lock and Dam built in 1937.[1]

"It's difficult to exaggerate the degree to which the hydrology of the Savannah River was modified," Dr. Amanda Wrona Meadows told me in March 2006. For years Meadows kept watch over the river for the Nature Conservancy of Georgia. The alterations for navigation proved mostly a waste of taxpayers' money. By 1980 shipping on the Savannah had virtually ceased, and the Corps abandoned navigation maintenance between the cities of Augusta and Savannah.[2]

The Savannah, though, had plenty of other burdens to bear—so many, in fact, that it is still one of the Southeast's most overworked waterways.

Meadows called it one of "the most highly stressed of Southeastern rivers." That's an understatement.

The river provides drinking water for two major Georgia metropolises, Augusta and Savannah; the cities of Beaufort and Hilton Head in South Carolina; and many smaller municipalities in the river basin. At the same time, it assimilates treated sewage from the urban areas. In addition, U.S. Environmental Protection Agency records show that industries legally discharged more than seven million pounds of toxic chemicals into the Savannah in 2009.[3]

In the river's uppermost section, the three big Corps of Engineers dams—Hartwell, built in 1963; Richard B. Russell, built in 1983; and Thurmond, built in 1954—and their huge reservoirs churn out electricity for hundreds of thousands of homes and factories. In Augusta the Savannah passes through a heavily industrialized area of chemical plants and other facilities that pipe their treated wastes into the river. About thirty-five miles downstream from Augusta, huge twin cooling towers mark the two nuclear reactors of the Vogtle nuclear plant operated by Georgia Power. The reactors are cooled by millions of gallons of water pumped from the Savannah. Two additional reactors are being built at the plant. Across the river from Vogtle, in South Carolina, sits the 310-square-mile Savannah River Site, once a top-secret facility operated by the U.S. Department of Energy. From the 1950s through the 1980s the site's five massive reactors generated tons of radioactive plutonium and tritium for thermonuclear bombs. The site once diverted hundreds of millions of gallons per day from the Savannah to produce heavy water for bomb making and to cool the reactors, which are no longer in operation. The sprawling site still uses huge volumes of the river's water for other purposes, such as decontaminating the massively polluted site.

The river, however, enters its most heavily used stretch as it approaches the city of Savannah near its mouth. One of the most industrialized areas in the South, Savannah harbors twenty hazardous waste sites that are on the federal Superfund watch list. The river itself forms the thirty-six-mile-long shipping channel for the Port of Savannah, the nation's tenth-busiest hub for oceangoing container ships. To accommodate the big vessels the channel has been widened extensively and dredged to a depth of forty-two feet. Now there are controversial plans to deepen it to forty-eight feet—more than twice the river's natural depth—to float even larger ships.

It should come as no surprise, then, that this greatly overburdened waterway has become seriously flawed for nearly its entire length. Getting most of the blame for the river's calamities are the big dams upstream. Even the Corps of Engineers acknowledges that its "operation of dams on the Savannah for the last 50 years has caused notable degradation of ecosystem integrity."[4]

"The dams on the Savannah River have caused an ecological chain reaction," Amanda Meadows explained to me in 2006. "Natural flow patterns have been altered, not only disrupting the riverine habitat for fish and birds, but also impairing the natural ecological functions of the floodplain forests and estuary, such as providing clean water and nutrients to the estuary that aid in the development of crabs and shrimp."

A 2003 report by a twelve-member team of University of Georgia researchers who studied the Savannah noted that "low flows have increased; peak flows have decreased; there is less frequent overbank flow and less extensive floodplain inundation. Maximum peak flows at Augusta are less than a third of pre-dam flows; these lower flows are less able to move sediment, shape the channel and deliver water to the floodplain."[5]

Especially hard hit, the researchers said, have been the river's sprawling bottomland swamps, as a rule the most productive parts of southeastern river basins. In great swards of swampland, new growth of native trees and other vegetation is either not occurring or has been considerably stymied by the disruptions in natural flood pulses. Natural floods in winter, for instance, are vital for seed dispersal in the swamps. Numerous fish species also have been cut off from vital spawning and foraging areas in the swamps. Before the big dams straddled the river, some eighty species of fish—including several species of bass, sunfish, suckers, catfish, darters, carp, and minnows—came to the floodplains to feed, reproduce, rear their young, and seek refuge from predators during seasonal floods. The fish timed their spawning to coincide with flooding, allowing their offspring to take advantage of the food-rich floodplain habitats. With seasonal inundations now out of synchrony, the swamps are left high and dry when they should be under water, and the fish have no way to get to their old spawning grounds. The decreased river flow into the estuary downstream has led to increased salinity, which in turn may affect the distribution, abundance, movements, and reproduction of more than ninety species of estuarine-dependent fish.

The Shortnose Sturgeon

The alterations to the Savannah have affected all of the migratory fish that leave their saline haunts to spawn upriver, but the biggest concern is for the endangered shortnose sturgeon, which requires fast-flowing fresh water in rocky areas of rivers to lay its eggs—habitats now ruined or blocked off by dams. The four-foot-long sturgeons once prospered in the Savannah and other southeastern rivers; now, the Savannah harbors only about twelve hundred to three thousand of them. Scientists are unsure how many of those present are the remnants of older populations and how many are juveniles stocked by scientists in the 1980s that have now reached reproductive age.[6]

Acipenser brevirostrum is one of Earth's oldest—it existed with dinosaurs—and most mysterious fishes. With a body covered by rows of bony plates, it even looks primitive. The fish has a broad, blunt, shovel-like snout and a wide, toothless, low-slung mouth that siphons worms, crustaceans, and other food from estuarine bottoms. Its short chin whiskers help it zero in on its food. Individuals can live as long as seventy years.

Shortnose sturgeons are diadromous fish; that is, they migrate from salty waters to spawn upriver in freshwater rapids. The shortnose's much larger relative, the Atlantic sturgeon, also inhabits the Savannah but does not need to come as far inland to spawn. Its numbers are dwindling, too, mostly because of overfishing; for that reason it was declared a federal endangered species in early 2012.

Cued by changes in light, temperature, and pulses of fresh water coming downstream, shortnose sturgeons move up the Savannah around February to lay thousands of sticky eggs in turbulent fresh water over gravel or rocky bottoms. After hatching, the larval fish seek cover and hide until their yolk sacs are absorbed and their sensory systems are fully developed. Around March, aided by spring freshwater surges, the young fish begin drifting downstream to the upper estuary and salt marshes, where they will remain for most of their lives.[7]

Historically, the shortnose sturgeon's spawning grounds stretched for more than a hundred miles in the Savannah's middle and upper sections—until the big dams were erected to generate electricity, control floods, and perform a variety of other tasks, but none related to protecting fish. The massive dams did their intended jobs well, even though it meant upsetting the river's natural flows.

The dams replaced the Savannah's natural, variable, seasonal flow patterns with a more even and predictable pattern—one good for meeting human needs but bad for species adapted to the river's natural pulses. The shoals where sturgeons and other migratory fish—American shad, hickory shad, herring, and the like—once congregated in spring to spawn disappeared. All that remains of their spawning habitat in the Savannah is about four miles of river near Augusta—just 4 percent of the original habitat. The sturgeons have a difficult time getting even that far. Blocking their way is the New Savannah Bluff Lock and Dam built just downriver from Augusta.[8]

The shortnose sturgeon has suffered a similar fate in other rivers. By 1967 its numbers had spiraled so low that it was one step from extinction, a dire situation that landed it on the federal endangered species list. Pollution, overfishing, overharvesting of its prized caviar, and the fact that it generally waits until late in life to spawn also have contributed to its downfall. But dams and locks remain the biggest reasons for its undoing.[9]

Downstream on the Savannah, in the estuary, life hasn't been any easier for the sturgeon. Constant ship-channel dredging has caused salinity levels to rise and dissolved oxygen levels to fall, robbing juvenile sturgeons of nursery areas in which they might feed and grow.[10]

HARBOR DREDGING HAS spawned other ecological disasters as well. It is believed to be the reason why the estuary's saline zone has moved several miles upstream, far beyond its historical confines. Swaths of rare freshwater marsh have converted to salt marsh as a result. Although salt marshes dominate the coastal environment, freshwater marshes, because of their high biological diversity, are also of great ecological importance.[11]

The Savannah estuary and surrounding marshes are still trying to recover from a serious blunder the Corps of Engineers made in 1977. The Corps constructed a "tide gate" on a 605-foot-long concrete spillway across a Savannah tributary, Back River, to maintain the ship channel's water depth. The gate was opened during incoming tides and closed during

Striped bass being tagged as part of a study in the Savannah River.

outgoing tides. The maneuvers forced the water behind the gate into the main shipping channel, where it helped prevent the buildup of silt, thereby reducing the need for dredging. Not anticipated was the dramatic rise in salinity levels in the estuary and the adjacent Savannah National Wildlife Refuge. Wide expanses of fragile freshwater marsh were transformed into salt marsh; scores of cypresses and other trees perished.[12]

The tide gate was a disaster for striped bass, nearly wiping out the once-abundant fish. Before the gate was built, the Savannah was home to the biggest populations of striped bass in Georgia and South Carolina. Generations of anglers had battled the stripers in the river. But after the gate was installed, striped bass began disappearing. The reason: the saltier water was destroying their eggs. Within a few years striped bass egg production had plummeted by more than 95 percent. The fishery collapsed. When the Corps in 1990 owned up to its big mistake, it ceased operating the tide gate. A few years later the striped bass fishery started recovering. Freshwater marshes also started recovering—but they are still nowhere near their status before the tide gate was built.[13]

Conservationists and scientists warn that even that modest recovery may now be in jeopardy. One new burden is the planned withdrawal of as much as 1 percent of the river's average annual flow for power generation at Plant Vogtle near Augusta, which is building two new nuclear reactors to complement the two already in operation. The new reactors are expected to be online before 2020. By then, however, massive development will have already taken its toll. Tens of thousands of new homes are expected within the Savannah River basin over the next couple of decades. In addition to producing more pollution, the development could heighten the already high risk of devastating floods. While the big dams on the Savannah initially reduced the chances of flooding in subdivisions and other developed areas along the river, rampant development since then has "bought back" the risk. The impervious surfaces associated with development cause torrents of storm water to gush into the river, and residential areas along the waterway are again threatened—even though the river's flow is only a third of what it was before the dams were built. More development in the basin will make the problem even greater.[14]

But the biggest cause of worry, river protectors say, is the plan to deepen the Savannah's thirty-six-mile-long ship channel all the way from the Atlantic Ocean to the Port of Savannah, upstream of the city's famous downtown district. Congress officially blessed the $551-million project in 2000, but bitter controversy still swirled around it in 2011 and the Corps of Engineers still lacked the permits needed to proceed.

A number of groups were opposed to the plan as it stood in late 2011. Savannah water authorities feared the project would make the water saltier and cause lead and copper to leach out of aging water pipes, thereby contaminating the city's drinking water. At least a dozen environmental organizations wanted to kill the plan altogether because they believed it would cause dissolved oxygen levels to plummet. For the shortnose sturgeon, the project could be the final nail in the coffin; the species could finally become extinct in the Savannah.[15] Wildlife biologists believed the deepening would wreak havoc on the nearby wildlife refuge.[16]

Trying to resolve the concerns, the Corps studied, sampled, surveyed, mapped, modeled, monitored, and even artificially oxygenated the river. Georgia environmental officials refused to sign off on the project until the Corps agreed to install "bubblers" to oxygenate the river.

An array of politicians, business leaders, and others lined up to support

The Savannah National Wildlife Refuge, a sanctuary for wading birds and migratory songbirds, is threatened by a plan to deepen the Savannah Harbor shipping channel.

the deepening project. Without it, they warned, the state's premier port will lose ground to other East Coast ports able to accommodate the next generation of super container ships. They insisted that the Corps must complete the deepening by 2014, when the refurbished Panama Canal will start accommodating the bigger ships.

The Corps, however, may first have to satisfy a sister federal agency.

ON A CLEAR DAY in late October I paddle a neon-blue kayak in one of the placid tidal creeks beribboning the Savannah National Wildlife Refuge. The refuge straddles the Georgia–South Carolina border adjacent to the Port of Savannah. Twelve-foot-long alligators bask in the warm autumn sunshine. A bald eagle soars overhead. Red-winged blackbirds dart through stands of wild rice sagging with ripened grain.

With its swaths of wild rice (remnants of former plantations), freshwater marsh, bottomland hardwood swamps, maritime forest, expansive salt marsh, tidal rivers, and creeks, the twenty-nine-thousand-acre refuge is one of the most important wildlife preserves on the East Coast—especially for migrating birds. Twenty-five species of warblers have been seen here during spring and fall migrations. During the winter, thousands of ducks fill the refuge's impoundments, including rarely seen cinnamon teal, Eurasian widgeons, and fulvous whistling ducks.

Adjacent to the refuge is the former Mulberry Grove Plantation, where Eli Whitney invented the cotton gin, the machine that ushered in the era of King Cotton and culminated in the Civil War. Jungle-like maritime forest covers most of the old plantation now.

Looming on the refuge's western horizon are some "man-made birds"—the huge steel gantry cranes that load and offload the big ships in the Port of Savannah. They are stark reminders that this is also a heavily industrialized area. The refuge's managing agency, the U.S. Fish and Wildlife Service, must maintain constant vigilance—and sometimes wage hard-nosed battles—to protect the sanctuary from the continuous channel dredging and the pollution from Savannah's industries.

So it was with considerable trepidation that the agency viewed the Corps's plans for gouging a deeper Savannah shipping channel. A massive study by the agency in 2008 indicated that the project might destroy 40 percent of the refuge's remaining freshwater marshes. Only about thirty-three hundred acres remain of the twelve thousand acres of freshwater marsh that once graced the Savannah River delta—primarily because of higher salinity levels from the dredging over the years. In the refuge alone, the six thousand acres of freshwater marsh it contained at its inaugural opening in 1927 had plummeted to twenty-eight hundred acres.[17]

"We simply cannot afford to lose any more freshwater marshes," Sam Hamilton, the service's southeast regional director in Atlanta when the report came out, told me in June 2008. (Hamilton died of a heart attack in January 2010 only months after President Barack Obama appointed him director of the entire agency.) The scarcity of such wetlands, Hamilton noted, and the great diversity of plants and animals they contain, made it imperative that all the remaining marshes be preserved. Most waterfowl species depend on the freshwater systems for food while wintering and preparing for their spring breeding season.

The Corps promised to devise mitigation methods to avert the damage that would be caused by the river deepening. But in its scathing report, the

Fish and Wildlife Service said that the Corps's damage-control proposals—such as artificially injecting oxygen into the water and creating new freshwater marshes elsewhere to compensate for those destroyed—were "unlikely to perform . . . as predicted." Furthermore, the report noted the Corps's poor track record in preserving wildlife—such as the ill-fated tide gate that almost destroyed the striped bass fishery.[18]

Nevertheless, the Corps has tried to make amends upstream for the harm that its big dams inflicted on the shortnose sturgeon and other species. Beginning in early spring 2004, in concert with the Nature Conservancy and state wildlife agencies, the Corps began testing a bold plan to help restore some of the river's natural flow. It let out four times more water than usual from its massive J. Strom Thurmond Dam at Clarks Hill, South Carolina, the key controller of water movement on the Savannah, in an effort to mimic the natural pulses of water that once came down the river in the spring. The initial releases showed promise in improving the river's ecology, and other releases were scheduled for each year after that, though not without controversy.

Ecologists hope that the effort will create better spawning conditions upstream for the sturgeon and other migratory fish, and give a cleansing flush to the estuary downstream. Also, by returning the Savannah to something resembling its natural rhythm, a major portion of the river's seventy thousand acres of floodplain and rich bottomland hardwood swamps might be revitalized.[19]

But no one knows for sure how the river's natural systems functioned during the pre-dam era. If the Corps had such information, it could better mimic the natural patterns of water released to suit the life cycles of the river's flora and fauna. To determine what those natural patterns might be, and what an unobstructed, natural flow in a similar river is like, scientists turned to the Altamaha, "perhaps the least regulated, most pristine large river system in the southeastern United States," according to Darold Batzer, the University of Georgia scientist who has intensively studied the waterway.[20] The Altamaha's flow, he noted, is still largely controlled by natural pulses; it is the major reason the Nature Conservancy named the river one of seventy-five "last great places" in the United States. Batzer has spent considerable time determining and understanding the fish, insects, and other species that thrive and interact on the Altamaha's floodplain.

Armed with such information, ecologists might better understand how the Savannah's floodplain should function.

Amanda Meadows called the implications of the Corps's study "huge." "We're not just doing this for the sturgeon. It's to help everything that depends on the [Savannah]. If we can determine how best to manage the water flows for the benefit of the sturgeon and other native species, then we can use this information to influence sustainable river management worldwide."

Word of the Savannah River project spread. Chinese researchers visited in 2005 to learn how they might go about restoring natural flow regimes to the Yangtze River, on which the Three Gorges Dam was built. In 2008 a delegation from Mozambique and Zimbabwe toured the Savannah looking for ways to help their Zambezi River.

Ecologists say that it's too early to know if the Corps's pursuits on the Savannah upstream will prove fully successful. It may be years before we know. No one believes the Savannah could be restored to its original plumbing. That would require shutting down and dismantling the big dams, and that will never happen. But there is great optimism that the ecosystems can make a strong comeback under the other options. "Although restoring a natural flow regime to the Savannah River may not be a feasible objective, alternatives to current flow management could enhance the ability of the river to support native fish populations," concluded a University of Georgia study.[21]

The Outcry

The Corps of Engineers, state agencies, and private organizations may not be allowed time enough to make that call. The first round of pulse-mimicking water releases in 2004 generated little public reaction — probably because the Corps, anticipating turning on the spigots, had stored additional water from winter rains in the Strom Thurmond reservoir. In later years, however, when a searing drought gripped the region, the public no longer remained quiet about all the extra water being let out of the big lakes to benefit a bunch of fish.

By 2008, homeowners, boaters, and owners of businesses lining the shores of Thurmond Lake and Lake Hartwell — the two Savannah reservoirs with shoreside development—were up in arms over the huge volumes of water being turned out of their lakes on behalf of animals few of them had ever seen. The sweeping expanses of dry lakebed resulting from the withering drought that had commenced in 2005 fueled the uproar. Lakeside dwellers increasingly saw their waterfront property morph into parched red clay, leaving boat docks high and dry and weeds growing where boats once bobbed in several feet of water. Homeowners joked about having to mow the grass around their boats.

The lakeside property owners grew increasingly disenchanted as more water was drawn out of their lakes—even though the Corps insisted that the draw-downs had lowered lake levels by only a few inches. Some of the most strident and well-organized protests came from the two-thousand-member Lake Hartwell Association, formed in 1990 to influence, among other things, "positive growth and development while preserving the quality of life for all lake users."

Statements from the group said that its members weren't without sympathy for the shortnose sturgeon, but they remained unconvinced that pumping more water downriver would benefit the creature. The property owners demanded that the Corps curtail the releases. To that end, they enlisted the help of congressmen on both sides of the river.

The Corps now was in a bind—environmentalists were demanding the water releases and lakeside homeowners were demanding that the water be held back. At one point, an exasperated Colonel Edward J. Kertis, then commander of the Corps's Savannah District, told an interviewer: "I am very sympathetic to the person that retired here from Boston, moved down here and bought a lakefront house and all of a sudden the lake's gone. I got it. But they are multipurpose reservoirs. They are put there so that the water is there when it's needed for some other purpose. And when that other purpose doesn't suit [the property owners], they are going to be angry. I understand that."[22]

In fall 2008, in a move that gladdened property owners but angered environmentalists, the Corps announced that it would substantially cut back the amount of water dispatched downstream from Thurmond Dam. The reason for its change of heart, the Corps acknowledged, was lack of "conclusive evidence" that releasing more water would benefit the sturgeon.

That was a poor call, because it prompted the National Oceanic and Atmospheric Administration's fisheries service to join the fray. The service said that although the Corps "did not have absolute proof" that extra water would help the sturgeon, it likewise had no evidence to prove otherwise—that the releases were of no benefit to the fish. NOAA demanded that the Corps "err on the side of caution" and turn more water out of the dam. The Corps complied, and in February 2009 pulses of fresh water were released from Strom Thurmond Dam and sent down the river on behalf of the shortnose sturgeon and other migratory fish.

That in turn aroused the big guns—the representatives to Congress from states surrounding the reservoirs. On the South Carolina side, Representative J. Gresham Barrett chastised NOAA and the Corps for putting the interests of fish ahead of people. He told his constituents at Lake Hartwell and Lake Thurmond that he might introduce legislation to amend the Endangered Species Act and allow for the protection of lakes and water supplies.[23] Representative J. Paul Broun, M.D., of Georgia also went on the record that "people are much more important than fish."[24]

CHAPTER EIGHT

An Endangered Culture

AFTER THE CIVIL WAR, legions of freed slaves who had toiled on the vast rice and cotton plantations of the Southeast coast formed close-knit societies. Many of their communities were carved from the old antebellum plantations. A rich, unique culture—the Gullah-Geechee—evolved among them. The name Gullah referred mostly to the people in South Carolina; Geechee, to those in Georgia.[1]

The Gullah-Geechee folk thrived on the remote sea islands of Georgia and South Carolina, turning to the broad estuaries, tidal rivers, and salt marshes for sustenance. Gullah fishermen knitted tough fishing nets with needles made of palmetto wood. The estuaries were theirs for fishing; the marshes theirs for shrimping, oystering, and crabbing. The maritime forests yielded wild game. The fertile black soil yielded fruits and vegetables. Many grew their own rice. They tended hogs, chickens, and cattle. And they formed fierce attachments to the land and water.

In isolated communities they conversed in their melodic dialect, incomprehensible to outsiders. With strong passion they sang moving spirituals in weathered, whitewashed wooden "praise houses"—their voices blending in harmonies reminiscent of their West African ancestors. They buried their dead in graves facing east so that the spirits could fly home to Africa. They wove beautiful baskets of native coastal sweetgrass that strongly resembled the sturdy straw baskets made by their African forebears.

Outside the sea islands and adjacent mainland areas the Gullah-Geechee culture was little known, and that may have been its salvation. Gullah-Geechee people on the islands traveled to and from the mainland, but outsiders seldom came into their isolated hamlets. The Gullah enclaves on the mainland, usually situated along tidal rivers, were separated from larger towns and cities by forests and poor roads. Because of the isolation, Gullah-Geechee folk largely kept intact their colorful creole language, folklore, cuisine, arts, rituals, and traditions. Through the early 1960s the islands, vast marshes, placid rivers, and oak-shrouded dirt roads remained relatively unchanged.[2]

Then progress came. Modern concrete spans began replacing the rickety old wooden drawbridges that connected the islands with the mainland. Four-lane highways replaced narrow country lanes. Miles of the rutted, bumpy dirt roads crisscrossing the islands were paved. Tall steel towers carried electric power lines over marsh and river—eliminating the annoying power losses that occurred when boats or bad weather knocked out the outdated transmission lines. The improved power lines also brought clear television reception for the first time. Relatively cheap air-conditioning provided merciful relief from summer's brutal heat and sticky humidity. Control programs reduced the hordes of vicious mosquitoes.[3]

In the late 1960s—all of a sudden, it seemed—the outside world discovered that the Southeast coast is a great place to live and visit. Like a magnet, the coast and the sea islands began drawing retirees and tourists from up north. In the 1980s and 1990s people flush with cash from the booming economy came from everywhere in search of homes with views of the salt marsh and estuary. They wanted their own private docks running down to the tidal creeks that wound behind their minimansions and three-car-garage vacation homes. To bar undesirables, they wanted iron gates erected at the entrances to their exclusive enclaves. And they wanted all the amenities that go along with the good life—golf courses, swimming pools, marinas, clubhouses, tennis courts, shopping centers, drive-thru banks, and trendy restaurants. Standing to make mountains of money from all this, developers began snapping up desirable land wherever they could.

Much of that desirable land belonged to Gullah-Geechee families. Developers found clever ways of separating reluctant-to-sell landowners from the land their families had occupied for generations. Some land was literally stolen from African American landowners. Others, unable to pay the skyrocketing property taxes because of the ritzy development taking place all around them, were forced to sell.[4]

Where blue-trimmed, tin-roofed bungalows once squatted, where the people once chatted on wooden benches and old chairs and upright drink crates under the shade of spreading oaks while they stitched cast nets and wove sweetgrass baskets, now stood the clubhouses and the golf courses and the gated subdivisions of the newcomers.

↓ ↓ ↓

THESE CHANGES HAVE had profound and devastating effects on the Gullah-Geechee culture. The very survival of the culture, once the essence of the Southeast coast, is in jeopardy. The close-knit societies are disintegrating. The lilting Gullah dialect is rapidly vanishing, and television and erudite educators who don't like dialects are major reasons why. The islands have lost black residents in droves. On John's Island, where I grew up, 80 percent of the residents were African Americans in the 1940s; according to the 2010 census, it's now only about 30 percent.

In his seminal 1999 work *The Gullah People and Their African Heritage*, author and historian William Pollitzer wrote of the declining culture: "The Gullah people face a crisis today as the demand for their land and marsh encroaches upon home and farm and threatens their way of life. They are ill-equipped to meet the challenges of a modern era."

In an unusual move, the National Trust for Historic Preservation in 2004 added the Gullah-Geechee culture, the Southeast coastline, and the sea islands to its list of the nation's "11 Most Endangered Historic Places." The designation described threats from new bridges and roads that "have opened the area to intensive development and tourism, and sprawling resorts, residential subdivisions and strip malls that are sprouting everywhere. Family cemeteries, archaeological sites and fishing grounds are being paved over or put off-limits by new owners, and familiar landmarks— stores, churches, schools and houses—are being demolished or replaced with new structures."[5]

If the Gullah-Geechee culture dies, the very soul of coastal Georgia and South Carolina will die with it. African Americans will lose their purest link to their past. If the culture disappears, the great salt marshes and estuaries will lose their spirituality; for if any people are inextricably tied to these tide-driven places, it is the Gullah-Geechee folk. "The area and its people are especially important to African Americans because we find in this sacred place physical, emotional and spiritual roots of our present day existence," Patricia Guthrie wrote in *Catching Sense: African American Communities on a South Carolina Sea Island.*[6]

One of the last great strongholds of the culture is Saint Helena Island near Beaufort, South Carolina. It was one of the earliest strongholds of slavery in the original thirteen American colonies. African Americans still own most of the lush, fifty-three-square-mile sea island—more than 80 percent of it, in fact; most of them are descendants of former slaves who purchased parcels of land after emancipation. People on Saint Helena still live their culture; they don't stage it for tourists. Every year, island people celebrate their heritage in a big Gullah festival.

Saint Helena

On a hot day in July, I am going to Saint Helena to learn more about Gullah's past—and perhaps gauge its future in the face of booming coastal development. Saint Helena is encircled by one of the largest and most beautiful sweeps of salt marsh on the Atlantic Seaboard. Weathered shrimp docks, many of them family enterprises, stand along the creeks and rivers that twist through the marsh.

As I cross the bridge from the mainland and drive across the narrow, twelve-mile-long island, I am treated to grand views of the marsh and creeks and shimmering estuaries. No wonder the Gullah population is so firmly fixed to this place, with its timeless splendor and promise of abundance from the sea.

"We are a sea people as well as a land people," explained Marquetta Goodwine, a lifelong Saint Helena resident and staunch Gullah protector. "We look at water as our bloodline and the land itself as part of our family and not just something you buy or sell."[7]

Saint Helena is said to be the last authentic African American community in the country. It is typical of the Gullah communities that evolved all along the Southeast coast following the Civil War. Family compounds—resembling African villages—dotted the landscape. A matriarch or patriarch kept his or her home in the center while children, grandchildren, and even great-grandchildren lived around the perimeter. A newlywed husband would bring his bride to the house where he grew up, and the couple would build their own dwelling in the "yard" of the man's parents

Saint Helena, South Carolina, is a stronghold of the
African American Gullah-Geechee culture.

or nearby. In this way, land on Saint Helena was handed down from generation to generation.[8]

Life was slow paced amid the tidal marshes, majestic live oaks, and
dirt roads. Transportation was by bateau, sailboat, mule, marsh tacky, ox-
drawn cart, and callused feet. Community residents practiced the customs
of their West African homeland, crafting coiled baskets of sweetgrass and
palmetto, knitting cast nets, and making strip quilts. Led by "wise men,"
they danced "ring shouts" like the Buzzard Lope to the rhythm of African
drumbeats, clapping, and foot stomping. Ring shouts were religiously inspired dances that bridged African culture with later spirituals and secular
blues.[9] The music making often took place in the small one-room "praise
houses" where spontaneous local meetings took place during the week,
supplementing the larger services in the churches on Sunday.

The people grew African red peas, butter beans, okra, yams, and other
vegetables, cooking them nearly always with rice—and often with oysters,
shrimp, fish, or wild game—into spicy gumbos. Foods were cooked on
wood-fueled stoves and fireplaces or in big "rice pots" over open fires. A
family's rice pot was a prized possession handed down from generation to
generation.

Granny midwives delivered babies and treated childhood ills, often with medicinal herbs grown in gardens or gathered from the woods and salt marsh. Children in the communities ran carefree under the protective watch of relatives, who were never far away. Most grievances and disputes among adults were settled in the churches and praise houses, where stern-faced ministers, deacons, and community elders sought not punishment but reconciliation between the aggrieved parties. Someone accused of letting his hog uproot a neighbor's garden might have to repay the neighbor with a mess of peas. Islanders who took cases to courts outside the community faced frowning disapproval from neighbors. Respect for elders and belief in the power of recently deceased kinfolk to punish wrongs also were paramount in Gullah communities.[10]

Though the people were devout Christians, their belief in cunjuh influenced nearly every aspect of Gullah-Geechee life, from birth to death. "Root doctors" supposedly could concoct powerful potions from herbs and roots and conjure up spells and "fixes" to heal or protect you from evil—or to inflict harm on your enemies. The forms and shape of the sinister beings of the cunjuh world varied from island to island. On Saint Helena, boo-hags were the disembodied spirits of old women who could ride you and sap your strength and cause you to fall seriously ill. Especially fearsome was the plat-eye, a hideous one-eyed ghost that could assume numerous forms.

The heart of the Gullah culture, though, was the language. Gullah probably arose independently in South Carolina and Georgia in the eighteenth and nineteenth centuries when African slaves on rice plantations developed their own creole patois to communicate with their white masters and with each other, combining features of English with their own West and Central African languages. The Gullah language flourished after the war in the isolated communities. Today, probably only a few dozen people still speak pure Gullah.[11]

The Net Weaver

Joseph "Crip" Legree Jr., eighty-seven, a lifelong Saint Helena resident, is a "living legacy" of Gullah—an honor bestowed on him in 2009 by the state of South Carolina for his work in preserving the cultural values and traditions of his ancestors. I am paying him a visit.

Joseph "Crip" Legree Jr., a lifelong resident of Saint
Helena Island and a master cast net weaver.

To get to his home I pass through the village of Frogmore in the center of Saint Helena. Frogmore harbors only a handful of buildings, but its fame has spread far and wide because of Frogmore stew, a highly seasoned, mouth-watering Gullah concoction of fresh-caught shrimp, sausage, clams, onions, newly shucked corn, redskin potatoes, and spices simmered together and then dumped onto a newspaper-covered table and eaten with the fingers. In my mind, it is the essence of the marshes.

I drive past the Penn Center, site of one of the country's first schools for freed slaves—now a Mecca of sorts for Gullah-Geechee folk and one of the most significant African American historical and cultural institutions in the country. During the 1960s Dr. Martin Luther King Jr. and members of the Southern Christian Leadership Conference used the Penn Center as a training site and as a retreat. They planned the 1963 march on Washington there.

I drive six miles down Lands End Road to its junction with Seaside Road, along which Legree and much of his family still live. Several of the homes are trimmed in blue. Seaside Road traverses the widest section of Saint Helena. The salt marsh is to my right. Oak-shaded dirt roads snake back into communities where people still live in family compounds more than 150 years after the demise of the plantations. Though most of the old plantation boundaries were erased long ago, their names persist—Frogmore, Ann Fripp, Tombee, Dr. White, and Bighouse.

I find Legree sitting on the small front porch of his blue-trimmed cinder-block bungalow off Seaside Road—only about fifty yards from where he was born and raised. "Come on in," he says in his Gullah-tinged lingo. He is gray-haired, tall, slim, and shirtless, the latter a concession to the muggy July heat. He says that his friends, family, and neighbors call him "Crip" because he broke his leg at age six and still walks with a slight limp. His family did not have the money for a doctor to properly treat the broken limb, which healed by itself. He never needed to see a doctor again until he was in his seventies, he says.

Some also call him "Captain Crip" because he has fished, shrimped, crabbed, and harvested oysters from local rivers and salt marshes for most of his life. One of fourteen children, he attended Frogmore School until third grade, when he began working the fields to help support his parents and siblings. "My Daddy tell me I had to get in the field and hoe 'tater," he says. He learned how to crab from his father, and was working the river by the time he was seventeen. He is the father of six living children and has twenty-three grandchildren and thirty great-grandchildren.

"Outlived two wives," he says as he brushes away a gnat. As we sit and talk he works on his latest cast net. He explains that he has probably made well over a thousand of them in his time. But they're for other people now, he says, because he seldom gets down to the river anymore.

Like most Gullah men, he always used his own homemade nets to catch shrimp and mullet. He would stand in the bow of his twelve-foot-long bateau in a tidal creek, sling one end of the folded net over his shoulder, and then twist his body to spin the net out over the water. Flying through the air, the net would unfold to form a perfect circle as it splashed into the murky water. Any creature—shrimp, crab, mullet, or stingray—within that circle was entrapped when Legree jerked the rope that closed the net. He would pull the net back up into his boat and empty its contents into a wide bucket.

He sold his catch to local markets and seafood dealers—and also provided bountiful fish and shrimp to his family and friends in their compounds along Seaside Road. When he wasn't in the creek, he and his chil-

Cast net made by a Gullah-Geechee resident on Sapelo Island, Georgia.

dren tended the garden in which he raised vegetables for the family table. A patch of sugar cane was ground at the mill and made into sweet syrup. A flock of chickens provided fresh eggs. Hogs were butchered on cold winter days for hams, pork chops, and ribs. A cow provided milk. Manure from the livestock and fertile marsh mud were used to fertilize the garden.

"We always had plenty to eat," Legree says.

On Sundays there were all-day services at Ebenezer Baptist Church with enthusiastic singing and clapping. Baptisms were in the tidal creek directly behind the church. Legree and his siblings were known for their singing. He still sings as he sits on the screened-in porch weaving his nets—or "building a net," as he puts it.

He learned to make the nets from his friend Harry Owens Jr. while they sat in a bateau waiting for the high tide to recede so they could get onto the exposed oyster beds. "The first net I tried to make wouldn't work; I made it so tight it wouldn't open up when you threw it," Legree says. But he quickly got the hang of it. He became a master net weaver, so good that he was given the Jean Laney Harris Folk Heritage Award, which recognizes South Carolinians for lifetime achievement in the folk arts.

Some see the work of Legree's worn hands as one of the Gullah culture's dying arts. Objects d'art or not, cast nets once were vital equipment for the nourishment and sustenance of Gullah-Geechee families. Hilton Head Island writer David Lauderdale called the nets "a delicate link to an era when sea island craftsmen made their own tools, clothes, cuisine, bateau, music, baskets, stories, songs, churches, homes, medicine and, yes, whiskey. It was a day of steady midwives, powerful deacons, roaming livestock, marsh tacky horses, rocking praise houses, sultry juke joints and bateau with oars."[12]

Legree still sits on his front porch and weaves his nets nearly every day in good weather. The net he is currently working on hangs from a nail hammered into a porch beam. Using a plastic "needle" from a local fish tackle store and a flat piece of wood resembling a large fingernail file, Legree laces knot after knot, his gnarled fingers moving at blurring speed. Nets with a mesh of about half an inch are for catching fish; smaller-mesh nets are for snaring shrimp. As Legree works, the gossamer pattern of a net quickly takes shape until it finally forms a circle eight to twelve feet in diameter. Legree makes it look easy, but the craft requires considerable skill and labor. It takes him about five days of steady knitting to produce a small net. When the net is finished, he weaves little lead weights called "bullets" into it to make it sink quickly into the water. He also adds an authentic cow-horn ring-slide through which to pull the net's rope.

He sells some of the nets at the Penn Center's museum shop or by personal order, with each net tailored to the buyer's height. They go for about $150 apiece. A community partner with the Penn Center for more than twenty years, Legree demonstrates his cast net weaving skills during the center's annual Heritage Days celebration in November.

These days, though, fewer people in the Gullah communities go into the river for fish, shrimp, and crabs. When they do go, they usually use machine-made monofilament nets imported from Japan or China. Legree says the machine-made nets are flimsy and don't last, but his nets last a lifetime. He would like to make sure that at least one of his many family members can make a cast net from start to finish and carry on the tradition. "Young folk ain't got time," he says. One of his grandsons, though, has picked up the skill and has begun working as his grandfather's apprentice. "He ain't as fast as me," Legree says with a wink.

When Legree isn't net making (which is rare), he sits on the porch and swaps tales with neighbors and family. In their Gullah tongue they reminisce about fishing on the river and hunting in the woods—and some-times about dodging game wardens and revenuers intent on destroying moonshine whisky operations.

Legree says one of his joys now, late in his life, is being surrounded by his extensive family and sharing his Gullah recipes at family gatherings. "I don't know no other life 'cept this one," he says. "I never left this island."

A MAJOR REASON why Saint Helena is still relatively undeveloped—and the Gullah lifestyle still prevails—is that the residents are fiercely de-termined not to allow their island to go the way of Hilton Head or Saint Simons—once-serene barrier islands that have been transformed into traffic-clogged, fast-food-franchised resorts top-heavy with condomini-ums, hotels, and strip malls. Afraid that similar pressures would bear down on them sooner or later, Saint Helena's Gullah residents in 1999 persuaded Beaufort County commissioners to designate a unique "Cultural Protec-tion Overlay District" for the island. It is intended to shield the island from the kind of choking growth that beset the Hilton Head area just across Port Royal Sound from Saint Helena's southern tip. The cultural protec-tion designation, which covers all of Saint Helena, discourages the con-struction of gated communities, golf courses, and resorts. In approving the designation, Beaufort County officials acknowledged that they were recognizing the Gullah culture as a unique part of their county's heritage.

Cultural protection or not, the feverish demand for developable land along the Southeast coast makes Saint Helena a juicy plum in developers' eyes. Several exclusive, predominantly white communities have already sprung up on the island. Lots on tidal creeks go for two hundred thousand dollars an acre or more. A typical Internet ad for land there touts Saint Helena as "a beautifully undeveloped waterfront paradise, where families enjoy a serene, rural retreat."

While Saint Helena Island itself is protected by the cultural district des-ignation, the smaller islands that surround it—Dataw, Fripp, Warsaw, Cat, and others—are outside the district's boundaries. Some of the islands are now gated communities with signs at their entrance gates warning "Private Property—Residents and Guests Only." For the Gullah people of Saint

Helena, who once freely roamed the islands to hunt and fish, such signs are spirit-withering reminders that their way of life is ebbing away.

Gullah folk say the newcomers don't comprehend their deep attachment for the land. "This land is valuable to us because it symbolizes freedom," says Emory Campbell, retired Penn Center director, who grew up on Hilton Head before a bridge connected it to the mainland—when most of the island was still populated by African Americans. "We're the ones who stayed here and withstood the heat, the mosquitoes, and the malaria. It hurts to see what happens when highways and streets are paved, access to waterways is privatized, and we are blocked out."[13]

Pierre McGowan, eighty-three, another lifelong Saint Helena resident and a keen observer of island life over the decades, made a grim assessment of the island's future in his 2000 book *The Gullah Mailman*: "The county development planners are trying to hold down development, but I believe they are too little, too late. The black landowners on St. Helena, who are in the majority, are very reluctant to sell, but in the end, money will move the land."[14]

McGowan noted that several subdivisions have already been built on Saint Helena. "And there are many more hidden away in developers' files, waiting for the right time to strike," he added. "In addition to developers with their large projects, there are already several thousand individuals . . . who have managed to pry loose small chunks of land from the local citizenry."

Ironically, the very large families that are hallmarks of Gullah culture are a big part of the problem. Extended African American families often collectively own land as "heirs' property," and many titles to black-owned land along the coast are hopelessly tangled affairs. Heirs who live far away in New York or Detroit or Chicago want to sell their inherited portion of the land, which many have never used or even seen, while their relatives living on the island desperately want to hold onto their family's legacy. "You see heirs fighting each other," says Jabari Moketsi, publisher of the biweekly *Gullah Sentinel* based in Beaufort.

Entangling matters even more, many African American landowners die without leaving a will, and the land passes on to heirs—often dozens of them—with unclear deeds. Taking advantage of the confusing situation, developers may buy only one heir's share of the property and then, by

Sign in a Gullah-Geechee community near Beaufort, South Carolina.

wielding a legal device called partitioning, file a legal partition and gain title to the entire parcel.

Representative James Clyburn of South Carolina, whose wife, Emily, is of Gullah origin, minces no words about his views of such practices. Most partitioning, he says, amounts to little more than robbing blacks of their property. "It is heart-wrenching to know the very legal system charged with protecting the rights of all Americans is being used to strip blacks of their rightful property ownership," said Clyburn, who was the House majority whip until Republicans took over in 2010.[15]

Clyburn was the impetus behind a major new project, approved by Congress in 2006, to save and protect the Gullah culture. The mandate directed the National Park Service to set up the ten-mile-wide Gullah-Geechee Cultural Heritage Corridor stretching from Wilmington, North Carolina, to Jacksonville, Florida. A fifteen-member commission—including representatives from the four coastal southeastern states—was established to oversee spending of up to ten million dollars for the project.

Only time will tell if the program is a success. "The long-term goal is to make sure we keep this culture part of who we are," Clyburn says. But if Gullah-owned land continues to be lost to others, he notes, "the rich history and heritage that make places like Saint Helena so unique may be lost to future generations. As the land is lost, so too is the Gullah culture that once dominated these islands."

↓ ↓ ↓

AT A FORUM held in an African American church on John's Island in July 2009, a queue of speakers offered suggestions on how the ten-million-dollar federal project could help to save the Gullah-Geechee culture from oblivion.

Several speakers asked that the corridor project develop a plan to provide legal protection to heirs' properties. In a poignant story, Benjamin Dennis IV of Charleston described how his great-grandfather paid fifty cents per acre for a twenty-two-acre farm on Daniel Island near Charleston more than a hundred years ago. Only half an acre of it is left, he said, "and every other week someone offers $900,000 for it. I'm proud to be a 'Geechee boy' and told my grandfather I would never sell it."

Willie B. Heyward, a sixty-three-year-old lawyer and a legal representative for the Gullah-Geechee corridor, explained to the group that the preservation of the lands vital to the Gullah-Geechee often comes down to "heritage versus money." Because Gullah is a land-based culture, preserving the land where the culture was born—and the places where it still thrives—is extremely important. But above all else, Heyward said, he hopes that the new Gullah-Geechee Cultural Heritage Corridor project will finally give the culture its due and give the rest of America the opportunity to learn about culture's legacy and its three hundred years of arts and traditions.

Gullah has not always enjoyed such respect, Heyward noted. He grew up on neighboring Wadmalaw Island, where Gullah culture was—and still is—a predominant way of life for African Americans. As a young college student in California he tried to avoid talking about his childhood, dreading that he would be shamed in front of his classmates when they learned of his background. "Gullah then wasn't something to be proud of, to be appreciated," Heyward said. "But we didn't know what we had at that time, didn't know how rich it was," he added. Now, he said, the Gullah-Geechee culture is not only respected, it is revered.[16]

The Basket Makers

At a Lowcountry festival on Edisto Island, South Carolina, on an overcast Sunday in May, Vera Manigault tugs gently at my arm and leads me to a young palmetto tree next to a salt marsh. "Let me show you what I'm talking about," she says. With a sharp knife, she whacks off a frond and deftly slices it into narrow strips. The palmetto strips, she explains, are used as binding in the beautiful sweetgrass baskets that she weaves and sells at festivals around the Lowcountry and at her roadside stand in Mount Pleasant, just east of Charleston.

Manigault, sixty-four, is a Gullah. The art of sewing sweetgrass baskets is unique to the Gullah-Geechee people, particularly those living around Charleston. The baskets that Manigault and an estimated three hundred other Gullah-Geechee descendants weave with great skill and care now form one of the most visible links remaining to their African culture and heritage. Strikingly similar baskets are still made in West Africa. Commanding prices ranging from less than fifty dollars to more than one thousand, the baskets now provide an income for many Gullah-Geechee folk.

Enslaved West Africans brought their basket-making knowledge with them three centuries ago when they crossed the Atlantic in slave ships. In the early days of southern coastal settlement, sweetgrass baskets were primarily utilitarian. "Fanner" baskets, for example, were wide winnowing trays used to throw rice grains into the air so that the breeze blew away the husks before the grains fell back into the basket. Baskets also were used in cotton picking; for storage; and to hold sewing supplies, laundry, breads, fruits, and babies.[17]

Today's baskets are still made for practical purposes, but they are also prized souvenirs and folk art collectibles. A well-made basket can last more than forty years.

"All the stuff we need to make our baskets grows right here in the Lowcountry," Manigault tells me. In addition to palmetto, other basic materials include long-leaf pine needles, black needlerush from the salt marsh—

The materials, tools, and finished products of a sweetgrass
basket maker on Sapelo Island, Georgia.

and the prime ingredient itself, sweetgrass, a long-bladed grass restricted
to the Southeast coast.

All of the materials save one are cheap and readily available. Sweetgrass,
however, the constituent needed in greatest quantity, has become difficult
to find. The biggest reason, the basket makers say, is that rapid development has cut them off from lands in rural areas where they used to harvest
the grass—lands that have become shopping malls, beach resorts, and
private communities with "No Trespassing" signs. Bulldozers and chainsaws have destroyed large colonies of the soft, pliable grass to make way for
development.

Known by botanists as *Muhlenbergia filipes*, and sometimes by its other
common name, "muhley grass," sweetgrass grows in clumps in the fringe
of land between salt marsh and woods, along the second dune line of
beaches, and in wet savannahs. Its delicate pink blooms add a soft, pastel
glow to marsh edges in late fall. The grass is harvested in the spring and
through the hottest part of summer by "pullers," usually the menfolk of a
basket-weaving family.[18]

The plant's increasing unavailability threatens to cripple sweetgrass weaving. "There is a real possibility that this culturally and economically significant art form may disappear if basket makers cannot find a reliable and affordable source of sweetgrass," concluded Marianne Burke in her report of a 2002 study. A research ecologist with the U.S. Forest Service, Burke and other researchers interviewed twenty-three longtime sweetgrass basket makers in the Charleston area, all of whom cited residential development as the biggest reason for dwindling sweetgrass supplies.[19]

In no other place has that impact been more palpable than in the epicenter of sweetgrass basket making, Mount Pleasant, just across the Cooper River from Charleston. U.S. Highway 17, which runs through Mount Pleasant, sports a sign proclaiming it the "Sweetgrass Basket Makers Highway." The thoroughfare runs past the moss-shrouded compounds of small homes and churches where Gullah folk have long kept their craft alive. The road is lined with dozens of weathered wooden outdoor stands displaying sweetgrass baskets and providing shelter to the weavers who patiently stitch their wares while waiting for customers.

↓ ↓ ↓

JUST A FEW years ago, sweetgrass harvesters in Mount Pleasant needed only to drive to the nearby marshes to gather the tall grass. But Mount Pleasant, population fifty-eight thousand, is South Carolina's fastest-growing town. Transplants attracted to the town for its climate and relatively low cost of living have tripled its population during the past two decades. Expensive homes now occupy most of the traditional sweetgrass harvesting spots, and the owners often won't let the basket weavers come through to pull the grass.[20]

Many basket makers say they have to drive long distances from Mount Pleasant to find adequate supplies. "I have been as far as Savannah," more than a hundred miles away, says Nakia Wigfall, executive director of the Sweet Grass Cultural Arts Festival, and "some weavers have gone as far as Florida." Others say they have to pay dealers exorbitant prices to supply them with the grass.

Angela Halfacre, a professor of political science at the College of Charleston who helped conduct the sweetgrass study, said the high prices dealers charge not only raise basket prices but also affect the craft's legacy.

Some basket makers say they can no longer afford to hand their children sweetgrass to practice with when the youngsters show an interest in learning the craft.[21]

Like other Gullah traditions, sweetgrass basket making is passed down from generation to generation. Young children begin by making the coiled bottoms and progress to making complete baskets. Manigault says she was five years old when she learned basket making from her great-aunt.

The sweetgrass scarcity has forced some weavers to substitute needlerush from the salt marsh. Needlerush, though, is a tough material to work with, and baskets made from it usually don't fetch as high a price as those crafted from sweetgrass.

Local governments and various organizations — and even some developers — have taken steps to set aside land for growing sweetgrass, although there is concern that the cultivated variety may not be as hardy as the wild type. Perhaps the best hope is that natural areas still harboring the plant can be protected and managed. Marianne Burke predicted that "the future of sweetgrass basketry may very well hinge on sustainable management or restoration plans that are conceived and developed in the near future."

Pin Point

On a sweltering day in September, I am on the outskirts of Savannah overlooking another sprawling salt marsh. In the distance, Skidaway Island squats low on the horizon. Winding through the marsh is the Moon River, made famous in the 1961 Oscar-winning ballad by Savannah native Johnny Mercer. Crossing the marsh and connecting Savannah to Skidaway is a busy thoroughfare known as the Diamond Causeway. I stand at the foot of the causeway where it intersects with narrow, oak-shaded Pin Point Avenue. The street is the main entrance to a small historic Gullah-Geechee enclave known as Pin Point, population four hundred. At the intersection, a tall blue-and-white sign dated 1991 tells passersby of the community's most famous son: "Pin Point, Birth place of Supreme Court Justice Clarence Thomas."

Descended from slaves who worked a three-thousand-acre rice plantation near Savannah, Thomas was born in Pin Point on June 23, 1948, in a shanty that had no bathroom, no running water, and no electricity except for a single light in the living room. When he was seven, his mother, Leola,

The old oyster factory at Pin Point, Georgia, a Gullah-Geechee community in Savannah where Supreme Court Justice Clarence Thomas was born.

who worked as a maid, sent him to live with his strict grandfather in Savannah. Thomas never returned to Pin Point except for brief visits. His sister still lives here.

"Pin Point was too small to be properly called a town," Thomas recalled in his 2007 book, *My Grandfather's Son: A Memoir*. "No more than a hundred people lived there, most of whom were related to me in one way or another. . . . Pin Point was at the water's edge, and just about everyone I knew did some kind of water-related work. Many of the men raked oysters during the winter and caught crabs and fish in the spring and summer. Their boats, which we called 'bateaus,' could be heard far away in the marshes, straining to carry home their heavy loads. They would slowly emerge from the labyrinth of surrounding creeks and pull up to the dock, where the day's haul was unloaded. The crabs went to the crab house to be cooked, while the oysters were tossed into a bin at the oyster 'factory' next door."[22]

Another native son, Arthur Sams, seventy-one, left Pin Point as a young man to join the Navy. After his service he lived nearly thirty years in California and elsewhere. When he retired, he came back here to live out the rest of his life. "Pin Point is in my blood," he says. "I always knew I'd come back."

Sams has offered to give me a tour of the community, and I am on my way to meet him. I drive down Pin Point Avenue, past the small bungalows and mobile homes shaded by live oaks and rustling palmetto trees, to meet Sams at the community's lone house of worship, Sweet Field of Eden Baptist Church. The whitewashed cement-block building, which replaced an old wooden sanctuary in 1961, is next to a weedy, headstone-filled cemetery where Sams's mother and other relatives are buried. "Sometimes I come down here to talk to my mother," he tells me. Close by are the remains of the old three-room school that Sams attended as a boy. "One room was for first through sixth grades, one room was where we ate, and the other was where they kept supplies and stuff; it was all heated by a wood stove."

Occupying about twenty-five acres on a peninsula pooching out into the salt marsh, Pin Point looks out on Shipyard Creek, a tidal stream ten miles southeast of downtown Savannah. Just beyond the creek and marsh is the Moon River. Like Sams, most of Pin Point's residents are descended from former slaves who once worked the big plantations on nearby Skidaway and Ossabaw islands. After emancipation, however, the ex-slaves could not buy land on the islands. Many of them wanted to be closer to the mainland anyway. Travel from the islands to the mainland was drudgery requiring nearly half a day of rowing or sailing.[23]

When a chance popped up in 1897 for them to purchase land near Savannah, several snatched the opportunity. A couple of white men offered to sell them lots carved from an old plantation at the place called Pin Point.

Within a decade the new owners had transformed Pin Point into a mainland Gullah-Geechee community of families who adhered to the traditions of their rich culture. Sams recalls the time when the community had no electricity or running water and residents used kerosene lamps for light, woodstoves for warmth, and outhouses to heed nature's call. Drinking water came from a common well. The children drew the water and toted it home in old lard buckets. Sams remembers he and his neighbors and kin being baptized in the same creek where they harvested crabs, shrimp, and fish and the children learned to swim. He reminisces about parishioners joyfully singing as they walked down to the creek for baptisms. The residents' lives were closely intertwined with the marsh and tidal creeks just a few yards from their back doors. Most of the women worked in the crab and oyster "factories"; the men worked the local creeks and rivers, harvesting crabs in summer and oysters in winter. "If you didn't work at the factory or go out in the bateaus, you made cash making the bateaus and nets and crab traps," Sams says.

In 1926 a seafood cannery, A. S. Varn & Son, opened in Pin Point. The "factory" became Pin Point's economic mainstay. Most of Pin Point's residents worked for Varn at some time or another. Many residents remember picking ten to fifteen pounds of crab-claw meat a day at the factory. An occasional summer visitor was Johnny Mercer, who came to listen to the workers sing spirituals as they worked. Some say that their singing had a major influence on Mercer's music.[24]

The factory closed in 1985, a victim of, among other things, economics and more stringent government requirements for canning and shipping seafood. The loss of the seafood plant was a huge blow to the community. Many feared that the glue holding Pin Point together was gone and that the place would become a footnote in some history book. Indeed, developers cast their eyes on Pin Point, imagining the money to be made from the now highly desirable waterfront property.

But Sams and other community leaders vowed that urban sprawl and deep-pocketed developers would not have Pin Point. They would protect their heritage and keep their community intact. They asked for help from anyone who could assist them—the government, conservation groups, and private backers. Their requests didn't fall on deaf ears. Pin Point was designated the first nonurban historic district in Chatham County, where Savannah is the county seat. Pin Point's old seafood factory was slated for new life as a museum to portray Pin Point's unique culture through exhibits, documentary films, and interactive displays. Now there is reason to hope that Pin Point will remain one of the last waterfront Gullah-Geechee communities on the mainland.

But the survival of another Georgia Gullah-Geechee enclave on a remote island remains a great uncertainty.

Sapelo Island

It's eight o'clock on an August morning and already sticky hot. I'm at the state-owned dock in Meridian, a blip on the map midway along Georgia's coast, ready to board the gleaming white ferry *Annemarie*. A half-hour ride will take me to Sapelo Island, which is separated from the mainland by more than five miles of salt marsh and winding tidal streams.

I'm not sure how many times I've been to Sapelo, but the anticipation of going always arouses a tingling sense of adventure. Perhaps it's because the barrier island is still isolated, reachable only by boat, and still mostly wild and undeveloped. Regardless of the reason, Sapelo, fifty miles south of Savannah, is one of the most intriguing places I have ever visited. It's home to Hog Hammock, probably the most famous, most-written-about Gullah-Geechee enclave on the entire Southeast coast.

I will stop by Hog Hammock and say hello to my friend Cornelia Walker Bailey, long the community's matriarch, a masterful storyteller and unofficial historian. For years she has struggled to preserve her culture and save Hog Hammock from falling into the hands of outsiders who, she fears, will obliterate the hamlet. Though the state of Georgia owns nearly all of Sapelo, Hog Hammock's residents possess their land in fee simple and can sell it to the highest bidder if they choose.

The *Annemarie* nestles gently alongside the barnacle-encrusted public dock on the Duplin River on Sapelo's lee side. The pungent marsh odor greets me; fiddler crabs scurry into holes in the muddy bank. I had called ahead to request that a Hog Hammock resident rent me his old truck. He said he would leave it—a mint green GMC pickup with missing hub-caps—near the dock area. The key will be in the ignition. I find a rusty, fender-dented truck that meets the description. I have no idea what year it was made. Its bottom is rusted out and ugly springs stick out of its cracked vinyl seat. The windshield is cracked in three places. Taped on the steering wheel is a handwritten note: "Do NOT take key out of ignition. It wont go back in." Surprisingly, the truck immediately cranks up. It has no muffler and no gas gauge. As I drive away, I find it has hardly any brakes, either.

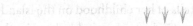

SIXTEEN THOUSAND ACRES of sand, wide beach, maritime forest, and boundless salt marsh, Sapelo is ten miles long and up to two miles wide—the fourth-largest barrier island in a shimmering string of thirteen coastal islands known as Georgia's Golden Isles. Hog Hammock, which occu-pies 434 acres of Sapelo's southern half, is the last intact Gullah-Geechee community left on Georgia's sea islands. It is a patchwork of small tin-roofed houses, trailers, a store, a tiny bar with a jukebox, and two Baptist churches. Its unpaved roads are sandy, rutted, and nearly impassable when it rains. Roosters crow in the yards; dogs run loose. Rusting automobile hulks sit here and there amid tall weeds and running vines.

Peacefulness, a mesmerizing charm, pervades Hog Hammock. Set amid groves of giant live oaks, soaring pines, and palmettos, its quaintness borders on picturesque. Nearly all of its sixty or so African American residents are direct descendants of West African slaves brought to Sapelo in the early 1800s to work the big cotton, sugar, and rice plantations owned by planter Thomas Spalding and his kin.

Spalding, a leading practitioner of scientific farming in his day, was said to be an agricultural genius. He practiced crop rotation, was one of the first to grow sea island cotton, and shepherded in Georgia's sugar industry. His adroit management skills and reputed humane treatment of his slaves made him one of the most influential planters on the Southeast coast. His slaves were managed not by the typical white overseers but by black supervisors, the most prominent of whom was Bilali, a Muslim and Spalding's second in charge on Sapelo.[25]

Cornelia Bailey, born on Sapelo in 1945, traces her ancestry directly back to Bilali. I find her walking back to her squat wooden house after checking on The Wallow, a spacious six-room guesthouse that she and her husband, Julius, built to lodge tourists. She and her family also run The Trough, the nearby tiny bar with the jukebox. Attached to the bar is a small gift shop.

Cornelia is a handsome woman with a commanding bearing and a face framed by a halo of white hair. I have known her for years. "Good to see you again," she says as we greet each other with a hearty hug. She proudly calls herself a "saltwater Geechee," one who grew up immersed in the sea island culture and speaking the rich patois. Her remarkable book, *God, Dr. Buzzard and the Bolito Man*, tells of her childhood on the island, when its people believed in three things: God; voodoo, symbolized by the "root man," Dr. Buzzard; and luck, personified by the Bolito Man. "We saw no conflict in that at all because we figured we needed a little extra luck," she wrote.[26]

Cornelia "was in paradise" as a little girl in the now-defunct Belle Marsh settlement on Sapelo. Her father, a skilled cast net weaver, hunted, fished, crabbed, shrimped, farmed, and trapped to feed his family. "I had everything a little girl could want—my family, one ox and a hog, orange and other fruit and nut trees, and lots of room to explore and the most beautiful marsh you'd ever want to see. The marsh was directly behind our house, about three hundred feet away. The high tides on Sapelo are so big that on an especially big tide like a spring tide . . . the whole marsh would be white with water." The air always smelled of the sea.[27]

The spirit world and magic were a part of Cornelia's everyday life, just as they were for her African ancestors. She learned to respect her elders and to believe that her ancestors are always with her. Like most of the older folks in Hog Hammock, Cornelia was delivered by a midwife, "Miss Katie" Underwood. One of Cornelia's seven children was the last child Miss Katie delivered before she retired. Sapelo's newest ferry was named in her honor.[28]

Cornelia likes to tell visitors that they are "com-yas" as opposed to "bin-yas." *Com-ya* is the Geechee term for newcomers. *Bin-ya*—as in "been here a long time"—refers to the longtime residents.

But "it's a dying form of life we have here," Cornelia also tells outsiders. "In some ways I relish the new way while at the same time I feel such a heavy loss for the vanishing of the old way." Young people are leaving. Some of Hog Hammock's land has fallen into the hands of "outsiders"; the residents who remain are struggling to hold on to their property and their unique heritage. "In 1974 there were 150 people," Cornelia says. "Now, we're down to 60 folks. I fear for the survival of my people on this island."

Well-heeled people who desire a piece of an unspoiled island have offered huge sums of money to Hog Hammock residents; some landowners have accepted the offers. In one deal, less than half an acre in Hog Hammock recently sold for $238,000. In some cases the land is "heir property" owned by people who left Sapelo years ago and have no intention of returning. Some have never even set foot on the island and have no qualms about parting with their inherited land for a princely sum. Most of the new owners, some of whom are building houses that are huge by Sapelo standards, are white.

Several current and former Hog Hammock residents, conservation groups, and even the state of Georgia have tried to come up with strategies to save the community and its culture. But all of the plans are fraught with glitches and shortcomings. The Gullah-Geechee Cultural Heritage

Corridor project, managed by the National Park Service, does not have the power to buy land. The Sapelo Island Cultural and Revitalization Society, founded in 1993 by Hog Hammock supporters to preserve the village, has a land trust but little money. The Sapelo Island Heritage Authority, created by the Georgia legislature to help Hog Hammock stay intact, has never had a budget.

Cornelia says saving the land is of utmost importance: "Culture is no good without land. We're holding on to the land so we can hold on to the culture."

The Uprooting

How Cornelia and other African Americans on Sapelo came to be confined to Hog Hammock is a story island residents still tell, sometimes with bitterness. At the beginning of the Civil War, the Spalding family owned more than 350 slave families and thousands of acres on Sapelo. After the war, dozens of the freed slaves purchased island property and congregated in several Gullah-Geechee settlements—Raccoon Bluff, Behavior, Shell Hammock, Lumber Landing, Hog Hammock, and Belle Marsh. Cornelia Bailey as a young girl lived in Belle Marsh on Sapelo's north end.

Spalding's descendants, though, still owned most of the island. In 1912 they sold their property to Howard Coffin, chief engineer of the Hudson Motor Company in Detroit. He built mansions on Sapelo and entertained such luminaries as Calvin Coolidge, Herbert Hoover, and aviator Charles Lindbergh, who landed his plane on the island in 1929. Coffin also founded the Sea Island Company, developer of The Cloister, an exclusive resort on Sea Island northeast of Saint Simons Island. On Sapelo, Coffin raised beef and dairy cattle, felled timber from the island's forests, and opened an oyster and shrimp cannery in 1922. Those operations employed most of the African Americans living on Sapelo at the time.[29]

Coffin's fortunes nosedived with the 1929 stock market crash, however, and in 1933 he sold his Sapelo holdings to another multimillionaire, Richard J. Reynolds Jr., heir to the Reynolds Tobacco Company of Winston-Salem, North Carolina. In the deal, Reynolds acquired nearly all of Sapelo except the settlements owned by black residents. Reynolds continued several of the projects initiated by Coffin, including logging, growing crops, and managing a dairy herd. He continued to employ Sapelo's

African Americans as well. On his own initiative he added new buildings to the island's south end, including two elaborate boathouses. He had Coffin's old farm buildings torn down and replaced with an architecturally acclaimed quadrangle of dairy and horse barns; one of the barns held a second-story movie theater that could seat a hundred people.[30]

Reynolds's long-range plans for Sapelo also included moving all of the black residents to one village—Hog Hammock—and demolishing their other settlements. He told the residents he could do more for them if they all lived in one community instead of being scattered about the island, so during the 1950s and 1960s most of the black landowners in other settlements on Sapelo sold or swapped their land to move to Hog Hammock and enjoy indoor plumbing and electric lights for the first time.[31]

Some of them, though, were decidedly against moving. But Reynolds was in a position to coerce. He literally controlled who was hired on the island, who got electricity, who could use the ferry, and who could build on Sapelo. Some say he wielded that power to force the holdouts—one of them being Hicks Walker, Cornelia Bailey's father—to move. Cornelia's book notes that a foreman for Reynolds strongly hinted to her father that he might lose his job on Sapelo if he did not relocate to Hog Hammock. For the sake of his family, Hicks Walker agreed to go.

Reynolds is now remembered on Sapelo mostly for a more generous and visionary act: the creation of the University of Georgia's Marine Institute. The scientific wisdom accumulated there would help save marshes worldwide.

CHAPTER NINE

The Institute

THE STORY OF how the University of Georgia Marine Institute came to be on Sapelo Island begins on a sunny morning in August 1948. Eugene Odum, then a rising star at the university in the emerging field of ecology, was bird-watching on the island with two colleagues. One of Odum's colleagues knew Sapelo's caretaker and had wrangled permission to visit there. The trio's main goal was to get a glimpse of a chachalaca, an exotic Mexican pheasant that Howard Coffin had introduced as a game bird on Sapelo in the 1920s.

"We never expected to see Richard Reynolds on the island that day," Odum later recalled. But while he and his fellow birders squinted through binoculars at a bird perched on a shrub, Reynolds and a couple of his workers drove up in a jeep. Odum's party introduced themselves, and Reynolds took an immediate liking to the scientists. He asked them to take a quick ride with him to the beach to check out a strange fish that had washed up there. Impressed with their knowledge, Reynolds invited them to his beachside cabana for lunch—and, as it turned out, to share a bottle of fine Scotch whiskey.

During the course of their conversation Reynolds told them that his cattle-raising, dairying, and timber ventures on Sapelo were not paying the taxes. He revealed that his latest moneymaking scheme was to open an exclusive retreat on the island for wealthy patrons. He asked the scientists if they also might have a use for the island. Yes, indeed, they said. Sapelo's vast unspoiled marshes and estuaries would make an ideal outdoor laboratory for research on coastal ecosystems.[1]

Sapelo Plantation, the hideaway retreat that Reynolds built, turned out to be a money loser and he shut it down. But he had not forgotten his ear-

Sapelo Island, Georgia, home to the University of Georgia's Marine Institute, is one of the fourteen barrier islands that make up the Golden Isles of Georgia.

lier conversation with the bird-watching scientists. He had continued to correspond with Odum, and the two of them had mulled over the possibility of setting up a marine biological research laboratory on Sapelo. Finally, in 1952, Reynolds invited then–University of Georgia President O. C. Aderhold to come to the island with a delegation of four scientists—including Odum—to discuss a proposal for such a venture. Reynolds made a strong pitch for the lab. A few days later, back on the UGA campus in Athens, Aderhold asked the scientists to send him in writing their ideas on how the university could use Sapelo. Of the four, only Odum was enthusiastic about the island's potential for research and education.[2] The others were lukewarm—some were even against it—and said the university already had enough research sites scattered around the state. Odum, never one to give up, persisted. At Aderhold's request, he and a colleague, Don Scott, drew up a blueprint for a laboratory on Sapelo to carry out basic studies "on the biological productivity of coastal waters and marshes." They proposed a fifty-thousand-dollar initial startup budget.

Eugene Odum (in lab coat) explains the value of marsh ecology to University of Georgia president O. C. Aderhold (wearing glasses) and Sapelo's owner, tobacco heir R. J. Reynolds Jr. Photo courtesy of the Marine Institute archives.

Reynolds found the idea "sound and feasible" and agreed to set up the Sapelo Island Agriculture and Forestry Foundation to support the lab. In early 1953 the foundation and the university signed a contract, and just like that the Sapelo Island Marine Biology Laboratory was up and running — the country's first center dedicated to the exploration of salt marsh and estuarine ecosystems. The initial budget was twenty-five thousand dollars to cover operating costs, field studies, and salaries. Odum, who had just published his milestone opus *Fundamentals of Ecology*, and his family spent the Thanksgiving holiday on Sapelo collecting the first of many samples of organisms from the salt marshes.[3]

In exuberant support, Reynolds turned over Sapelo's whole south end — marshes, maritime forest, and magnificent beach — to the scientists. Just as important, he also gave them exclusive use of the south end's complex of buildings, which would house the laboratory, offices, and living quarters.

The livestock were turned out of the big dairy barn, and workers set about converting it into a hall for scientific research. This barn was no quaint little outbuilding. Built of heavy masonry and reinforced concrete, it had hot and cold running water and steam heat. The ground floor boasted a tiled milking parlor and a photographer's darkroom — and of course there was the one-hundred-seat movie theater on the second floor.

The milking room became a "wet lab" with tanks to keep research specimens alive. The old cattle trough system was converted to maintain a flow of seawater from an adjacent tidal creek to the tanks. Cow stalls and adjacent rooms became researchers' offices. Odum once recalled that several tons of feed had been left in the loft over the converted offices, and rats scurried everywhere. A diesel generator supplied the electricity. The building's only air-conditioned room became the instrument room. At first, the only devices in it were a balance and a colorimeter used to determine the concentration of a known substance in a solution.[4]

No marine laboratory is complete without a research vessel, of course. Again Reynolds rose to the occasion, putting his sixty-five-foot, wood-hulled boat the *Kit Jones*, built on Sapelo and launched in 1940, at the researchers' disposal. In addition to being used in offshore studies as far out to sea as the Gulf Stream, the vessel was also employed as a ferry to haul people and supplies to and from the island and to tow barges carrying heavy equipment.

Even before the lab opened its doors, its scientific advisers were trying to decide on the initial research priorities. The field was wide open: little was known at the time about the Southeast's salt marshes. The prevailing notion was that marshes and other wetlands were wastelands good only for "improvement." An example of that mentality was just outside the new laboratory's back door, where Reynolds had ditched, diked, and drained a large swath of salt marsh next to his old barn to create a cow pasture.

After prolonged rounds of coffee-fueled discussions, the advisers decided that the lab's initial focus should be finding answers to two broad questions: What was the importance of the great expanses of marsh, and what was the nature of the marsh's hydrology, including the tides?

With those questions in mind, the lab's directors began making the first faculty appointments. Most of those chosen were newly minted PhDs. Among them were Robert Ragotzkie, a University of Wisconsin hydrologist; Lawrence Pomeroy, a zoologist; Edward Kuenzler, a marine biologist; and John Teal, an ecosystem ecologist. All of them would go on to become luminaries in the fields of marsh and estuarine ecology. Teal's 1962 paper "Energy Flow in the Salt Marsh" became the basis of research for the numerous scientists who followed him. In 1969 Teal and his wife, Mildred, wrote *Life and Death of the Salt Marsh*, which became—and remains—

a classic work explaining the fascinating processes of salt marshes. The book also described the effects of human pollution and development on the fragile landscapes and made convincing arguments for salt marsh conservation.

Not everything functioned smoothly in the laboratory's early days. Sapelo's remoteness posed transportation and other logistical problems. Researchers and their families suffered from the social isolation. Telephone service might be disrupted for days, even weeks, when underwater cables broke. Electrical power from the ornery diesel generator was limited and unpredictable. Laboratory and field equipment was in short supply.

But what the researchers had in great supply were pluck, ingenuity, and enthusiasm. And they had thousands of acres of pristine salt marsh and estuary to explore and study. They made do with what they had, designing experiments that could be done within the limits of their meager equipment—buckets, shovels, measuring sticks, grass clippers, and the like. Soon they were gaining new insights into—and an immense appreciation for—the complex world of the salt marsh and estuary.

Others began taking notice of their work. Federal and private grants started trickling in. The money purchased new equipment that allowed more elaborate experiments. The scientists observed marsh ecosystems at a local scale and learned that the marshes, estuaries, coastal ocean, and land interact as one great natural system. Early on, they learned that the ebbs and flows of the tides are crucial to stimulating marsh growth, which in turn is vital for feeding the young of an array of fish and shellfish.

The scientists were astounded by the marsh's prodigious productivity. Sapelo's marshes, they concluded, ranked with the most productive ecosystems on the planet. Equally impressive was the nine-foot tidal range, which the scientists surmised was in some way involved with the marsh's amazing richness. The rising tide, they found, ferries in a rich subsidy of nutrients and sediments from off the land and elsewhere; the falling tide flushes salts, toxins, and other wastes out of the marsh. The scientists studied spartina, which covers 90 percent of Sapelo's marshes, to determine how it tolerates salinity levels lethal to most other plants. They discovered that the great marsh expanses were not as uniform as they looked, that the marsh can be divided into zones depending on how long each one is flooded daily.

Early researchers on Sapelo Island: (left to right) Larry Pomeroy, Robert McRorie, Eugene P. Odum, and Donald Scott in the doorway of the Marine Institute (1958). Photo courtesy of the Marine Institute archives.

They began charting the food webs of marsh and estuary, studying how microbes break marsh grass down into detritus—bits small enough to be gobbled up by tiny organisms that are, in turn, consumed by larger creatures, all within the context of an open and ever-changing environment. They began to figure out how nitrogen, sulfur, phosphorus, and carbon are used and recycled in the marsh and estuary—and discovered that microbes are at the heart of the recycling processes.

Even Reynolds's attempt to turn a section of salt marsh into a cow pasture became fodder for research. The scientists concluded that the impounded marsh would never support a lush cover of terrestrial green grass; the salty clay was too acidic and inhospitable. They persuaded Reynolds to open the dike separating the marsh from a tidal creek and let seawater flow in once again. Within a few years, without human intervention, the spartina was growing there in luxuriant swaths. Clearly, the restoration of impaired salt marshes was possible.

By 1958 the five-year-old Marine Biology Laboratory was garnering national, even international, renown, and the researchers made the bold decision to host the first ever salt marsh research conference. The conference would bring fifty-five leading scientists to Sapelo from as far away as New Zealand, update them on what had been learned there, and set the agenda for future research. Even though transporting and housing that many scientists was a logistical nightmare, the conference was a huge success. Some called it a turning point in salt marsh and estuarine ecology research. That remarkable meeting is still talked about today.

"The conference brought together people who had never interacted: geologists, botanists, marine chemists," said Lawrence Pomeroy, now retired, who helped lead research on Sapelo from 1954 through the 1970s. He attended the 1958 gathering and was part of the team that published the conference proceedings a year later.[5]

"So there was both an excitement of seeing the system as a whole and, at the same time, reactions were a bit tentative because we were suddenly bombarded by many unfamiliar viewpoints. We were all busy revising our viewpoints—assimilating what other people knew about marshes. I think [the conference's] value, beyond the effect on the thinking of the participants, was to successfully make a statement that salt marshes are a legitimate, significant subject of research."[6]

The pioneering studies on Sapelo became the early building blocks of ecosystem ecology and landscape ecology as well as the emerging fields of conservation ecology and restoration ecology. Over the years, Sapelo research has produced more than one thousand scientific papers. Jim Alberts, a former director of the institute, noted, "One can travel the world and wherever there are researchers who study marshes, they are aware of Sapelo Island and the pioneering and continuing knowledge gains that are the legacy of the researchers who have been there. Indeed, very few of them would not jump at the chance to come again and work at Sapelo."[7]

The early investigations on Sapelo reinforced and strongly influenced Odum's fundamental concepts of ecology: the ecosystem is the basic unit of nature; the living Earth is a global set of interlaced ecosystems; biological diversity increases ecosystem stability; nature tends toward stability in its mature stages; and the whole is greater than the sum of its parts. His pioneering work earned Odum worldwide respect and the honorary title "father of modern ecology" from his peers.

From humble beginnings, then, Sapelo became a revered name in marine science worldwide. In 1959 the laboratory's name was changed officially to the University of Georgia Marine Institute. R. J. Reynolds Jr. would not live to see Sapelo achieve its full glory. He died in 1964 at age fifty-eight from severe emphysema brought on by a lifelong addiction to smoking. In 1976 the foundation he created also changed its name and amended its purpose—it became the Sapelo Island Foundation and turned toward charitable activities. The University of Georgia began picking up the tab for most of the institute's operations, which became a line item in the university's budget.

In his will Reynolds left all of Sapelo—except Hog Hammock—to his young widow, Annemarie Schmidt Reynolds, the last of his four wives. In separate deals in 1969 and 1976 she sold Sapelo to the state of Georgia, conveying 97 percent of the island to state ownership. That set the stage for the exceptional honor conferred on the island in December 1976 when the National Oceanic and Atmospheric Administration designated it the nation's second national estuarine research reserve. NOAA called the new sanctuary a "Christmas present to the people of the nation." The seventy-four-hundred-acre reserve includes extensive tracts of unspoiled salt marsh, marsh hammocks, a maritime forest, a scenic stretch of sandy beach, and the entire Duplin River estuary on the island's back side. "The creation of the Sapelo estuarine research reserve ensured the continued integrity of Sapelo's south end as a platform for scientific research," noted Buddy Sullivan, the reserve's director.[8]

The early research on Sapelo and the state's promise of permanent protection for the island were largely responsible for NOAA's decision to establish the research reserve there. Plus, the U.S. government had contributed four million dollars toward Georgia's acquisition of the island. Sapelo was also chosen because it is representative of the short, wide barrier islands that fringe the coasts of Georgia and South Carolina.

Congress created the estuarine reserve system in 1971 after two federal studies revealed that nearly all the nation's estuaries were being destroyed, ruined, or diminished by runaway development and pollution. The first reserve, created in 1974, was in Coos Bay, Oregon; now there are twenty-seven. The reserve system is a network of protected coastal areas set aside for education, conservation, and long-term research—in effect, living laboratories for scientists. The protected areas are used as standards to measure the impacts of human activities on the coast. The federal gov-

ernment provides funding and technical backup; the states ante up match-
ing funds, personnel, and managerial oversight. Each reserve is operated
by a state agency or a university; in Sapelo's case it is the Georgia Department of Natural Resources.

The University of Georgia Marine Institute found itself within the confines of the new sanctuary and had to make new arrangements to use the
land. The institute agreed to lease 1,575 acres of the reserve from the state
for a dollar a year. The institute and the reserve began cooperating on scientific endeavors, although their relationship was not always cordial.

↓ ↓ ↓

RENOWNED FOR THEIR unique natural beauty, barrier islands fringe
most of the Southeast coast. Geologists call them barrier islands because
they sit between the open ocean and the mainland. By their very nature,
barrier islands are in constant flux, always being reshaped by wind, waves,
currents, and tides. Depending on the relative strengths of those forces,
barrier islands assume radically different forms. A quick glance at a map
reveals a distinct difference between the barrier islands of Georgia and
southern South Carolina and those of North Carolina and northeast Florida. The former are generally short and wide, whereas the latter are long
and skinny.[9]

Located midway on the eastern fringe of McIntosh County, halfway
along Georgia's coast and at dead center of the South Atlantic Bight,
Sapelo Island is bounded by the winding Sapelo River to the north; the
broad, choppy waters of Doboy Sound to the south; the Atlantic Ocean
to the east; and, to the west, the Duplin River, which really is a large tidal
creek.

If you walk across Sapelo starting at the ocean's edge, you will encounter the sequence of ecosystems typical of barrier islands along the coasts of
Georgia and South Carolina. First is the gently sloping beach, nearly two
football fields wide at low tide—a magnificent stretch of fine quartz sand,
hard packed and sugary white. The large tidal range, low wave energy, and
tidal sands create the broad expanse of beach. Shorebirds by the thousands
congregate there to rest and eat the countless invertebrates that wiggle and
burrow in the sand. On moonlit summer nights, ponderous loggerhead
sea turtles laboriously crawl up to lay their eggs in the soft sand.

Closest to the beach is a wall of young "primary dunes" sculpted by wind and waves and anchored by sea oats and other hearty plants. The dunes' faces are steep and largely bare of plants. They are the island's first line of defense against wind and storms from the sea. Farther back stand older, larger, steeper secondary dunes of soft, powdery sand. Between the primary and secondary dunes are swales of thick grasses, sedges, and shrubs such as wax myrtle that attract seed-eating birds, rabbits, and other small mammals.

Moving inland, past the dunes, you enter the majestic maritime forest that stretches across the island—the result of Sapelo's great width and relative stability. Giant live oaks dominate the cool, shady forest. Other large-canopy trees include southern magnolia, pine, sweetgum, and palmetto, many of them festooned with woody vines. Shrubs and smaller trees such as American holly, cherry laurel, red bay, saw palmetto, sparkleberry, wax myrtle, and yaupon holly form the forest's understory. Not all of Sapelo's forest is dominated by hardwoods, although initially it was. In areas once under cultivation, secondary pine stands still rule. Eventually, they, too, will give way to the trees of the maritime forest.

The forest marches down to the edge of Sapelo's back side, which faces the mainland. Beginning there and spreading unbounded more than five miles to the mainland is the splendid salt marsh, nearly all of it covered by spartina. Sparkling creeks dissect the marsh; tree-covered hammocks punctuate the horizon.

Shaped and maintained by the tides, the barrier islands protect the salt marsh from sea storms and scouring currents; the marsh, nurtured and cleansed by the tides, buffers the islands and helps keep them intact from relentless erosion. The estuaries trap nutrients and sediment from the land and deliver them to the marsh via the tides. Food from the fertilized marsh sustains life in the estuary. Impairment of one part of this great connecting system affects all the others.

Eugene Odum came to this stark realization during his early forays on Sapelo, when he explored the twisting tidal creeks cutting through the vast salt marsh. "The notion came to us, in those early days, that we were in the arteries of an energy-absorbing system whose heart was the pumping action of the tides," he later said. "The entire complex of barrier islands, marshes, creeks, and river mouths was a single operational unit linked together by the tide. If we were right, each part of the system would have to be dependent for its life-sustaining energy not only on the direct rays of the sun, but also on the energies of the tides."[10]

As it turned out, they were right.

↓ ↓ ↓

BY ALL ACCOUNTS, John Teal presented the most remarkable paper at the three-day conference held on Sapelo in 1958. He was offering, he said, a new understanding of how a salt marsh functions. Teal hypothesized that the ebb tides sweep nearly half of spartina's annual production out of the marsh and into the estuary and coastal waters, where it becomes the basic staple for a host of marine fish and shellfish. At that point, no one knew for sure how much—if anything—the marsh contributes to ecosystems outside its confines; most scientists believed that rivers and the sea itself supply most of the nutrition. In essence, Teal was proposing that salt marshes were the engines driving marine productivity—that they were essential to the survival and well-being of coastal fisheries as far as five or six miles offshore. Without the marshes, Teal suggested, the estuaries of the Southeast would support only a fraction of the abundant sea life that teemed within them.

Teal had come to the fledgling University of Georgia Marine Institute from Harvard in 1955 as a postdoctoral associate to replace a scientist who left Sapelo after one year. As a graduate student he had studied energy flow in ecosystems—how natural systems harness and consume energy. On Sapelo, it seemed only natural that he would study how energy moves through the marsh and estuary—how green plants and microalgae capture the sun's energy and produce new biomass that nourishes other creatures in the food web. Teal focused on the most obvious green plant in Sapelo's marshes, spartina.

Earlier studies had shown that insects and other organisms eat only about 5 percent of the living spartina, which dies back in the fall and slowly decays into detritus. Teal's research allowed him to account for the fate of about 55 percent of the aboveground spartina biomass in the marsh. It was being consumed in the marsh itself—before it ever reached the estuary—by microbes, animals, and other marsh organisms. But to his surprise, Teal couldn't account for the other 45 percent. In other words, if the marsh was producing 10 tons of spartina per acre, about 5.5 tons of that were being consumed in the marsh, leaving 4.5 tons unaccounted for.

Teal concluded that "the [ebb] tides remove 45 percent of the production before the marsh consumers have a chance to use it and in so doing, permit the estuaries to support an abundance of animals." He estimated that the seaward-exported detritus "can support about twice as much animal life in the estuaries as is found in the marsh itself."[11] It was a revolutionary conclusion, and it would stimulate new research around the world as scientists tried to prove it, expand on it, and apply it to their particular locales.

Meanwhile, Eugene Odum was pursuing parallel research. In the late 1960s he and graduate student Armando de la Cruz measured the concentration of detritus suspended in the water at the mouth of a salt marsh creek on Sapelo. They found that the concentration was about twice as high on the falling (ebb) tide as on the rising tide. Microscopic examinations also suggested that more than 90 percent of the detritus originated from spartina. The conclusion was inescapable: Georgia's marshes were exporting a massive amount of organic detritus.[12]

That study helped lead Odum to what he called his "outwelling hypothesis," which was similar to Teal's hypothesis except that Odum applied it to mangrove forests and other coastal systems as well. In any event, he believed the export of large amounts of nutritious detritus from these systems to be essential to life in coastal waters. In using the term *outwelling* for the first time during a brief commentary at a scientific conference in Rhode Island in 1968, Odum stressed its similarity to upwelling, the phenomenon by which nutrients rise to the surface from deep in the ocean and support teeming fisheries, as occurs off the coast of Peru. "The most fertile zones in coastal waters capable of supporting expanded fisheries result either from upwelling of nutrients from deep water, or from outwelling of nutrients or organic detritus from shallow water nutrient-traps such as reefs, banks, seaweed or sea grass beds, algal mats and salt marshes," Odum said.[13]

Odum had more substantial data to support his hypothesis than Teal had for his, and so outwelling became one of the most studied—and controversial—concepts in salt marsh and estuarine ecology. During the past forty years, no other hypothesis has stimulated as much coastal research worldwide. Legions of scientists have spent great sums of research money and long hours in dozens of estuaries around the world trying to prove—or disprove—it. That research furthered estuarine science and in some cases yielded startling new hypotheses. In pivotal studies, Lawrence Pomeroy, Evelyn Haines Sherr, Scott Nixon, and other marine researchers on Sapelo found that the lowly one-celled algae—diatoms, dinoflagellates, and phytoplankton—may rival or even exceed spartina's net primary production in marshes. Once regarded as of little consequence in marsh output, algae, too, now had to be factored into calculations to gauge a marsh's productivity.

The majority of the investigations of outwelling have been indeterminate at best. Odum himself came to cast doubts on some of his earlier notions. At a marine environmental conference in Rhode Island in 1986, for example, he stated: "On the basis of our early work at Sapelo, we thought that the salt marsh estuaries exported large quantities of detritus, but now we are not so sure if it's POC (particulate organic carbon), DOC (dissolved organic carbon), or living biomass that outwells, if indeed there is a net export at all. There is likely wide regional variation in import and export flows of carbon and nutrients along our coastline."[14]

The prevailing evidence now suggests that both *Spartina alterniflora* and algae contribute substantially to the nourishment of life in the estuaries and nearshore waters of the Southeast—depending on the marsh's location, size, shape, age, tidal forces, and other factors. Moreover, nutrients exported from the marshes and estuaries stimulate the growth of phytoplankton that contributes to the overall food supply in nearshore ocean waters. The marsh's productivity may also be "outwelled" in the guts and tissues of the small creatures that feed in them rather than directly as detritus and nutrients.[15]

"There is no doubt that outwelling occurs in the South Atlantic bight where salt marshes are extensive and extremely productive, and tidal amplitudes large," Odum wrote in 2000 after reviewing a number of outwelling studies. "In these areas, marshes are definitely exporting 'hot spots.'"[16]

REWIND TO 1968, when Odum and others wielded an early version of outwelling—along with other findings from fifteen years of research at

Sapelo—to persuade a pack of staunchly conservative Georgia lawmakers and a governor known for his rigid racial segregation policies to pass monumental legislation that protected Georgia's salt marshes. Georgia's action would serve as a model for marsh protection in other nations around the world.

CHAPTER TEN

Protecting the Marsh?

I N 1968 THE GIANT Kerr-McGee Corporation of Oklahoma quietly and methodically bought thousands of acres of marshlands, including several small islands, on Georgia's coast. That July the company revealed its intentions. It applied to the Georgia State Mineral Leasing Commission for a lease to strip-mine phosphate on the sea islands and in the marshes, river bottoms, and seabed out to the three-mile limit, an area encompassing twenty-five thousand acres near Savannah in Chatham County.[1]

The company said it would take three to five million tons of phosphate per year from Georgia's marshes and estuaries, three to five times more than was being mined at its strip mines in neighboring Florida at the time. The plan in Georgia was to dig through 70 to 120 feet of overburden to reach the phosphate beds lying deep under the marshes. The dredge spoil—more than thirty million cubic yards of shell-flecked mud and sand per year—would be dumped onto the marsh to create dry land, which would then become twenty square miles of prime real estate. The marsh itself would be destroyed. The phosphate ore would be hauled to Oklahoma and processed into fertilizer. The sales would boost the company's fortunes, and Georgia would get some two million dollars a year in taxes and fees.[2]

When word of the plan got out, shock waves sizzled up and down the coast and all the way inland to the gold-domed capitol in Atlanta. It was said that when R. S. "Rock" Howard, then head of Georgia's Water Quality Board, heard of it, people half a mile away could hear the outraged roar erupting from his office. Howard, who had a reputation as a rabid defender of Georgia's environment, vowed that Kerr-McGee would strip-mine the marshes only "over my dead body." He immediately started calling close colleagues—powerful movers and shakers in state government—telling them in no uncertain terms that Kerr-McGee's proposal would ruin Georgia's beautiful coast. Newspapers quickly picked up on the brewing controversy. Articles and strong editorials sounded the alarm.

In the end, Kerr-McGee was stopped by a group of outraged Georgia citizens, ecologists, legislators, conservationists, schoolchildren, fishermen, water experts, lawyers, and others galvanized into action by the sheer magnitude of the project. They successfully waged a fierce campaign against the would-be despoiler of the marshlands. Then, vowing that Georgia's coast would never again be vulnerable to the kind of wanton destruction seen in other states, they rallied behind the passage of new legislation in 1970 to permanently protect the state's four hundred thousand acres of tidal marshes. With some reluctance, Governor Lester Maddox signed the new Coastal Marshlands Protection Act into law.

Without question, the law eventually generated by Kerr-McGee's proposal is the single biggest reason why Georgia's marshes have remained intact and fully functional over the decades in spite of efforts by developers, industry tycoons, and others to fill, drain, or otherwise "improve" them. Other U.S. coastal states and nations around the world have emulated Georgia to protect their own remaining marshes and estuaries from ruin, with varying success.

BUT IN 1968, not everyone was against Kerr-McGee's plan to strip-mine the marshes. Many welcomed the project. Local politicians, labor unions, and business bigwigs in coastal counties saw immense potential for new jobs and revenue. Realtors salivated over the prospect of new waterfront property arising from marshy wasteland. Governor Maddox himself favored the mining. The opponents of strip-mining had an arduous task ahead, and they approached it from several directions.

A fuming Rock Howard argued that the deep digging could breach freshwater aquifers, allow saltwater intrusion, and contaminate drinking water supplies for much of coastal Georgia. Fred Marland, an oceanographer at the Marine Institute on Sapelo Island, warned that phosphate extended over a large area beneath the Southeast coast, and granting the lease would set a dangerous precedent. He urged his colleagues to contribute any scientific "ammunition" they could muster to show the environmental folly of the mining operation.[3]

Heeding the public outcry, Maddox assembled a blue-ribbon panel to evaluate the consequences of mining. The panel agreed to conduct a thorough environmental, geological, and cost-benefit assessment.

Among those on the panel was Eugene Odum, who at about that time was bringing to light the crucial biological value of the salt marsh, including his outwelling hypothesis, which assumed the marshes to be vital for life in the estuaries and coastal ocean waters. He urged his fellow panel members to scrutinize the scientific research data amassed during fifteen years of studying the marshes and estuaries of Sapelo Island. The data suggested that the mining operations could severely deplete oxygen levels in the water and cause widespread suffocation of shrimp, crabs, fish, and other creatures of marsh and estuary. The studies also backed up Howard's contention that the mining could puncture freshwater aquifers and taint Georgia's drinking water.[4]

While the panel was wrapping up its final report in the fall of 1968, a fortuitous event took place at the exclusive Cloister resort on Sea Island near Brunswick. Spurred on by the Kerr-McGee squabble, politicians, scientists, and businessmen gathered there for what was billed as the Conference on the Future of Marshlands and Sea Islands. Odum was a featured speaker. He saw the conference as a key opportunity to show the need for conserving Georgia's coastline and sea islands and denying Kerr-McGee a license to mine. Armed with data gleaned from years of scientific endeavor on Sapelo, Odum waxed eloquent on the "interlacing pattern of marshes and tidal creeks, some of the most productive natural systems on Earth":

> In Georgia, the salt marshes are the biological heart of the estuary; they must be protected so that the open water portion of the system can be used for seafood harvest, recreation, transportation, mineral regeneration, and other needs of human society. If marshes are safely in a protective category, then the sea islands can also be saved. . . .
>
> The inner recesses of marshes and small creeks are the seafood nursery, the most fertile part of the estuaries. . . . More organic matter is made here by photosynthesis than can possibly be used in place, so, there is a tremendous export of materials from these parts of the marsh into the deeper wa-

ters where the food energy supports a whole host of additional organisms as well as later stages of species that originate in the nursery.

In essence, Odum was alluding to his outwelling hypothesis. Some say he used it prematurely—before he had all of the scientific data necessary to support it in hand—to convince those at the two-day conference that the marshes of Georgia must be saved. Years later, two of his colleagues argued that "the outwelling concept may have been so useful to curtail the then rampant destruction of tidal salt marshes, that little could have stood in the way of its uncritical acceptance."[5] Premature or not, the hypothesis was widely quoted and cited at the time.

Shortly after Odum gave his talk, the advisory panel, in a remarkably objective report, using strong science and incontrovertible facts, showed that the mining was decidedly not good for Georgia environmentally or economically. The panel stressed the value of the tidal marshes, the threat posed by phosphate mining to the state's fisheries, and the questionable economic benefits of the project.

Kerr-McGee's lease request was denied.

The battle was won, but the war was far from over. Kerr-McGee made it plain that it would try again for a lease. And other companies had their own designs for the "useless marsh." A huge pulp and paper company wanted to drain and fill swaths of marsh and plant pine trees in them. A Brunswick chemical company wanted to dump tons of waste dirt and sand into the marshes.

Odum and others understood that the environmental assaults would never end until the marshes were legally protected under a strong, enforceable law. Without legal protection, they feared, individuals and corporations bent on financial gain would ruin a vast portion of Georgia's coastal wetlands beyond recovery. The advisory panel recommended the creation of a permanent state agency to fend off would-be destroyers of the marshes. In effect, the responsibility of preserving Georgia's marshes was being handed off to the Georgia General Assembly and to a governor better known for riding his bicycle backward than for protecting the environment.

Many of the state's most powerful lawmakers didn't want anything to do with such a political hot potato, but some courageous legislators were willing to tackle the issue head-on. Prominent among the latter group was

Representative Reid W. Harris, a young title lawyer from Brunswick. Like thousands of other schoolchildren in Georgia and South Carolina, he had memorized Sidney Lanier's "The Marshes of Glynn" in junior high school. He had seen how phosphate strip-mining had left parts of Florida's landscape devastated by deep, sterile pits and silt-clogged streams, and he vowed it would not happen to Georgia's coast. In addition, he was persuaded by the ample scientific data from Sapelo, which showed the immeasurable value and benefits of Georgia's marshes for wildlife and people.[6]

With the help of Marland and others, Harris drafted a tough bill to prohibit any person from removing, filling, dredging, draining, or otherwise altering any marshland in Georgia without first obtaining a permit. A new state agency would be set up to review the environmental soundness of permit requests. Recommendations would be passed on to a three-person committee, which would decide if the permit should be granted. If the application did not meet strict environmental criteria, no permit would be issued. The act would prohibit anything that "unreasonably interferes with the conservation of fish, shrimp, oysters, crabs, clams, or other marine life, wildlife or other resources, including but not limited to water and oxygen supply," or "otherwise alters" the salt marsh. The act also would declare most of Georgia's four hundred thousand acres of salt marsh state property because the king of England had held dominion over the marsh when Georgia was still a British colony. Even individuals who could establish a title to swaths of marshland could not legally impair the marsh for their private gain.[7]

Early in the 1969 Georgia legislative session, Harris introduced the Coastal Marshlands Protection Act and launched it on a perilous path through the legislative chambers. Harris would need powerful allies to face the various chambers of commerce, labor unions, developers, coastal banks, heavy equipment dealers, paper mill companies, and other powerful groups and corporations arrayed against him. The bill "created an uproar in my home district and other coastal communities," Harris recalled. "My poor daddy caught hell and my brother, too." Opponents of the bill pulled money from the First National Bank of Brunswick, where his father, Augustus M. Harris Sr., was president and chairman. Harris himself became an outcast in his own law firm and felt forced to resign.[8]

But Harris also had his legion of supporters. No sooner had he introduced his measure than a vocal and highly influential cadre of scientists, conservationists, garden club members, fishermen, college students, and others started lining up behind him. Several of them were stalwarts of Georgia's early environmental movement, including Jane Yarn, later an adviser to President Jimmy Carter, and Ogden Doremus, a lawyer who became a mentor to countless young greenies who would fondly call him "Mr. Environment." But in the forefront was Eugene Odum, who by then had become one of the world's most renowned ecologists. Touting his early outwelling concept, Odum patiently explained to anyone who would listen how the salt marshes are indispensable for feeding fish and shellfish in the estuaries.

Betty Jean Craige's biography of Odum tells of his involvement in the campaign:

> Students at the University of Georgia, many of them associated with the Institute of Ecology, formed the Save Our Marshes Committee and recruited Odum to help them explain the function of the ecosystem to Georgia voters. Odum wrote a fact sheet describing the salt marshes as nursery grounds for marine animals and listing what the marshes provided for human beings: food, recreation, erosion control, open space, and income. And he converted the marshland resource into dollars to show its economic value to the state. "The most productive agricultural crops in the world can produce no more total organic matter than the Georgia marshes where the tide does the work of fertilization and cultivation—free," he said. The marshes should be valued at a minimum of $2,000 per acre, he continued, because indirectly the marshes produced a yearly income (in 1970 dollars) of $100 per acre, totaling $40 million per year for the whole coast. "It would take almost $1 billion in the bank to produce an income equal to the yearly income from your marshes."[9]

Tremendous public support began to swell behind Harris's bill. News articles, editorials, and feature stories about the beauty and importance of the salt marshes appeared in newspapers throughout the state. *Life*, *Time*, and other national magazines covered the issue in feature spreads. "Save Our Marshes" bumper stickers showed up on cars; buttons bearing similar messages appeared on men's lapels and women's blouses.

The Georgia House passed the bill, by committee substitute, in 1969, but the measure never reached the Senate floor. Instead, it would be taken up again in the 1970 legislative session, when the clamor for its passage became even more strident.

Odum was in his element. He was "working with students on a cause he held dear, teaching the public about ecosystems, talking with legislators and testifying at public hearings. At a 'Conservation Teach-in' held in January [1970] at the University of Georgia, Odum concluded his lesson on the value of the saltwater wetlands with a comment that was widely quoted: Filling in the Georgia marshes or 'allowing them to be whittled away,' he said, 'is as senseless as filling in San Francisco Bay.'"[10]

On February 6, 1970, the Georgia Senate, whose members had sided with developers the year before, unanimously passed the Coastal Marshlands Protection Act. Three days later the House overwhelmingly approved it. Clearly influenced by Odum's concepts, the lawmakers acknowledged the value of Georgia's salt marshes and estuaries:

> The estuarine area of Georgia is the habitat of many species of marine life and wildlife that cannot survive without the food supplied by the marshlands. . . . This coastal marshlands resource system is costly, if not impossible, to reconstruct or rehabilitate once adversely affected by man. It is important to conserve this system for the present and future use and enjoyment of all citizens and visitors to this state. Activities and structures in the coastal marshlands must be regulated to ensure that the values and functions of the coastal marshlands are not impaired and to fulfill the responsibilities of each generation as public trustees of the coastal marshlands for succeeding generations.[11]

The measure did allow for some exemptions, such as power companies maintaining power lines across marshes, maintenance of public highways by the state Department of Transportation, and the building of private docks by those who owned upland property adjacent to the marsh. But the most destructive projects, such as dredging or filling the marsh, were prohibited.

It was left to Maddox to sign the bill into law. At first he threatened to veto it. To him, the act represented just another attempt by government to interfere with unfettered private development on the Georgia coast. But on March 27, 1970, the last possible day that he could legally sign a bill, Maddox became the governor who bestowed permanent protection on Georgia's marshes, spurred on by the "three barrels full of mail" that he had received supporting the act.[12] That did not stop him, though, from tossing the pen over his shoulder and onto the floor after signing the bill.[13]

Odum later would say that one of the lessons learned from the save-the-marshes campaign was that "the legislative system works when there is strong public mood for decision—and this mood must have a rational basis if legislative action is to have a long-term effect."[14] Without the years of research on Sapelo, he said, the marsh protection bill would never have gotten off the ground. "If we had not had the first fifteen years, and a wild marsh to work in, we would not have learned what we did and the marsh might have died without our knowing what we had lost."[15]

As for Reid Harris, sore feelings against what he had done were still simmering on the coast, and he never sought public office again. But in 2009, nearly forty years after the marsh protection law was passed, he received the Rock Howard Award, which is given annually by the Georgia DNR to a person who has made great contributions to sustain, enhance, protect, and conserve Georgia's natural, historical, and cultural resources. "Without his tireless efforts, Georgia's irreplaceable marshes today would be polluted, mined, filled and otherwise largely destroyed," the DNR representative said in presenting the award to Harris.

Kerr-McGee never again sought a permit on the Georgia coast. In 1990 it gave the Nature Conservancy the two islands it had bought for strip-mining. The Nature Conservancy then sold Little Tybee and Cabbage islands to the state of Georgia for $1.5 million and used the proceeds to help preserve a pristine remnant of tallgrass prairie in Kansas.[16]

In 1981 the Georgia legislature passed another monumental piece of legislation—the Shore Protection Act. In effect, the act extended the state's stewardship of the coast beyond the marshlands and provided vital protection for the state's beaches, beach dunes, sandbars, and offshore shoals. The act also established a five-person committee to issue permits for projects that might affect the ecosystem.

Counterattacks

The Coastal Marshlands Protection Act has been one of Georgia's most enduring environmental laws—and one of the strongest in the nation. Because of the law, Georgia's marshes are in almost the same condition as they were in 1970. A 1988 University of Georgia study of the act's effectiveness found it to be "working well."[17]

But two decades later, a gathering force of property developers and others began finding the law a serious impediment to their plans. Many of the developers' allies, including several former state officials, wanted to see the Coastal Marshlands Protection Act limited.

Perhaps conservationists and other supporters should have anticipated such challenges. But the measure's early framers were more intent at the time on stopping industry abuse of the marshlands. Who could have foreseen that the biggest threat would become runaway population growth?

By 2008 a law that had withstood numerous legal challenges and had become nearly sacrosanct in Georgia was facing an uncertain future because of rule changes and a major court decision that favored developers. The situation prompted influential Georgia political analyst Bill Shipp to write in a syndicated newspaper column: "The Marshlands Protection Act has served Georgians well as a statute aimed at protecting an important national and state resource. But the times, they are a-changing. Real estate development is exploding along Georgia's coast. A new generation of wheeler-dealer lobbyists and cavalier politicians has taken control of the state Capitol. Everywhere you look, developers are rolling out plans for gigantic subdivisions and shopping centers. Many of these new gold-seekers view the marshlands as Georgia's last frontier—a wild and watery space to be filled, developed and overpopulated."[18]

THE FIRST BIG challenge to the law actually came in 2001. Theodore Jockisch, a retired Atlanta dentist turned developer, proposed building numerous high-end homes and a large marina on three unspoiled marsh hammocks near Savannah as part of a larger development called Emerald Pointe. But if it were to be successful, the development would need three bridges spanning the salt marsh and linking the hammocks to the mainland. Without the bridges there would be no way for homeowners to drive over to the hammocks. The state Marshlands Protection Committee, which had become a unit of the Georgia DNR, granted Jockisch a permit to build the spans, claiming that the bridges by themselves would have negligible environmental impacts on the marsh. The committee did not look at the possible impacts of the entire development—including the dozens of new houses Jockisch proposed to build—claiming not to have the authority under the law to regulate developments on high ground such as marsh hammocks. Three environmental groups disputed that interpretation of the law and appealed the committee's decision before an administrative law judge. The judge ruled against them.

The groups argued that storm runoff laced with fertilizers, pesticides, oil, and other contaminants flowing off rooftops, lawns, roads, and parking lots in the subdivision would pollute the marsh, alter salinity levels, and endanger marsh habitats. The committee should therefore have considered the environmental consequences of the entire project and not just the bridges, the groups said.

Superior Court Judge Constance Russell agreed with the environmentalists and ruled in their favor. She said that the Marshlands Protection Committee, in issuing the permit, had indeed violated the 1970 marsh protection act. "Bridges are not roads to nowhere," she quipped. "Analyzing the propriety of issuing permits for bridges and activities in the marshes in isolation from the larger purpose of the activity or structure does violence [to what the act intended]."[19]

Jockisch determined to fight on. To environmentalists' consternation, state officials stepped in on his side. Jockisch—and the state of Georgia supporting him—challenged Russell's decision in the Georgia Court of Appeals. To outraged environmentalists a state official explained that the Marshlands Protection Committee didn't have the expertise or manpower to exercise authority over uplands. But no matter; in early 2004 the Court of Appeals rejected the requests for appellate review. The state Supreme Court then also declined to intervene.

Jubilant environmentalists toasted their victory, seeing the Superior Court's ruling as broadening the mandate and the authority of the 1970 act. The committee would henceforth have to widen its horizons and consider the impact of an entire project on Georgia's marshes—not just the portion on or over the marsh. They celebrated too soon. The builders and their powerful allies vowed to fight the decision—and they would be successful.

THE TURNING POINT came in March 2005. The Marshlands Protection Committee granted a permit to another Atlanta-based developer, Land Resources, to build a massive development along the Intracoastal

Waterway near Saint Marys, Georgia, close to the Florida state line and directly across from the Cumberland Island National Seashore. Called Cumberland Harbour, the gated community would have up to twelve hundred homes and commercial facilities on one thousand acres of a soggy, maritime forest–covered peninsula surrounded by a sweeping salt marsh. Lots with breathtaking views of marsh and estuary would sell for up to $750,000. Land Resources also planned to build dozens of private docks, three community docks, and two large marinas to moor or store as many as eight hundred boats of all sizes. It would be the largest marina project ever permitted in Georgia.

Once again the committee (now expanded from three to five members) acknowledged that it had reviewed only the impacts on the marsh from the marina portion of the project—not the impacts from the entire development—even though the earlier Emerald Pointe ruling established the panel's right to take into account the whole project and stipulate in a permit how the developer should protect the marsh.

Because the committee had not exercised that authority, the environmental groups appealed the Cumberland Harbour permit before an administrative law judge. Their argument was similar to the one that had won them victory in the Emerald Pointe case: The state is obligated to protect the marshes from the upland components of a project as well as from structures that jut out into the marsh. In essence, the groups wanted the state to make sure the developer took the steps necessary to control storm runoff from rooftops, streets, and other structures on the high-ground portion of the development. That would probably entail the installation of other expensive control systems—beyond those already planned—and thereby considerably slash the developer's profit.

Once again the state joined the developer in fighting the appeal, saying that the committee lacked the legal authority to regulate development on uplands. The administrative law judge disagreed and ruled in favor of the environmentalists. For a second time, they celebrated a win.

Once again, however, the state and the developer challenged the ruling in the Georgia Court of Appeals. This time the court agreed to take up the case, and the environmentalists cooled their heels while the court pondered the matter.

The other side didn't wait for the court's decision. The Georgia DNR and its sixteen-member governing board, top-heavy with pro-development sympathizers, took the issue into their own hands. As the rule-setting body for the Marshlands Protection Committee, the DNR board suggested a new set of regulations "to help guide" the committee. The board explained that the new rules would apply to the uplands portion of marsh-front developments and help clarify the authority of the 1970 law and give better guidance for permit issuing. The rules would give the DNR something to enforce, said Susan Shipman, who headed the DNR's Coastal Resources Division: "This brings new standards where there were no standards."[20]

Ever suspicious, the environmentalists and their allies sensed a backdoor attempt to weaken the marsh protection law. Jim Stokes, the head of the Georgia Conservancy, suspected that "these developers, and those who respond to their political influence, are trying to use the rule-making process to circumvent existing law and court rulings that they find disagreeable."[21]

At first glance, the new rules the DNR proposed appeared to strengthen the marsh protection law by regulating some upland components of marsh-front developments. They required, for instance, that developers maintain a fifty-foot-wide vegetation buffer between the marsh and parking lots, restrooms, sidewalks, storage sheds, and other structures connected directly to a new project's marinas and community docks. The purpose of the vegetation buffer would be to slow storm water and filter out pollutants before the runoff reached the marsh. The rules required that green space be retained "where practicable and appropriate" and that storm-water controls "must be utilized to the maximum extent practicable." Developers would be obligated to shoot for a goal of no more than 15 percent impervious surface in the marina portion of a project.

When the environmentalists looked again, they found the rules to be riddled with loopholes. The new rules would actually weaken the marsh protection act, not bolster it. For one thing, the proposed buffer requirement wouldn't pertain to private homes, condos, swimming pools, and gazebos on high ground adjacent to a marsh—even though the earlier court rulings said the committee should consider such structures when evaluating a permit request. The DNR board claimed that other state laws, such as the erosion and sediment act, regulated those structures.

"These rules have been designed to benefit a select few at the expense of the marsh," the Georgia Conservancy protested to the board. They "fail to protect the marsh from stormwater runoff and other sources of pol-

A Liberty County, Georgia, salt marsh kept largely intact
by Georgia's Coastal Marshlands Protection Act.

lution from developments. The proposed rules don't have standards for
enforcement and have ignored accepted science. Science shows that at ten
percent impervious surface, harm to the salt marsh and coastal streams are
detected. These rules don't provide an enforceable limit on impervious
surface."[22]

The environmentalists received unexpected support from more than
thirty state legislators who urged the DNR board to at least delay implementing the rules until the Appeals Court ruled in the Cumberland Harbour case, which was expected to clarify the extent of the committee's authority. The court's decision could affect the direction of marsh protection
for generations to come.

But the DNR board did not wait. It approved the new rules, which became effective in March 2007. It was a stinging defeat for the environmentalists. But it wasn't the only one. The Georgia Court of Appeals ruled
against them in the Cumberland Harbour case. Dissatisfied, they appealed
to the Georgia Supreme Court—the first time a marsh protection case
had ever come before the high court. In November 2008 the Supreme

Court also ruled against them by a vote of five to two. The court's majority opinion said the Georgia General Assembly in 1970 had not intended to "establish the [marsh protection] committee as the 'super regulator' of any and all development in the coastal areas of the state."[23]

The decision was a huge blow for the environmentalists—and for the salt marshes they were trying to protect. "The Supreme Court . . . left nearly 400,000 acres of one of the world's most productive natural resources in uncertain hands," lamented Chris DeScherer, a senior attorney for the Southern Environmental Law Center, which represented the environmental groups. The ruling, he said, "limits what had been one of the strongest available tools to . . . balance ecological protection with economic development as the Georgia coast continues to grow."[24]

Vernon "Jim" Henry, who was a coastal geologist and an original member of the Marshlands Protection Committee, believed that politicians, bureaucrats, and developers had acted in concert to weaken the law. "Politics and greed have overcome scientific knowledge and consideration for the public good in the proper management and protection of marshlands and estuarine waters by the Georgia Department of Natural Resources," he told me before he died in 2010. "It is quite obvious that over the years . . . a permit applicant has changed from being a supplicant to a customer, and finally to being a client or even a partner in the doling out of public property for private development."[25]

Meanwhile, in South Carolina . . .

While scientists, conservationists, lawmakers, and others in Georgia scurried to save that state's salt marshes from phosphate mining, a battle just as bitter and hard fought was about to erupt in South Carolina. In a well-orchestrated press conference in October 1969, executives with the giant German chemical firm Badische, Anilin- und Soda-Fabrik (BASF) peremptorily announced that the company was going to build a four-hundred-million-dollar plant on Victoria Bluff, a pristine eighteen-hundred-acre site near Hilton Head Island in Beaufort County. Covered mostly by a maritime forest, Victoria Bluff bordered the placid Colleton River, which flowed through thousands of acres of unspoiled salt marsh and emptied into Port Royal Sound, one of few pristine estuaries remaining on the Southeast coast.

The sprawling complex would turn out trainloads of raw materials for various kinds of plastics, dyes, and other products and would generate hundreds, perhaps thousands, of new jobs. Though the press conference was the first public revelation of BASF's plan, it had been no secret among state and local public officials. Backroom negotiations had been taking place for some time between the company and the officials. To entice BASF to the South Carolina coast, the officials had promised the firm a five-year exemption from state and local taxes. They also had assembled the land for the plant and were selling it to the company at a near giveaway price. A new thirteen-mile-long rail line and a four-lane highway, subsidized by taxpayers, would be built to the plant. A deepwater port would be developed with public funds to accommodate tankers bringing in an average of forty thousand barrels of naphtha—a flammable mixture of hydrocarbons distilled from petroleum and coal tar—per day to feed the plant's manufacturing processes.

The officials viewed what they had achieved—bringing a well-heeled international company and scores of new jobs into an area of South Carolina then wrestling with widespread poverty and a grim economic outlook—as a stunning victory. They fully expected the public to applaud them for the good deed. And indeed, many South Carolinians rejoiced over the prospect of jobs and other benefits. The NAACP said it expected the plant to be a source of badly needed jobs for local black citizens.[26]

The government officials and BASF executives were thus taken aback by a stinging backlash that erupted a few days after the big announcement. Homeowners in Hilton Head's posh resorts, only two miles away from the proposed plant site, cried foul. They said that pollution spewed from the plant would ruin surrounding marshes and estuaries, sully the air, and wipe out private property values. They quickly organized into the Hilton Head Island Community Association and formed an alliance with local shrimpers, crabbers, and oystermen who feared the pollution would destroy sea life in Port Royal Sound and put them out of business.[27]

The alliance would need a powerful leader unfazed by the deep-pocketed corporation and public officials wielding enormous power. They found him in Charles Fraser, the cocky developer of Hilton Head's exclusive Sea Pines Plantation. Fraser feared that the plant could ruin all that he had tried to do on Hilton Head. Sea Pines Plantation, built in the 1950s and 1960s, had won national acclaim for tastefully preserving trees, scenic beauty, and wilderness while blending in golf courses, shopping areas, and subdivisions. Fraser had connections to powerful people in the state and federal governments and in journalism, conservation, and legal circles. He would pull all of those strings in fighting BASF. He also persuaded some of his fellow wealthy developers to join the fight.[28]

He hastily organized his allies into a research effort to examine the ramifications of the pollution from the BASF plant. Eugene Odum, then helping to lead the battle against Kerr-McGee in Georgia, was asked to provide an ecological assessment. The plant's opponents were alarmed by what they found. Most of the maritime forest on Victoria Bluff would be clear-cut. A ten-mile-long shipping channel would be dredged in Port Royal Sound. The thousands of barrels of naphtha that the company would bring in each day could cause widespread devastation if a spill occurred. The plant would draw up to one hundred million gallons of water per day—as much as a good-sized city used—from aquifers and from the Savannah River. Canals would be dug to carry the river water to the plant. In return, the plant would pump two and a half million gallons of poorly treated wastewater per day into Port Royal Sound. (The local governments had pledged to create a special utility district for the plant's wastewater treatment.) Particularly alarming was BASF's track record in Europe. Its Ludwigshafen, Germany, plant dumped ninety million gallons of acidic effluent into the Rhine River every day; its Antwerp, Belgium, plant was blamed for helping to make the surrounding water unfit for fishing and swimming.[29]

Governor Robert McNair of South Carolina, who vigorously supported the plant, tried to allay such concerns. "We have assurances that the company is vitally concerned about the ecology and beauty of the area and that steps are being taken to satisfy all legal, environmental and industrial requirements in safeguarding the air and water from pollutants," McNair said.[30] Company executives promised that the plant would obey all regulations governing pollution. The opposition was not reassured. They replied that South Carolina's lax enforcement of already weak, loophole-ridden antipollution laws gave them no assurance at all that the plant could be run safely. Their battle cry became "BASF: Bad Air, Sick Fish."

In early 1970 savvy lawyers hired by Fraser sought a legal injunction against BASF. The action was filed in behalf of a predominantly black Hilton Head Fishing Cooperative, whose members contended that pollution from the plant would endanger their way of life. The injunction would provide more time to study the potential environmental impacts of the plant.

Fraser hired a full-time publicist to rally media coverage. As news media spread the word about the controversy, opposition to the plant heated up. The plant's opponents had a distinct advantage in the environmental consciousness that was gripping much of the nation in 1970. Rachel Carson's momentous book *Silent Spring*, published in 1962, had convincingly driven home the point that pollution was imperiling the nation's air, land, and water, and people were beginning to understand that the damage would be irreparable if not curtailed. The nation also was getting ready for its first Earth Day (which took place on April 22, 1970). In addition, Congress was set to pass the powerful new Clean Air Act and was putting the finishing touches on bills to create the U.S. Environmental Protection Agency and the National Oceanic and Atmospheric Administration.

Journalists from Washington and national publications began covering the BASF battle, using it as a prime example of the perils facing the nation from industrial pollution. The Sierra Club, the National Audubon Society, and other big environmental groups joined the fray. College students staged protests in downtown Beaufort, chanting, "Progress without pollution."

The pressure began to pay off. Governor McNair publicly backed away from his support of the plant and ordered the state Water Resources Commission to assess the effects of chemical wastes on the water and nearby marshes. A bill was introduced into the South Carolina General Assembly to delay construction of the plant by at least six months. In late January 1970 *Time* magazine reported, "The message is beginning to reach BASF's Manhattan headquarters."

Then another BASF foe reared up: Secretary of the Interior Walter J. Hickel, a former developer and governor of Alaska. At that time, Interior had authority over the states to enforce federal clean water laws if individual states did not toe the line. With Congress debating the creation of the EPA and passage of the Clean Air Act, Hickel reportedly was looking for ways to dramatize and bolster the nation's environmental policies.

In a scathing letter to Hans Lautenschlager, president of BASF's American affiliate, in late March 1970 Hickel made it abundantly clear that his agency would not tolerate any pollution from the plant. Furthermore, Interior would strongly oppose the plant's construction unless assurances for safeguards were forthcoming. So far, he noted, the agency had not received such assurances. "The area in question is a splendid estuary, virtually free of pollution," Hickel wrote. "This Department would strenuously oppose any action which would result in degradation of that water quality." In effect, Hickel was saying that if South Carolina did not enforce the clean water laws, the federal government would step in and do it for the state.

Particularly worried about the damage that dredging could inflict on Port Royal Sound, Hickel warned, "This Department will oppose strenuously any proposal for channel dredging which would cause environmental damage or which would cause a significant increase in environmental hazards" to the estuary. He also warned that the daily handling of huge amounts of naphtha and other petrochemicals would pose an immense threat to the marshes and estuary.

Hickel's letter turned the tide. BASF realized that the battle to build the plant might not be worth the expense and the bad press the company would reap. Any doubt that the antiplant faction had won was dispelled in April 1970 when a shrimp trawler named *Captain Dave* sailed from Beaufort to Washington with twenty-five pounds of fresh Port Royal shrimp and a petition bearing forty-five thousand signatures opposing the BASF plant. Meeting the vessel at the dock in Washington were Hickel and other dignitaries and a phalanx of TV and newspaper reporters.

After Hickel's intervention, BASF halted its plans for Victoria Bluff. Later, a BASF executive reportedly acknowledged that pollution from the plant could indeed have done considerable damage to the surrounding estuary and marshes. The author of *German Industry and Global Enterprise, BASF: The History of a Company* (2004) cited the minutes from an April 1970 company board meeting in which company officials acknowledged that it would be impossible to overcome pollution problems at Victoria Bluff because the plant would have had to dispose of eighty thousand tons of neutral salts a year, "a level beyond the carrying capacity of the Colleton River."[31]

In a December 1982 interview for an oral history project, former governor McNair acknowledged that the project had not been properly studied for possible adverse effects. "We had overlooked the attitude of people about the impact of something like this on the seafood, shrimp and all of this, and hadn't done enough homework."[32]

The skirmishes over Victoria Bluff, however, did not end with BASF's pullout. The Houston-based company Brown & Root (a division of Halliburton) proposed building a plant that would produce giant offshore oil rigs to explore for oil off the Southeast coast. The rigs, up to 240 feet long and 800 feet high, would be towed through Port Royal Sound, and that would require the dredging of a shipping channel. The Chicago Bridge & Iron Company acquired 775 acres next to the Brown & Root site on which it planned to build high-pressure containers as tall as a ten-story building to ship liquefied natural gas. It, too, would need a dredged shipping channel.

The environmentalist forces mobilized against the new round of industrial threats, raising the same arguments that had helped them win the BASF fight: the plants would endanger marshes and estuaries and wipe out fisheries. But this time the companies' plans were thwarted more by politics and economics than by environmentalists. Federal obstacles to oil drilling in the South Atlantic Bight caused Brown & Root to back off on its project, and falling demand for liquefied natural gas shipping containers prompted Chicago Bridge & Iron to abandon its plans. The final battle was against an Indiana company that wanted to set up a boat-building plant at Victoria Bluff. It, too, was turned back after a rancorous battle.

In the end, conservationists and environmentalists might have won a pyrrhic victory. In 1989 a development firm acquired the 775 acres where the Chicago Bridge & Iron Company had wanted to build its plant. Instead of heavy industry, an exclusive gated subdivision, Colleton River Plantation, sprang up on the site, replete with some 395 swanky houses dotted around a Jack Nicklaus–designed golf course with a clubhouse and other luxury amenities. In 1995 the developer of Colleton opened Belfair Plantation right next door—an even more upscale community built around thirty-six Fazio-designed holes. Then came two more upmarket developments, the Crescent and Eagle's Pointe, and their golf courses. The floodgates had been opened to rampant development.

There was one silver lining to this cloud. About eleven hundred acres of the old BASF land would be protected by the state from schemes to convert it to industry use or subdivisions. Today, the Victoria Bluff Heritage Preserve is open to the public for hiking through a maritime forest and a rare pine–saw palmetto ecosystem. Occasionally in the fall, the preserve also is open to hunting.

Ψ Ψ Ψ

LIKE THE KERR-MCGEE battle in Georgia, the battle against BASF in South Carolina sparked worry that the Palmetto State lacked strong legal protection for its marshes and estuaries and an effective system to regulate impacts on them. A diverse group of legislators, conservationists, and others set about to rectify the gaping deficiency, but it would take them several years to push through the legislation necessary to set up that protection.

Twice, in fact, the South Carolina legislature passed "tidelands" bills to safeguard coastal marshes, estuaries, beaches, and oceanfront sand dunes, but each time the measures were vetoed by then-Governor James B. Edwards. A major sticking point for Edwards was the question of marsh ownership. The state's attorney general held that a 1928 case had established the precedent for private ownership of marshland. Under that decision, private ownership of lands between the high and low tides could be established only through titles traceable to a grant of South Carolina's colonial Lords Proprietors, a king's grant, or a state grant. Edwards sought exemptions for people who could demonstrate title to tidelands within state public trust jurisdiction. (The lack of such exemptions had stalled tidelands protection legislation in South Carolina since the late 1950s.)[33]

Finally, in 1977, a compromise was reached. The agreement would allow a private individual to sue the state to validate a claim of marshland ownership. The legislation also would exclude upland portions of a coastal project from permit consideration—the issue that would cause the bitter disputes in Georgia. This time the measure was palatable to Edwards, and he signed the South Carolina Coastal Tidelands and Wetlands Act in May 1977.

The new law created the eighteen-member Coastal Council to "develop and implement a comprehensive coastal management program and a permitting system for the critical areas in the eight coastal counties of South Carolina." The "critical areas" included marshlands, estuaries, beaches, and primary and secondary dunes. In 1988 the Coastal Council successfully pushed the Beachfront Management Act through the South Carolina legislature. The act adopted the policy of "retreat" from the ocean and banned new seawalls. It also triggered the landmark *Lucas v. South Carolina*

Coastal Council case, in which David Lucas, who owned two beachfront lots on the Isle of Palms east of Charleston, sued the council because it prevented him from building on the property. The council claimed that Lucas's proposed construction was in one of the critical areas—the dunes area—protected by the 1988 beachfront protection law. Lucas appealed all the way to the U.S. Supreme Court, which found that the act did deprive his land of all its "economically beneficial use." The state eventually settled with Lucas and purchased the lots.[34]

During a state government restructuring in 1993, the Coastal Council was renamed the Office of Ocean and Coastal Resource Management (OCRM) and became a division of the state Department of Health and Environmental Control. The OCRM makes all initial permit decisions. Initial appeals are heard by administrative law judges and, if not resolved, then by the Coastal Council. The DHEC board serves as the agency's ultimate authority on coastal policy.

The report card on South Carolina's coastal protection laws has been mixed. Initially, complaints about permit decisions under the laws came mostly from developers who wanted to build closer to the ocean and put more docks in the marsh and more condominiums on filled wetlands. Jimmy Chandler, the director of the South Carolina Environmental Law Project and South Carolina's foremost environmental lawyer until his untimely death in 2009, said that for many years the OCRM worked reasonably well administering the law and protecting the coast. But then the agency began to backslide. A few years ago Chandler was led to remark: "It now seems to me that our coastal management system has gone terribly awry. In recent years, we have seen trends that indicate to us that the agency has lost its focus, lost its sense of mission and is now characterized by poor judgment, inconsistency, and day-to-day confusion."[35]

Chandler said his complaint was prompted by the inordinate number of appeals his group was forced to file because of mistakes the OCRM made in issuing permits and certifying coastal projects. Progress has since been made, he said, "but there is still a lot of work to be done."

EVEN THOUGH STATE laws and agencies are charged with protecting the coastal environment, land-use decisions made by city and county governments have enormous impacts on coastal systems. Land-use ordinances at the city and county levels determine the location and layout of development. State and federal agencies can do very little to control sprawl.

And indeed, it is sprawl—not strip mines and giant chemical plants— that now poses the biggest threat to the salt marshes and estuaries of the Southeast and the myriad creatures that live in them. The oyster, one of the most important species of salt marsh and estuary, is among the creatures bearing the brunt of assaults on coastal ecosystems.

CHAPTER ELEVEN

Saving the Oyster

THE EASTERN OYSTER is not a handsome creature; when its hinged shell is tightly shut, it looks more like a rock than a living animal. Pry it open and it's hardly more appealing. And yet this featureless blob is one of the most vital animals in the salt marsh and estuary. Without it, many other marine species would suffer and perhaps even perish. Oysters clean the water, recycle nutrients, and regulate energy flow—all functions critical to keeping estuaries and salt marshes healthy and balanced. Oyster meat is nutritious food for a host of other creatures. The dense, rugged reefs that oysters build provide vital shelter for scores of fish, crabs, plants, and invertebrates—a veritable marine metropolis. Scientists are still adding to our knowledge of the reefs' range of ecological services. *Crassostrea virginica* is thus a keystone species that exerts considerable influence over the vitality of its entire ecosystem.

Oysters are voracious filter feeders, straining out phytoplankton, bacteria, detritus, and other nutritious matter from seawater, which they pump in copious quantities across their gills at high tide. In this simple act of eating, an oyster three to four inches long can strain four or more gallons of water—hundreds of times its body volume—in an hour. On a warm summer day, an adult oyster can suck up and spit out twenty-five to fifty gallons of water while consuming plankton and other food and ejecting indigestible material. Three young oysters can match the filtering efficiency of one adult.[1]

In the act of filtering, oysters remove huge amounts of suspended particles from tidal water, thereby rendering cloudy, murky water remarkably cleaner and clearer. You can see this clarity around a reef when scores of oysters are feeding at the same time. In a sense, the oyster's function is

An intertidal oyster reef in the Sapelo River, Georgia.

similar to that of the human kidney, which filters wastes from blood and helps regulate blood flow in the body.

Great reefs of oysters scattered throughout an estuary may be capable of filtering all of the estuary's waters in a matter of days. Roger Newell of the University of Maryland estimated that when the Chesapeake Bay was at peak health prior to 1870 and oyster reefs flourished throughout the bay, the mollusks could filter the entire bay's waters during the summer in about three to six days. Today, with the polluted bay's oyster population at only about 1 percent of its original number, it takes nearly a year for the surviving shellfish to filter all the water.[2]

Overfishing, pollution, disease, and other human-induced ills virtually wiped out the Chesapeake's vast oyster beds. So far have oyster numbers fallen there that an environmental scientist in 2005 petitioned the federal government to list the oyster as an endangered species. Federal wildlife officials gave serious thought to the request before a public uproar—and a realization that such a listing would shut down the nation's entire oyster industry—prompted the petitioner to withdraw his proposal. Nevertheless, a 2009 report by the Nature Conservancy indicates that the oyster is in steep decline worldwide for the same reasons that brought down the Chesapeake population. Eighty-five percent of the world's oyster reefs have disappeared during the past century, and many of the surviving reefs are in sad shape.[3]

If the report is accurate, estuaries, salt marshes, and entire oceans are in serious trouble. When oyster reefs disappear, the myriad ecological services they render to marine ecosystems go with them. Without adequate numbers of thriving, fully functional oyster reefs, troubled estuaries like the Chesapeake will probably never return to glowing health—although oyster reef restoration alone will not be the final solution to an estuary's ills.[4] If more oyster reefs disappear and no new ones take their place, the environmental well-being of many other estuaries also will spiral downward.[5]

Several oyster experts disagree with the Nature Conservancy's report about the extent of reef loss along the Southeast coast, saying that it has not been as dire as the 85–90 percent suggested. Yet the region's oyster reefs without doubt have suffered. The Shellfish Research Laboratory of the University of Georgia's Marine Extension Service, for example, reported that "Georgia's oyster populations were once immense, however overfishing, habitat degradation, and disease have considerably impacted these estuarine communities."[6] Although the experts do not agree on the extent of the damage in the Southeast, most strongly back vigorous "oyster restoration reef" programs that are trying to rebuild reefs all along the coast.

The Oyster

An oyster shell's two halves are hinged at the base. Each half is called a valve; hence the oyster is classified as a bivalve mollusk. When an oyster living in an intertidal reef is exposed to air, it must keep its shell tightly closed to prevent its tissues from drying out. It does this by contracting its adductor muscle, which is attached to each valve. The amazingly strong muscle accounts for 20–40 percent of the oyster's soft tissue weight. If you've ever tried to pry open an oyster, you've encountered the muscle's grip—there's no gap at all between the firmly closed valves.

When the tide comes in and submerges the oyster, it relaxes its adductor muscle and the shell swings open like a space shuttle opening its "clamshell" cargo bay doors. The oyster rapidly beats small, hairlike whips called cilia on its gills to draw in water. The gills filter oxygen from the water and also separate food particles from silt and other indigestible materials suspended in the water. The unconsumed particles collect on, and become coated with, mucus on the gills, forming dense, tiny pellets—known collectively as pseudofeces—that are discharged into the water without passing through the oyster's gut. The cilia conduct the retained food—mostly bits of phytoplankton—to the oyster's mouth and then to its stomach. After digesting its meal, the oyster expels the wastes as feces.

The feces and pseudofeces are particularly high in nitrogen accumulated from the organisms and material filtered from the water. When bacteria process the oyster's waste material, much of the nitrogen returns to the ecosystem as ammonia and other compounds. In limited amounts, some of these compounds are essential for growth of spartina and phytoplankton. About 20 percent of the compounds are "denitrified" by special bacteria in the mud and released as nitrogen gas that bubbles up through the water and escapes into the air.

Denitrification helps keep an estuary's nitrogen levels in check. Too much nitrogen in the system would lead to eutrophication, which promotes unrestrained phytoplankton growth and can result in dangerously low dissolved oxygen levels, or hypoxia, in the estuary. Oysters can have a double-whammy effect in helping control eutrophication: their filtration not only removes nitrogen from the water, it also takes out excess phytoplankton that rob the water of oxygen.

The eastern oyster's admirable filtering feats are only part of its great worth to estuaries and salt marshes. Also of utmost importance is individuals' urge to aggregate and live together in dense reefs that help maintain the physical and biological integrity of coastal ecosystems. Only in recent decades have scientists gained a full appreciation of an oyster reef's full range of ecological services. Perhaps if the reefs' full importance had been appreciated much earlier, many of our estuaries would be facing a brighter future.

On a Reef

On a bone-numbing cold day in January, I'm with my eighty-two-year-old friend Edgar "Sonny" Timmons Sr. picking oysters at low tide. We're on a

Edgar "Sonny" Timmons Sr. of McIntosh County, Georgia, spent
most of his life harvesting seafood from local coastal waters.

small reef in a tidal creek twisting thorough the sprawling salt marshes of
Georgia's McIntosh County. Far across the winter-brown marsh I can see
the low outline of Sapelo Island. An about face reveals the Harris Neck
National Wildlife Refuge on the far horizon.

Captain Sonny, as he's known in these parts, has come to harvest a few
bushels of oysters for some folks in Savannah who are having a backyard
oyster roast. He subleases the reef from our mutual clam-farming friend,
Charlie Phillips, who leases it from the state. Captain Sonny's family was
among the Geechee folk evicted from Harris Neck by the government during World War II to build a military airfield. Clad in a bright yellow slicker
over warm clothing, he works with a nimbleness that I cannot match,
though I am twenty years younger. "Been doing this most of my life," says
Captain Sonny. "I love it out here." He suddenly points upstream—a mink
is swimming across the creek. "Most people never see one," he says.

Wielding an ordinary claw hammer, Captain Sonny, his skill honed
by years of experience, quickly breaks up tightly glued clusters of choice
oysters and knocks away dead shells stuck to them. He tosses the keep-
ers into a blue plastic pail. My job is to tote the full container back to the
boat, a Carolina skiff, and empty the muddy contents into bushel baskets.

It's not easy work, for I must step gingerly between the densely packed, razor-sharp oysters. Walking atop them is nigh impossible. The topmost oysters project upward like fingers, long, slender, and narrow. When I step down between them, my boot-clad feet sink ankle-deep into the thick mud, which tries to suck off the footwear and leave my feet at the mercy of the flesh-slicing shells.

Helping Captain Sonny, though, allows me to fulfill another mission— to get a close-up look at a typical intertidal oyster reef similar to those that fringe the banks of tidal creeks and rivers all along the Southeast coast. If the oyster is a keystone species of salt marsh and estuary, the oyster reef is the ecosystem's cornerstone.

The oysters' strong affinity for one another is what leads to their extensive reef building. A reef may be years, even decades, in the making as new oysters latch onto old ones and create new layers. The resulting three-dimensional, honeycombed structure is the hardest natural edifice in the otherwise soft, muddy sediments of the surrounding marsh and estuary. For that reason, oyster reefs are the temperate zone's equivalent of tropical coral reefs. Both kinds of reef enhance water quality; both help protect the land from erosion and damage from howling storms; both teem with life, supporting a remarkable assemblage of species seeking food and shelter.

The species diversity associated with a southeastern intertidal oyster reef is incredible—as many as three hundred species by some counts. Captain Sonny points to one of them—a small crab, less than an inch long, scooting for cover among the oyster shells. "A little mud crab," he says. "There's lots of other little things here that I don't even know the name of. They're quick to hide."

The oyster reef, in short, is an ecological community that includes not only multitudes of tightly aggregated oysters—living and dead—but a bevy of other creatures as well. They range from full-time residents, which use the reef as primary habitat, to transients, which come in with the tide and hunt for small prey around the structure. Some of the species are found throughout the estuary, others only around oysters. Minnow-like gobies, blennies, toadfish, and skilletfish use oyster reefs as primary habitats—places where they can grow, forage, breed, and hide from predators. The fish attach their eggs to the undersides of old oyster shells, relying on the reef's craggy architecture and numerous cracks and crannies to protect

Captain Sonny harvesting oysters from a reef in an
unnamed creek off the Sapelo River in Georgia.

their young. Somehow, they find enough moisture in and around the reef
to survive at low tide, when the reef is exposed to air.

Little snails scour the oyster reef for food. Tiny crustaceans—amphipods and copepods—graze and nibble on films of algae growing on the
oyster shells. Several mud crab species find more safety from predators
on a reef than on the surrounding bare, open-bottom habitat. The most
numerous of the crabs is the flat back mud crab, less than an inch long,
which grazes on the layers of algae and detritus that glaze oyster shells
and may feed on young oysters, marine worms, and other crustaceans as
well. At low tide it retreats into its burrow or finds a tiny crevice within the
reef. The tiny pea crab lives inside the shells of living oysters. It doesn't kill
them, but it does steal their food. The stone crab, though, is a major oyster
predator, using its bulky claws to crush the shells of living oysters and get
to their meat. Stone crabs build their burrows below the low-tide mark
around oyster reefs. The burrows afford protection for molting crabs and
egg-incubating females.

Polychaete worms are usually present in crannies between and beneath a reef's oyster shells. The most common is the clam worm, which eats zooplankton. Another is the blister worm, which can bore into oyster shells, weaken them, and make them more susceptible to predators. The mud tube worm browses on detritus and uses its tentacles to filter plankton from the water.

Other filter feeders on oyster reefs include the hooked mussel, ribbed mussel, sponges, and barnacles, all of which firmly attach themselves to oyster shells. The barnacle is found at the reef's highest points because it can tolerate exposure to air longer than most. The nonoyster filter feeders take advantage of the same currents as the oyster to strain out food, thus greatly enhancing the reef's filtration capacity.

The oyster springtail, an insect, hides in crevices between oysters at high tide, breathing oxygen trapped by hairs on its fuzzy body. At low tide it must watch for boat-tailed grackles, which swoop down to munch on springtails.

Another bird, the American oystercatcher, preys on oysters, although it takes only nominal numbers. When feeding, the oystercatcher wades along a slightly submerged reef where the oysters are feeding with their shells open. With quick thrusts of its long, bright orange, razor-sharp bill, the oystercatcher severs the adductor muscle and dines on the oyster meat. Once prized for its handsome feathers to decorate ladies' hats, the oystercatcher's populations are still at low levels.

Other birds that commonly forage on the reefs include herons, egrets, terns, gulls, dowitchers, and curlews. Raccoons also often frequent reefs when the tide is out. The oyster's adductor muscle is no match for the raccoon's powerful teeth and claws.

On the small reef where Captain Sonny and I harvest oysters, the rising tide will deliver a whole new cast of transient characters: shrimp, juvenile fish, and others seeking food and safe haven in the reef's labyrinthine tunnels and cavities. Following them in will be the large predators—diamondback terrapins, blue crabs, sheepsheads, red drums, croakers, and others. The big fish attract human anglers, who often find good fishing around reefs.

Water filtration and habitat provision, though, only begin to describe an oyster reef's full range of ecological services. The reefs stabilize tidal creeks and stream bottoms. They dissipate the erosion-causing energy of natural waves and those from speeding boats. Beyond the marsh, reefs serve as natural breakwaters that guard the mainland shore during storms. By slowing down tidal currents, the reefs cause suspended dirt and other matter to settle out—thus further increasing water clarity beyond the effects of filtration. In this way, reefs may profoundly affect the suitability of adjacent areas for other species. Clearer water, for instance, can increase light penetration and promote growth of bottom-dwelling diatoms and other microscopic algae, which further stabilize sediments.

Oysters even help in curtailing global warming by sequestering carbon in their hard calcium carbonate shells.

Reef Building

Over most of its geographic range, the eastern oyster occurs in subtidal reefs that remain submerged during both low tide and high tide. But along the Southeast coast, from Cape Hatteras, North Carolina, to Cape Canaveral, Florida, the dense reefs are almost exclusively intertidal and are exposed to the air for several hours at low tide. One reason intertidal reefs dominate in the Southeast is that there is simply more intertidal area as a result of the region's six- to nine-foot tidal range and lack of topographical relief. The higher tides effectively flush adjacent marsh areas and enrich the water with algae, detritus, and other organic material that nourish oysters.[7]

Generally, intertidal oysters suffer less from predators than do oysters on subtidal beds. Richard Dame, a marine scientist, explained that "most oyster reefs [in the Southeast] are intertidal because in the high-salinity estuaries of this area, marine predators such as oyster drills and boring sponges decimate subtidal oyster populations."[8] Intertidal reefs are not similarly decimated because the predators suffer more from exposure at low tide than do the oysters.

Other possible explanations for intertidal oysters' prevalence on the Southeast coast include the presence of more suitable substrates on intertidal reefs for young oyster attachment; more available food; water currents more suitable for feeding; higher survival of young; the exclusion of many disease-causing organisms; and, perhaps, genetic differences. The intertidal oysters' colonial lifestyle and mutual interdependence also are factors in the prevalence of their reefs.[9]

Differences between subtidal and intertidal reefs make for distinct differences in the oysters themselves. The intertidal mollusks tend to form clusters, while subtidal oysters do not. Intertidal oyster shells are typically thin, elongated, and irregularly shaped; subtidal mollusks tend to have regular, heavy shells. Intertidal oysters are more suitable for canning; subtidal oysters are more often steamed or served on the half shell.

Oyster density on an intertidal reef almost defies comprehension. One survey found well over five thousand young and old oysters—four and a half bushels—in one square yard of reef. Despite the myriad other creatures that live in and on a reef, oysters still account for nearly 90 percent of the biomass.[10]

Oyster reefs don't occur randomly. They develop where chemical and physical conditions are favorable for oyster growth, safety, and reproduction. They seldom build up in areas of high wave energy or in tiny creeks that lack good tidal flushing. First, there must be something hard (not soft mud or shifting sand) to which young oysters can attach. Then, water currents must be strong enough to ferry in food at a steady clip and wash away sediments and reef inhabitants' wastes. The water flow also must be of sufficient strength to disperse oyster larvae. Other conditions also must be met, including tolerable sediment levels, water temperature, dissolved oxygen, and salinity.[11]

Eastern oysters, though, are hardy and tenacious. They can withstand high turbidity and low oxygen levels in the water for several days at a time. They can survive freezing winter temperatures and blazing summer heat; they can tolerate—at least temporarily—salinity levels ranging from brackish to stronger than seawater strength.[12]

A new reef may get its start when oyster larvae attach to a bit of shell or wood—or even a tin can, tire, or old chunk of concrete—on a mudflat. Once attached, the oysters become sessile; that is, they remain there for life. New oysters attach to the older ones, pushing them into the mud and smothering them, but in turn providing a firm substrate for oysters yet to come. The reefs keep building up in this manner. It is a self-sustaining process that provides for long-term growth. Unlike a tropical coral reef ecosystem, which can lose several species of coral and still survive, the oyster reef will collapse without a healthy population of younger oysters growing on the old and dead ones.

Oyster reefs often are narrow, linear structures shaped by currents. In size, they may range from a dozen square feet to dozens of acres. Some may stretch nearly a mile and rise several feet high. When I was growing up on the South Carolina coast, slate-gray oyster beds lined the banks of nearly every tidal creek and river. In the eighteenth and nineteenth centuries, many reefs were so massive that they posed navigation hazards. The still-standing Cockspur Island Lighthouse near Savannah was built directly on top of an oyster reef.

The production of multitudes of new oysters each year is what keeps oyster reefs vigorous and viable. Oysters reproduce during warm-weather months when temperature and light cues prompt male oysters to release sperm, which then triggers female oysters to release their eggs. A single female can produce up to one hundred million eggs every year. When thousands of oysters release trillions of sperm cells and eggs into the water in an orchestrated fashion, the water around the reef can turn cloudy white. Within hours of joining with a sperm, a fertilized egg develops a shell. Oyster larvae, each the size of a pepper grain, emerge from the eggs soon afterward. Tidal currents help disperse the free-swimming larvae.

After two or three weeks the larvae use their tiny, probing feet to find a hard surface on which to settle. They may be attracted to existing oyster reefs by a chemical, possibly ammonia, associated with the reefs. Once settled, the baby oyster's foot excretes cement-like glue that fastens the tiny creature to the hard surface. The attached larvae, a little less than an inch in length, are called spats. Only one to a few in a million larvae make it to the spat stage. Predators such as copepods, fish, and crustaceans eat many of them, and many die when they don't find a hard substrate for attachment. Even the spats are still vulnerable to predators such as crabs. By the time they are about two inches in size they have built hard shells of calcium carbonate, diminishing their vulnerability to predators.[13]

Oysters, which usually reach maturity in one year, are protandric, meaning that during their first year they spawn as males. As they enlarge over the next two or three years and develop greater energy reserves, they release eggs — as females. On the Southeast's intertidal beds, oysters reach harvestable size in about three years.

THE OYSTER EVOLVED about 190 million years ago, during the Jurassic period when the first dinosaurs were roaming the land. From that time until the modern age it survived essentially unchanged. But while millions of years of natural upheavals left the eastern oyster nearly unscathed, the mollusk may finally have met its match in *Homo sapiens*.

"We're seeing an unprecedented and alarming decline in the condition of oyster reefs, a critically important habitat in the world's bays and estuaries," Mike Beck, the Nature Conservancy's senior marine scientist, wrote in the organization's 2009 report *Shellfish Reefs at Risk*. Scientists on five continents had a hand in writing the report.[14]

The report says that reasons for the oyster's predicament are similar worldwide. The main one is decades of overfishing—taking the shellfish at unsustainable levels. Many other factors have also contributed—and are still contributing—to the oyster's downfall:

> Destructive fishing practices that directly alter the physical structure of reefs have been implicated in rapid declines in both [oyster] fisheries productivity and overall reef condition in many estuaries. Fishing practices involving translocation and introduction of non-native shellfish within and between bays have increased the incidence and severity of disease and parasite outbreaks that have all but eliminated fisheries in many coastal areas. Coastal development activities including filling ("land-reclamation") and dredging of shipping channels have also taken a toll on reefs. Likewise, activities occurring upstream continue to cause problems as human populations increase in coastal watersheds. Altered river flows, construction of dams, poorly managed agriculture, and urban development can all impact the quality and quantity of water and sediments that affect whether shellfish reefs persist or perish.[15]

The report takes special note of North America's eastern oyster. Pollution and diseases such as MSX (*Haplosporidium nelsoni*) and dermo (*Perkinsus marinus*) have been especially destructive, wiping out as much as 95 percent of stocks in estuaries as far apart as Long Island Sound and the Louisiana delta. The loss in the Chesapeake Bay was catastrophic—more than 90 percent of historic oyster reef acreage in what once was one of the world's most amazingly productive bodies of water.[16]

Most of the Southeast received a poor to fair rating in the report, meaning that "only" 50–90 percent of the reefs have vanished. Craig Hardy of North Carolina's Department of Marine Fisheries said that figure is true for his state. But several other oyster experts in the region find it way too high and dispute it.

Randal Walker, director of the University of Georgia's Marine Extension Service, is one of the skeptics. Oyster reefs have indeed been destroyed in Georgia, he told me, but not to the extent portrayed by the Nature Conservancy study. In 2010 Walker and some colleagues undertook their own survey of Georgia's oyster reefs using GIS systems and related sampling technology. They concluded that Georgia's reef loss during the past century was lower by orders of magnitude than the Nature Conservancy report suggested. "There is no question that oyster populations have been dramatically reduced, but endangered or facing extinction? Nonsense," Walker says.

Nevertheless, Walker and his colleagues in Georgia and elsewhere along the Southeast coast adamantly support intensive efforts to restore oyster reefs. For one thing, Walker notes: "On a coast where septic tanks are the major sewage treatment process for most coastal counties, and we have an ever-increasing coastal population, oyster reefs can help offset the negative environmental impacts of an ever-increasing coastal sewage and population problem."

Reef Restoration

Recognizing the vast importance of oyster reefs, most coastal states are backing ambitious projects to create new reefs. "If we can restore and protect our oysters, we'll restore and protect our coast as well," Todd Miller of the North Carolina Coastal Federation told me. Most of the restoration efforts aim to replenish suitable areas of rivers and creeks using old oyster shells to lure baby oysters.

Initially, the projects' focus was to increase the amount of harvestable oysters for consumption. But with growing awareness of the oyster's keystone species status, more emphasis is being placed on restoring reefs for the sake of the oyster's ecological functions—though that emphasis is not yet widespread.

Most reef restoration endeavors so far show promise in creating new reefs, but the projects are expensive, time consuming, and hampered by a major shortage of a key component: old oyster shells. For decades, oyster harvesters, canneries, restaurant operators, and others have failed to return old oyster shells to rivers and creeks from which live oysters were taken. The empty shells have been—and still are—diverted to other purposes such as construction, road paving, and chicken feed supplements. Untold tons have ended up in landfills, where they serve no purpose at all. The result is a dearth of hard surfaces to which baby oysters can attach, grow into adults, and maintain reef health.

The lack of shells has left restoration program managers literally begging restaurants, oyster roast hosts, and others to recycle their empty shells. Radio and TV ads, billboards, newspaper notices, and other public appeals ask anyone—restaurants, wholesale seafood dealers, and party givers—with a few old oyster shells to donate them to the restoration cause.

↓ ↓ ↓

THE FIRST STEP in building a reef is to find a suitable site for the deployment of cultch, the hard material that provides a settling place for oyster larvae. A suitable spot would be one where salinity, temperature, water flow, and other conditions allow oysters to thrive. Gently sloping creek banks are preferred over steep ones, and the site must be accessible to the volunteers who haul the bags of oyster shells to the sites and monitor the reefs.[17] Cultch material might include cement-coated bamboo stakes and PVC pipe, oak limb bundles, or chunks of cement. The most desirable material by far, however, is recycled oyster shell, which new oysters zoom in on as attachment sites.

In Georgia, the cultch shells are hauled to one of several shell-recycling centers along the coast and allowed to dry in the sun for several months. The process removes any remaining tissue and possible pathogens—and foul odor—from the shells. Once the shells are cured and ready for planting at a new reef site, volunteers shovel them into biodegradable mesh bags, which create a stable, three-dimensional unit conducive to recruitment of young oysters.

Despite the public appeals for recycled shells, many reef restoration programs have difficulty finding as many as they need. South Carolina, which runs one of the nation's most vigorous reef restoration programs, has turned to importing at least half of its recycled shells from Gulf Coast states, which usually have a surplus.

In neighboring North Carolina, state legislators in 2006 passed a new law to encourage shell donations. The law gives taxpayers a state tax break of one dollar for each bushel of oyster shells provided to the state's restoration program. The measure also prohibits disposal of oyster shells in landfills and bans state agencies from using shells for paving, landscaping, or any other purpose other than reef restoration.

The new reefs themselves have a good success rate. South Carolina scientists found that crabs, mussels, and other creatures typical of natural reefs—in addition to oysters—had become abundant at several restored reefs within a couple of years. Spartina was growing behind many of the new reefs, meaning that the structures were preventing erosion and helping to stabilize the marsh.[18] Florida biologists reported that seven acres of "oyster mats" laid down in the Mosquito River Lagoon in the Canaveral National Seashore turned into healthy oyster reefs within a year; more than one hundred species were using the new structures.[19]

But whether oyster reef restoration will become the salvation of estuaries—and of the oyster itself—remains uncertain. A looming problem is the green porcelain crab, an invasive South American species that has showed up in massive numbers. The dime-size, filter-feeding crab threatens to crowd out native reef species and compete with oysters for food and space.

Some researchers believe that many reef restoration efforts eventually will fail because the problems that caused the oyster loss in the first place—siltation, disease, polluted water, overharvesting, and habitat destruction—are not being addressed.[20] "Oyster restoration cannot be successful without responsible development, farming and forestry practices, wastewater treatment and stormwater runoff controls," said Craig Hardy of North Carolina's Department of Marine Fisheries. "In short, we have to address all the factors that have contributed to the decline in order to be successful in restoration."[21]

A Town's Dilemma

Of the many varieties of the eastern oyster that grow in the dense reefs along the U.S. East and Gulf coasts, the May River oyster in South Carolina is a culinary superstar. Though not a large oyster, it is acclaimed for its exceptional sweetness, which speaks of the rich tidal waters in which it thrives. In his *Pat Conroy Cookbook: Recipes and Stories of My Life*, the author best known for his riveting novels writes about eating the prized oysters raw out of the May River on a frosty morning: "Of all the oyster bars I have frequented in my life, none came close to the sheer deliciousness of those tide-swollen oysters I consumed that long-ago morning, which tasted of seawater and a slight cucumber aftertaste."[22]

The river that sustains this praiseworthy mollusk bends and twists sharply for about fifteen miles, snaking through the historic town of Bluffton only a few miles from where BASF wanted to build its chemical plant. The tranquil stream continues through great swards of salt marsh and then into Calibogue Sound, the broad estuary that separates Hilton Head Island from the mainland.

On a chilly October morning, I stand on Bluffton's public dock and absorb the superb beauty of the May River at high tide. Just downstream, the river makes a dramatic, almost ninety-degree turn as it heads out to sea. Just upriver, a cluster of white shrimp trawlers lies moored to the dock of the Bluffton Oyster Company, the last oyster shucking-house left on the South Carolina coast. Across the river, an immense salt marsh stretches, just starting to turn its autumnal golden brown.

A few hours from now the tide will recede, exposing the great oyster reefs lining the creek and river banks, and the oyster pickers will return to the marsh. Wielding hammers and culling irons and dragging plastic pails, they will tread onto the razor-sharp beds to gather the morsels for which the May River is famous.

The daily shellfish harvesting in fall and winter is an inherent part of Bluffton's lifestyle and economy—a celebrated tradition long observed by generations of local families. The tradition, though, may be endangered. As the Nature Conservancy's 2009 report noted, the outlook for the eastern oyster has not been good of late. Unbridled development and the ensuing environmental calamities have jeopardized oyster-growing streams considered pristine only a few years ago. The May River is one of them.

I have come to the May, billed as one of the Southeast's cleanest tidal rivers, to see how its famous oysters are coping with the region's tremendous growth.

THE MAY IS not a true river in the sense of being fed by freshwater streams. Like many tidal rivers along this stretch of South Carolina's coast, the May is essentially a tidal slough of the ocean invading the land. Most of its fresh water flows directly off the land. The region's eight- to nine-foot tides push vast amounts of clean ocean water over its banks twice daily—a dramatic water exchange that prevents heavy rains from diminishing the river's salinity, which oyster lovers believe contributes to the May oysters' famed succulence.

In addition to its oysters and superb beauty, the May has been justly famous in South Carolina's Lowcountry for its cleanliness. The South Carolina Department of Health and Environmental Control designated the May an outstanding resource water for that reason. Such purity is rare these days for a waterway on the Southeast coast. It has made the May River a source of outstanding civic pride in Bluffton, which, as its name suggests, perches on a bluff overlooking the river. Besides oysters, other life abounds in the May. Crab pot floats dot its surface; hordes of shrimp churn the water; dolphins frolic in it.

"I remember how proud we all were when we found that the May River was among only a select few bodies of water on the entire East Coast that could boast an A-plus rating," wrote Collins Doughtie, outdoors writer for the *Bluffton Packet*. "We fought industry and won. We reveled whenever a story in some national publication used the May River as an example of the right way to develop in harmony with nature."[23]

But in February 2009 Blufftonians learned overnight that their precious waterway was not the super-clean stream they believed it to be. Weston Newton, who represented Bluffton on the Beaufort County Council, informed his fellow citizens that "there is a very high probability that a portion of the formerly pristine May River estuary will soon be closed to shellfish harvesting." Rising fecal coliform bacteria levels in the May's upper stretches had caused state regulators to consider "this unprecedented action."[24] While fecal coliform bacteria—which comes from the intestines of warm-blooded animals, including geese, dogs, and humans—does not necessarily cause illness itself, its presence indicates that microbes that do cause human illness may be in the water.

The unexpected announcement left Blufftonians shocked and angry. "To say I was stunned is an understatement," Doughtie said. "I was absolutely floored and frankly, mad as hell." Numerous other Blufftonians felt the same way. Dozens of them—oyster shuckers, oyster pickers, politicians, merchants, businesspeople, socialites, writers, teachers, artists, and charter boat captains—piled into cars and a bus and headed to Beaufort, the county seat, to plead with county officials to save the May River.

Three months later, however, the unthinkable happened. Regulators with the South Carolina Department of Health and Environmental Control announced that they indeed were closing shellfish harvesting in the May River's headwater creeks for at least a year because of bacterial contamination. The headwaters would be declared a "restricted area," meaning that the water quality did not meet state and federal standards and the oysters were unsafe to eat. Anyone who ate the tainted mollusks would risk stomachache or diarrhea or, even worse, hepatitis, typhoid, or some other nasty infection. The officials were basing their decision on three years of data showing rising fecal coliform levels in the headwater creeks. Furthermore, a four-mile stretch of the May River downstream from the headwaters and extending to the fringes of Bluffton's historic district would be designated "conditionally approved." Shellfishing would be prohibited when storms dumped more than 1.1 inches of rain in the area and would be allowed again only when water sampling indicated bacteria levels were again within safe limits for shellfish harvesting. The sampling process usually took two weeks.[25]

Portions of the May River were thus joining the dubious list of some one-third of South Carolina's shellfishing grounds saddled with a shellfish-harvesting restriction of some kind. Some attributed the May River's bacteria burden to gaggles of geese in the river's upper reaches; some said it was from dogs, cats, and horses; some blamed leaky septic tanks; some said it was from a faulty septic system at a campground.

No doubt all of those factors contributed to the problem. But it was Fred Holland, the scientist who had headed the much-heralded tidal creeks study in Charleston, who cut to the chase: "Bluffton's waterways are being impacted by the sprawling development of the last several years," he told the Bluffton Town Council on August 18, 2009, when he was invited to speak there. "The time has come to make the hard choices that will ultimately shape Bluffton's future. The pressing question for every resident, property owner, and elected official: how badly do we want to save this river and our way of life? If we want to maintain Bluffton's unique heritage and sense of place, it's time to bravely move the town in a new direction."

"The amount of hard stuff [roads, rooftops, and parking lots] in a watershed is critical and a good indicator of whether you can eat the shellfish or swim in the water," Holland said. "At ten percent impervious surface, you are going to be closing oyster beds . . . only a little bit more and it is not safe for swimming." The Coastal Conservation League calculated that the impervious coverage in the May River watershed in 2009 was already 11.9 percent, nearly 2 percent above the 10-percent threshold. The league further estimated that if existing development plans were carried out, the impervious coverage would reach 21 percent within the next decade or two—"and edible May River oysters will be a thing of the past."[26]

The gloomy messages shouldn't have surprised the local officials. Holland said he had presented his data to the Beaufort County Council on at least ten different occasions since 1995.

THE MAY RIVER'S 25,600-acre watershed encompasses one of the fastest-growing areas in the Southeast. Retirees, northern transplants, and first-time homeowners alike are drawn by the salubrious climate, outstanding beauty, recreational venues, and the resort amenities on nearby Hilton Head. The surrounding estuaries and rivers and tidal creeks offer some of the best fishing and boating on the East Coast. Golf courses designed by some of the biggest names in the sport seem to be as numerous as the fast-food franchises sprouting at nearly every highway intersection. So many gated communities have popped up in the area that gatehouse security guard is one of the top employment opportunities.

The phenomenal growth has meant profound changes for the once-drowsy town of Bluffton, first settled in the early 1800s. By 1830 the town, cooled by gentle summer breezes blowing off the river, had become a summer haven for wealthy white planters and their families trying to escape the heat, the drudgery of plantation life, and the malaria spread by mosquitoes in the swampy coastal areas. The May River was a route for riverboats bringing in goods and supplies from Savannah on a weekly basis. During the Civil War, Union forces pillaged and burned the town. Only seventeen structures survived; ten of them still stand today inside Bluffton's historic district.

After the war Bluffton became a major distribution center because of its prime river location. Ships ran regularly between Hilton Head and Savannah, importing farm supplies and exporting local crops. A thriving seafood

industry sprang up in the area. Vacationers discovered the recreational of-
ferings of the area, and tourism prospered. Then, in the 1950s, Charles Fraser built his resort on nearby Hilton Head and sparked an extraordinary
growth spurt. Along a fifteen-mile stretch of U.S. 278 starting at the bridge
at Hilton Head, grand, unspoiled vistas of salt marsh, maritime forest, and
estuary began giving way to mass development. The growth ultimately
engulfed Bluffton.

In the mid-1990s the town's official boundaries still encompassed only
about one square mile. But new subdivisions were springing up all around
the tiny town. The first big development was built in 1994—Del Webb's
Sun City, a gated housing development for retirees that eventually har-
bored forty-two hundred houses. At the time, it and nearly all of the new
developments were in unincorporated Beaufort County, outside Bluffton's
city limits. That was when Bluffton's officials decided they could no longer
afford to let the breakneck growth continue without making an effort to
control it. At stake was the health of the May River, and a healthy river
was the key to a healthy town.[27] The prospect of an increased tax base was
another incentive.

So Bluffton drew up plans to annex surrounding areas on both sides of
the May River. The town struck a deal with the Union Camp Corporation,
which wanted to develop two big tracts near the town—including a scenic
nineteen-thousand-acre forested parcel called Palmetto Bluff—into gated
communities with thousands of homes. Many people had hoped that Palmetto Bluff would be permanently protected in its natural state under a
Beaufort County land-use plan. But that was not to be. Local voters approved the annexation plan 151–91 in 1998, and Palmetto Bluff became
Bluffton's newest community. In one fell swoop, Bluffton had acquired
sixty-six hundred new residential units and six hundred acres of new commercial space.

The town kept adding on. By 2009 it covered thirty-four thousand
acres, about fifty-three square miles. Almost overnight it became South
Carolina's fifth-largest city in landmass. Its limits today stretch several
miles from the original old town. Its largest community, the exclusive Palmetto Bluff, is eight miles west. Bluffton's total population has increased
from 400 to about 13,500 residents in about fifteen years.[28] (Interestingly,
the town never annexed Del Webb's Sun City.)

Once the surrounding areas were within the city's fold, city leaders took steps to protect the May River—restricting private docks, limiting boat storage to dry storage only, and requiring that construction be set back from the river. Government agencies and civic groups applauded the city for its vision. The town, though, apparently did not do enough. Critics said its zoning rules allowed developers to put more houses on smaller lots—creating areas with a much higher density level than the county allowed. The higher density generated more storm runoff, which was not good for the May River.

↓ ↓ ↓

THE GROWTH AROUND Bluffton so far, however, may be only a smidgen of what is to come. Development plans for the area over the next thirty years include construction of about twenty thousand residences on lots ranging in size from half an acre to about three acres and more than eight hundred acres of commercial establishments and parks. That bit of information comes from a 2004 study of the May River conducted by state and federal researchers. Bluffton's elected officials commissioned the study to determine "the status of the May River before significant land use changes occur." It would "enable the town of Bluffton to continue monitoring the system in the hopes of limiting the impacts of major-development on the May River Estuary."[29]

In 2009, however, five years after the study was handed to the officials, the town was trying to figure out what went wrong. "If our report card is the river, we have obviously failed," Weston Newton said in May 2009. With the May River already sullied, priorities had to be reshuffled. The major aim became reversing the damage to the river and taking steps to prevent it from getting worse. Toward that end the town came up with the "May River Headwaters War Plan," which consisted of reducing pollution, sampling water quality in key areas, and identifying sources of contamination. Town and county funds helped finance the $3 million, three-year plan. The state also agreed to kick in $483,500, but only if the town refined its proposal to implement certain practices to reduce runoff pollution. The South Carolina Coastal Conservation League also offered its own "comprehensive plan" to help save the river. The nonprofit group suggested changing development patterns to keep impervious coverage in the May's watershed at or below 10 percent.[30]

Other stringent efforts, such as a county-wide storm-water control plan designed to keep runoff at predevelopment levels, were instigated. Whether the efforts ultimately will bring the ailing May River back to full health—and keep it that way—remains to be seen. It will be neither easy nor cheap.

In 2010, in fact, Bluffton got another jolt. The four-mile stretch of the May that had been "conditionally approved" for shellfish harvesting in 2009 had shown no improvement. Fecal coliform levels had worsened, and state regulators shut it down for the 2010 season. Some nine hundred acres of the May's most productive oyster grounds were now off-limits.[31]

The question now was: Will it get any worse?

As Fred Holland noted at a public meeting in Bluffton, "One of the problems with development is it's society's choice for what they want. It's my job as a scientist to tell them what the consequences are. There is no easy answer. People are coming, and they've got to have a place to live. You need to be smart about how you do it or you will lose ecological services. It will ultimately get down to whether you can swim in the water or eat the seafood."

Bluffton, of course, is only one example of the sprawl swallowing up sleepy little fishing villages and maritime forests and old tomato farms and pecan orchards all along the Southeast coast. Sad to say, before it's all over, untold numbers of once bountiful streams may be fit only for the hardiest marine creatures and pollution-tolerant worms.

Oysters, once an economic mainstay on the Southeast coast, may be relics of the past.

Oysters and the Economy

Humans have been slurping down oysters for thousands of years. Many cultures consider them an aphrodisiac. Ancient Greeks served oysters as an aperitif. Romans imported them from England, placed them in saltwater pools, and fattened them up by feeding them wine and pastries.

In the Late Archaic period, some four thousand years ago, oysters were a basic foodstuff for Native Americans. Great heaps of shells on Southeast coastal barrier islands testify to their voracious appetite for the mollusks. One of the most dramatic of these mounds is on Sapelo Island, where an oyster shell ring measures fifteen feet high and two hundred feet in diameter.

Early colonial settlers on the East Coast were astounded by the size of the oysters and the vast extent of the oyster beds. Oysters helped them survive harsh, bone-chilling winters when food was scarce. Slaves on coastal plantations relished them rolled in cornmeal and fried. Mounds of oyster shells accumulated around slave cabins on many a plantation. A major reason why early settlers beseeched the king and colonial authorities for ownership of salt marshes was to gain exclusive control over oyster harvesting.

The early residents passed on their love of oysters to their descendants. Steamboats, railroads, and express "oyster wagons" facilitated quick shipment of perishable oysters into the nation's landlocked interior, hundreds of miles from the sea. Abraham Lincoln was said to host oyster parties at his home in Illinois.

By 1880 millions of Americans, rich and poor, were consuming great quantities of oysters, which were cheaper than beef, chicken, or fish. Philadelphians reportedly slurped down an average of six a week, and twelve a week during oyster-harvesting season. New Yorkers were so enthusiastic over the "luscious bivalve" that they prepared it in almost every conceivable way: "Oysters picked, stewed, baked, roasted, fried, and scalloped; oysters made into soups, patties, and puddings; oysters with condiments and without condiments; oysters for breakfast, dinner, supper; oysters without stint or limit, fresh as the pure air, and almost as abundant, are daily offered to the palates of the Manhattanese, and appreciated with all the gratitude which such a bounty of nature ought to inspire."[32] Elsewhere in the country oysters and oyster stew were staples in saloons and other eateries. Nearly every town of any size had its oyster saloon, oyster parlor, oyster bar, or oyster lunchroom.

It was the canning industry, though, that made the oyster a staple of the American diet. Thanks to steam-powered equipment, oysters preserved in metal cans could be shipped around the country. America's first oyster-canning establishment opened in Baltimore around 1820 to can the famed oysters of Chesapeake Bay. By 1850 oyster canning was a thriving industry all around the bay. As more and more canneries opened, oyster harvests in the Chesapeake soared from seven hundred thousand bushels in 1839 to twenty million bushels in the mid-1880s.

The heavy harvesting was seriously depleting oyster populations in the Chesapeake and elsewhere in the Northeast. New York's oysters already had been wiped out or made unfit to eat by a combination of overfishing and pollution. Thus the industry began turning to the vast intertidal oyster beds of the Southeast to help meet the demand.[33]

Intertidal oysters, though, are generally difficult to shuck unless they are steamed—and thus are more suitable for canning than for eating on the half shell. Thus, oyster canneries began springing up all along the Southeast coast. There was a market, too, for the region's raw shucked oysters. A sizable number of shucking-houses also dotted the coast in the early 1900s. But it was the canned oyster with which the Southeast made its biggest mark in the oyster industry.[34]

In its heyday between 1900 and 1930, the Southeast's oyster-canning business was one of the country's largest. The region's output routinely topped ten million pounds of oysters per year, peaking in 1908 when the production was nearly twenty million pounds, and thousands of people, including children as young as seven or eight, toiled in the canneries.

In 1905 South Carolina ranked second in the nation in the number of oyster canneries and third in the value of its canned oysters. Neighboring Georgia caught up fast. By 1908 Georgia led the country in oyster production with eight million pounds.[35] In 1913 eighteen canneries and five wholesale raw oyster dealers were scattered along Georgia's hundred-mile-long coast.[36] South Carolina had fourteen canneries—five of them in Charleston and six in the Beaufort area. North Carolina had seven canneries and five shucking-houses. Most of Florida's oyster industry was on its Gulf coast, centered on Apalachicola. Tons of oyster shells from southeastern "oyster factories" went into paving U.S. Highway 17, which prior to the construction of I-95 was the main north–south thoroughfare along the Atlantic Coast.

The biggest oyster cannery operator in the Southeast was the Savannah-based L. P. Maggioni and Company, founded by Italian immigrants in the late 1890s. The company built more than a dozen oyster canneries on the coasts of Georgia, South Carolina, and northeast Florida. One of its largest operations was on Daufuskie Island—the island on which Pat Conroy based his early novel *The River Is Wide* and the later movie *Conrack*. In the decades before World War II, Daufuskie's canneries provided a livelihood for more than six hundred people, most of them Gullahs.[37] Entire settlements resembling mill towns replete with "company stores" sprang up around the canneries to house workers.

To run at top productivity and efficiency, a cannery needed several hundred bushels of oysters per day. During fall and winter, Gullah men went out in their flat-bottomed wooden bateaus and used short-handled "grabs" or long-handled tongs to harvest the shellfish. When their bateaus were full, the oyster pickers either rowed them directly to the canneries or transferred their harvest to the mother boat, which could deliver hundreds of bushels of oysters at a time to the canning plant.[38]

South Carolina Oyster Industry: A History, by Victor Burrell Jr., provides a glimpse of a typical oyster cannery's operations. When the oysters reached the factory, they were unloaded, washed, and then shoveled into ten-bushel "steam cars" that ran on rails into the "steam chest." Steam was injected into the chest under pressure, and the oysters were held there for ten to twelve minutes, which was usually long enough to open the shells. The cars were rolled out the other end of the steam chest, and women standing on each side of the car picked the oyster meat from the open shells and dropped it into metal containers hanging over the car's sides. "The cooked oyster meats were washed and placed in tin plated metal cans," the book continues. "After brine was added to the filled cans, the cans were sealed and loaded into a large metal basket, which was placed in a retort and heated under pressure to sterilize the contents. After cooling, the cans were labeled and placed in cases for shipment."[39]

The Southeast's oyster-canning industry prospered until the beginning of World War II, when a new national economy based on heavy industry emerged. Numerous opportunities for good-paying wages in effect robbed the oyster canneries of the cheap labor that once had kept the plants humming. Before the war, farm jobs and cannery work were about the only types of labor available to African Americans along the Southeast coast. After the war, thousands of cannery workers migrated to New York, Detroit, and Philadelphia to take factory jobs with fatter paychecks. Those who stayed in the South also had other higher-paying job options.

Without cheap labor the canneries could not afford to stay open. At the same time, pollution associated with industries and development became a looming threat. Government regulators banned shellfish harvesting in thousands of tainted acres of salt marsh, tidal creeks, and estuaries. In some cases pollution killed entire oyster beds. Daufuskie Island's thriving canning business met its end in the 1950s when industrial discharges into the Savannah River contaminated the salt marshes and estuaries—the cost of the tremendous growth that followed the war.[40]

By the mid-1960s nearly every oyster cannery on the southeastern seaboard had shut down. The last one—on Lady's Island in Beaufort County—pulled the plug in 1986. The golden age of the oyster-canning industry was history. Gone, too, were nearly all of the shucking-houses that specialized in raw oysters. Big, bleached-white heaps of discarded oyster shells, wind-and-tide-battered dock pilings, and empty sagging, rotting creek-side buildings are all that remain of them.

But one oyster business refused to die. The Bluffton Oyster Company, a still-humming shucking-house, is the only one left on the South Carolina coast and one of the last in the United States. It is housed in a white-painted concrete-block building that squats amid high mounds of old oyster shells on the east bank of the May River at the end of Wharf Street.

The Last Oyster House

Larry and Tina Toomer, both fifty-three, are the co-owners of the venerable establishment, which has occupied the four-acre site since well before World War II. Before the war, oyster shells discarded by the company were used to pave Bluffton's streets. The company still purveys the May River's largess—shrimp, blue crabs, clams, and, of course, oysters. In the cold winter months people come from all over to pick up bushels of oysters for backyard oyster roasts. "We'll be here as long as we have good water," vows Larry, whose family has been immersed in the oyster business for three generations. As such, he and Tina are perhaps the people with the most to lose as the May River continues to be sullied by breakneck development and more restrictions are imposed on shellfish harvesting. To get their take on the situation, I visit them at their oyster house on a chilly but sunny October day.

I find Larry, whose thick, wavy hair is prematurely gray, standing behind the counter chatting with customers who are buying oysters harvested that morning from the river. "Our oysters have the most unique, delicious taste of any oyster anywhere," Larry tells them. While he tends to business, I look around the rustic building.

Permeating the place is the alluring aroma of a fresh seafood shop, a blend of smells from sea and salt marsh, from blue crabs, shrimp, oysters, and clams. For seafood lovers, it's perfume. I peer into the damp, chilly oyster-shucking room, which has a sloping concrete floor and is kept cold

The Bluffton Oyster Company in Bluffton, South Carolina, one of the last
remaining oyster shucking-houses on the Southeast coast.

because of government regulations. Two elderly women—sisters named
Ernestine and Daisy—stand at a long concrete table, nimbly working on
piles of oysters brought in by oyster pickers earlier today. With ordinary
claw hammers they break the tough oyster shells; with small knives they
quickly pry out the meat. *Click, click, click,* go their hammers. Dressed in
long white aprons, white rubber boots, and gloves, they softly sing and
hum gospel songs as they work. They perform their tasks with efficiency
and dexterity honed by years of experience. Daisy has been shucking oysters for fifty years, Ernestine for more than thirty. If oyster shucking is an
art, these women are divas, perhaps among the last to possess that skill.
They plop the slippery morsels into stainless steel cans and toss the empty
shells onto large shell piles on the tables. They push the cans of oyster meat
and juice through a small window separating the shucking room from the
measuring-and-packing room, where a worker washes the contents and
weeds out small shells at a special skimming table. After draining the water,
he weighs the meat in eight-pound "dry packs," which contain nothing but
meat. The meat is refrigerated until it is delivered to individual customers,
restaurants, and grocery stores. In season, the company packs an average of
fifty gallons per day, eight hundred to one thousand oysters per gallon.

The oyster pickers, all men and most of them Gullahs, are independent contractors who work at their own speed. A dozen or so oyster pickers toil all through autumn, winter, and early spring—the official oyster-picking season—to supply Toomer with May River oysters. Most of the pickers are highly experienced; many have been oystering for much of their lives. They work the areas of the river and marsh where Toomer holds commercial leases for shellfish harvesting. Most of them have dealt with the Toomers for years, building up strong, solid trust. Some speak of Larry as if he were family. Gracing the public entrance to the Bluffton Oyster Company is a foyer with a sign denoting it "Tyrone's Porch." The Toomers built it as a memorial to Tyrone Smith, a young Gullah oysterman who drowned while collecting oysters for the company.

At low tide, often out in bone-wracking wind and cold, the pickers maneuver their highly stable Carolina skiffs to the edges of the dense intertidal oyster beds lining the river, creeks, and salt marsh. Few now use the old wooden bateaus that were the standard work vessels in the area only a few years ago.

Except for the boats, oyster-harvesting methods have changed little in more than a century. The pickers slog across the reefs, often bogging up to their shinbones in the thick, sucking mud. Bending over for hours on end, they use hammers, heavy cast-iron tongs, or small three-pronged rakes to break off singles, doubles, or compact clusters of oysters from the beds.

When the incoming tide submerges the oyster beds, the pickers turn their loaded skiffs toward the Bluffton Oyster Company's dock. With the help of a motorized chain hoist, they heave their mud-caked oyster bushels onto the dock. Dockworkers hose down the shellfish with fresh water to wash off the mud. The clean oysters are then shoveled into wheelbarrows and wheeled into the shucking room, where Daisy and Ernestine take charge of them.

THE SHELLFISH-HARVESTING restrictions imposed in the May River were a bitter pill for Larry and Tina to swallow. They had been worried about that possibility for some time in the face of Bluffton's booming growth. Larry's commercial leases include both the headwater creeks that were restricted from harvest in 2010 and the stretch of river that was shut

Workers at the Bluffton Oyster Company wash the mud from oysters harvested a few hours earlier from the May River in South Carolina.

down a year later. Larry says that restricting harvesting in the headwaters was not a major problem for his business; his oyster pickers rarely go there because the water is too shallow. But closing the other stretch of river was a major blow. "It definitely hurts our production area; there's no question about that," he says.

If anyone knows how tough the commercial seafood business can be, and how the odds—labor shortages, pollution, government regulations—seem stacked against you all of the time, it is Larry Toomer. "I can deal with regulations, and I'm not afraid of working hard," he says. A father of five grown or nearly grown children, he often puts in sixteen-hour days.

He also knows, though, how rewarding the business can be. He grew up on the banks of Skull Creek on Hilton Head Island in a family that made its living shellfishing. "I started going into the river harvesting oysters when I was eight, right in front of the house," he said. "I started running a crab boat by myself when I was twelve. When I was thirteen, I was pulling 125 to 150 traps a day by myself."

He went to school in Bluffton, crossing the two-lane swing bridge that in 1956 joined Hilton Head to the mainland. "I bought my first shrimp boat when I was twenty, scared to death—$1,460 a month payments," he says.

But he had the same drive and bustle as his grandfather, father, and uncles, nearly all of whom had their own oyster-shucking plants or oyster canneries. Simpson Toomer, who had labored for Savannah-based oyster tycoon Ralph Maggioni on Daufuskie Island in the early 1910s before opening his own competing oyster cannery, was his grandfather. Although Maggioni's three corporations controlled most of the oyster beds, Simpson succeeded. Three of Simpson's four sons carried on his oyster operation until rising labor costs and other factors drove them out of business.[41]

Larry's kinfolk taught him all aspects of oyster production—how to pick them from riverbanks, how to run the shucking-house, wholesaling, retailing, catering, and protecting the shellfish beds. Larry was making a living at shrimping with his eighty-eight-foot shrimp trawler in 1991 when the owners of the Bluffton Oyster Company hired him to manage the struggling business. The group of five owners had bought the operation from a group of Gullah oyster pickers and shuckers who had rescued it from closing in 1969 and named it the Bluffton Oyster Co-op. They did it to protect their jobs when the previous owner died and his children no longer wanted to run it. Larry began turning the sputtering business around. Eventually, he and Tina became the co-owners of the company. The Beaufort County Land Trust, a preservation group, bought the property on which the company sits for $2.3 million. Once the property was in the county's hands, Larry and Tina signed a long-term lease to keep the Bluffton Oyster Company at its historic location. It was a satisfactory arrangement. The trust said it wanted to preserve one of Bluffton's most historic places and maintain the oyster-shucking operation that is still one of the city's claims to fame. At the same time, saving the site also protected one of the most beautiful views of the May River along its entire length.

Now, visitors come there not only to buy fresh seafood but also to see what an authentic traditional "oyster factory"—like those once strung along the Southeast coast—looks like. To supply a steady product, Larry and Tina now operate two shrimp boats, a couple of crab boats, and several oyster boats. The Bluffton Oyster Company still holds state permit

S.C. 10, representing the tenth commercial oyster permit issued in South Carolina.

Business remains strong, but Larry and Tina worry it might not always be that way. "Our major, major concern is protecting our water quality," Larry says. "We make our living selling a local product—the oysters, the crabs, the shrimp. Without clean water, the oysters are the first to go."

CHAPTER TWELVE

Saving the Marsh

SEVERAL TIMES A WEEK, Randy Buck runs a boat with an ailing outboard motor up and down the Jerico River in coastal Georgia to help diagnose the engine's problems. "It's like an automobile mechanic taking a car out for a test drive," he says. Buck makes a living fixing outboard motors at his cluttered boatyard next to the Jerico in Liberty County.

During the test runs, he seldom fails to notice the expansive salt marsh stretching like a waving meadow on each side of the tidal river. "I know that marsh like the back of my hand," he says.

In early 2002 Randy began noticing something strange and a bit scary: Large patches of spartina along the river and tidal creeks were turning a sickly yellow. Each time he passed, they seemed to be sicker. Then the marsh started shriveling and dying.

"We started seeing the marsh balding just like a head going bald," Buck says. Instead of wind-tussled marsh grass turning green in spring and golden amber in fall, whole sections were withering and dying—becoming lifeless brown stubble poking out of the mud. "We had seen small bare spots in the marsh before, but these areas were fairly large." In fact, they looked like a barren moonscape of brown, mostly bare mud.

Worried about the dead marsh, Buck called the Georgia Department of Natural Resources at its coastal division's headquarters in Brunswick. Taking his call was Jan Mackinnon, a young DNR biologist. She immediately went to the Jerico to see for herself. Buck took her up and down the river in his boat for a close look.

"I was in shock," Mackinnon recalled when I later spoke to her. "I had never seen anything like it." The scene was just as Buck had described it—several miles of dead and receding marsh along creek banks as well as many acres of dying marsh along the Jerico. A large patch of dead marsh also was visible from I-95 near where a bridge crosses over the Jerico River midway along Georgia's coast. A marsh once covered with healthy marsh grass had become several dozen acres of barren mud. In some areas the bare mud was already eroding into the water. "It looked as though someone had come along and sprayed Roundup in the marsh," Mackinnon said.

With photos in hand, she returned to her office in Brunswick to show her colleagues. When they saw the pictures, it was their turn to be shocked. Word of the dead and dying marsh spread quickly along the Georgia coast. The Georgia DNR rallied biologists, ecologists, and marine scientists at universities, Sapelo Island, the Skidaway Institute of Oceanography, and other institutions to find out what was plaguing the marsh. They quickly learned that the marsh dieback was occurring all along the state's coast. All six coastal counties had open mudflats where spartina had once grown. Both spartina's aboveground aerial shoots and its tough belowground rhizomes were dying. Black needlerush in the high marsh zones was also affected. At several sites the mud was completely bare. At others, a few scraggly plants remained like wispy strands of hair stubbornly clinging to a bald head. In all, the mysterious malady had laid bare more than two thousand acres covering some forty sites—ranging in size from a few acres to dozens of acres—of once robust, wind-rippled marsh.

What was killing these hardy plants—species long adapted to the harsh environment of the salt marsh? Was the dieback spreading? Would entire square miles of healthy marsh end up as bare, ugly, eroding mudflats? Could it be the first signs of an ecological catastrophe such as the blight that a century ago had killed off the American chestnut? Such a specter was frightening to contemplate. Answers were needed immediately.

"A widespread die-off would have huge consequences for coastal resources," Mackinnon warned. Marine nursery habitats would be wiped out and food webs horribly broken. Entire populations of shrimp, crabs, and fish—and the birds and other animals that depend on them—would vanish. Spartina also is the biological glue that holds the marsh together. Without it, marsh soil would slough off into creeks and rivers, clogging them with tons of sediment and literally choking the life out of them. Without the marsh to protect them, mainland areas would be highly vulnerable to flooding. Coastal property values would plummet as spectacular marsh vistas began to look like bombed-out battlefields. Tourism would nosedive.

The researchers learned of similar die-offs in other states, including South Carolina, Florida, and Louisiana. More than one hundred thousand acres had died in Louisiana since May 2000. Scientists in those states were equally stumped as to the cause of the dieback. David Whitaker, a marine biologist for the state of South Carolina for more than twenty-six years, said it was the worst die-off he had ever seen in his state. "As I drove along the coast, it was clear that whatever the cause, the die-off was widespread," he said.

All manner of possible culprits were suggested to explain the Georgia die-off—a killer fungus, perhaps, or an unknown herbicide, a genetic change, a steep decline of blue crabs, or a sharp increase in marsh snails that ravaged the marsh grass. A strong possibility, researchers speculated, was the searing drought that had started in 1998 and was still gripping Georgia in 2002. No one at first, though, could connect a prolonged dry spell with a marsh die-off.

A cadre of researchers labored to get to the root of the marsh problem and devise strategies to stop the dieback. Even the usually glacial Georgia Assembly in Atlanta recognized the seriousness of the situation and formed a study committee to investigate it.

"We were like forensic scientists trying to go back and figure out what happened to the marsh," biologist Chandra Franklin of Savannah State University, one of the scientists who investigated the die-offs, told me. "We knew that spartina is not a delicate plant. If acres of it were dying, it had to be that something drastic was happening to it."

But what? Microbial studies of dead plant tissue turned up no lethal fungus or other unusual microorganisms. Pesticides and other pollutants were dismissed, primarily because the affected sites were widespread, and some were in remote areas. Also ruled out was hypersalinity in the soil. In one trial, healthy spartina plants propagated and grown in a greenhouse were planted in both healthy marsh soil and soil taken from die-off sites, and were watered regularly to mimic rainfall. The plants grew well in both soils. Curiously, however, still-living underground spartina rhizomes taken from the die-off areas would not resprout when watered, suggesting that whatever was causing the die-offs had damaged the plants beyond recovery.

Then Franklin made a significant finding: The dead marsh plants' xylem vessels, which transport water from roots to plant tissue, were clogged with an unknown yellowish-brown substance. The gunk, he surmised, was hindering water movement within the plants, resulting in their death. He and fellow researchers worked diligently to determine the composition of the mystery substance. When they learned what it was, they were able to come up with a reliable explanation for the marsh dieback. According to their hypothesis, the prolonged drought had induced pH changes in the marsh mud that resulted in "higher mobility" of metals, such as iron, that are commonly found in the mud. The marsh plants absorbed higher amounts of these metals than they could deal with, and the excess metals accumulated in the plants' xylem vessels and inhibited water flow.[1]

It was a logical explanation backed up by good evidence. The hypothesis was reinforced when regular rainfall patterns returned and the drought ended, and spartina began naturally rebounding in most of the hard-hit areas. "Those along the Jerico River seemed to turn green again," said Randy Buck. The pace of rebound, however, was not uniform—some areas resprouted much faster than others. Nevertheless, the growth brought a cautious sigh of relief from researchers and coastal residents worried about the wholesale disappearance of their beloved marshes. At least they had a plausible explanation for the marsh disappearance.

When another severe drought latched onto the Southeast in 2007, another round of marsh die-offs hit Georgia and South Carolina, though not necessarily in the same spots as in 2002. This time the researchers, though still apprehensive, were not caught off-guard. The new die-offs were more evidence that drought was the primary cause.

Still unknown, though, was exactly how drought triggered changes in the marsh soil that led to the widespread marsh loss. That uncertainty still haunts the scientists, who have continued their studies to tease out answers. Some believe that other mechanisms also might have contributed to the diebacks. "The bottom line is that our marshes are so important that we cannot take their functions for granted," Mackinnon said.

Marauding Snails

Brian Silliman, an assistant professor of zoology at the University of Florida, thought he had an answer early on to the marsh malady. Based on salt marsh studies he conducted on Sapelo and in Louisiana, Silliman sug-

Periwinkle snails climb spartina during high tide in a South Carolina salt marsh.

gested that at least some of the unprecedented die-offs were due to a combination of the drought and unrestrained gluttony in one of the marsh's most common creatures, the periwinkle snail.[2]

These half-inch-long snails ordinarily live in ecological accord with salt marshes, munching unceasingly on dead spartina tissue and decay fungi growing on the still-standing dead marsh grass. But when drought stresses salt marshes, Silliman hypothesized, it can trigger the formation of "traveling fronts of grazing snails" that literally mow down both dead and living spartina. Silliman said that in some areas the "runaway consumption"—which spread fungi to healthy stands of grass—caused nearly as much destruction as drought and, in some areas, slowed the postdrought recovery. "The snails can transform a healthy marsh to mudflats in a matter of months," Silliman said.[3]

He went on to make another bold assertion—that the snails actually regulate the growth of spartina through a biological concept known as "top-down control." Marine scientists had long believed that the forces regulating spartina growth are primarily "bottom-up," that is, strongly dependent on nutrient supplies and physical factors such as salinity and oxygen. Silliman, however, said his studies showed that the control was top-down: consumers—in this case the snails—regulate spartina production. If he proved right, marine ecologists might be forced to alter their concepts of basic salt marsh processes.

When Silliman and his colleagues described their findings in the December 16, 2005, issue of the prestigious journal *Science*, the hypotheses garnered widespread attention in newspapers, magazines, and other popular media. In scientific realms it triggered considerable controversy. Skeptics noted that periwinkle snails and salt marshes have coexisted for thousands of years and found it hard to fathom how the creatures could turn suddenly into agents of mass destruction. "Snails may have exacerbated the problem," marine ecologist Merryl Alber told me. "But I don't think they had a major role. There are a lot of pressures on Georgia's salt marshes. And the drought we had was a once-in-a-hundred-year event, so we really don't have anything to compare it to."

Perhaps the biggest blow to Silliman's hypothesis was other researchers' failure to find the legions of snails that Silliman had seen in Georgia's marshes. For that reason, the Georgia Department of Natural Resources rejected the periwinkle snails as a cause of the die-offs. In a report prepared in 2008 for the Georgia DNR, Alber said: "The majority of dieback areas (and the most extensively affected sites) were at inland locations with low snail densities. . . . It is possible that snails can expand or even initiate salt marsh dieback when they are in high enough densities, [but] we have never observed the densities reported by Silliman."[4]

The controversy, though, conferred star status—if only fleeting—on the lowly periwinkle snail and drew attention to its close relation with spartina. The periwinkle (*Littoraria irrorata*) is one of three common marine snail species of southeastern salt marshes, the others being the coffee-bean snail and the mud snail. Sporting a conical, spiral, pale gray shell, the periwinkle is found throughout the salt marsh but is usually most prevalent in the marsh's midsection, presumably because fewer predators such as blue crabs venture there.

The snail's mouth is equipped with a strange rasping structure called a radula—a muscle with rows of ultrasharp, hooked teeth with which it scrapes fungi off spartina and other surfaces. After it scrapes up fungi and dead spartina tissue, the snail folds the radula lengthwise in its mouth, mixes the fungi with mucus, and pulls the slimy glop into its stomach.

Like all gastropods, the periwinkle has a single, fleshy, muscular foot. Attached to the bottom of its lone limb is a horny protective shield called the operculum, which allows the periwinkle to seal itself tightly inside its shell to prevent drying out. At low tide, periwinkles spend much of their time low on spartina stalks or on the mud itself. But when the tide comes in, they instinctively ascend the stalks. They know when to become upwardly mobile because their innate biological clocks are timed to the tides' ups and downs. The snails begin their ascent even before the tidewater arrives, seeking safety from one of their major predators, the blue crab, which lurks in the water below and grabs unwary snails. The crabs have even been known to shake a spartina stalk to dislodge a clinging snail.

There is another big reason why periwinkles climb spartina. Steve Newell, a former University of Georgia marine mycologist who pioneered studies of snails and fungi in Sapelo's marshes, found that periwinkles also climb spartina to eat fungi that grow on the upper leaves. "It's probably the main reason they climb the plant," he told me.

"Farmers in the Shell"

Newell spent the bulk of his career in the muddy marshes of Sapelo pursuing a class of fungi known as ascomycetes, so named because they produce spores in specialized holding cells called "asci." Newell became a leading expert on the organisms and learned that several ascomycete species carry out most of the initial decay in dead spartina, and thus are central to detritus production. Indeed, several of the fungi species were able to break down and digest the toughest components of spartina tissue—cellulose and lignin, which make up more than 80 percent of the plant but are indigestible for most organisms. He also discovered that the fungi are the periwinkles' food of choice. Because of that, he concluded, the snails are "a prominent avenue by which the fungi flow into the marsh food web."[5]

Newell met Silliman, who was conducting his own studies on periwinkles in Sapelo's marshes, and the two hooked up for a new study. They would scrutinize periwinkles in the laboratory as well as in the marshes to clarify and verify the relationships between the snails and the fungi. "We wondered whether periwinkles could eat living spartina leaves if fungi were present in them," Newell noted. He and Silliman knew, of course, that the snails eat the fungi that decompose dead and dying spartina while it still stands in the salt marsh. But their field observations seemed to indicate that the periwinkles grazed on living spartina as well.

Then the researchers made a remarkable discovery: the periwinkles were not eating the live spartina at all—they actually were munching on fungi growing on the leaves. But even more astonishing, the snails appeared to be regulating the fungi's growth. As strange as it sounded, the gastropods were sowing, fertilizing, and nurturing their own food and then harvesting it; in essence, they were farming. "A farmer in the shell" is how one report later described it. The periwinkles were scraping the living spartina leaf tissue with their sawlike bands of teeth to prepare it for fungi cultivation. Then the snails deposited feces laden with fungal spores and nutrients onto the wounded blades. "The wounds reduce the plant's defensive capabilities, and the fungi take hold," Newell concluded. "The snails return to the wound and eat the fungus that has grown in it."[6]

It was the first evidence that a lowly creature other than insects engages in farming. When the study was published in the *Proceedings of the National Academy of Sciences* in December 2003, the idea of a snail engaging in a primitive form of agriculture fanned the imagination; articles on the research appeared in newspapers and magazines around the world.

Beyond revealing a fascinating biological system, Newell and Silliman's findings had another implication. They were evidence that a marine snail species could exert ecological control in an ecosystem, a living salt marsh, by initiating and encouraging fungal growth. The researchers noted that fungal infestation stunted spartina's growth. The snails appeared to be controlling spartina growth to a greater extent than the plant could do on its own.[7] That evidence and other findings would lead Silliman to propose his hypothesis of top-down control in the salt marsh. Several scientists who have examined the hypothesis, however, give it little credence.[8]

The Macrofauna of the Marsh

Periwinkle snails are not the only marsh animals that have a cozy relationship with spartina. The scarcity or overabundance of any of several other common salt marsh creatures—fiddler crabs, ribbed mussels, grass shrimp, mummichogs, and others (collectively known as "macrofauna")—may also trigger upheavals in marsh productivity. Over the millennia, these animals have coevolved with salt marshes and forged intricate mutual-benefit relationships. Spartina helps nurture and protect the diminutive animals, which flourish in mud, creek, tidal pool, and other marsh niches. As if to return the favor, the macrofauna help nurture spartina to a greater lushness. If the animals are to flourish in the marsh, spartina must flourish as well.

The complex links between the animals and marsh grass haven't always been appreciated. Like periwinkle snails, these lowly creatures, despite

Fiddler crabs in a South Carolina salt marsh.

their considerable numbers, have often been overlooked. "The role of plant-animal interactions in mediating marsh productivity and growth is virtually unexplored," lamented Mark Bertness of Brown University in a 1984 paper. That situation has slowly been turning around as scientists have come to realize that the macrofauna perform key tasks in keeping marshes intact and functioning as finely tuned ecosystems.[9]

"Animals that burrow in marsh sediment, deposit-feed on marsh soils, or filter-feed on marsh waters and deposit their wastes on the marsh surface, all influence sediments and may have an important impact on the primary production of marsh vegetation," Bertness explained. Take fiddler crabs, for instance. The three fiddler species found in southeastern salt marshes—the mud fiddler, or Atlantic marsh fiddler; the sand fiddler; and the red-jointed fiddler—are easily the most numerous macrofauna in the marsh. One acre of healthy spartina marsh may harbor nearly a million fiddlers. As such, the crabs, which congregate in huge "herds" on mud and sand, are an essential element of energy flow through the marsh. They may consume up to a third of the marsh's net output—detritus, algae, bacteria, fungi, and other matter. Of that amount, 10 percent may be assimilated into their carapace-covered bodies for growth. Most of the rest is expelled as pseudofeces and nitrogen-rich fecal pellets, which add nutrients to the soil and fertilize spartina. The tiny lumps of pseudofeces and cylindrical fecal pellets may literally blanket the marsh floor and persist through successive tidal cycles.[10]

Spartina's roots, in turn, give the soil an ideal consistency for the fiddlers' inch-wide, foot-and-a-half-deep burrows, where they mate, hide from predators, and escape from tide and temperature extremes. The maze of burrows is immeasurably valuable to the entire ecosystem. In digging and maintaining their tunnels, fiddlers haul up sediment to the surface, roll it into small balls, and pile it at the entrance to their holes. This process draws oxygen into the soil, enhancing the growth of spartina and microbes. Moreover, the constant excavating tills and processes nutrients and other chemicals in the mud, much as earthworms' activities do on land. The burrows allow the plants' roots to penetrate deeper into the mud and help stabilize the marsh. In addition, the burrowing reduces toxic sulfide accumulation in the mud, which otherwise stunts spartina growth. Studies by Bertness and others show that when fiddlers are excluded from experimental marsh plots, aboveground spartina growth markedly decreases.

The burrows, too, can harbor meiofauna, the marsh's tiniest burrowing animals, which include minute worms, hydroids, and shrimplike crustaceans. For every fiddler there may be hundreds or thousands of meiofaunal animals. The presence of fiddler crabs, then, indicates a much greater abundance of marsh life.

In some marshes fiddler burrowing can be so intense that it undermines and causes the collapse of creek banks. At first blush, this might seem destructive, but the collapse actually might increase the surface area for spartina to grow and facilitate tidal flow to other areas of the marsh.[11]

Finally, the fiddlers themselves are an important food source for the large predators that come to the marsh for sustenance—blue crabs, red drums, sheepsheads, rails, egrets, marsh hens, herons, and raccoons. (Fiddlers are the bait of choice for anglers fishing for sheepshead.) Hence, the meek, scurrying creatures are a critical link in the food web. More than 40 percent of fiddlers in a marsh may disappear each year into the guts of hungry predators.

ANOTHER HUMBLE CREATURE that succors spartina is the filter-feeding ribbed mussel, named for the ridges on its shell that resemble ribs. Like the oyster, it is a bivalve mollusk. In fact, the four-inch-long, brownish-yellow

mussel is second only to the oyster as the marsh's most efficient water fil-
terer. Ribbed mussels can be found poking out of the mud throughout
the marsh, wherever there is sufficient water for their gills to strain. They
especially favor the low marsh, where the dense, taller vegetation shades
them from intense sunlight; they can be packed quite densely there. On
the other hand, they are safer from predators in the high marsh, although
their growth rate is slower.

In pursuing its steady diet of phytoplankton and detritus, a single mussel may filter a gallon of tidal water per hour at high tide. So good are
mussels at filtering, Steve Newell says on his website, that "they can cause
opaque flood-tide water moving onto the marsh to become visibly clear
within several minutes."[12] Although mussels attach themselves via their
strong, hairlike byssal threads to oyster reefs, to each other, or to any other
hard object in the marsh, they most often adhere to spartina's roots and
rhizomes. The tight linkage helps the mussels thwart predators such as
raccoons. More important for the marsh, by latching steadfastly onto spartina's underground parts, mussels strengthen the marsh grass and thereby
help stabilize the sediment. In effect, the mussels engage in a kind of marsh
building. Also like fiddler crabs, mussels deposit mud and other indigestible wastes onto the surrounding sediment that builds up soil nitrogen and
stimulates spartina growth.

Eventually, the cast-off mud forms low clumps around clusters of mussels. When the mud gets too high, the mussels, unlike sessile oysters, can
detach themselves and then reattach elsewhere. Younger mussels can move
easily about a clump of spartina to find a suitable spot. Older mussels are
not so mobile—they are gradually buried until they find themselves sitting at the bottom of a hole kept open by their pumping.

Like oysters, old ribbed mussels create habitat for other species,
such as amphipods and barnacles, that find mussel shells good sites for
attachment.

THE HALF-INCH-LONG grass shrimp, another common member of the
marsh macrofauna, is nearly transparent, a trait that often makes it inconspicuous despite its great abundance. If the grass shrimp truly were to disappear from the marsh, however, the loss would be an ecological tragedy.

Without the tiny shrimp, vital food pathways would collapse, because it is a hub in energy and nutrient flow through the marsh.

Grass shrimp live mostly in tidal creeks near the bottom, but their numbers usually surpass those of all the other macrofauna in the streams. At high tide they take refuge amongst the spartina — or in an oyster reef, if one is handy — to hide from their numerous predators.

The grass shrimp grazes on plants, especially the one-celled algae coating spartina stems and other surfaces, and as such may be an important algae regulator. The shrimp also preys on meiofauna and other small organisms — nematodes, polychaete worms, and arthropods — of marsh and creek. And lest it go hungry, it also eats detritus. As a "detritivore" the grass shrimp benefits countless other marsh organisms. It accelerates spartina decomposition by plucking away at decaying stem and leaf fragments and breaking them into even smaller bits that become colonized by bacteria, fungi, diatoms, and other microbes. By this action the shrimp makes spartina-derived detritus more palatable and nutritious to a host of other creatures, many of which will become food for larger animals.[13]

The grass shrimp excretes copious wastes for such a little animal, including ammonia and phosphate. This is beneficial for the marsh, too: The nutrients aid the growth of spartina and microalgae, the marsh's "primary producers."

The grass shrimp itself is also a highly sought-after morsel. Red drums, spotted sea trout, striped bass, croakers, and mummichogs are among the higher-level consumers. As prey for the large fish, the shrimp fills another essential role — the transfer of energy from the primary producer level in the food web to higher consumer levels.

RIVALING THE GRASS shrimp both in abundance and as prey for other animals in tidal creeks is the little mummichog. It belongs to a family of tiny fish called killifish that includes several saltwater minnow species — or bull minnows, as people along the Southeast coast know them. Killifish also are called baitfish because they are commonly used for that purpose. Many a coastal angler maintains a minnow trap in a shallow creek to have a steady supply of baitfish.

Any minnow-like fish you see in a southeastern tidal creek is most likely a mummichog. Its abundance and ability to adapt to a wide range of conditions make it almost ubiquitous. Like other macrofauna it is a year-round resident of the streams.

The word *mummichog* comes from an Indian word meaning "going in crowds," a reference to the fish's tendency to swim in schools of several hundred or more. Breeding males are easily distinguished from females by their brilliant pigmentation and vertical stripes. Females are generally much paler than males. The females lay their eggs at night in April through August inside old oyster and mussel shells and on spartina leaves and stems—but only in places reached by the spring tides that occur every two weeks. The eggs, protected by a tough cover, hatch when they are moistened by the higher tides.

At high tide, mummichogs move into spartina marshes to feed. They usually forage on the bottom, even though their upward-tilted mouth is specialized for feeding at the surface—and for breathing air if oxygen levels get too low in the water. Occasionally, the receding tide traps several mummichogs in a marsh puddle, where they stay until the tide comes back in. If stranded on bare mud, they can flop their way for several yards to a drain or small creek.

As much as four inches long, the chunky little minnow is omnivorous; that is, it eats everything—detritus, small crustaceans, marine worms, plankton, small mollusks, and even other fish smaller than itself. It is also a scavenger—mummichogs may be seen congregating and nibbling on a dead fish or other carrion in the water. Particularly beneficial to humans is the mummichog's appetite for mosquito larvae. A single mummichog can eat more than two thousand mosquito larvae in a day. Not only does the little minnow help keep mosquitoes in check, it also may help prevent the spread of dangerous mosquito-borne diseases such as eastern equine encephalitis and West Nile virus.

The mummichog is one of the most remarkably tolerant species of the estuary and salt marsh—able to endure a gamut of fluctuating environmental conditions that would be fatal to other creatures. It can survive in water saltier than seawater or nearly as fresh as tap water. It can withstand temperature swings from forty-three degrees to ninety-five degrees Fahrenheit. If temperatures dip below freezing, it can burrow eight inches into the mud or move into deep channels. It can survive in water low in dissolved oxygen and high in pollutants. It usually is the only fish species still alive in severely contaminated urban creeks.[14]

The mummichog is a basic staple in coastal food webs — a standard menu item for blue crabs, larger fish, and seabirds and wading birds, especially herons and egrets, for which it may form the bulk of the diet. As nutrition for other creatures, the mummichog becomes a means of transferring productivity from the marsh to the estuary, an offshoot of Eugene Odum's outwelling hypothesis.[15]

THE ABUNDANT PRESENCE of all these crawling, burrowing, scurrying animals — periwinkle snails, fiddler crabs, ribbed mussels, grass shrimp, and mummichogs — tells an observer that all is well in a salt marsh. Without them, it would not be a true marsh. So when a marsh is ruined by pollution or wantonly destroyed by humans and these animals perish or are forced to leave, what usually remains is a sadly depleted, dysfunctional ecosystem. That's why a host of scientists and engineers who work to restore impaired salt marshes anxiously look for the return of these unsung creatures to a recovered wetland — they are a good sign that a once-desecrated marsh may be returning to its former productivity.

CHAPTER THIRTEEN

Rice Fields and Causeways

NATURE'S FORMIDABLE POWER—searing droughts and shrieking hurricanes—can wreak havoc on salt marshes, but the greatest danger stems from what humans do to them. When nature deals a harsh blow, marshes often bounce back on their own, as they did from the drought-inflicted diebacks. But when humans build a road across a marsh or dredge it or "reclaim" it to expand a city, the destruction usually is forever. Reviving the marsh may be like trying to resuscitate the dead. The Georgia legislature said as much in 1970 when it passed the landmark Coastal Marshlands Protection Act: "The coastal marshlands resource system is costly, if not impossible, to reconstruct or rehabilitate once adversely affected by man."[1]

Perhaps half of America's original 7.4 million acres of tidal marshes have now been destroyed, with most of the destruction taking place between 1950 and the mid-1970s. In the Northeast, where the pressures of industry and development began as early as the late nineteenth century, the destruction is almost complete. The loss hasn't been as severe in the Southeast, partly because of the huge extent of the marshes and less pressure from commercial and industrial development and pollution. Still, losses have been substantial.[2]

The excavation of straight-line drainage ditches through the marshes to control mosquitoes and the building of dikes to create watertight impoundments for rice growing account for most of the losses. About 14–16 percent of South Carolina's coastal marshes are still impoundments. In many instances the dikes enclose an entire marsh–tidal creek system in which water control structures called trunks regulate water levels, water exchange, and salinity. Before the Civil War, most of the impoundments

Former rice fields, now part of the Caw Caw Interpretive Center near Charleston, South Carolina, were once part of a fifty-five-hundred-acre rice plantation that flourished in the late 1700s and early 1800s.

were built to grow rice; afterward, they were rebuilt and maintained mostly to lure ducks and other waterfowl for hunters. Whatever their purpose, the impoundments negate the natural functions of a tidal marsh, although wildlife biologists praise them for their benefits to waterfowl.[3]

The vast majority of marsh destruction, however, has been due to the filling of marshes—so-called reclamation—to create more dry land for houses, industry, agriculture, roads, and urban expansion. When I was growing up near Charleston in the 1950s, an endless parade of clanking garbage trucks unceremoniously dumped the city's refuse onto a wide salt marsh along the Ashley River near the Citadel. The putrefying wastes, which attracted swirling flocks of gulls and other scavengers, were covered with thousands of tons of fill dirt, ultimately creating more dry land for the city's expansion. Charleston and other coastal cities were largely built that way.

Today, that practice would enrage coastal ecologists and other marsh protectors and incur a flurry of lawsuits, although such a project would probably never be permitted in the first place. A string of federal and state laws and regulations now supposedly reflect the general public's appreciation for the function and value of marshes. Willful salt marsh destruction has been greatly minimized over the past forty years as a result.

Nevertheless, supposedly legitimate reasons to destroy a marsh often arise—to build or widen a highway, construct a new airport runway, or lay a new rail line, for example. In such cases "mitigation" has become a powerful facilitator. To get a permit to dredge or fill in a marsh for what is deemed a necessary purpose and for which wetland loss cannot be avoided, builders now invoke mitigation. They promise to create new marsh, preserve an existing one elsewhere, or restore a comparable piece of degraded wetland to compensate for the loss.

Mitigation got its big boost in 1990 when the George H. W. Bush administration mandated "no net loss" of wetlands for the nation. The rule pertained to all wetlands, fresh water as well as salt water. In 1998, in what some deemed one-upmanship, the Clinton administration called for a "net gain" of one hundred thousand acres of wetlands per year beginning in 2005. Not to be outdone, President George W. Bush devised his own save-the-wetlands strategy: on Earth Day 2004 he pledged that his administration would protect another three million acres of wetlands in five years.

To facilitate wetlands mitigation and help ensure that the "no net loss" edict would be obeyed, developers, land managers, and bureaucrats came up with a clever scheme. They created a system of "mitigation banks" in which landowners create new wetlands or restore old ones—and then sell them as "credits" to developers who need to satisfy permit requirements. In effect, the credits serve as replacement wetlands for those being destroyed. It's having your cake and eating it too.

A whole new industry has sprung up around mitigation banking. An entrepreneur, for instance, acquires land that used to be a marsh or swamp or bog, and restores it. Government regulators calculate how many mitigation credits the land is worth, and the buyer can sell it to a developer. By simply paying the "banker," a developer can dodge the expense and headache of doing the restoration work himself.

Restoring a salt marsh, in fact, can be devilishly hard to do, depending on whether you are simply breaching a dike or rerouting entire roads and the courses of tidal creeks. Even more difficult is "building" a new marsh.

On the fast-growing Southeast coast, where strong marsh protection laws often stand like brick walls blocking new development, mitigation banks have become many a developer's salvation. When the U.S. Army Corps of Engineers in 2008 approved a plan to create Georgia's first salt marsh mitigation bank, developers and bureaucrats alike celebrated. To create the bank the Corps promised to return a ninety-acre swath of freshwater marsh to its original status as a salt marsh. The former salt marsh, adjacent to the Savannah River in the city of Savannah, had been badly damaged by the massive Islands Expressway project, which choked off saltwater flow into the wetland. Fresh water washing off from nearby developments replaced the seawater, and cattails replaced the once-lush spartina. To return the wetland to a salt marsh, the Corps will create a winding feeder creek system and install several state-of-the-art culverts under the roadway to bring salt water back in. Taxpayers will foot the bill. The Corps expects the wetland to be a fully functional salt marsh by 2012—and eligible as a "credit" for someone needing permission to destroy a marsh elsewhere.

The Corps is upbeat about the mitigation bank concept. "It is banks like this one that will provide valuable habitat for many different species of salt water fishes and crustaceans while supporting many birds such as the belted kingfisher and blue heron," Colonel Ed Kertis, commander of the Corps' Savannah district, said in 2009.[4]

Not everyone agrees with the colonel. Mitigation has raised a slew of nagging questions. Is it really acceptable to destroy a healthy marsh, even though the same number of acres will be created or restored at another site? Does it make ecological sense to restore a marsh so that one can be destroyed elsewhere? Which is more important, the existing marsh that will be destroyed or the one that will replace it? "Frankly, there seems little point in spending large sums restoring degraded salt marshes if developers and road builders and others can fill, drain, or otherwise ruin healthy salt marshes with little or no restriction," an exasperated government ecologist told me. "It's really a lose-lose situation for wetlands."

Which raises more hard questions: Can a restored marsh or one created from scratch ever perform the myriad functions of a natural, intact marsh? Successful wetland mitigation requires that the mitigation land be functional. But duplicating the biological richness and productivity of a natural salt marsh is awfully tricky. It's not as simple as just moving things around on the landscape. It requires, for instance, an understanding of how all marsh organisms, including microscopic ones, interact. "Restored wetlands must successfully replace lost acres and functions," said Rebecca Kihslinger, a science policy analyst for the Environmental Law Institute in Washington, D.C. She reviewed several studies of restoration projects and concluded in a 2008 report that "mitigation wetlands often do not replace the functions and types of wetlands destroyed."[5]

If You Build It, Will They Come?

So, how do you determine if salt marsh restoration is successful? If you restore it, will the oysters, snails, fiddler crabs, mummichogs, grass shrimp, ribbed mussels, and other keystone creatures return in their original numbers? Will spartina be as productive as it is in an undisturbed marsh? Will diatoms and other benthic algae once again cover the mud? Will the innumerable microbes that process minerals repopulate the restored marsh? Can blue crabs and shrimp and red drum find nourishment there?

Finding the answers to those questions requires tedious work and a pile of money. "In many . . . cases, there has been little, if any, follow-up to measure the success of a restoration project," said Judith Weis of Rutgers University in *Salt Marshes: A Natural and Unnatural History*. Defining success, then, is one of the most vexing aspects of a salt marsh restoration project. Another problem is that marsh restoration is still more a trial-and-error undertaking than a cookbook procedure—in Weis's words, "more of an art than science."[6]

So far, restoration has received mixed reviews. Some coastal ecologists at the University of Georgia adamantly maintain that once a marsh is drained, dredged, diked, or smothered, chances are slim that it will ever regain the vibrancy of a natural marsh, no matter how meticulous the restoration.[7] But the consensus among experts is that restoration can work if done carefully and scientifically. It can revive a dysfunctional marsh to equal in vitality and productivity a healthy, never-before-degraded marsh. The policy adopted by the Society of Wetlands Scientists states that the effort must be supported by "good science, design, construction and maintenance."[8]

A few studies on mitigation outcomes suggest that restored salt marshes can perform many of the same ecosystem functions as natural marshes. Scientists from the University of Rhode Island who compared the diets of mummichogs in a restored marsh and those in an unsullied marsh to help determine the success or failure of the restoration found that the fish were similar in weights, lengths, gut fullness, and diet composition whether they lived in the restored marsh or the still-intact marsh—suggesting that the rehabilitated marsh was functioning like the natural one. "Results from this study show that restored wetlands can respond quickly to tidal restoration," said Mary Jane James-Pirri, who headed the study, adding that "the community structure of salt marshes may become established within one year after restoration."[9]

Other scientists remain skeptical. Fred Holland, retired director of the Hollings Marine Laboratory in Charleston, told me that he has "yet to see a case where a restored wetland functions as well as a natural one that was relatively undisturbed. We may get close [to full restoration], but we are not there. Mainly restoration takes time and we rarely want to wait the many years required to recoup functionality."

From Rice Field to Marsh

The tidal marshes that were impounded to become rice fields were mostly brackish salt marshes, where salinities may range from about one to fourteen parts per thousand. They occur naturally in the upper ends of estuaries wherever rivers contribute a significant input of fresh water. The more fresh water coming down the river, the closer the brackish zone is to the coast. Brackish marshes, rich in nutrients, are important ecosystems in their own right because they are transitional habitats between freshwater marshes and highly saline marshes and harbor species from both. The red-jointed fiddler crab, more tolerant of fresh water than its two fellow fiddler species of southeastern marshes, inhabits brackish areas. The young of blue crabs, shrimp, and other marine species may utilize brackish marshes as nurseries. These areas also are essential nurseries for juvenile Atlantic sturgeon and for nearly all age classes of the endangered shortnose sturgeon, particularly from spring through fall.

For rice growing, earthen dikes were built deep in the marshes to block off the brackish water that pushed ahead of the ocean tides, and wooden floodgates and trunks hollowed from cypress logs functioned as culverts to flood or drain fresh water as needed. The fresh water usually was drawn from a holding pond dug for water storage.

The rice industry was prominent in the economies of Georgia and South Carolina in the century prior to the Civil War. After the war, labor shortages, competition from Gulf state growers, and the carving up of plantations by new owners helped bring about the decline of rice culture in the two states. The ultimate blow came from a string of severe hurricanes between 1893 and 1911 that breached dikes, destroyed crops, and poisoned the fields with salt water. The rice culture on the Southeast coast was history. But a considerable number of the old fields were rebuilt by new plantation owners and reborn as impoundments for waterfowl and fish for the benefit of sportsmen.

In 1997 the Georgia Department of Transportation needed a former four-hundred-acre rice paddy along the Ogeechee to offset the loss of tidal wetlands that would be destroyed when the agency widened a stretch of U.S. 17 between Savannah and the nearby town of Richmond Hill. The impoundment was about a mile downstream from the road-widening site. Soon after the DOT bought the tract, bellowing earth-moving machines chugged in and ripped open the earthen dikes. Immediately, the saltier Ogeechee River water, laden with nutrients and sediments, began running unimpeded into the impoundment, which still sported floating lily pads and other freshwater plants. Changes were fast and dramatic. Before the breaching, the impoundment's water levels fluctuated only slightly; very little water got in or out. After the breaching, the tidal range in the old rice field quickly shot up—by nearly seven feet over the course of a few weeks. Spartina seeds washed in and soon sprouted.[10]

A scientific team led by coastal geologist Clark Alexander of the Skidaway Institute of Oceanography in Savannah began keeping track of the project, following its progression from freshwater impoundment to brackish marsh. "Typically in these remediation projects you build it and then go away, and don't look at how successful it has become," Alexander told me. "This project is one of the first in the Southeast to follow an entire project to see if the salt marsh is coming back to its full function."

It may take years to draw a final conclusion, but one thing the researchers have concluded with certainty is that some things cannot be changed simply by breaching the dikes and flooding the impoundment with seawater. The rigid checkerboard configuration of the restored marsh's old rice-field drainage system remains, and it is markedly different from the twisting tidal creeks that are hallmarks of natural marshes. The unbending channels have less shoreline, and their edges are much steeper than those of natural creeks. Both characteristics make it tough for fish, crabs, shrimp, and other water creatures to move on and off the flooded marsh to forage and dodge predators. The unswervingly straight channels persist even when old impoundments have been abandoned for more than a century. They virtually never regress to a natural meandering flow without human help. "One thing this study tells us is that if you want those natural meandering types of patterns, you will have to build them yourself," Alexander said.

Expressways across the Marsh

The expansive salt marshes that indent the Atlantic shoreline once made travel by land a time-consuming ordeal. Travelers wanting to get from one place to another had to take long, circuitous routes to circumvent wide stretches of tidal marsh. Vehicle access to a sea island was nigh impossible without a way of getting across the marsh.

The answer was to build sturdy causeways of dirt, mud, and sand over the marshes. To construct a causeway, marsh mud was dredged and dumped alongside the roadbed, and sand and other materials were brought in to fill the dredged area. Today, hundreds of asphalt-covered causeways, some supporting coastal interstate highways such as I-95, stretch for miles across the vast marshes of the Atlantic shore. They have made coastal travel quick, easy, and efficient. They connect coastal communities and cities to the rest of the world. They open up once-remote maritime forests, quaint fishing villages, and sea islands to lucrative development.

But the salt marshes paid dearly for the roadbeds in their midst, which disrupted essential tidal flow patterns across entire square miles of marshland. Existing tidal creeks were routinely filled and cut off from oceanic tidal flow. As a result, highly productive low marsh became less-productive high marsh. Thousands of acres of *Spartina alterniflora* converted to black needlerush. In many areas, high marsh became dry land. Many swaths of marsh converted to open, stagnant water. Populations of once-abundant marsh plants and animals plummeted or disappeared altogether. Invasive weeds such as *Phragmites australis,* common reed grass, replaced spartina and changed the function and structure of the marshes. Some estuarine ecosystems were eliminated entirely because of causeway-induced changes.[11]

The damage caused by the Diamond Causeway between Savannah and Skidaway Island, built in the late 1960s, is typical. Running north–south across the expansive salt marsh and spanning the Moon and Skidaway rivers, the two-mile-long causeway links the gated golf communities, oceanography institute, and state park on Skidaway to the city. Building it caused considerable injury to the marsh—particularly to the long stretches of marsh surrounding the Isle of Hope, a high-ground peninsula between the Moon and Skidaway rivers and one of Savannah's most picturesque districts.

Built by the usual dredge-and-fill method, the Diamond Causeway dramatically altered tidal flows and caused wide swaths of marshland on the north side to convert from an undisturbed, functioning low marsh to a sparsely vegetated high marsh with many barren salt flats. Dredge material dumped on the marsh became dry land that sprouted trees. The changes jeopardized the historical integrity of one of Georgia's most noteworthy places, Wormsloe Plantation, a large estate on the Isle of Hope established in 1736 by Noble Jones, one of Georgia's colonial founders. Now an official Georgia historic site open to the public, Wormsloe's boundaries encompass much of the impaired marsh.[12]

The marsh suffered a similar fate south of the causeway, and an entire Gullah-Geechee community, Pin Point, was hurt as well. The causeway covered Butter Bean Beach, a spot where Pin Point residents swam and picnicked. Silt choked tidal creeks and smothered oyster beds, and shrimp and blue crabs became less plentiful. "It affected water flow in the creeks and river to Pin Point, and it changed the marsh," longtime dweller Arthur Sams told me. "The marsh now definitely is not the grand marsh we had here before the causeway."

ONLY IN RECENT years have scientists and engineers begun to understand the enormity of the damage causeway construction causes. David Whitaker of the South Carolina DNR reported that "the overall net impact of causeways in salt marshes has been a loss of primary and secondary productivity in the ecosystems. The cumulative effect of these marsh alterations has never been computed. But the total has, no doubt, been significant—resulting in reductions in *Spartina* and fishery resource production."[13]

Marsh experts in other state and federal agencies along the Atlantic Seaboard agree with Whitaker. Now, their aim is to restore scores of salt marshes and estuaries ruined by causeways, generally by digging up stretches of causeways and replacing them with bridges and culverts to bring back unimpeded tidal flow—the driving force of a marsh ecosystem. To restore the marsh impaired by the Diamond Causeway in Savannah, engineers have proposed installing more culverts under the roadway, removing the fill material dumped onto the marsh during construction, reconnecting old tidal channels and designing new ones, and replanting *Spartina alterniflora*. "In conducting this restoration, not only can we restore ecosystem function, but we can restore the landscape of this historically rich setting," vows an engineering study of the proposed restoration.[14]

Whitaker headed a project in South Carolina that planned to breach a portion of a half-mile causeway over a salt marsh and replace the gap with a bridge. Built in 1940, the paved two-lane causeway links Edisto Island, a sea island about thirty miles south of Charleston, to Edisto Beach, a barrier island that is part resort, part popular state park. The causeway split the once highly fertile three-hundred-acre salt marsh through which meandering Scott Creek ran. The tidal creek itself originally was a single productive estuarine system connected directly to the ocean by small inlets. The causeway blocked off the tidal flow into the creek and the entire marsh, creating two separate systems.[15]

Whitaker and his colleagues documented the damage in a 2007 report:

> The . . . causeway significantly reduced tidal current flow rates and volumes, and consequently resulted in deposition of fine sediments and filling in of Scott Creek and associated secondary creeks and tidal marsh. As the tidal creeks filled in, particularly those near the causeway, they began to lose biological function. Prior to the causeway's construction, salt marsh in the vicinity was likely comprised largely of healthy stands of smooth cordgrass (*Spartina alterniflora*). As the marsh filled and increased in elevation, there was a transition to less productive high-marsh plant communities and a total loss of marsh plants in some areas. This resulted in a net loss of pri-

mary productivity. Concurrent with this loss of marsh, shallow water tidal creeks were lost and along with them, optimal nursery habitat for fishes, crustaceans and piscivorous [fish-eating] wading birds.[16]

The project designers said they hoped a successful marsh restoration would "illustrate the potential for rehabilitating a marsh system that had been degraded because of causeway construction. A successful project could demonstrate to coastal managers and the public at large that . . . some of the consequences of coastal development can be successfully mitigated."

Ironically, however, a successful restoration at Scott Creek could mean the death of another marsh elsewhere. There was a chance that the restored marsh would be used as mitigation credits for new marsh-destroying highway projects.

CHAPTER FOURTEEN

Bridging the Marsh

O N A SUNNY DAY in early November I'm again on the Stono River near my old home on John's Island, South Carolina, cruising down the tranquil stream in a small johnboat on the rising tide. My destination is directly ahead—a small marsh hammock of about five acres surrounded by a salt marsh tinged a mellow brown. I ease the boat up to the marsh edge and kill the little Mercury engine. With a stout paddle, I push, prod, and pole through the spartina until the boat's aluminum bow scrapes against a sandy salt flat. From there it's only a short walk through a patch of glasswort to the island's edge.

In the near distance is the Limehouse Bridge, which speeds cars over the river and across the marsh to John's Island. Across the river from the island is a sprawling waterfront subdivision with the standard docks and boathouses jutting into the river. Looking across the marsh, I can see my old home place in the distance. Fiddler crabs scuttle out of the way as I walk. A boat-tailed grackle flaps overhead. A small flock of cedar waxwings lights among a thicket of the red cedars that cover the island. Surprisingly, I also spy some good-sized sycamore trees, a couple of palmettos, and a lone pecan tree near the center of the island.

Thousands of isolated marsh islands like this one dot the immense salt marshes stretching along the Southeast coast. Most are nameless and devoid of human habitation. They range in size from less than an acre to up to a thousand acres. The vast majority of them are in South Carolina and Georgia, popping up from the salt marshes that lie between barrier islands and the mainland or along estuaries and tidal rivers. South Carolina harbors some thirty-five hundred of these hammocks, most of them south of Charleston and nearly half of them less than an acre in size.[1] Georgia

Salt pan and marsh hammock in the marshes of Glynn near Brunswick, Georgia.

has about sixteen hundred.[2] Together, marsh hammocks in the two states cover an estimated forty thousand acres of high land surrounded by tidal marsh.

Until a couple of decades ago, marsh islands drew little attention from scientists and the general public. One of the scientist exceptions was Eugene Odum, who considered marsh hammocks an integral part of the coastal marsh ecosystem.[3] For the most part, however, marsh hammocks got little respect. They don't have the wide sandy beaches of barrier islands; they're mostly accessible only by boat—and then, in most cases, only at high tide. They were mostly the domain of hunters, fishermen, and Scout troops who built crude camps or pitched tents under the sheltering trees.

In the mid-1990s, however, hammocks came into vogue. With developers running out of room on the coast, especially on the highly developed shores of South Carolina and Florida, hammocks became much more appealing. Land once considered unbuildable took on a new appeal. Well-heeled people wanting commanding views of marsh and estuary were willing to pay a hefty price for a lot on a marsh island. In 2003 actors Ben Affleck and Jennifer Lopez reportedly paid about seven million dollars to purchase an eighty-three-acre estate on Hampton Island in Liberty County, Georgia. The hammock now is being developed as an exclusive "conservation-minded retreat"—replete with a unique illuminated waterway to accommodate night-flying seaplanes.[4]

Scientists and conservationists viewed the newfound interest in hammocks with apprehension. They knew that no development, no matter how cautiously it is done, is without some harm to the environment, especially when that environment is a salt marsh. In sounding an early alarm on hammock development, conservationists embraced the work of scientists such as Odum, who viewed hammocks as life rafts for marsh and migratory species because they offer unspoiled nesting and feeding grounds and provide a refuge on higher ground when seasonal and storm tides wash over the marsh. "Any development of these islands . . . it's not that you are messing up one of the hammocks, it's that you're going to affect the whole marsh," Odum warned.[5]

The high cost of providing access to marsh hammocks had always been a major deterrent to developing them. If the islands were to become attractive to cash-flush investors, there would have to be some way of driving automobiles over to the isolated patches of high ground. Causeways essentially were out. It had become nearly impossible to get a permit to build a causeway across a marsh because of the ecological damage they cause. The only alternative was a bridge; but bridges are expensive. As real estate prices continued to soar, however, the cost of building a bridge to develop a hammock suddenly seemed a good investment. A South Carolina DNR report warned in 2003 that "hammocks that have been protected by their remoteness and inaccessibility are now threatened with development, in part, because exceptionally high values of real estate make it cost-effective to construct bridges or to ferry building materials."[6]

Between 1973 (when permitting requirements first kicked in) and 2000, Georgia's Coastal Marshlands Protection Committee had granted only about twenty-five bridge permits, most for spans only a few hundred feet long to reach hammocks directly adjacent to the mainland. Most of those islands had already been developed or were approved for development. Altogether, in 2000, slightly more than a hundred privately owned islands had bridges or causeways—or both—linking them to the mainland. Many of the structures were built before Georgia's Coastal Marshlands Protection Act was passed in 1970. The situation was similar for South Carolina.[7]

Then the dam broke. Requests for permits to build bridges to dozens of other marsh hammocks began flooding the marsh protection officials of both states. For a variety of reasons, officials seemed inclined to grant most of the permits—which scared the dickens out of ecologists, conservationists, and other marsh lovers. The untold numbers of houses, paved streets, septic systems, marinas, and other development on mere slivers of land in the middle of salt marshes would ruin entire expanses of marsh. Of equal concern, conservationists feared that leapfrogging development from island to island, bound by a web of bridges and roadways, would spoil some of the grandest vistas left on the planet.

"Because we have some of the last marshes on the East Coast and hammocks are such an integral part of that ecosystem, the unfettered development of the hammocks could be the tipping point," cautioned Patty McIntosh, formerly the coastal leader for the Georgia Conservancy. "We could look back some day and say, 'That's where we lost our marshes.'"[8] She and others warned that the rush to hammock development had to be halted.

In Georgia, the battle line was drawn in early 2001 with the Emerald Pointe project. Atlanta developer Theodore Jockisch wanted to build three twenty-two-foot-wide bridges to link three marsh hammocks that he owned and planned to develop near Savannah. In granting the permit, the Marshlands Protection Committee had determined that the bridges by themselves would not substantially alter the marsh.[9]

In a highly publicized lawsuit opposing the permit, environmentalists contended that the bridges would do considerable harm to the marsh and would disrupt the entire marine ecosystem.[10] If the Emerald Pointe project got the green light, the environmentalist groups said, bridges and houses on hundreds of other marsh hammocks along Georgia's coast would be inevitable, and the damage incalculable. They cited scientific reports to back them up. "As [marsh] islands are developed," a report from the University of Georgia concluded, "the cumulative impacts caused by small-scale construction of home sites, roads, bridges and septic fields may alter the environment to such an extent that natural hydrologic and ecological processes are no longer possible."[11]

Support for the antidevelopment crowd came from an unexpected

Bridge to a marsh hammock in Camden County, Georgia.

corner. At the time the environmentalists were challenging the Emerald Pointe permit, Scenic America listed Georgia's hammocks among America's ten most endangered habitats. The influential Washington-based organization recognizes endangered places of beauty or distinctive community character "that face both a pending threat and a potential solution."[12] Its designation for Georgia garnered front-page headlines and drew national attention to the plight of marsh islands.

Meanwhile, South Carolina's environmentalists drew their own line in the sand with the Park Island development. At issue was a developer's request to build a 1,430-foot-long bridge over a picturesque tidal creek and marsh to an undeveloped thirty-acre hammock near Charleston. The developer wanted to clear the trees and build thirty-three upscale homes on the forest-covered hammock.[13]

Each case wound up in its respective state supreme court, but with decidedly different results. Georgia's environmentalists celebrated victory while the developer in South Carolina won and forced the state to redraw its hammock-protection rules.

But long before the two high courts rendered their crucial decisions, conservationists and other would-be hammock defenders realized that they faced a serious shortcoming: They knew very little about the ecology, hydrology, and geology of marsh hammocks, mostly because few scientists had ever paid attention to the spits of land. If they were to effectively preserve and protect marsh hammocks, they had to able to make a strong case for their ecological importance—as Eugene Odum and his supporters had done for salt marshes in 1970 when Georgia adopted the Coastal Marshlands Protection Act. As Odum noted at the time, the salt marsh information was grounded in fifteen years of studies on Sapelo Island.

An exhaustive survey of research journals and other data turned up very little scientific information about the hammocks. Confusion even reigned over who owned many of the islands—the state under its original concept of the king's domain, or private individuals and corporations through original king's grants. Moreover, the states had no official definition of a marsh hammock. There had been no need for one: developers and others had not previously shown any major interest in the hammocks. The islands' remoteness and inaccessibility had made them safe from development—or so nearly everyone had thought.

The permit granted to build the three bridges at Emerald Pointe shattered that notion. It was a jangling wakeup call—hundreds of marsh islands now might be in danger of developers' bulldozers and hammers. That message was not lost on the parent agency of the Georgia Marshlands Protection Committee, the state Department of Natural Resources. Agency officials acknowledged that with pressure rising to develop more hammocks—and with more lawsuits possibly in the offing—there had to be a better way of protecting the marsh islands.

To devise a protection plan the Georgia DNR in February 2001 created the fifteen-member Coastal Marsh Hammocks Advisory Council. Made up mostly of environmentalists and scientists, the council's assignment was difficult and controversial from the start. It was to come up with ways to "mitigate development" on marsh islands and provide more protection for them under the Coastal Marshlands Protection Act—without running afoul of private property rights. The council would push for new studies to understand the ecological significance of marsh hammocks. Until its final report was handed in and digested by the DNR, there would be a moratorium on issuing new bridge-to-hammock permits.[14]

Marsh hammocks came under the closest scientific scrutiny they had ever enjoyed. Researchers associated with governments, universities, and environmental groups carried out intensive surveys of the flora and fauna of Georgia's hammocks. Similar surveys would follow in South Carolina. The vigorous inspections confirmed and enhanced Eugene Odum's notion that marsh islands are essential habitats intimately tied in with the intricate functions of salt marshes.

"Through our extensive survey, we found these habitats to be much more biologically diverse than what we originally thought," biologist Billy McCord told me. McCord had helped lead studies of some 340 marsh hammocks in South Carolina. One of them was the little hammock I visited next to my old home place on John's Island.

MOST MARSH HAMMOCKS, especially the larger ones comprising hundreds of acres, were molded over the past several thousand years by the same natural forces—wind, tide, erosion, and rising sea levels—that shape and form barrier islands. Geologists believe that many of the larger hammocks, especially those within a mile of the ocean, derive from barrier islands because the hammocks have ancient dune ridges. Many of the smaller islands may be the remains of old barrier islands that have broken up over time—especially the swarms of hammocks ten acres or less in size that make up the bulk of the Southeast's marsh islands. One geological report labels the smaller hammocks as mostly "erosional remnants of pre-existing upland."[15]

Some hammocks, however, are the result of human activity, particularly those along the Intracoastal Waterway where the Army Corps of Engineers once dumped tons of muck into the marshes while dredging a shipping channel. Some of the islands were born in the era of sailing ships. Georgia coastal historian Buddy Sullivan wrote that "ballast islands sprang up along the tidal rivers as European ships unloaded ballast in exchange for cargoes of timber."[16]

The vegetation of marsh hammocks ranges from a few salt-twisted cedars, wax myrtles, and salt-tolerant shrubs on the smaller islands to jungle-like maritime forests of live oaks, magnolias, sweet gums, pines, and other trees on the larger hammocks. The larger islands also may harbor freshwater ponds, ancient dune ridges, and unexplored archaeological sites. Nearly every hammock has a narrow collar of salt-shrub thickets growing along the marsh edge.

"The key here is the absence of salt," McCord explained. "In the salt marsh and estuaries, salt defines the ecology. But as one moves inland and upward in elevation away from the marsh, as onto these marsh hammocks, there is rapid change in habitats because of diminishing impacts of salt." Every island, though, has its own character. Several may be archaeological treasure hoards containing pre-European Indian pottery, shell mounds, middens, and ceremonial rings. Over time, the accumulated shells may have increased the amount of calcium in the hammock soil, helping to support unusual plant communities, including sugar maples. In centuries past, plantation owners farmed several of the larger marsh islands because of the enriched soil. Some hammocks still show faint traces of rows and furrows from when planters grew sea-island cotton and other crops on them. Runaway slaves sometimes occupied smaller noncultivated hammocks. After the Civil War, sawmills rose on some of the hammocks with maritime forests and deep-water access.

But regardless of how they were formed or formerly used, marsh hammocks—small and large—are crucial components of salt marshes, especially as important safe havens for wildlife. A report by the Southern Environmental Law Center, one of the groups that conducted the hammock studies in Georgia, notes that "Georgia's marsh hammocks provide a secluded sanctuary for wildlife, away from the coastal mainland that has become increasingly congested with development, traffic, and noise." The center had a vital stake in the hammocks—its lawyers represented the three environmental groups that sued in the Emerald Pointe case. "Hammocks serve as roosting grounds for birds as they rest while feeding in the marsh," the report continues. "They also serve as nesting grounds for colonies of ibises, herons, wood storks (an endangered species) and other colonial nesters. Through their behavior, the birds reveal that the marshland—including the hammocks—is a single habitat."[17]

The biologists who explored South Carolina's hammocks found an array of plants and animals that far exceeded their expectations. "Really amazing," McCord said. His ramblings on dozens of hammocks at the behest of the South Carolina DNR made McCord an undisputed authority on marsh islands.

He and fellow researchers recorded more than 530 plant species, 90 invertebrate species (primarily butterflies and dragonflies), and 224 vertebrates, including 161 bird species, among which was the bald eagle. Sixty-two of the vertebrate species were listed as priority conservation species for South Carolina.[18]

Diamondback terrapins were found nesting in hammocks with sandy banks or dunes. Virtually every hammock they visited, even the smallest, had signs of deer—which are excellent swimmers that feed mainly at night on the mainland and the larger developed islands. McCord noted that the deer may take shelter on hammocks during the day to escape dogs and other bothers. Bobcats, minks, and river otters were using the marsh islands for food, shelter, and territory. Temporary depressions that flood with rainwater were providing essential freshwater habitat for a surprising number of frogs and salamanders. With enough fresh water, these populations may have sustained themselves for generations. Since amphibians cannot cross salt water, McCord surmised that any disturbance of these wetlands could doom the local population.[19]

At least sixty bird species, including several wading bird species in rookeries located in isolated marshes, were using the hammock islands as breeding and nesting grounds. On some hammocks, great egrets and snowy egrets were so numerous that at high tide during late summer and early fall, after the young had dispersed from their nests, the birds' plumage literally turned the islands' green canopies white. But perhaps the hammocks' most important role, researchers learned, was as vital resting and refueling stops for migrating neotropical songbirds such as tanagers, warblers, thrushes, buntings, and orioles—about seventy-five species in all. These birds spend the winter in Central and South America and on Caribbean islands and migrate to North America in the spring to breed and raise their young. In the fall they make the arduous trek back to the tropics. During their migrations the birds fly in huge waves at night, when the weather is cooler and the threat from hawks and other raptors is minimal. At the first hint of daylight they start looking for places with dense cover and abundant food in which to land and spend the day resting, refueling, and hiding from predators.[20]

McCord said that marsh hammocks "are of invaluable importance to these birds." The vegetation on hammocks often grows in nearly impenetrable thickets, and insects, fruits, and seeds often are abundant there. In addition, few of the hammocks have feral housecats, among the most devastating predators of songbirds.

Two hundred years ago, McCord noted, such habitat was widespread on barrier islands and the adjacent mainland. But mushrooming development obliterated much of the wild space along the coast. "People don't want their houses in the middle of dense thickets, nor are they typically tolerant of shrubs that may obstruct their view of the marsh or coastal waters," he said. The habitat loss helps explain an interesting discovery: birds occur in higher diversity and concentrations on hammocks in developed areas, such as Charleston, than on hammocks in less-built-up areas farther south. McCord hypothesized that the birds have been pushed over to the only unspoiled sanctuaries still left to them, the marsh hammocks.

For one bird in particular, marsh hammocks may mean salvation. Dazzling in its red, green, yellow, and blue plumage, the adult male painted bunting inspires awe among bird enthusiasts. Ornithologist, conservationist, and South Carolina native Alexander Sprunt Jr. gushed: "For flaming, jewel-like radiance, the nonpareil, as we know it in the South, literally fulfills the name: it is 'without an equal.'" But despite the sparrow-sized bird's brilliant plumage, scientists largely overlooked the species until about a decade ago, when they realized the bunting was disappearing from much of its range. The reasons for the decline remain unclear, but habitat loss likely tops the list. Painted buntings require coastal habitats such as maritime forests and maritime shrub thickets near salt marshes—the very places where people like to build houses. Now this bunting is high on the list of priority species most in need of conservation in both South Carolina and Georgia.

With their habitat being erased by development, painted buntings are seeking refuge wherever they can find it, McCord said. His observations showed that marsh hammocks with mixed habitats—including lots of grasses and shrubs—are very favorable sites for the painted bunting. That would help explain why he found painted buntings on twenty-two of the twenty-five hammock islands he surveyed during the 2004 breeding season. Apparently they can find desirable breeding habitat on most hammock islands of two or three acres or larger.[21]

"I can guarantee that there is an 80 percent probability that if you go to an undeveloped hammock with three acres of forest on it during May through August, there will be at least one breeding pair of painted buntings on it," McCord said.

✟ ✟ ✟

THE COASTAL MARSH Hammocks Advisory Council appointed by the Georgia DNR in 2001 delivered its official report a year later. "Development of marsh hammocks can destroy valuable wildlife habitat and significantly alter Georgia's famous coastal landscape," the council concluded. The members were very concerned that too many bridges built to access marsh hammocks will "create significant habitat loss for a number of important wildlife and plant species." It offered several recommendations: adopt strict guidelines for building bridges that connect hammocks to the mainland or to another hammock; prohibit development altogether on hammocks less than ten acres in size; don't permit bridges to hammocks just to afford access to other hammocks; on hammocks where development is allowed, mandate a vegetative buffer at least fifty feet wide between the marsh and any pavement or structure.[22]

Predictably, the panel's suggestions did not sit well with would-be developers, who besieged state officials and legislators with protests. The most consistent complaint was that restricting hammock development would violate private property rights. At first, the Georgia DNR said it would hold public hearings on the council's recommendations and then draw up proposed legislation to introduce into the General Assembly. But the development crowd's hue and cry gave the DNR cold feet. The agency then came up with another tried-and-true tactic—form another advisory group.

The second group appointed by the DNR was described as more broadly representative of "stakeholders" who would address unresolved issues and "refine" the first group's recommendations. Simply called the "stakeholders group," the panel consisted of twenty-four members. This time the DNR made sure the panel included developers, property owners, government regulators, realtors, marina owners, tourism operators, fishermen, and plain citizens in addition to environmentalists.

The stakeholders group's report came out in 2003, a year after the group was appointed. Like the first advisory council, the stakeholders group also offered recommendations for regulating bridge building. Among them were: don't allow developers to build a bridge or roadway to a hammock less than three acres in size and more than fifty feet away from the mainland or the closest barrier island; for hammocks up to fifteen acres, prohibit bridges that would affect more than one-tenth of an acre of marshland.

Again the developers clamored "foul play." The DNR was playing with a hot potato. In the end, the final say went to the sixteen-member Board of Natural Resources, the DNR's governing body—a group composed largely of people with connections to the development industry. Disregarding the recommendations of the two advisory groups, the board decided on a handful of limited administrative rules and guidelines that it said would enhance marsh protection. The DNR board also insisted that it could adopt the rules without involving the state legislature and without having to amend the state's marsh protection act. The only new rule of any significance passed by the board was the requirement of a fifty-foot vegetative buffer between the marsh and structures connected to a marina, such as maintenance sheds and parking lots. Even that, however, seemed in jeopardy. While the board was passing the new buffer rule, the DNR's staff was being told to come up with ways to help developers who owned narrow, hard-to-develop lots find a way around the new regulation.[23]

The board never discussed the two advisory groups' specific recommendations for regulating bridges and protecting small hammocks. Several environmentalists questioned whether the creation of the panels had been a sham: Did the state of Georgia ever have any intention of regulating marsh hammock development?

The state has never given a clear answer.

Meanwhile, in South Carolina . . .

South Carolina's turning point came in early 2005, when its state supreme court, ruling on the Park Island bridge-building case, wiped out the state's regulations for limiting access to marsh hammocks. It had started in 1998, when LandTec of Charleston asked the state for a permit to build a bridge to the pristine thirty-acre hammock on the Wando River near Charleston. South Carolina's Office of Ocean and Coastal Resource Management (OCRM) approved the permit in 1999, saying that it had no legal reason to deny it. The developer prepared to proceed with building thirty-three homes on the unspoiled hammock.[24]

At that point the South Carolina Coastal Conservation League stepped in and challenged the permit for roughly the same reasons that Georgia's environmentalists had protested the Emerald Pointe permit. South Carolinians feared that if the Park Island project proceeded, developers would find it far easier to erect bridges to—and subdivisions on—numerous other marsh islands. "If this bridge is allowed," warned Nancy Vinson, the league's program director, "there will be no stopping a bridge to every marsh hammock. This is going to open the floodgates to turning our beautiful marshes into access highways to crowded houses on every little island."

The league's challenge claimed that South Carolina's marsh protection law technically disallowed bridges to "small islands." A circuit court judge agreed and ruled in the environmentalists' favor. The developer appealed; the case wound up in South Carolina's supreme court.

In 2005 the court ruled that the developer should be allowed the permit because Park Island was not really a small island. Furthermore, the court ruled South Carolina's small-island regulations invalid because they did not define what a small island was. "Small-island regulation fails for vagueness," the justices wrote. In effect, the supreme court had in one fell swoop tossed out South Carolina's hammock protection rules.[25]

Distraught environmentalists and state regulators found themselves scrambling to come up with new hammock-protection rules that would pass muster in the state legislature.[26] The South Carolina Department of Health and Environmental Control hastily put together a panel of developers, realtors, environmentalists, regulators, and others to hammer out new guidelines for marsh island access. That not all hammocks could be protected was a foregone conclusion; sooner or later, several of them would have bridges. The question was: How many hammocks could be spared from bulldozers and chainsaws? The group's resulting proposals would prohibit bridges to all but about 250 of South Carolina's 3,500 marsh islands. Bridge length would be restricted. On islands where bridges would be allowed, stronger standards for docks, lighting, and buffers were recommended. Also proposed were requirements for the use of native vegetation in landscaping to prevent invasive plants from taking over the islands.

The proposed guidelines were dispatched to the state capital in

Columbia, where lawmakers—and lobbyists for development interests—got hold of them. The legislators didn't like everything they saw. They adopted most of the recommended standards for bridges to hammocks but removed the requirements for buffers, native vegetation, lighting, and other specifications on developed hammocks.

As one state regulator noted: "The good news was that the legislators restricted bridges only to a couple of hundred islands; the vast majority of them would not be subject to bridges. The bad news was that even if you can't build a bridge to a hammock, you can still do anything you want to it, such as cutting down all the trees or planting anything you want on it."[27]

As for Park Island, its website now boasts that it is one of the Charleston area's most exclusive gated communities—a "lush, pristine property with beautiful salt marsh"—and homes starting at one million dollars. The website also touts the island's teeming wildlife.

Billy McCord took exception to the latter: "Prior to the development of Park Island, there were very likely several nesting pairs of painted buntings there, but I doubt that there are any buntings breeding there now."

Docking the Marsh

Having a house with a glorious view of a salt marsh, tidal creek, or estuary is good—but it isn't enough. Most people also desire the other main amenity of a home by the water—a private dock on which they can cast a line, launch a boat, or watch the sun go down while sipping a cocktail.

You can hardly blame them. I probably spent half my boyhood on the wobbly little dock in back of my home on John's Island. How I loved that dock. My older brothers, my daddy, and I spent days on end on the rickety structure made of scrap lumber and old pilings. According to the tide, we crabbed, cast a net, fished for sheepshead and mullet, or dove into the water to cool off on a blistering summer day. The little boat that we kept tied up there rested on the black mud at low tide. From the dock I could smell the mud and listen to the snapping shrimp and watch the long-legged birds as they foraged along the creek. Sometimes I sat on the dock just daydreaming, wondering what I'd do when I grew up and which of the exotic places I read about in *National Geographic* I'd visit. I often came down to the dock at night and gazed at the moon and planets through my little telescope. The sky was so dark back then that I could see the Milky

Aerial shot of docks along a tidal creek in Chatham County, Georgia. Photo courtesy of the Georgia Department of Natural Resources.

Way stretched clear across the sky. In the daytime I could train my telescope on the fancy yachts heading down the Stono on their way to Florida for the social season. Once I saw a gorgeous woman in a skimpy bathing suit standing on a passing yacht's deck. She blew me a kiss, and I was in love.

So I can hardly blame someone for wanting a dock.

The problem is that there are just too many of them. Thousands and thousands of docks now crowd the salt marshes. In many areas, docks are so prolific that they have become surly blights robbing the marsh of its natural splendor. Along many once-picturesque tidal creeks, so many docks vie for space that the marsh is barely visible. Dock after dock after dock, so close together that you quickly lose count if you are trying to tally them.

"Dock authorizations are now the single most frequently sought permit from coastal managers," a NOAA report notes.[28] A significant segment of the public believes coastal homeowners have a "right" to a dock. A 2001 survey by the South Carolina DNR showed that 90 percent of coastal South Carolinians queried wanted a dock, 86 percent felt docks increased their property value, and 73 percent thought they should be allowed to build one.[29]

Most coastal sites with easy access to deep water were snapped up long ago. As less ideal sites are developed, docks must be made longer and longer just to reach a tiny creek with enough water to float a boat at high tide. Ecologists and a sizable portion of the public fear that the thousands of docks, many of the newer ones more than three football fields long, are doing irreparable damage to the marsh. "With each new request for a dock permit, public concerns about the cumulative environmental impacts of dock proliferation on the coastal environment have increased," a South Carolina DNR study notes.[30]

Common sense would dictate that scores of docks stretching out side by side are not good for a marsh. Several University of Georgia marine scientists conducted a study of dock impacts for the National Park Service and concluded that "docks and similar structures have the potential to contribute directly and indirectly to water quality problems in several ways, including leaching of preservatives from dock pilings and release of long-chain polyaromatic hydrocarbon pollutants from boat traffic (through combustion and fuel spills). Physical disturbances caused by construction or boat activity can also contribute to erosion and sedimentation. In addition, docks can reduce the density of marsh vegetation by shading, which affects overall marsh productivity."[31]

IN 2004 SCIENTISTS from the Hollings Marine Laboratory in Charleston studied thirty-two docks of all sizes along tidal creeks in the Charleston area and found that docks built over salt marshes shaded out nearly three-fourths of the sun-loving spartina beneath them. They pointed out that the amount of marsh lost to a single dock might seem insignificant compared with the some 350,000 acres of salt marsh spread along the entire South Carolina coast. But when the cumulative effect of thousands of docks is taken into account, the loss of spartina can be significant. In the decade prior to the completion of the South Carolina study, some seven thousand new coastal docks were approved in the state. The researchers calculated that some 150 acres of marsh were lost because of them. Since then, thousands more docks have been approved, and thousands more are

Marsh wrack in a South Carolina salt marsh.

expected to be built as growth continues to soar along South Carolina's coast. Without doubt, more marsh will be lost to docks and similar structures. The overall loss could amount to as much as 2 percent of the state's total marshland. In some highly developed locales it could be 5 percent or more—a loss that would seriously jeopardize the natural functions of the entire ecosystem.[32]

A 2004 study by researchers at Georgia's Skidaway Institute produced similar results. Researchers scrutinized scores of docks jutting out over the marsh around Wilmington Island, a highly developed Savannah neighborhood. The number of docks there had jumped by nearly 75 percent between 1970 and 2000—from 174 to 301. The researchers concluded that the cumulative dock-shading effect could have significant adverse impact on "the carbon budget of the marsh, which provides critical habitat for many commercially important species."[33]

Researchers now fear that the longer docks may cause another kind of marsh die-off. Evidence suggests that the so-called megadocks may block the natural movement of wrack—large, raftlike mats of decaying spartina.

Marsh wrack occurs naturally all along the southeastern shore. When spartina dies back in the fall, the stems and leaves eventually topple to the marsh floor—just as dead leaves fall from trees in autumn. Most of the decaying spartina will become detritus. But a sizable amount of intact leaves and stalks floats out with the tides and into tidal creeks, where it tends to bunch up and form wrack. Much of this decaying matter eventually makes its way into the estuary and then into the near ocean, where it adds carbon to coastal waters. Some, however, washes back up on barrier island beaches, where it plays a vital role in trapping windblown sand and laying the foundations for sand dunes.

The long docks may disrupt wrack's natural movements and cause inordinate amounts of it to accumulate around the structures, literally suffocating the healthy marsh. The Skidaway study suggests that wrack accumulation around long docks may be five times more damaging to the marsh than shading.[34]

GOVERNMENT REGULATORS SAY that the results of various dock studies back up what they have deduced from their field observations: the growing plethora of coastal docks is bad for the marsh. Nevertheless, legislators and policy-making boards, who set the rules by which the regulators must abide, have been reluctant to rein in dock building to any significant extent lest they be accused of curtailing private property rights—a paramount issue in the strongly conservative Southeast. Georgia officials say that in issuing permits to build structures in the marsh, the state's objective should be "balancing protection of the marsh with private property rights."

Some conservationists see permitting private recreational docks as tantamount to giving away public property. Most of the public, they note, probably doesn't realize that most private docks are built over public property—the salt marshes. "On the coast, we the people of Georgia own the marshes," insisted Chandra Brown of Georgia's Ogeechee Riverkeeper. "By giving them away, we're turning public property into private property."

Georgia's strong adherence to property rights is the main reason that private docks are exempt under the state's 1970 marsh protection law. The only structures over which the law has jurisdiction are so-called community docks (owned and used by several homeowners or groups) and marinas. Most of the permitting for private docks—the ones that cover the marshes by the thousands in Georgia—is delegated to the U.S. Army

Corps of Engineers, although the state reserves the right to sign off on longer docks, such as those extending 750 feet or more. Even then, the Georgia DNR promised in new rules in 2009 to "fast-track" review of most dock-building requests.[35]

Which led Deborah Sheppard, director of the Altamaha Riverkeeper, to tell me: "The whole system that allows dock building over our salt marshes in Georgia is badly flawed. Even those of us who keep watch daily on this activity find the regulatory process awfully confusing and maddening. So, we see no end to dock proliferation in Georgia."

CHAPTER FIFTEEN

The Ultimate Price

SOME CREATURES HAVE paid dearly—extinction—because of marsh destruction, pollution, and other coastal ills. Others may be headed that way if their environments do not improve. These are the stories of three of them.

For the dusky seaside sparrow, the end came with a lonely twitter. Always reclusive in the Florida salt marshes it once inhabited, the subspecies became extinct on June 16, 1987. The last individual, a twelve-year-old male named Orange Band, died in a cage at Disney World's zoological park. Its final resting place—the repository of the last of its kind—is a glass bottle in the Ornithology Collection at the Florida Museum of Natural History.[1]

Only the second bird to become extinct since the U.S. Endangered Species Act was passed in 1973, the dusky seaside's obituary reflected that it was the victim of America's space program, a superhighway, Florida development, years of bureaucratic indecision—and diking of its salt marsh habitat to control mosquitoes.

The dusky seaside sparrow might be an extreme case, but its end was the ultimate price that most salt marsh creatures pay when their habitat is destroyed or radically altered. "What killed the sparrows of Merritt Island? In a word, improvements," explains a January 2009 *National Geographic* article. "No one ate the dusky seaside sparrow or hunted it for sport. Its nests weren't vandalized, nor was it suddenly preyed upon by a newly introduced predator. But by spraying with DDT to control mosquitoes and building impoundments that allowed freshwater vegetation to take over the salt marshes, humans adjusted the ecosystem—hoping to improve their own lives—and discovered, too late, how finely attuned to its home in the cordgrass the dusky seaside sparrow really was."[2]

Have we learned anything from the dusky seaside sparrow's passing? Not very much, say ecologists. Habitat destruction, overfishing, and pollution continue to take heavy tolls on species of salt marsh and estuary— to the point where some of them could go the way of the dusky seaside sparrow.

First discovered in Florida's Brevard County in 1872, the nonmigratory dusky seaside sparrow apparently never strayed outside a ten-mile radius of the spartina marshes along the lagoons of Merritt Island and the upper Saint Johns River. The canary-sized bird spent most of its time on the marsh floor. Its black-and-white plumage made it the most distinctive subspecies of all the seaside sparrows that range the coastal salt marshes from New England to Mexico. Birdwatchers came to Merritt Island from far and wide to add it to their "life list."

The little bird's demise actually began in 1940 when DDT was sprayed extensively on the salt marshes to control mosquitoes. The pesticide entered the ecosystem's food web and caused the dusky seaside population to decline from two thousand breeding pairs to six hundred.

Then, in the late 1960s, NASA selected Merritt Island and the surrounding area as the site for the nation's spaceport, now called the Kennedy Space Center. To make the place habitable for the humans who would work there, however, something had to be done about the great swarms of vicious mosquitoes. To accomplish that, authorities built an extensive system of dikes and levees to flood the marshes and wipe out the mosquitoes, which bred in the mud. In the process the authorities also drowned the marshes that supported the largest colony of dusky seaside sparrows. The ground-feeding dusky, though used to periodic flooding by the tides, could not tolerate prolonged periods of inundation. With its nesting grounds devastated, its numbers plummeted further.

In 1963 the U.S. Fish and Wildlife Service, which assumed management of NASA's lands in Florida, established the 140,000-acre Merritt Island National Wildlife Refuge. The agency's biologists and refuge managers looked with great alarm on the downward spiral of the dusky seaside sparrow population and sought to reverse the decline. Doing so, though, would require curtailing the intensive mosquito control programs—which presented a major dilemma because America at the time was caught up in the ambitious "race for space." Anything that might interfere with this great flag-waving project met with sneering resistance.

By the time Americans landed on the moon in 1969, only thirty-five pairs of dusky seaside sparrows remained. Clearly the little bird was headed for annihilation unless a last-ditch effort was mounted to save it. The refuge's managers finally hammered out a joint management program with the local mosquito control district that permitted the removal of three dikes to restore a large portion of the marsh. But for the dusky seaside sparrow, it was too late; too few remained for the population to recover. In 1977 biologists sadly observed what was believed to be the last dusky in Merritt Island's marshes.

A second, smaller colony of the birds near Possum Bluff on the Saint Johns River also met its end at the hands of humans. The colony plunged into a steep decline in the early 1970s because of drainage projects, a succession of destructive wildfires, and the extension of the Beeline Expressway built to speed traffic from Florida's Space Coast to fast-growing Orlando. "One day there was a marsh," said Florida Audubon ornithologist Herbert Kale, who led a losing fight against the expressway, "and the next there was a highway."

By 1979 only six of the Possum Bluff colony's duskies remained. In a desperate attempt to save the subspecies, biologists captured five of the six birds. The quintet of duskies was intended to be the nucleus of a flock that would perpetuate the subspecies in captivity. There was just one problem. All five were males. The last female had been sighted in 1975. The five males were brought to Disney World's Discovery Island to live out their remaining days. Old age took its toll. By March 31, 1986, only Orange Band, named for the band on one of his legs, remained. A year later, he died. The dusky seaside sparrow was declared officially extinct in 1990.[3]

Two geneticists from the University of Georgia who later analyzed Orange Band's remains announced that the colonies' passing was not a huge loss because Orange Band's genetic makeup was nearly the same as that of other seaside sparrow subspecies. There was no valid scientific reason, they said, for classifying the dusky seaside as a distinct subspecies. In a paper published in a February 1989 issue of *Science*, they concluded that the costly effort to save and protect the bird under the 1973 Endangered Species Act was "well-intentioned but misdirected."[4]

Others disagreed. Kale, who had worked tirelessly to save the dusky, said its distinctive plumage, darker than that of its cousins, and its isolation from other seaside sparrows alone justified trying to protect it.

But whether the dusky seaside sparrow was a subspecies, a distinctive race, or some other taxonomic subcategory, one fact remains: It is gone forever, a victim of encroaching humans who knowingly destroyed its salt marsh habitat and acted too late to save it. The question now is: What might be next? The painted bunting? Other seaside sparrow subspecies?

As their names suggest, seaside sparrows are nearly always birds of coastal salt and brackish marshes. Ecologists say that the sparrows' strict preference for maritime wetlands makes them a good "indicator species" of the health of salt marshes. Where marshes are in good condition, the birds are abundant; where marshes are degraded, they are scarce or absent.

By that measure, many marshes are not doing well. Of the nine recognized subspecies of seaside sparrow, two are extinct: the dusky and the Smyrna, which lived along Florida's northeast coast from Amelia Island to New Smyrna. Currently on the endangered species list is the Cape Sable seaside sparrow, which once inhabited the Cape Sable area of southwestern Florida but is now confined to a portion of the Everglades.[5]

The subspecies found along the coasts of Georgia and South Carolina is the MacGillivray's seaside sparrow. Of this bird, *The Breeding Bird Atlas of Georgia* notes:

> Although there is extensive saltmarsh habitat on Georgia's coast . . . natural and human-generated threats to this habitat could have significant impacts on the Seaside Sparrow. Hurricanes or tropical storms could destroy or alter much of the saltmarsh, and rising sea levels could eliminate or degrade much of the marsh. Other threats include sedimentation from construction activities, agriculture, and logging; alteration of hydrology from groundwater withdrawal on the mainland and from construction of causeways to islands or marsh hammocks; pollution of food resources; and increases in the number of predators, such as Fish Crows and raccoons, as a result of increased human populations and activity near the coast. A more recent concern is the die-off of large patches of saltmarsh apparently caused by metal toxicity to cordgrass, which results from lower than normal pH brought on by drought conditions, and infestations by large numbers of periwinkle snails.[6]

The McGillivray's seaside sparrow has an especially strong affinity to the salt marsh. It forages for insects, spiders, tiny crabs, and seeds on the marsh floor, along banks of tidal creeks, and at the edges of wrack piles.

A diamondback terrapin retrieved from a salt marsh along the Edisto River in South Carolina.

Around April, females build their cup-shaped nests in the territories of their male partners. Woven from marsh grasses, the nests usually are located in areas with short to medium spartina, black needlerush, and occasionally glasswort. Sparrow pairs often nest in close proximity to one another and rarely show aggression. The two to five eggs laid in each nest are incubated for about two weeks; the babies fledge about ten days after hatching.[7]

In essence, the marsh provides the seaside sparrow with everything it needs to survive. Destroy the marsh, and you destroy the bird.

The Diamondback Terrapin

The colorful, beautifully patterned diamondback terrapin is the world's only turtle exclusively adapted to life in the salt marsh. The species occurs over an extraordinary geographic range of several thousand miles, from Maine to Texas along the Atlantic and Gulf coasts. Historically, it reached its greatest abundance in the vast salt marshes of the Southeast. Now it is vanishing.[8]

Despite its extensive range, the diamondback survives only in isolated pockets among fragmented habitats; thus its total area of occupancy and its numbers are dwindling.[9] A sure sign of spring on the coast used to be dozens of terrapins poking their thumb-size heads out of tidal creeks in March, when they were emerging from their winter slumber. Now, terrapins have vanished from many of those creeks.

The terrapin currently has no federal protection. The various coastal states where it occurs have their own conservation safeguards in place, but they vary from state to state and deal mainly with overfishing.

The terrapin's downslide can be blamed in part on the same adversities—habitat loss, marsh destruction, pollution, and overfishing—that plague so many other marine creatures. Much of its misfortune, though, is due to its lifestyle. Each year, automobiles crush untold numbers of female diamondback terrapins as they plod across barrier island causeways in search of suitable egg-laying spots. Thousands more, mostly males and juveniles, drown when they are accidentally ensnared in crab traps and can't escape.

All of this, together with the fact that terrapins mature slowly and don't reproduce until they are five to eight years old, makes survival especially doubtful for the species. Wildlife biologists fear that without strong conservation rules to protect the terrapin, it will slide toward the same fate as the dusky seaside sparrow. "The decline in terrapins may mean more than merely the loss of a spectacular turtle," said Whit Gibbons, a University of Georgia ecologist who has chronicled terrapin losses in the marshes of Georgia and the Carolinas since 1983. "Terrapins may be harbingers of a deeper-lying problem: that the coastal marshes themselves are being environmentally stressed beyond a sustainable limit, an issue that bears scrutiny. Whatever the cause, terrapins are in far fewer numbers in the creeks we have studied, and presumably the same holds for unstudied areas along much of the coast."[10]

About the size of a small dinner plate, the terrapin has many devoted admirers—researchers, teachers, students, coastal residents, and vacationers.[11] "The diamondback terrapin is my favorite wild animal," Gibbons declared. "Imagine a reptile with the dreamy eyes of a golden retriever and the unassuming face of a manatee. Add the docile temperament of a lamb and the beauty of a seashell."[12]

Its name comes from the diamond-shaped plates that form the pleasing pattern on the turtle's carapace. The underside, or plastron, is greenish yellow or gray, and the skin is whitish gray with black spots and squiggles. The diamondback's face appears frozen in a perpetual grin; its webbed feet and strong claws are excellent for digging. An adult female terrapin's shell can be as much as nine inches long, two to three times larger than a male's, which is only a little larger than a person's hand.[13]

Terrapins hibernate in creek bank mud during winter and mate from mid-May through June. Five to eighteen eggs are laid in May through early August in sand above the high-tide mark. The eggs hatch in sixty to one hundred days, and the one-inch hatchlings that survive predators and other misfortunes to reach adulthood will have a long life expectancy— thirty years or more.

Food-wise, terrapins eat fiddler crabs, baby blue crabs, and other small invertebrates—just about anything they can swallow, including carrion. They have a particularly hearty appetite for periwinkle snails.[14]

Terrapins exhibit extreme fidelity to their home creek, seldom straying more than one hundred yards. Even ferocious hurricanes can't drive them away. When Hurricane Hugo hit the South Carolina coast in 1989 with winds up to 140 miles per hour, diamondback terrapins weathered the violent storm with minimal loss, even though the fierce winds ravaged their streams.[15]

What did nearly wipe out the terrapin more than a century ago was human gluttony. Its savory meat has long been considered a delicacy. During America's history, terrapins, like oysters, fed the desperately poor as well as the well-to-do. Terrapins sustained slaves on tidewater plantations and poor families living in remote coastal communities. Continental Army soldiers trudging through coastal marshes snatched up terrapins to cook and eat. From the late 1800s until the Great Depression, terrapin soup was a popular menu item in highbrow East Coast restaurants where affluent diners slurped the sherry-laced brew from bowls made just for that purpose. Early in the twentieth century, a diamondback terrapin fishery on Georgia's coast provided meat for the soup. As demand increased for the animals, prices soared and the diamondback terrapin was hunted nearly to extinction. The species was saved only when the terrapin fad faded out in the 1920s. Its populations began to rebound, but the species didn't really fully recover until about 1970.

Now, diamondback terrapins are again in serious decline. Coastal development has spawned roads, traffic, and pollution. Development whittles away nesting habitat. Construction of homes, docks, and marinas silts up many tidal creeks and makes them nearly uninhabitable for terrapins. Highway death is a huge threat. Between May and July, when terrapins are most apt to nest, cars flatten scores of egg-laying females trying to cross marsh-spanning causeways and coastal highways in search of nesting sites. It is not unusual in nesting season to see the bloody carcasses of egg-laden females lying belly-up on causeways. "It's terribly heartbreaking to see the slaughter," Rene Heidt, who runs a tour boat service on the resort island of Tybee near Savannah, told me. "You feel so helpless." On many summer days she has found more than a dozen dead terrapins on the four-and-a-half-mile-long causeway that links Tybee to Savannah.

Heidt helped start a project to prevent terrapin deaths in the Savannah area. Participants in "Project Diamondback" pledge to patrol coastal roads to rescue terrapins and urge drivers to avoid hitting the animals if possible. The terrapin protectors also promise to pluck still-viable eggs from the dead and injured turtles and artificially incubate them. Hatchlings are released into the wild. The effort has met with limited success. Retrieving the turtles and their eggs is both labor-intensive and dangerous. Rescuers risk their own lives when they try to grab smashed terrapins along busy thoroughfares of speeding cars. Concerned about human life and limb, some local police discourage terrapin-retrieval efforts.

"The odds seem so stacked against the little animal," said Heidt as we boated along a tidal river near Tybee. As she spoke, we passed numerous brightly painted floats lining each side of the river. Each float marked a submerged crab trap of a commercial crabber. Heidt said she was willing to bet that some of the submerged traps had terrapins in them. Occasionally, we saw old traps half buried in the mud, obviously lost or abandoned by their former owners.

"Crab traps now are the biggest killers of diamondback terrapins," Heidt said. "They're taking a terrible toll."

FEW OF THE numerous tidal creeks and rivers twisting through the Southeast's great salt marshes are without the floats of crab traps, or pots, belonging to commercial crabbers. Blue crabs bring in millions of dollars in revenue for the region. In 2009 Georgia had 146 licensed commercial blue crabbers who set out some 17,850 crab traps—an average of 122 per crabber, according to the Georgia DNR. South Carolina had 280 licensed crabbers. The figures do not include the thousands of traps—no one has an exact number—that belong to "recreational crabbers," coastal residents and vacationers who drop one or two crab pots off a dock to catch a bushel or so for an occasional meal.

Blue crab traps on a Georgia dock, ready to be deployed in a tidal river. Many diamondback terrapins drown in such traps.

The boxlike, two-foot-by-two-foot traps used by both commercial and recreational crabbers usually are made of wire mesh or entirely out of metal. Each usually contains two to four narrow openings that allow crabs to enter but prevent their exit. The problem is that the traps—commercial and recreational—can be death traps for diamondback terrapins. Lured perhaps by the smell of rotting crab bait, the air-breathing reptiles crawl into the traps. Most are males and juveniles whose smaller size allows them to slip through the narrow slits. Also part of their undoing is that they are social creatures. They like to congregate. Once a terrapin is in a trap, it will attract others. A female small enough to enter the trap may give off sex pheromones that entice males. The result: they all die together. Once they're in, they can't get out. Terrapins can hold their breath for a few hours, but untold numbers drown before the crabber returns to check the trap.

It isn't uncommon to find dead terrapins in a crab pot, sometimes in overwhelming numbers. A South Carolina biologist discovered ninety-five dead terrapins in a single trap. A Georgia researcher in 2007 found ninety-four drowned turtles in a single trap in a tidal creek of the marshes of Glynn. The weight of so many dead animals made it almost impossible for one person to pull up the traps by hand.[16]

And those are just the ones researchers know about. No one knows exactly how many terrapins die in crab traps, because authorities check few traps. Doing so can be a legal issue. State laws make it a prosecutable offense for anyone other than licensed crabbers and their employees to pull up commercial crab traps or tamper with them in any way. Most crabbers, on the other hand, shy away from voluntarily reporting entrapped terrapins. But studies, surveys, and anecdotal observations indicate that the number of terrapins that die in crab traps every year is substantial, a loss great enough to imperil the species' survival.

Especially dangerous are "ghost traps," crab pots that have been lost or abandoned for one reason or another but still rest on shallow creek bottoms and elsewhere in the salt marsh and still lure terrapins to their deaths. "These 'ghost traps' can do endless harm to diamondback terrapins and other marsh wildlife," said Gibbons. In some coastal areas of North Carolina, researchers found as many as five ghost traps for every active trap.[17]

Most of the derelict traps probably are discards of weekend and vacationing crabbers, Gibbons said. In fact, he said, "commercial crab trappers may not be responsible for most terrapin deaths. They check their traps fairly often. Visiting tourists abandon thousands of recreational crab traps each year in all coastal states. They come down a couple of times a year, throw a trap off the end of a dock, and leave it in the water. They are unaware of the trouble they can cause. But they kill terrapins and a lot of other animals as well. We've also found blue crabs, small sharks—even dead otters—in these ghost traps. They're deadly to wildlife."[18] The vinyl coating used on many pots slows their breakdown and allows these traps to keep catching and killing animals for years after they're lost or abandoned. The human population explosion along the coast means thousands more recreational crabbers using—and perhaps abandoning—crab pots. The small, narrow creeks close to uplands that new coastal residents prefer are the same habitats favored by terrapins. The turtles, though, are so homebound they won't move to other creeks, even when crab pots pose a danger, Gibbons said. "Crab traps in tidal creeks can be devastating to terrapins."

AN INTENSE, ENERGETIC man whose drawl bespeaks his native Alabama, Gibbons began his research on diamondback terrapins on a day in 1983 when his young son Michael caught a terrapin in the marshes of Kiawah Island on South Carolina's coast. An exclusive resort barrier island top-heavy with championship golf courses and million-dollar mansions, Kiawah borders the Atlantic Ocean but is otherwise surrounded by sprawling tidal marshes interlaced with twisting tidal creeks.

For their investigations, Gibbons and his fellow researchers chose four creeks, all less than a mile long. One was aptly named Terrapin Creek. Twice a year the researchers trekked to Kiawah's marshes to drag the creeks with seine nets and trammel nets to capture the turtles. The snared animals were measured for sex, weight, and size and marked for individual identification before being released. More than three thousand terrapins have been captured and released since the study began, and fifteen hundred of them have been recaptured.

As the years went by, fewer and fewer terrapins showed up in the nets; fewer turtle heads poked out of the water in spring. The declines were dramatic. Where the researchers once saw twenty or so terrapin heads popping above a creek's surface, only one or two heads can be seen now. Oyster Creek, which yielded as many as two hundred turtles in 1990, now contains only a fraction of that number. And virtually all of the captured turtles are old.[19]

The most intensively sampled creek, Fiddler Creek, also showed a steady decline—from about 400 terrapins in 1989 to fewer than 100 in 2010. But it was Terrapin Creek that experienced the most marked declines. When the Kiawah study kicked off in 1983, the half-mile-long stream was home to an estimated 250–400 terrapins. Since 1990 the creek has produced only two captures—the same turtle both times.[20]

The research project continues—the longest continuous diamondback terrapin study in the nation. In effect, the results show that young turtles are not replacing those that die, which could lead to local extinction, explained Michael Dorcas, a herpetologist from Davidson College in North Carolina who now leads most of the Kiawah studies. He and Gibbons noted in a report that the most striking decreases have been in the creeks close to access points where people fish, deploy their crab traps, and launch boats. A large dock built in 1983 on the Kiawah River just across from the mouth of Terrapin Creek "increased human access to this creek and is likely what contributed to the drastic terrapin population decline," the researchers wrote.[21]

Interestingly, for many years, the only one of the four creeks that didn't show a detectable decline in terrapins was Sandy Creek, the stream most distant from any human access point. It offered hope that diamondback terrapins could survive quite well in streams away from intense development. Now, even that stream seems to be losing its terrapins, Dorcas told me.

The causes for Kiawah's terrapin declines include the litany of problems plaguing the animals up and down the coast—disruption of nesting habitats, road mortality, and increased sedimentation resulting in choked-up streams. High sedimentation since 1983 is evident in most creeks around Kiawah Island, Gibbons said. But the overriding cause of diamondback terrapin decline is crab trap mortality; the results of the ongoing Kiawah studies provide solid evidence for that. "A high proportion of young turtles and males become trapped in crab traps and drown, resulting in shifts towards larger and older individual, mostly females, within the population," Gibbons and fellow scientists concluded in a 2007 report.[22] Such drastic population shifts are not conducive to the species' survival, Gibbons said.

ALTERNATIVE CRAB TRAP designs have been proposed to reduce terrapin drowning. A simple, cheap, effective terrapin-protection method already exists: the so-called bycatch reduction device, or terrapin excluder, a two-inch-by-six-inch wire or plastic mechanism that easily attaches to existing crab traps. It lets crabs in but keeps terrapins out. Studies in New Jersey, Delaware, South Carolina, and elsewhere suggest that the devices reduce or even eliminate accidental catch of terrapins while having little effect on the crab intake. Some research has shown that the crab catch actually may increase if crab pots are fitted with the excluders.[23]

Fishery biologists in Georgia and the Carolinas have urged crabbers, commercial and recreational, to voluntarily retrofit their crap pots with excluder devices. Such requests have met with little response, even when the states and local jurisdictions have offered to install the devices for free. "The main reason, I believe, is that people generally are reluctant to change age-old ways," Paul Woolf, a member of Tybee Island's City Council, told me. Most people, he added, probably are still unaware of the terrapin's struggle to survive. In 2009 Woolf persuaded the Georgia DNR to provide two thousand excluder devices for distribution free to crabbers who participated in a pilot project to demonstrate the gizmo's effectiveness. The project was aimed primarily at recreational crabbers, but commercial crabbers were welcome as well. "We got few takers," said Woolf, who acknowledged that the general lack of interest puzzled him. "I still have a box of the devices sitting at my house."

Whit Gibbons, despite witnessing the diamondback terrapin's alarming decline over the past twenty-seven years, remains optimistic. "I know that attitudes can change when people become aware of the terrapins' plight," he said. "And there are a lot of good efforts out there to let them know what's happening and how they can help."

Nevertheless, the conclusion of the report he and his colleagues wrote about their Kiawah Island research is a stark warning: "Unless prudent measures are implemented throughout the range of the terrapin, continued population declines are likely. The comeback of the species in the first half of the 20th century has given us a second chance to preserve an important macro-consumer of the salt marsh ecosystem and a culturally significant reptile. We may not get a third chance."[24]

The Red Drum

That same grim assessment could be made for the Southeast coast's most sought-after fish, the red drum. Known for its distinctive reddish-amber color and the black spot on its tail, the red drum (also call redfish, spot-tailed bass, and channel bass) became so popular a few decades ago that the fishing and marine industry came out with specialized boats, gear, and tackle just for red drum anglers. Today, red drum tournaments vie with bass tournaments in popularity.

The high esteem for the fish stems in part from its reputation as a fierce fighter. It can be caught year-round and will take most kinds of bait, both natural and artificial. It can be hooked from a boat in an estuary, caught in the surf at the beach, or stalked in a flooded salt marsh in less than a foot of water at high tide. A bottom-feeder, the red drum is one of few predatory fish that will boldly venture into a marsh on a spring tide in search of its dinner. It is especially fond of fiddler crabs. Amongst the dense spartina stalks the red drum will position itself over a fiddler's hole—standing on its head with its entire tail waving out of the water—and literally try to suck the hapless creature from its home. Anglers call this antic "tailing."

Red drum being
tagged for a study in
the Edisto River in
South Carolina.

If its prey tries to escape, the fish will create quite a commotion—splashing, wallowing, twisting, and huffing its entire back out of the water as it tries to latch onto its meal. A fishing guide once told me that stalking the shallow grass flats for red drum is the ultimate challenge for wade anglers, although mountain trout anglers would probably argue that point.

The red drum is also one of the tastiest fish in the Southeast, which nearly led to its demise a few decades ago. When New Orleans master chef Paul Prudhomme started serving blackened redfish in the 1980s, it sparked a nationwide fad; restaurants couldn't get enough of the fish. Red drum landings reflected the huge demand. In 1984 commercial red drum harvests totaled 4.8 million pounds. In 1986, when blackened redfish became a regular menu item across the country, the harvest jumped to 14.5 million pounds.[25] The fishery could not bear such pressure, and redfish numbers went into a tailspin. By 1988 only about 528,000 pounds of red drum were harvested. Demand was still high, but there were not enough fish in coastal waters to meet it. Complicating the situation was the fact that redfish do not mature and spawn until they are four years of age, which increases the risk of overfishing and harvesting before they can reproduce.

Fishery biologists feared that the red drum population was headed for a collapse. The federal government and Atlantic and Gulf coast states in 1988 clamped down on red drum fishing, which until then had been largely unregulated. The U.S. government slapped a moratorium on both recreational and commercial red drum fishing in the Exclusive Economic

Zone, which extends three to two hundred miles off the U.S. coastline (beginning nine miles off the shores of Florida and Texas). Individual states implemented bag and size limits on red drum caught in state waters, which extend up to three miles offshore. Florida, where red drum fishing was particularly heavy, went from no regulation on commercial red drum harvesting to a complete ban, and set a daily bag limit on recreational fishing of one per person, with a size limit of sixteen to twenty-two inches. In addition, Florida shut down its red drum fishery for three months of the year to give the fish population time to recuperate.

The stringent state and federal restrictions reined in the downward spiral, and red drum populations slowly began to recover. The comeback, though, was not nearly as fast as many had hoped. In October 2007 the concern went all the way to the White House. President George W. Bush signed an executive order officially labeling the red drum (along with the striped bass) a game fish in the Exclusive Economic Zone, in effect banning commercial harvest of the species in waters controlled by the federal government.[26]

In signing the mandate Bush said of the red drum: "What happened to this particular fish was that it became popular to eat. The restaurants found it to be good food and it became a popular dish and they got overfished. Unfortunately, the red drum species is still trying to recover. That's why I'm going to take this additional step, because the recovery is not complete. In the waters from North Carolina to the tip of Florida, the numbers are still too low."[27]

Bush also urged individual coastal states that had not already done so to confer game fish status on red drums in state waters. "I hope the state officials take a serious look at game fish designation; it is an effective tool to protect endangered or dwindling species," Bush said. "It prohibits commercial sales, which removes the incentive to catch the fish for anything other than recreational purposes."[28]

Some state fisheries officials saw Bush's order as political grandstanding, noting that the federal government's 1988 moratorium already prohibited red drum fishing in federal waters. Others, though, praised the president for reaffirming the importance of the red drum fishery, which annually generates millions of dollars in revenue for coastal communities. If the moratorium were lifted in the future, they said, the red drum's game fish status would shield it from commercial harvesting.

As of 2010, neither the states nor the federal government seemed in-clined to loosen their red drum fishing restrictions. Although recreational anglers insisted there were plenty of red drums to be caught in the South-east's coastal waters, it was difficult to determine from the various studies, surveys, and reports compiled by the states whether the fish was recover-ing, holding its own, or declining. The Atlantic States Marine Fisheries Commission, formed in 1942 by the fifteen East Coast states to coordinate the conservation and management of their fisheries, still classified the red drum as overfished. Commission officials said they didn't have enough data to determine if the classification needed upgrading.

In certain locales, however, depending on whom you talked to, the out-look for the red drum was rosy, fair to middling, or bleak. "In Georgia, our red drum population is healthy," a fisheries expert with the state DNR told me. On the other hand, some of his colleagues said an uptick in fishing pressure on red drums was cause for concern in the state. The Georgia legislature in 2009 rejected a bill to make the red drum a game fish, even though many anglers had signed petitions urging the bill's passage. Several lawmakers argued that game fish status would prohibit anglers from selling their red drum catches and making a few extra bucks. Georgia's daily bag limit of five red drums, fourteen to twenty-three inches long, per person is the most liberal of all states on the Atlantic Coast. Georgia's anglers also may sell their red drum catch.

In neighboring South Carolina, where the red drum has been a game fish since 1985, the daily red drum bag limit in 2010 was three fish, fifteen to twenty-three inches long, per person. North Carolina's red drum limit was one fish, eighteen to twenty-seven inches long, per person daily. The state allowed limited commercial red drum fishing, which angered many recreational fishermen who must abide by the more stringent bag limit. North Carolina fishery officials said their red drum management efforts have ended overfishing "and recovery is well under way."

Fishing pressure on the red drum, however, is not expected to let up in most of the Southeast. If anything, it is likely to grow. A large proportion of the tens of thousands of people moving to the Southeast coast are lured there by the prospect of good fishing. Recent surveys in Georgia show that red drum fishing is on the rise. In addition, technological advances in boats and fishing gear have greatly improved the ability of anglers to pursue red drum and other saltwater fish.

Even if overfishing should become less of a problem, the fish will continue to face other threats that challenge its survival. Coastal development will bring more runoff pollution and will alter freshwater flow to salt marshes and estuaries. As more salt marsh is destroyed or degraded from the constant gnawing away of state marsh protection laws, essential habitat will be lost.

↓ ↓ ↓

THE RED DRUM, like more than 80 percent of the other seafood species along the Southeast coast, depends on the salt marsh and tidal creeks during its early life. Life begins for the red drum well off the coast, where the eggs hatch from August through October. Tidal currents transport the larvae into the estuaries and far back into the tidal creeks and salt marshes. During their first winter they remain in the marsh, relatively shielded from predatory fish. The following spring and summer the young fish make their way into rivers and estuaries. At this stage, and for the next three to five years, they remain within the estuaries, feeding mainly on shrimp and crabs. One eight-pound red drum may consume as many as twenty-five hundred crabs in a year. This is the time when the majority of red drums are caught by anglers. The targeting of these immature red drum greatly increases the risk of overfishing before the fish can reproduce.

Red drums reach maturity at about fifteen pounds. At that point they leave the estuaries through the inlets between barrier islands and venture into the ocean. The young adults join other adults in schools of fish that range in age from five to forty years and number in the hundreds—and perhaps thousands. That fact explains why the largest red drums caught each year are oceangoing and are generally caught by surf anglers. The schools of red drum spawn and lay new caches of eggs to start the cycle all over again.

On the Atlantic Seaboard, red drums historically were found as far north as Massachusetts. Today the distribution extends only from the Chesapeake to Florida. Whether the species can ever be restored to its full historic range is doubtful. The goal of fishery managers now is to keep the current range from shrinking.

CHAPTER SIXTEEN

Living on the Edge

S INCE 2004, scientists have pursued dozens of Atlantic bottlenose dolphins in the picturesque tidal creeks and rivers—collectively known as the Turtle River–Brunswick River Estuary—winding through poet Sidney Lanier's famous marshes of Glynn in Georgia. They fire retrievable darts into the animals' sleek hides for skin and blubber samples. They capture the creatures in sturdy nets and give them on-the-spot, head-to-fluke checkups as thorough as many humans get. And they do postmortems on the dead dolphins that occasionally wash up on mud-flats and beaches.

Pollution is the reason for these studies. With its four national-priority Superfund sites and several other hazardous waste dumps, the Brunswick area is one of the most contaminated coastal areas in the South. Over the years, discharges, leaks, and seeps from the sites have tainted marshes, tidal creeks, and adjacent uplands with all manner of harmful, long-lived chemicals. A joint report published in 2009 by researchers at Savannah State University, the Skidaway Institute of Oceanography, NOAA's Hollings Marine Laboratory in Charleston, and other institutions declared the Turtle River–Brunswick River estuary to be "severely contaminated."[1]

Funded mostly by the federal government, the researchers wanted to know if—and how—the toxic chemicals are affecting the dolphins, a sentinel species in coastal waters. If dolphins are not doing well, humans and other mammals may be at risk, too.

During the summer of 2009 scientists working on the Georgia Dolphin Health Assessment made a chilling discovery: the Brunswick dolphins carried "unprecedented levels" of a class of toxic chemicals known as polychlorinated biphenyls, or PCBs. In fact, the levels were the highest ever reported in marine wildlife. Compared with a typical count of sixty-four parts per million in East Coast dolphins, the Brunswick animals had on average four hundred parts per million. Some had counts as high as twenty-nine hundred parts per million, a record. "When we received the lab results for the Georgia dolphins, we were alarmed by the contaminant levels," noted Lori Schwacke, a wildlife epidemiologist at the Hollings Marine Lab. "In the Brunswick dolphins, the PCB levels are even higher than those seen in transient killer . . . whales from the Pacific Coast, which feed on other marine mammals, and are thus higher in the food chain."[2]

After testing the Brunswick animals, the scientists moved thirty miles up the coast to examine dolphins living in the waters around the Sapelo Island National Estuarine Research Reserve, known for its unspoiled creeks and salt marshes. Contaminant levels there were expected to be much lower. "We originally moved up there thinking we wanted to investigate health impacts of these contaminants and that this would be a good control site," Schwacke told me.

But the scientists were in for another shock. PCB levels in the animals around Sapelo were around 140 parts per million—much higher than expected, though lower than those in the Brunswick dolphins. And perhaps just as surprising, the dolphins had to be picking up the chemicals near Sapelo. The researchers tracked the movements of tagged dolphins and found that they rarely ranged far from their home estuary.[3]

The findings suggest that the pollutants are moving along the coast through the marine food web. Creatures low in the food web such as mummichogs and fiddler crabs accumulate the chemicals in their bodies from sediments and detritus of sullied marshes and tidal creeks around Brunswick. Foraging fish such as mullet, croakers, and spot enter the marsh, eat the tainted organisms, and then move out into surrounding waters. There, dolphins, at the top of the food web, eat the contaminated fish and amass the long-lived chemicals in their bodies, an insidious process known as biomagnification.[4]

The term PCB encompasses a raft of industrial chemicals once used widely as coolants and lubricants. They were banned in the United States in the late 1970s because they are dangerous to humans—causing, among other things, immune system suppression, impaired reproduction, poor cognitive development, hormone disruption, and possibly cancer. But because the chemicals may have half-lives of decades or more, they are still

Researcher Erin Pulster photographing dolphins going after bycatch
tossed from a shrimp trawler near Jekyll Island, Georgia.

sullying the environment. "The contaminants found in Brunswick are very
persistent, and dolphins are unable to metabolize these higher chlorinated
PCBS," reported Erin Pulster, who conducted some of the earlier dolphin
work as a graduate student at Savannah State University.[5]

WERE THE GEORGIA dolphins actually suffering ill effects from the pollution? An answer came in August 2009 from the Georgia Dolphin Health
Assessment project, which captured and examined twenty-nine dolphins.
The researchers found decreased thyroid hormone levels, elevated liver
enzymes, and symptoms of compromised immune systems—all of which
could make the beguiling creatures vulnerable to life-threatening maladies.

Schwacke put the findings in perspective in a NOAA report: "From
simple appearance the Georgia estuarine dolphin stock is thriving or at
least sustainable, but in reality many of these dolphins are living on the
edge. The fact that they're harboring critically high burdens of chemi-

cals with known toxic effects suggests that they are extremely vulnerable to further stressors. A viral or bacterial pathogen could push them over the edge, initiating an epidemic which devastates the stock. A number of disease epidemics have previously resulted in mass die-offs of dolphins or other marine mammals, and exposure to legacy contaminants such as PCBs is believed to have contributed to these die-offs and exacerbated the effects."

Schwacke also suggested the significance of the findings for humans: "We've demonstrated that PCBs which have leached into the Georgia estuaries are not simply settling into the marine sediments near the site or being washed into the ocean where they're diluted, they're making their way into the coastal food web. The extreme concentrations measured in these dolphins prompts questions about the potential chemical hazards for people who consume local seafood."

PCBs were not the only banned substances detected at high levels in the dolphins. Toxaphene, a chemical cousin of PCBs and once the nation's most widely used pesticide, also was found in the animals at levels above thresholds at which health impairment may occur. Toxaphene came into wide use after 1972 when DDT was banned because of the massive environmental damage it caused. Like PCBs, toxaphene can damage the immune system, injure the kidneys and liver, harm the adrenal gland, cause birth defects, damage the lungs and nervous system, and possibly induce cancer. In addition, toxaphene wreaks havoc in the environment. Low levels of toxaphene residues may affect reproduction and cause genetic damage in grass shrimp, cause serious fish deformities, and trigger fish kills. Government scientists in the early 1970s noticed that toxaphene-contaminated catfish growing in fish farms in the South developed a curious curvature of the spine that in many cases broke the fish's back and stunted growth by up to 30 percent. The government banned toxaphene in the 1980s.[6]

Toxaphene also persists in the environment for many years and, through biomagnification, builds up in ever-increasing amounts in the food web. High toxaphene concentrations are still found at all levels of the food web in the waterways and salt marshes around Brunswick—in worms, fiddler crabs, marsh hens, finfish, and dolphins.[7]

While the scientists were amazed at how high the levels of PCBs and toxaphene were in the dolphins, they already knew the source of the chemicals: they were once emitted by the tons from several chemical plants in

Brunswick. The PCBs in the dolphins and fish were traced to the notorious LCP Chemicals plant, which operated in a Brunswick neighborhood until 1994 churning out chlor-alkalai, a paper-whitening bleach. The old Hercules, Inc., factory just north of Brunswick produced thousands of tons of toxaphene between 1948 and 1980 and dumped the wastes into nearby tidal creeks.

The LCP and Hercules sites have been on the EPA's list of national-priority Superfund sites since the mid-1990s. Millions of dollars have been spent to clean up the sites, but progress has been slow and success limited.

The LCP Site

By anyone's measure, the former Linden Chemical and Plastics (LCP) plant just west of Brunswick is the most horrific of the city's four Superfund sites and one of the worst in the nation. It is a prime example of how lack of environmental vigilance and weak enforcement of regulations can allow a dangerous situation to get so out of hand that it becomes a threat to human health and the environment for decades into the future. The events that took place there also show how damage to a salt marsh can have widespread severe environmental repercussions for years to come.

About 85 percent of the LCP Superfund site's eight hundred acres is salt marsh adjacent to the placid Turtle River. The site includes all of Purvis Creek—the Turtle River's main tributary—and numerous smaller tidal streams that discharge into Purvis. The sinuous creeks once were popular fishing spots for locals. Now, health authorities warn people not to eat mullet and croakers from Purvis Creek and its tributaries because fish are still being tainted by the pollution.[8]

The site was polluted long before LCP began producing bleach in 1956. Beginning around 1919, an oil refinery, a paint-manufacturing plant, and other polluting industries operated on the site at one time or another. Initially, the LCP plant operated as Allied Signal, now a subsidiary of Honeywell International, Inc. After 1979 the plant, now owned by the Hanlin Group, Inc., based in New Jersey, operated as LCP Chemicals–Georgia, producing potent paper-whitening bleach for the nearby Georgia Pacific pulp and paper mill.[9]

Running twenty-four hours a day year-round, the plant also produced hydrochloric acid, hydrogen gas, and caustic soda for local industries. Some 150 workers toiled in the plant's two "cell buildings," each about the size of a football field. Each building held fifty mercury "cells" that churned out the products. Tons of a relatively rare type of highly chlorinated PCB known as Arochlor 1268 were used in each plant to lubricate graphite electrodes in the processing equipment.[10]

The operation produced inordinate amounts of caustic by-products. Court documents report that "the production process generated hazardous wastes, including elemental mercury, mercury-contaminated sludge, wastewater, chlorine contaminated wastewater, and extremely caustic wastes with high pH values."[11]

Until the 1970s, though, when Congress created the U.S. Environmental Protection Agency and passed bedrock antipollution laws, the LCP site and several other plants like it in the South had gone largely unregulated— even though local residents complained of foul odors, bad-tasting water, and sick wildlife. Georgia wildlife biologists wrote in 1975 that "reports of sick water birds are not uncommon in the Brunswick area." The birds' symptoms appeared to be neurological, including difficulty in walking and standing and inability to control muscle movements.[12]

Georgia's regulatory scrutiny of LCP picked up only in the late 1980s, mostly because of complaints from local officials and residents who feared that the plant was befouling drinking water. Georgia environmental authorities found serious lapses at the plant—but not serious enough to shut it down. Instead, they allowed LCP to install a wastewater treatment system and issued a permit to discharge processed effluents into Purvis Creek. The plant was also authorized to store wastewater in holding tanks in the cell rooms to await treatment. The cell rooms, made of concrete, were built with a downward slope that was supposed to divert the wastewater to a sump and then into the holding tanks. The sump itself was little more than a grate-covered hole in the floor.[13]

Court documents show that the waste disposal scheme was terribly deficient from the very beginning. Although LCP managers told state and federal regulators that the treatment system would continuously process seventy gallons per minute, its true capacity was only half that amount. By 1990 the sprawling plant was in serious financial straits. To slash operating costs, managers took shortcuts—including circumventing the waste disposal system and falsifying records. Plant maintenance began to deteriorate. Replacement parts were not made available. Flocculating chemicals needed for the waste treatment system were not ordered.

Unable to handle the waste loads, the plant's system began overflowing, literally inundating the facility with liquid refuse laden with PCBs, mercury, chlorine, and other dangerous ingredients. Plant managers resorted to other means of disposal, legal and otherwise. At one point desperate managers ordered workers to flush some of the wastes into old tanks partly filled with oil and mud from previous operations. The unlawful storage further contaminated the wastewater with oil and rendered it unsuitable for processing. Some of the waste was diverted illegally to old railroad tank cars. Hundreds of tons of highly contaminated sludge ended up in unlined pits dug into the ground adjacent to the salt marsh and in the marsh itself. Rain and extra-high tides sometimes breached the illegal pits.[14]

Court records show that at least three days a week the caustic, skin-burning water was dumped onto a cell room floor, even though the bosses knew it could leak through the floor into the ground. Workers had to wade up to their ankles through the nasty mess, protected only by rubber gloves and rubber shoes. The wastes spilled from cell room doorways and leaked through cracked foundations, ultimately dissolving the soil beneath the building and leaving a hole big enough to hold a school bus. The leaking wastes pooled onto the ground outside the building at such a rate that employees commonly referred to it as "the lake." Sand was piled around the buildings in a last-ditch effort to contain the wastes.

The dangerous conditions had the workers fearing for their lives. Their fears were justified. Records show that the wastewater was caustic enough to have caused severe burns. Inhaling the mercury and corrosive vapors could have been lethal. At first the employees were reluctant to take their complaints to authorities for fear of losing decent-paying jobs. Also, the company was issuing a steady stream of promises that the problems would be fixed and things would get better. Instead, things got worse. Finally, several workers filed complaints with the U.S. Occupational Safety and Health Administration. "They were in real fear of their life. They were willing to be suspended or fired rather than go into that water," an OSHA official later testified.

When OSHA inspectors showed up in August 1992, they were appalled by what they found. Workers were slogging through toxic wastewater, inhaling toxic fumes and lacking protective breathing devices and other basic safety equipment. The inspectors deemed the plant's condition a "willful violation" of worker health and safety laws. But apparently even that was not bad enough to warrant shutting down a plant that was considered vital to Brunswick's economy. LCP was ordered "to erect a boardwalk system above the water level around all the equipment until the water c[ould] be eliminated permanently." In response, LCP managers ordered wooden elevated walkways constructed in the cell rooms to prevent the workers from touching water on the floor and to reduce their risk of electrical shock and chemical burns. Despite the serious situation, the OSHA inspectors did not refer the case to environmental regulators because the inspectors said they found no evidence of waste being dumped improperly. "I'm disappointed they didn't tell us," a top EPA official said later in court.[15]

The situation got even worse. Shortly after the wooden walkways were built, wastewater started rising above the wood, again endangering workers.[16] When state and federal environmental authorities were finally summoned to the plant, they were stunned by what they found.

In February 1994 the Georgia Environmental Protection Division pulled LCP's wastewater discharge permit because of the company's brazen violations of environmental regulations. The plant was shut down, idling 150 workers, a blow to the local economy. Local environmentalists and LCP workers wondered why the regulators, who were aware of LCP's shortcomings as early as 1990, had not acted sooner. Glynn County commissioners considered suing the state of Georgia for letting conditions get so out of hand, but dropped the notion.

EPA investigators found so many pollutants that within a year the agency declared the eight-hundred-acre site a national-priority Superfund site, characterizing the extensive contamination as the worst known in the Southeast and perhaps in the nation.[17] In all, more than 37 tons of PCBs and at least 190 tons—some estimates are as high as 440 tons—of mercury may have seeped into Purvis Creek and surrounding marshes and uplands.[18]

MERCURY WAS INITIALLY the pollutant of biggest concern at the LCP Superfund site. It was used extensively in the plant's chlor-alkali cells to conduct an electrical charge that extracted chlorine from salt. Pure mercury is a highly toxic liquid metal that volatizes readily and can trigger all manner of health problems if inhaled or absorbed through the skin. Moderate exposures can cause tremors, mood swings, irritability, nervousness, insomnia, muscle weakness, headaches, and impaired performance on cognitive function tests. Higher exposures may lead to kidney, brain, and immune system damage; respiratory failure; and death.[19]

LCP's employees not only encountered mercury when they waded through wastewater; it also dripped from cell room ceilings, landing on their backs and soaking through their clothes. Explosions and mercury-laced gas clouds routinely chased them out of plant buildings.

Even a tiny amount of mercury can cause significant harm to the environment. A report from the Natural Resources Defense Council notes that "deposition of only 1/70th of a teaspoon of mercury a year could be enough to contaminate a 25-acre lake."[20] Investigators with the EPA and the U.S. Fish and Wildlife Service estimated that LCP had dumped a whopping three hundred thousand *pounds* of mercury into Purvis Creek alone between the mid-1980s and 1994. A similar amount had seeped into the salt marsh and soil around the plant—one of the worst episodes of mercury contamination in the country.

Once elemental mercury gets into water and wet soil, specialized bacteria and other microbes convert it into methylmercury, which is readily absorbed and stored by living things. Methylmercury also accumulates in the food web. Fish absorb it from polluted water as it passes over their gills. Investigators found high levels of methylmercury in fiddlers, mummichogs, blue crabs, oysters, shrimp, finfish, and other creatures during their initial examination of the LCP site.[21]

People generally are exposed to methylmercury when they eat fish and shellfish containing it. Most at risk of damage are fetuses, infants, and young children. An EPA briefing paper warns that "methylmercury exposure in the womb, which can result from a mother's consumption of fish and shellfish that contain methylmercury, can adversely affect a baby's growing brain and nervous system."[22]

Mercury has the same insidious effect on wildlife—turtles, alligators, otters, mink, eagles, ospreys, ducks, and wading birds—that eat contaminated fish. At high levels of exposure, methylmercury can reduce reproduction, slow growth and development, affect courtship and mating behavior, and even kill. Unfortunately, wildlife cannot read health advisories or change their eating habits to avoid mercury pollution.

Scientists in Brunswick found eggshell thinning and genetic and bone abnormalities in marsh hens living in the salt marsh contaminated by LCP's pollution. But it was mercury poisoning in an endangered species, the wood stork, that helped nail LCP and send seven of its officers and managers to jail. Wood storks, which feed on small fish in salt marshes, tidal creeks, and other wetlands, have been federally protected as endangered since 1984. Only about five thousand pairs breed each year. Agents and biologists with the U.S. Fish and Wildlife Service's field office in Brunswick detected the mercury-laden storks around the time the EPA was getting ready to declare the LCP plant a Superfund site. The birds were living in rookeries as far away as Saint Simons Island, eight miles downstream from LCP. The biologists found that the mercury had caused nerve damage and disrupted the large wading birds' normal mating habits—a serious concern when a poor breeding effort could jeopardize the species' survival.

Special Agent Patrick McIntosh, who worked in the agency's Savannah law enforcement office, helped trace the mercury to LCP. Through numerous long interviews and painstaking scrutiny of hundreds of boxes of company records, McIntosh compiled evidence showing that from the mid-1980s until its closure, the LCP plant dumped nearly 150 tons of mercury into Purvis Creek and the surrounding tidal marshes. The investigation also revealed that the dumping occurred with the knowledge and sanction of company and plant officials, and that plant workers had been unlawfully exposed to mercury and other contaminants.[23]

In addition to criminal violations of myriad federal environmental and worker safety laws, the Hanlin Group and LCP's managers also were charged with breaching the Endangered Species Act. The government claimed that mercury poisoning caused an impairment in the wood storks that constituted an illegal "take" under the Endangered Species Act.

In the ensuing criminal cases, Christian A. Hansen Jr., LCP's former chief executive officer, was sentenced to nine years in federal prison and fined twenty thousand dollars for multiple environmental violations and endangering employees. His son, Randall Hansen, the company's former chief operating officer, was sentenced to forty-six months in prison and also fined twenty thousand dollars. Former plant manager Alfred R. Taylor received a six-and-a-half-year sentence. Four other plant managers who pleaded guilty also were ordered to serve time.

The sentences remain some of the stiffest ever imposed in the United States for criminal violation of environmental laws. "This case represents a horror story for the company involved and the industry," said the EPA's head law enforcer, Earl Devaney, in 1998 when the managers were being hauled to jail. The managers knew what they were doing was wrong "and went ahead and did it anyway," he said.[24]

The Cleanup

When the EPA declared the LCP factory a Superfund site, the agency deemed the site's previous owners—Honeywell (formerly Allied Signal), Atlantic Richfield, and Georgia Power—responsible for most of the cleanup, but under EPA's supervision. Under the tough Superfund law, a contaminated site's previous owners can be held liable for the pollution and ensuring cleanup costs. The Hanlin Group, LCP's parent company, had declared bankruptcy.[25]

Today the old plant site is a grassy, table-flat field surrounded by a chain-link fence. Red signs warn "Danger" and "Keep Out." For a long time, only workers garbed in head-to-toe protective suits were allowed on the site. When cleanup operations commenced in the mid-1990s, the plant's decrepit cell rooms, storage tanks, administrative offices, and other buildings were demolished. More than 250,000 tons of soils and sediments laced with mercury, PCBs, lead, and other toxic chemicals were removed from forty acres of high ground. Some 25 tons of wastes were dug from thirteen acres of contaminated marsh flats, and twenty-six hundred linear feet of tidal channels were restored. Most of the filthy material was shipped by rail to landfills and other disposal facilities.[26]

So far, the cleanup has cost more than sixty million dollars, most of it borne by the "responsible parties." A portion, however, has been charged to taxpayers. EPA's ultimate aim is to make the site safe and clean enough for the community or a private business to use. That may take many more years, if it can ever be done. New health and environmental threats keep popping up. In 2002, for example, a million-gallon caustic brine plume was discovered seventy feet underground on the site. Suspended in groundwater, the plume contained mercury, arsenic, and chromium—chemicals that cause brain and kidney damage. It threatened to trickle down another six hundred feet to the vital Floridan aquifer, from which Brunswick and Glynn County draw drinking water.[27]

↡ ↡ ↡

WHILE THE CLEANUP was under way, Honeywell and the site's other former owners were settling several big lawsuits by local residents, former workers, and Glynn County itself for damages caused by LCP's pollution. The county was awarded twenty-five million dollars in compensation for the endangerment of its water supply, salt marshes, and other natural assets. Several former LCP plant workers were awarded twenty million dollars for having to work under dangerous, oppressive conditions at the plant. In a third lawsuit, twenty-five million dollars went to 120 local landowners whose properties adjacent to LCP had declined in value because of the contamination and whose health allegedly had been endangered by eating fish contaminated by the toxins LCP released.

One of the owners was Reba Reyna, sixty-nine, who lived only some twenty-five feet from the contaminated marsh. "I know that what the pollution has done is [it has] killed everything in our marsh back here," she said. In early 2010 she was a candidate for a seat on the Glynn County Commission.

The recent discovery of high PCB and toxaphene levels in Brunswick's dolphins has sparked new concerns. Residents of other coastal communities fear that the contamination may be heading their way. Lori Schwacke, the NOAA scientist who helped lead Georgia's dolphin research, confirmed that the contamination might indeed spread up and down the East Coast as polluted prey fish move about. "The contaminants aren't settling in the sediment or moving out in the ocean. They're actually moving into the coastal food web," she said.

Sooner or later, many of the hundreds of human-made chemicals we're now exposed to every day in our homes, offices, schools, and cars will join DDT, PCBs, and toxaphene on the list of banned products. Meanwhile, new chemicals will come onto the market, and many will also end up in our estuaries. An obvious question arises: At what point will our estuaries, tidal creeks, and salt marshes be so overwhelmed that they no longer can function? Will they someday become toxic no-man's-lands? Or will their amazing resiliency save us and the environment?

The Savannah River Site

On a low retaining wall along traffic-heavy DeKalb Avenue in the Lake Claire neighborhood of northeast Atlanta, a magnificent mural longer than a football field greets passersby. In dramatic fashion it depicts the two major river basins—the Altamaha and the Chattahoochee—that drain Atlanta and most of its suburbs as the rivers flow to the sea.

It is appropriate that the painting is on DeKalb Avenue. The thoroughfare follows the Eastern Subcontinental Divide, a major geological feature that separates the two river basins. If you could stand in the middle of the street with a bucket of water in each hand and face west toward downtown Atlanta, the water you dumped to the right would end up in the Chattahoochee River, which flows to the Gulf of Mexico, and the water tossed to the left would end up in the Altamaha and ultimately the Atlantic Ocean.

The mural shows the two rivers beginning as sparkling streams—the Chattahoochee in North Georgia's mountains and the Altamaha in Georgia's Piedmont. As they wind to the sea, they pass through swamps, farmland, forests, rocky shoals, small communities, and bustling cities—all depicted in the painting. Native animals that depend on the rivers appear in colorful settings. Finally, the mural shows the rivers reaching the sea, where dolphins romp in the estuaries.

The mural helps drive home a point that many people in Atlanta have probably never considered: all things are connected. Much of the industrial, agricultural, and domestic wastes spewing from pipes or running off the land into a river can make their way far down the river to its mouth and into the estuary. The Altamaha's mouth is more than two hundred miles downstream from Atlanta, but a large portion of the city's pollution may end up there.[28]

Salt marshes are in a particularly precarious position because the pollution of entire watersheds ultimately ends up in them. All rivers have watersheds, which can cover tremendously large areas. The Altamaha's watershed drains one-fourth of Georgia. Any foul material that makes its way into the river's tributaries could end up in the salt marshes fringing the estuary. Proof of that comes from an environmental calamity that occurred on the Savannah River in December 1991 when the Department of Energy's Savannah River Site accidentally released nuclear reactor cooling water containing radioactive tritium. Five nuclear reactors at the Savannah River Site once churned out tons of tritium and plutonium, the main ingredients of hydrogen bombs. Tritium, an isotope of hydrogen—and the H in H-bomb—fuses during a nuclear explosion and releases mind-boggling amounts of hot, destructive energy.

In the unintentional release of the tritium-laced water scientists found a silver lining. It was a golden opportunity to follow a readily detectable pollutant as it made its way down a river and into the estuary, tidal creeks, and salt marshes and then possibly out to sea. Using sensors and other devices, researchers followed the radioactive plume more than 150 miles downriver. Through tidal action, the pollution eventually spread from the Savannah River to a zone of interconnecting creeks and marshes 60 miles to the south along the Georgia coast. The tides flushed out most of the radioactive water within days, but some tritium lingered longer, locked up in the marsh. "It turns out the salt marshes had absorbed a portion of the tritium," said Skidaway researcher Jack Blanton.[29]

Spartina and other marsh plants can metabolize and break down many pollutants into less harmful forms. Marsh and estuarine sediments can absorb harmful chemicals and bury them in the mud, thereby minimizing their toxic effects and rendering them less likely to be transferred up food chains. But there is a limit to what the marsh can do. If pollutant loads continue at high levels, the marsh can become so overburdened that it loses its capacity to serve as a waste treatment plant, and the pollutants can move into the food web.

Persistent toxins such as heavy metals (e.g., mercury, copper, zinc, cadmium, lead, and selenium) and pesticides in particular can produce profound changes when they accumulate in salt marshes and tidal creeks. A reduction in populations of bottom-dwelling worms, crustaceans, bivalves, and the like may not be immediately obvious, but other impacts—such as the loss of oyster beds—are more apparent. Creatures such as fiddler crabs that constantly scoop up mud while eating are potentially at higher risk of exposure to heavy metals in sediments.

Several types of heavy metals are essential for good health in minute amounts but toxic at higher concentrations. Heavy metals inhibit enzymes that dictate or influence behavior and activities such as pursuing mates, evading predators, and foraging. Foraging activity of fiddler crabs exposed to heavy metals may decrease by as much as two-thirds. Fiddler crabs are key indicators of salt marsh health. If a pollutant hurts fiddlers, it's likely to hurt a wide range of other marine creatures as well. The fish, birds, and small mammals that prey on tainted fiddlers also may end up with impaired health and reproductive potential.[30]

Mummichogs are another indicator species that may suggest a marsh's health status. The little fish may become befuddled and more vulnerable to predators in marshes contaminated with heavy metals, especially mercury and cadmium. In oysters, cadmium interferes with the ability to take in adequate amounts of oxygen when water temperatures rise—potentially an enormous problem in the future in the face of rising sea temperatures brought on by climate change.[31]

↓ ↓ ↓

THE WATERSHEDS, estuaries, creeks, and salt marshes connected to the Southeast's rivers are constantly besieged by pesticides, herbicides, and fertilizers from runoff from farms, suburban lawns, golf courses, and pine plantations. Although DDT, toxaphene, Dieldrin, and aldrin—all once commonly used pesticides in the United States—are now banned because they pose significant hazards to people and the environment, other pesticides have taken their place. Is there any reason to believe that these new products are safer than the old ones?

A current herbicide star is atrazine, an organic, chlorine-based compound that is the second most widely used weed-killer in the country. Some eighty million pounds of it are used on American crops each year. Introduced in 1958, it became highly popular among corn, sorghum, and sugarcane growers because of its relative cheapness and the fact that it lasts for about forty days in the soil and can be applied before, during, or after planting. It also is used on lawns and golf courses in the South.

But atrazine is now the target of criticism from environmentalists and scientists. James Pinckney of the University of South Carolina reported that "atrazine may be having significant effects on South Carolina's wetlands and salt marshes" and noted that it has caused widespread contamination of waterways and drinking water supplies.[32] A 2005 study by researchers from the University of Texas revealed that exposure to atrazine and its products at levels commonly found in the environment significantly reduced the growth rate of red drum larvae.[33] Several scientific studies have linked atrazine to sexual abnormalities and limb deformities in frogs and fish at concentrations as low as one part per billion.[34] It is also known to kill algae and the microorganisms that make up the base of aquatic food webs; and in conjunction with other pesticides and herbicides it suppresses animals' immune systems.

Nevertheless, the EPA has said the scientific evidence on atrazine is still insufficient to compel restricting it—let alone banning it, as several environmental groups want. Not so, though, with the European Union, which declared atrazine a harmful "endocrine disrupter" and banned its use as of 2005.

↓ ↓ ↓

RICHARD F. LEE and Keith Maruya at the Skidaway Oceanographic Institute scrutinized the concentrations of atrazine and a host of other pesticides in tidal creeks and marshes to determine the major sources of contaminants in the Southeast's rivers and estuaries. They found five major sources of pollutants with "the potential to harm coastal estuaries and the near-shore environment":

- Heavy industry, particularly pulp and paper mills and chemical plants that spew heavy metals and persistent toxic contaminants into estuaries and salt marshes.
- Silviculture, which uses huge amounts of pesticides and other chemicals to maintain vast pine plantations.
- Agriculture, which uses some three dozen pesticides to grow soybeans, corn, cotton, wheat, and peanuts. The total use of these pesticides ranges from one thousand to six thousand pounds per acre per year.
- Golf courses, which cover more than 150,000 acres in Georgia, South Carolina, and North Carolina. Many are directly adjacent to estuaries.
- Cities and suburbs, whose extensive networks of hard surfaces cause millions of gallons of pollution-laden storm water to surge into streams during even moderate rainfall. Pesticides and herbicides used by homeowners also enter the watershed and accumulate in estuaries.[35]

CHAPTER SEVENTEEN

The Last Season

S THE SOUTHEAST'S great oyster reefs and canning industry faded in the early 1900s, a new commercial fishery was emerging—shrimping. Old World fishermen from Spain, Portugal, and Sicily were drawn to the Southeast coast, particularly the area around Fernandina Beach, Florida, by the abundant, delicious shrimp. At the time, shrimping was a laborious and exhausting endeavor with little financial return. Catching shrimp in any desirable quantity required the use of cumbersome, heavy haul-seine nets pulled by rowboat or sailboat. If shrimping were to become a profitable pursuit, more efficient harvesting methods had to be devised.

The modern shrimping industry was born in 1902 when Sollecito "Mike" Salvador, a Sicilian-born immigrant to Fernandina Beach, hooked a small gasoline engine onto his rowing skiff. The one-cylinder engine provided enough power to pull a seine net quickly and efficiently across the sea floor and haul in more shrimp with less exertion. Salvador saw the potential for a mass shrimp market. He formed his own seafood supply business, the Salvador Fish Company, in 1906 and was soon joined by his two brothers-in-law, Salvatore Versaggi and Antonio Poli, and their friend Joseph Gianino, all Sicilian immigrants. The partners realized early on that they would have to expand the market if they were to make a decent income from catching and selling shrimp.[1]

Their timing proved fortunate. Ice-making machines, refrigeration, and refrigerated train transportation—the keys to shipping fresh shrimp to markets as far away as New York City and Chicago—were just coming into use. Versaggi moved to New York and made valuable contacts at the

Fulton Fish Market for the future distribution of shrimp from Fernandina. Soon, shrimp from down South were finding their way onto tables in distant restaurants and homes. Americans all across the nation developed a hearty appetite for shrimp, and the market quickly increased tenfold.

During the early days the plentiful shrimp were easy to catch with the unrefined seine nets towed by the small motor-driven skiffs. But as the market for shrimp expanded, shrimping technology had to improve to meet the demand. Billy Corkum, who had come to Fernandina Beach from Boston, came up with an answer in 1913. He was familiar with a baglike, cone-shaped net with iron-weighted "doors" originally developed in England. The doors held the net's mouth open while it was dragged on the sea floor. Called the "otter trawl," the net had found its way into the New England cod fishery. Corkum made a few modifications, and the otter trawl's wide mouth and bottom-hugging design allowed shrimpers to haul in many more bushels of shrimp than the old-style seines.[2] Most shrimp boats today use essentially the same net.

The otter net also allowed shrimpers to greatly widen their shrimping territories. Until then, shrimping had been primarily an inshore fishery because seine nets were not efficient in the offshore waters where shrimp concentrations were densest. The otter net changed that by enabling shrimpers to fish in the deeper waters. Other improvements followed, including development of the diesel engine and sturdier, longer-lasting nets. The advances streamlined shrimp catching even more and substantially increased harvests and profits.

The shrimping industry changed again when Greek immigrants brought their expert boat-building skills to north Florida. Soon, boats custom-designed for shrimping were working the offshore waters. The new trawlers, built with low deadrises and very rounded bottoms, held more ice, fuel, and shrimp. They were much larger, too; by World War II it wasn't uncommon to see newly built boats forty-five to fifty feet long sliding down the ways.

Other fishermen saw the opportunity to make their fortunes in shrimp, and shrimping fever spread, especially among Old World newcomers. Portuguese immigrants founded the shrimping industry in Brunswick, Georgia, in the 1920s. Brunswick ultimately vied with Fernandina and Saint Augustine for the title "Shrimp Capital of the World." The first shrimp-packing house in South Carolina opened in 1924 in Port Royal near Beaufort, and shrimping soon became a mainstay of that state's economy.

Improvements to shrimping technology continued. The otter trawl was modified to include "wings" that helped guide the shrimp into the net's mouth. Researchers with the University of Georgia Marine Extension Service's Fisheries Station in Brunswick worked with local shrimpers to create the twin trawl system, which enabled shrimp boats to use a net on each side of the vessel and efficiently haul in even more shrimp. By the mid-1970s, twin trawls were being used throughout the world.

Over the years, shrimp boats became picturesque icons of the South. Charleston-based novelist Mary Alice Monroe called them "part of the southern landscape, culture, and heritage."[3] Artists and photographers captured gleaming white trawlers dragging their nets in the coastal waters or moored to rickety, barnacled wooden docks along tranquil tidal creeks in settings reminiscent of Old World fishing villages. At night, the lights of dozens of shrimp trawlers twinkled on the dark horizon. Visitors often remarked that they looked like a city shimmering on the water.

In addition to their fishing skills, Portuguese immigrants also brought from the Old World the traditional "Blessing of the Fleet," a colorful ceremony held at the start of the shrimping season in which local clergymen blessed decorated shrimp trawlers for a safe and bountiful harvest. The ceremonies evolved into major annual festivals in many coastal communities.

A Dying Industry

The shrimping tradition and heritage are fast disappearing. Only a fraction of the scores of shrimp trawlers that once worked the Southeast's coastal waters now leave their docks (if they are lucky enough to have a dock to leave from) during shrimping season. High fuel costs, increased government regulation, foreign competition, and farm-raised shrimp are big reasons for the downward slide of the Southeast's shrimping industry. Waterfront condominiums, restaurants, and marinas have replaced the old docks, weather-beaten packing sheds, and other waterfront structures where shrimpers bought fuel and ice, received dealer credit, and sold their catch.[4]

The numbers tell the story. Since the industry's heyday in the 1980s, the number of licensed shrimpers has declined by 75 percent or more. South Carolina licensed more than fifteen hundred shrimp boats in the early 1980s but only about four hundred in 2010.[5] Georgia sold about one thousand commercial shrimp boat licenses in 1983 and only 121 in 2010.[6]

Fewer working boats, of course, mean smaller harvests. For the ten-year period 1993–2002, the annual commercial landings of white, brown, and pink shrimp in Georgia averaged 4.3 million pounds, valued at $16.2 million. In 2009 the state's shrimpers harvested only 2.2 million pounds worth about $6.4 million.[7]

It's not that our appetite for shrimp has waned. Shrimp several years ago surpassed oysters and tuna as America's most popular seafood.[8] The average annual shrimp consumption in 2009 was 4.1 pounds per person.[9] But only about 15 percent of the shrimp consumed in the United States comes from U.S. sources. The rest is imported, with at least half coming from aquaculture operations in Thailand, Ecuador, India, and other countries.[10]

Ambitious efforts by groups such as the Georgia Shrimpers Association to promote their higher-costing wild-caught shrimp have met with limited success. The shrimpers insist that wild shrimp from the Atlantic are sweeter, tastier, firmer, and safer to eat than the cheaper farm-raised varieties. Customers know they are eating wild shrimp by a certification seal posted in restaurant doors and windows and printed on menus. The seal guarantees the shrimp came from the Atlantic, was processed and packaged in certified facilities, and meets quality taste standards. But so far, shrimp-eating Americans—and the restaurants and markets that serve them—haven't gone overboard for the wild type.

Among other possible reasons why Americans are not buying wild-caught shrimp may be conservationists' criticism of the indiscriminate way the shrimp are caught. For every pound of shrimp the trawls bring up from the bottom, nearly three pounds of finfish, sharks, squid, stingrays, horseshoe crabs, and other creatures—the "bycatch"—are scooped up as well. Most of the bycatch dies on deck and is swept overboard. Protected sea turtles also are part of the bycatch, although federal law now requires shrimpers to attach turtle excluder devices (TEDs) to their nets to allow the air-breathing reptiles to escape. Certified bycatch reduction devices also have become available and are now required in every coastal state. The devices can substantially reduce the unwanted catch, but shrimpers complain that they also let as much as 8–10 percent of the caught shrimp escape.[11]

The Wild Shrimp

The primary targets of commercial shrimpers belong to two species, the white shrimp and the brown shrimp—both members of the prawn family, Penaeidae. Of the two, the white shrimp is by far the most abundant and biggest moneymaker in Georgia, South Carolina, and northeast Florida, representing some two-thirds of the total shrimp catch. The proportion is reversed in North Carolina, where the brown shrimp predominates. Another penaeid species, the pink shrimp, also is netted and marketed in the Southeast but is not nearly as abundant as the other two species and so does not figure prominently in the commercial catch. Placed side by side, fresh white shrimp appear lighter in body color than brown or pink shrimps—thus their common names.

Their complex and amazing eight-to-nine-month life cycles are relatively similar. Mating and spawning occur twenty to eighty feet deep in the ocean from the beaches to about five miles offshore. White shrimp typically begin spawning in May and early June; brown shrimp begin mostly in October and November. During mating, the male transfers a packet of sperm called a spermatophore to the female, who uses it to fertilize as many as a million eggs that sink to the ocean floor after being released. The eggs hatch within twenty-four hours, and the larvae move freely into the water and become part of the oceanic plankton. After going through eleven larval stages in ocean water, the young shrimp reach the postlarval stage and finally look like ultratiny versions of adult shrimp.

During the second postlarval stage, the young shrimp ride the flood tides into the estuaries, where they move upstream, settle at the bottom of tidal creeks, and enter the juvenile stage. During high tide they move onto the marsh surface and feed in the dense vegetation, which protects them. They will eat almost anything—plant or animal—they encounter. Rapid growth marks this stage—upward of two inches per month. At about four inches in length the juveniles become subadults and move into the deeper waters of the estuary, where they may remain for several months. They continue to grow, though not as rapidly as in the juvenile stage.

Shrimp trawlers tied up at docks at Darien, Georgia.

Less than 2 percent of all spawned eggs reach adulthood because of high mortality rates from predation, weather, and water conditions. Myriad factors interact to affect the quantity and quality of shrimp, including temperature, salinity, and circulation. Wide swings in salinity or prolonged cold weather can wipe out huge numbers. In the winter of 2000–2001, prolonged cool water temperatures of about forty-six degrees destroyed an estimated 97–99 percent of South Carolina's shrimp population, and shrimpers qualified for federal disaster assistance. It took two seasons for the shrimp to rebound. Freshwater inflow, however, may be the dominant factor influencing the abundance and growth of the young shrimp. Ideal shrimp nursery habitat has water of low to moderate salinity.

From early summer to the end of December, depending on the species, the adult shrimp start moving through the sounds to deeper waters offshore in order to spawn. As the shrimp move seaward, shrimp boats are out every day trying to haul them in.[12] Once they reach the ocean the shrimp disperse into deep ocean waters several miles offshore, making it impractical for shrimp trawlers to go after them. Thus the shrimping season in the Southeast usually closes in early January and does not reopen until May or June.[13]

Shrimp Boats for Sale

At the western end of Brunswick's historic Gloucester Street, which runs through the heart of the city, lies Mary Ross Waterfront Park, named after a member of one of the city's old shrimping families. From here you can get a grand view of Brunswick's shrimp boat fleet moored in the tranquil East River. The Portuguese immigrants who started the shrimping industry in the 1930s built their extensive docks near here. It is also here that the city's annual Blessing of the Fleet takes place on Mother's Day, around the start of the shrimping season.

As late as a decade ago, this place would have been one of the busiest sites along Georgia's coast from May through December. Well before sunrise, dozens of white-hulled, sixty-foot-long shrimp trawlers, laden with thousands of gallons of diesel fuel and hundreds of pounds of ice, would be chugging out to the estuaries and the nearshore ocean just beyond the barrier island beaches for a full day of shrimping. As the boats headed out, crew members, or "strikers," would be eating big breakfasts of scrambled eggs, grits, and bacon washed down by copious amounts of coffee. Many of the boats would stay out for seventeen or eighteen hours straight, their "outriggers" spread like giant gull wings, steadily dragging their nets on the bottom at three to four knots per hour, scooping up hundreds or—on a good day—thousands of pounds of shrimp and other sea life. As the loaded nets were winched in and their squirming catch emptied onto the deck, the crew would work quickly to separate the shrimp and any other marketable organisms from the bycatch. If time permitted, deckhands sitting on wooden stools would cull and "head" the shrimp before dumping them on the ice in the hold—or, on some of the fancier boats, flash-freezing them. The unwanted bycatch would be swept overboard. By late evening the boats, followed by flocks of gulls and pods of dolphins looking for free meals as crews washed off decks and cleaned nets, would return to the docks and unload the iced-down catch at dockside packinghouses. A dozen or more workers would wash, sort, grade, and head the shrimp still with heads, and then pack them in boxes with more ice. After that, the succulent, wild-caught Georgia shrimp would be dispatched to markets all over the Eastern Seaboard.

But it's not that way any more. Few shrimp boats now leave the docks. There is no *Forrest Gump* happy ending here. Dozens of idle shrimp trawlers moored along the city's waterfront are rotting, their wooden hulls being chewed away by voracious marine worms that remain uncontrolled because boat owners can't afford to apply preventive treatment. The steel-hulled vessels are little better off; as they stay tied up at the docks for months on end their hulls accumulate layers of barnacles and algae.

Several owners told me they would like to sell their boats if they could. Some said they even would give them away—if they could find a taker. But there are no takers to be found. For most owners, shrimp boats have become liabilities. If a vessel sinks, the owner by law must pay to recover it, an effort that could cost fifty thousand dollars or more. Owners who can't afford to retrieve their sunken vessels face severe penalties, such as losing their commercial fishing license.

Shrimping along the Southeast coast has become a losing proposition for most trawler owners. In recent years packinghouses generally have been paying shrimpers between one and three dollars a pound depending on market demand for wild-caught shrimp. Shrimp prices shot up temporarily in 2010, but it took a devastating oil spill in the Gulf of Mexico to make that happen. Overall, the price that shrimpers get for their toil and sweat has become so miserably low that hundreds of veteran independent shrimpers, from generations of families long dependent on the sea for livelihoods, have simply given up and are trying to find work elsewhere.

Aboard the Lady Jane

Larry Credle, a Brunswick boat captain, experienced firsthand the thrills and joys of the heyday—and then the precipitous decline—of the Southeast coast's shrimping industry. "For all practical purposes, the shrimping industry is a thing of the past," he tells me. "The huge costs of shrimping, competition with imported foreign shrimp and farm-raised shrimp, and the terribly low prices for domestic wild-caught shrimp have spelled the end for the industry."

As he speaks, he steers his refurbished shrimp trawler, the *Lady Jane*, in Saint Simons Sound on a late November evening. Sidney Lanier's marshes of Glynn stretch to the darkening horizon. On board are some thirty or so paying passengers. In 2004, after more than forty years of shrimping and fishing, Credle saw no future in the business. So he converted his sixty-foot, steel-hulled trawler into a tourist boat that can carry as many as forty-nine passengers. The Coast Guard–approved boat is still rigged with shrimp nets and other standard equipment and trappings of a commercial trawler, but now Credle and his crew deploy the nets only for about fifteen minutes at a time to drag the bottom and give passengers a sense of what life is like on a real working shrimp boat.

"Most of them have no clue of how a shrimp trawler operates," Credle says. "Many of them tell me it's an eye-opening experience for them." The two-hour cruises are also science lessons because the fish and other sea life that the *Lady Jane*'s nets haul up show passengers the great diversity of life in the salt marshes' winding creeks and sounds. As the nets come up, gulls and pelicans by the dozens circle the boat.

Credle fits the role of a shrimp boat skipper. A graying beard fringes his chiseled face, leathery and tanned from years in sun and wind. He comes from a long line of seafarers and commercial fishermen. His father, grandfather, and generations of Credles before them all worked on or lived near the sea. Credle even claims that his ancestors sailed with Captain Edward Teach, better known as the notorious pirate Blackbeard, in the early 1700s. Credle was eight years old when he began shrimping with his father, George, off North Carolina's Outer Banks. But shrimping, a tough enough chore in Brunswick's temperate climate, was even harder work there. "You'd leave on Sunday and stay out on the water all week until Friday afternoon," Credle says. In 1964 his father moved the family and their boats to Brunswick because he saw better shrimping opportunities there. "Here, you could work from dawn to dusk and still go home at night."

Credle has numerous friends and acquaintances in the shrimping industry—or at least who once were in it—in Brunswick and all along the Georgia and South Carolina coasts. "I'm afraid that most of them still in the business are fooling themselves," he tells me as I stand with him in the *Lady Jane*'s wheelhouse. "The industry is all but dead."

Just off the Saint Simons Island Lighthouse, Credle turns his boat around and we head back to the dock in Brunswick. As we plod along, the marshes of Glynn stretch to the far horizon all around us. Two dolphins

An old dock in Brunswick, Georgia.

romp in the water just off the bow. The setting sun over the marsh colors the sky a beautiful glowing pink. "Just look at that," Credle says. "I don't know how many times I've seen that, but I never get tired of it."

AS WE STEAM along on a wide, twisting tidal creek on an incoming tide through the marshes, Credle rambles on about the business that once was such an ingrained part of his life.

> Back when we got here in 1964, you could make a good living at shrimping. We got about a dollar twenty-five a pound for shrimp then, but fuel cost only between thirteen and twenty-four cents a gallon. Now, it's up around three dollars a gallon. My fuel tank holds ten thousand gallons, so it costs me thirty thousand dollars to fill up. You do the math: this boat uses about twenty-eight gallons of fuel an hour, and during shrimping season we went out every day and usually stayed out seventeen hours each day. It has become just about impossible to make a living as a shrimper. . . .
>
> Nets cost only about six hundred dollars back then; now a new one costs about three thousand. . . .

The pay for our catch went like this: The packinghouse got a third, the boat captain got a third, and the crew got a third. . . .

You have other costs, like insurance. It's nearly impossible to get insurance on a wood-hulled boat now. Most banks don't want to talk to you if you own a wood-hull. Then, you have engine repairs and maintenance. The same thing with nets. . . .

Most of the packinghouses would let us tie up our boats at their docks for free or a small charge. But when the cost of shrimp got so low, it became much more profitable for the packinghouses to sell to developers, and so the shrimp boats lost their docking spaces. Several of the packinghouses still in business are buying imported shrimp instead of locally caught shrimp. The imported shrimp are cheaper. The shrimpers in the other countries don't have to worry about the strict government rules and regulations that we have to comply with. . . .

During summer and fall the waters around here used to look like a city from the lights of so many shrimp boats. Now, even in the peak of shrimping season, you might see only about ten boats. . . .

Only about seven years ago, the Department of Natural Resources sold about 400 commercial shrimping licenses. Then about two or three years ago it was down to about 160. Now, it's down to about 100. But even if somebody gets a licenses, that doesn't mean he will actually do any shrimping. . . .

There is some hope. I believe that if some of these guys can hang on, wild-caught white shrimp will become a gourmet item—"Sweet Georgia White Shrimp." There will be a demand for those shrimp. The taste and texture of wild-caught Georgia shrimp are far superior to the farm-raised shrimp and the imported ones.

CHAPTER EIGHTEEN

The Beloved Land

F EW NATURAL PLACES on the East Coast can match South Carolina's ACE Basin—it is remote, biologically rich, and superbly beautiful. Three of South Carolina's most scenic free-flowing rivers—the Ashepoo, Combahee, and Edisto—join here to form one of the largest, least-developed watersheds on the Eastern Seaboard. Gently flowing to the sea, the blackwater streams meander in turn past cypress swamps, historic plantations, old rice fields, fertile farmland, maritime forests, barrier islands, and abundant salt marshes. They empty into one of the Southeast's most productive estuaries, Saint Helena Sound.

Encompassing some 1.6 million acres south of Charleston, the ACE Basin watershed is a prime example of a landscape where developmental sprawl has been stymied. It is not all pristine. Biologists are quick to point out that much of the drainage area has for centuries supported agriculture, logging, hunting, and fishing. "This place has seen the ax, fire, the whole thing," Dean Harrigal, a wildlife biologist and ACE Basin project coordinator for South Carolina's Department of Natural Resources, told me. "There are trees getting cut right now. This is a living, breathing, working landscape where a traditional Lowcountry way of life still goes on."

Even so, the Nature Conservancy considers huge swaths of the ACE Basin still unspoiled enough to designate it a world treasure under the Last Great Places program. The U.S. Fish and Wildlife Service, in recognition of the basin's key importance for migrating and wintering waterfowl, selected it for a flagship project of the North American Waterfowl Management Plan. Scientists come here to gather baseline data in order to monitor changes in the physical and biological processes of the entire coast.

A few years ago, biologists were dumbfounded when they spied two

Botany Bay Plantation in the ACE River Basin in South Carolina.

pairs of statuesque, snow white birds preening in a marshy area of the ACE Basin—whooping cranes, among the rarest and most endangered creatures on Earth. Until then, the five-foot-tall birds, once on the very brink of extinction, had not been seen in South Carolina for decades. Their return affirmed the ACE Basin's pivotal importance as an outstanding ecosystem.

One reason the basin has remained largely intact is that the three winding rivers and their associated wetlands greatly impede human movements. Very little of the basin is accessible by road. In addition, after the Civil War, wealthy sportsmen from up north purchased many of the old plantations as hunting retreats and managed the newly acquired properties for a wide range of wildlife.

The land stewardship tradition continued through the twentieth century. "The ACE Basin is somewhat unique in that it represents an attempt to prevent, rather than mitigate or retard, widespread degradation and loss of critical ecological resources," noted University of South Carolina biologist Daniel L. Tufford.[1]

Upstream, the basin's rivers and creeks turn brackish, then fresh, coalescing into a web of isolated headwaters surrounded by the mellowed remnants of colonial-era rice plantations. Downstream, the basin's coastal portion is characterized by sea islands, marsh islands, and barrier islands interlaced with estuaries, extensive salt marshes, tidal creeks, and oyster reefs.

The salt marsh dominates in the basin's eastern side. At low tide, glistening oyster reefs and mud flats emerge. When the tide returns, schools of red drum and other marine life move into the warm shallows. Fishermen ply the flats for the red drum and flounder.

In the basin's western reaches the fresh water pushes back the salt. Spartina is replaced by yellow sawgrass and towering old cypress trees—a wetland haven for alligators, bald eagles, and all manner of waterfowl. In winter, flocks of wood ducks, teal, and other fast flyers concentrate in bottomlands, cypress swamps, and flooded old rice fields on private hunting preserves.

The basin, though, encompasses more than just rich natural habitats. It is rife with historic plantations, forts, cemeteries, churches, crossroad country stores, all mellowed with time, all part of the rural terrain, blending in and adding a special beauty of their own to the natural landscape. The basin provided strategic military footholds during the Revolutionary and Civil wars. Before the latter it was the center of rice cultivation in the South. The remaining freshwater impoundments represent some of the last vestiges of the rice plantation culture that flourished here. Because of their strategic benefit to waterfowl, the old rice fields have been tapped for protection under the North American Waterfowl Management Plan.

Two hundred and six thousand acres of this resplendent basin are now protected—an area embracing a national estuarine research reserve, a national wildlife refuge, two state wildlife management areas, and other publicly accessible areas. The protected swaths also include some ninety thousand acres in conservation easements, in which private and corporate landowners pledge minimal development of their lands in exchange for tax breaks and other considerations.

It took one of the most remarkable conservation feats ever seen in America to save this magnificent place—a grassroots effort that has become a model for conservation throughout the country. Private landowners in the ACE Basin helped get the ball rolling, fervently supporting the efforts of government agencies and conservation organizations—entities that haven't always walked arm in arm—to preserve a natural and rural landscape fast fading elsewhere in the South. All the more remarkable is that the preservation took place, and is still taking place, in a state where private property rights are tantamount to religion.

The battle to save the basin is only half won, though. The ever-present threat of development looms. Plans are under way to complete the widening of U.S. Highway 17 from a two-lane country road to a four-lane parkway through the basin, a necessary safety move but one that also is expected to foster development. In addition, exotic invasive species threaten to overwhelm much of the basin's verdant landscape and crowd out native plants and animals to the point where some might disappear. Rising sea levels resulting from climate change already are taking a toll, tainting groundwater and some freshwater wetlands with salt.

Such threats, of course, cast their gloomy shadows all along the Southeast coast. The ACE Basin, however, represents hope, a place where once-opposing factions united to protect the land simply for its beauty, fecundity, and natural richness. Future generations will come here to see how the Southeast coast looked when it was a subtropical Eden that inspired legions of poets, artists, and writers.

Visionaries on a Mission

The movement to protect the ACE Basin commenced in 1988 when Ducks Unlimited, the Nature Conservancy, the South Carolina DNR, the U.S. Fish and Wildlife Service, and powerful private landowners formed a loose-knit coalition known as the ACE Basin Task Force. It was a diverse group—some of the members had even squabbled with one another in the past over environmental and conservation issues.[2]

But this time they were of a common mind: to maintain the ACE Basin's natural beauty and rural makeup by promoting wise management of the land and continuing traditional uses such as farming, timber harvesting, and hunting on a sustainable basis. To succeed, these visionaries knew they needed the full cooperation of every member of the group, especially the landowners. But all of them wondered if the landowners and others could get along long well enough to accomplish these important goals.

That question was answered on September 13, 1989, a week before Hurricane Hugo roared ashore and ripped up the South Carolina coast. Some say the task force got its real start that sunny day. The would-be preservationists gathered under the massive oaks of one of the ACE Basin's historic plantations, Willtown Bluff, on the Edisto River. Their primary aim was to fight a plan for what they greatly feared would be a sprawling, Hilton Head–like development plopped in their midst. Some out-of-state developers wanted to build more than a thousand houses around a golf course and marina on Edisto Island, three miles downriver from where the group was gathered.[3] If the development proceeded, it was certain to breed other development that sooner or later would engulf most of the ACE Basin.

"We were drawing a line in the sand," recalled Charles Lane, a Charleston realtor and staunch conservationist who grew up on Willtown Bluff. "We saw what was coming, and it was unacceptable." The ACE Basin, he and others vowed, was not going to go the way of Hilton Head.

The group made a solemn pledge and agreed on a strategy to fight the development—and in doing so sowed the seeds for victory. Ultimately, the development project was killed when its permit was revoked as a violation of the federal Clean Water Act. To save the land from future development plans, the Nature Conservancy of South Carolina bought it.

Something even more far-reaching, however, came out of the gathering that day. A powerful new movement was born. From that day on, the ACE Basin Task Force was hell-bent on preserving their ways of life and the land they loved for future generations.

"We simply looked at a map of the entire watershed and then marked off an area within it that we thought was in the greatest need of protection," said Lane, who became the task force's chairman. "We then decided that we would try to protect as much of that area as we could."

That area encompassed some 350,000 acres of marshes, islands, bottomland hardwood swamps, forested uplands, maritime forest, old rice fields, farmland, commercial timberland, and other landscapes and ecosystems. The plan quickly became known as the ACE Basin Project and became synonymous with the ACE Basin Task Force.

The task force's initial goal was to protect 90,000 acres of the ACE Basin project. That mark was reached in just a few years—a dizzying pace that surprised even the staunchest conservationists. The goal was reset to 200,000 acres. That goal was exceeded by early 2010 with the protection of some 208,000 acres. "And we're not through yet," Lane said.

"This is a work in progress which Ducks Unlimited and other conservation organizations have used as a template," said Matthew Connolly, retired executive director of DU. "The beauty and wonderment of the area has not changed, nor has the way of life. The people of the ACE Basin have done something very unique, and [they] did it . . . through mutual respect for all the parties involved."[4]

In addition to the state and federal agencies, conservation organizations, and a handful of landowners who initially formed the task force, the movement now includes 113 private landowners, the Lowcountry Open Land Trust, the Nemours Wildlife Foundation, and Mead Westvaco (a timber and paper company). South Carolina DNR director John Frampton called the partnership unprecedented. "This is probably the first project in the United States that really had the private landowners, state, federal government, and nonprofits all working together," he told me.

All along, however, the landowners have been the driving force behind the ACE Basin Project. Initially, a small group of them began reaching out to others about the need to protect their land permanently through conservation easements. Under the terms of the easements, owners and their descendants retain title to the land but agree to maintain it in its natural state and for traditional uses. In return they get a substantial tax break.

The fact that the first group was widely respected within the community and able to influence others helped the cause. Several of the landowners were members of families who had held onto plantations within the ACE Basin for decades and had strong ties with other owners throughout the area. Many of them were outdoor lovers more interested in maintaining their way of life than making a profit on their land. Practicing what they were preaching, they got the ball rolling when they attached conservation easements to their vast holdings. The first was Ted Turner, the billionaire media mogul who owns the fifty-three-hundred-acre Hope Plantation in the middle of the ACE Basin. Shortly afterward Charles Lane and his family placed an easement on their Willtown Bluff Plantation. Other landowners quickly followed their example, in turn convincing their neighbors to resign the development rights to their land through easements.[5]

"The Task Force's unconventional method for protecting the ACE Basin made private landowners the foot-soldiers on a grassroots mission to encourage their fellow landowners to protect their properties through donated conservation easements," Lane said. "One tract at a time, this patchwork quilt of voluntary land protection began. What bound us was . . . a great love of the land, the woods, the waters, the salt marshes. There is an incredibly strong land ethic in South Carolina. I believe that if you love the land, you're going to do what you can to protect it. If we lose this, we have lost who we are."

Success bred success. Senator Ernest Hollings pledged backing from Washington. Publishing giant Gaylord Donnelley, who had already given nearly eight thousand acres to wildlife groups in the 1980s, put an additional ten thousand acres under easements. Soon, *easement* was the buzzword at cocktail parties, candlelight dinners, and oyster roasts of the Lowcountry elite. Landowners who didn't place an easement on their large holdings were politely shunned. For the most part, however, it seemed that big landowners could not wait to jump on the conservation bandwagon on behalf of the ACE Basin. In 2010 Norfolk Southern Railroad Company pledged to protect from development 12,500 acres of ecologically significant land—the Brosnan Forest timber and wildlife preserve—through a conservation easement with the Lowcountry Open Land Trust. The easement is thought to be one of the largest in the Southeast and the largest ever by a corporation in South Carolina.[6]

It won't be the last. The Nature Conservancy's most ambitious North American project now is the protection of a seven-hundred-thousand-acre green space along the lower Savannah River that would create a contiguous natural area space from the ACE Basin to the river. Studies showing the presence of large, intact, contiguous tracts of vital wildlife habitat in the area provided the incentive. Such unfragmented natural areas are vital to the survival of wildlife species such as the black bear and several species of songbirds.

"You need [to protect] 35 percent of land to maintain wildlife, quality of life, good fishing, clean water, and the environmental integrity of a place," said Lane. "That will leave developers with 65 percent of the state. They should be happy with that."

Loving the Land

Perhaps the first effort to develop the ACE Basin began in the 1680s when South Carolina's second town was founded on a bluff above the Edisto River. Originally called New London, it was formed by a splinter group from the original Charles Towne founded in 1670. In the five-hundred-acre hamlet, later called Willtown, settlers neatly laid out streets, blocks, and some 250 lots for homes, businesses, schools, and government functions.

The settlement grew to include a boat dock, several small shops, and two churches. From the 1690s through the 1730s Willtown was an important landmark on the Carolina frontier.[7] But unlike the first settlement, now called Charleston, Willtown ultimately failed. The reasons are not completely clear, but competition from new settlements, isolation, deadly malaria, and plundering British troops during the Revolutionary War probably were major culprits. Whatever the reasons, Willtown by 1800 had become a mere historical footnote in the Lowcountry's vibrant history.[8]

In the eighteenth and nineteenth centuries the ACE Basin became the domain of several planters who grew rice, cotton, and indigo on its river bluffs and fertile floodplains. The enormous rice plantations harnessed the tidal flow of the rivers and creeks. Ownership of the land remained in large tracts until the double blow of the Civil War and hurricanes spelled the end of the plantation society late in the 1800s. Northern industrialists such as the Du Ponts, Fords, and others bought up the land, eager to own the new status symbol—a plantation down south. The new owners maintained their large landholdings for hunting, fishing, cattle farming, silviculture, and other uses, but most of the large plantations remained undeveloped—despite the influx of people who were finding the South Carolina coast a highly desirable place to live. The wealthy landowners had a chance to sell to developers, but most of them opted not to do so—fortunate decisions that later set the groundwork for the ACE Basin Project.

Southerners played a huge role in the basin's preservation as well. Charleston banker Hugh Lane Sr. bought a chunk of Willtown Bluff in 1942 and kept buying bigger tracts for the rest of his life. He finally came to own the house and grounds of the old plantation in the 1970s. His son, Charles Lane, fifty-three, fondly tells stories of happy weekends there. On Friday afternoons, he recalled, the family piled into their station wagon and left Charleston for the country. "When I was a boy, there were few greater pleasures than hunting ducks with my father along the Edisto's black water, hoping to bag a pintail," he told me. "Willtown Bluff was my idea of heaven."

After graduating from college, Lane left the Lowcountry and eventually became an executive for the Fluor Corporation. But his old home lured him back. Shortly after moving back to Charleston in 1987 he came across a newspaper article that disturbed him greatly. A wealthy land speculator, Michael Tang, had received a state permit to build a massive resort and marina on Prospect Hill Plantation, a tract of more than one thousand acres along the Edisto River adjacent to Willtown Bluff. Tang's development plans also called for more than a thousand new homes.

It scared Lane half to death. Here was what he feared most—developers coming in and forever spoiling some of the greatest natural beauty and richness on Earth. He already was worried about Charleston's growth, which was creeping ever nearer to Willtown. Stark reminders of that were the traffic lights that were appearing with ever greater frequency along U.S. Highway 17 South, a major coastal highway. And now Hilton Head seemed to be coming to Edisto. The development would be the ruination of Willtown if it weren't stopped.

Lane hooked up with Dana Beach, whose Coastal Conservation League was getting off the ground at about the same time. Lane found a powerful, smart, and well-connected ally in Beach, who a year before, on behalf of the Sierra Club, had written a formal request that the scenic waters of the Edisto River be given a top protective designation as an outstanding resource water.

Beach was confident that Tang's permit could be successfully appealed before South Carolina's Department of Health and Environmental Control. Lane was not as confident, but the appeal indeed was successful and the battle was won. Buoyed by the victory, the conservationists and landowners set their sights on preserving the ACE Basin. They planned to use a novel method: mixing voluntary conservation easements with private and public land donations. The model "set a standard of how to get conservation done on a large scale using collaboration between private landowners, conservation groups and government agencies," said Mark Robertson, executive director of the Nature Conservancy in South Carolina, in an interview.[9]

Will the same strategy work in the future? That question troubles conservationists. No one is sure if the easements will be legally binding on future owners of the land. So far, at least, none of the easements has been challenged in court. ACE Basin property prices are soaring, however, and succeeding generations may be tempted to take the money in spite of their ancestors' love for the land.

The conservationists, though, fired up by their accomplishments so far, are confident they can deal with any problems that may arise. Beach notes that the public felt helpless to stop coastal development in the 1980s, but

the ACE Basin Project destroyed that notion. "The [project's] real importance is that it has given many people for the first time hope that a place of
great importance is not inevitably going to be developed," Beach said in a
newspaper interview.[10]

A Lowcountry Paradise

I ponder the ACE Basin story on a sunny morning in May while driving
on two-lane, tree-canopied South Carolina Highway 174, the main route
across Edisto Island in the heart of the ACE Basin. Edisto, south of Charleston, is one of South Carolina's largest sea islands and was once home to
sprawling cotton plantations. Now, as a result of the endeavors of the
ACE Basin Project, local land trusts, and others, about half of the island's
forty-eight thousand acres will remain far into the future as woods, farms,
salt marsh, and natural beach.

The highway takes me past the visible results of the conservationists'
achievements: long stretches of salt marsh, maritime forest, tidal creeks,
tomato and melon fields, historic churches and cemeteries, huge live oaks,
old plantation homes, fruit and vegetable stalls, sweetgrass basket stands,
country stores, and other rural icons fast disappearing elsewhere in the
Deep South. Some of my Seabrook ancestors are buried in the old grave-
yards along this route. The highway terminates at Edisto Beach with a superb view of the Atlantic Ocean.

The road itself has received its own brand of protection. In 2009 a
seventeen-mile stretch of S.C. 174 was officially designated a national scenic byway, meaning that the splendid views I'm seeing now will be around
for future generations to enjoy.

My destination this morning is the old Botany Bay Plantation, a 4,630-
acre tract donated by its late owner, hotel magnate John Meyer, to the state
of South Carolina in 1977. Opened to the public in 2008, it represents a
slice of the ACE Basin's biological richness and cultural legacy: old live
oaks, sunflower-filled farm fields, an expansive lake, the ruins of an 1800s
plantation house and slave quarters, duck ponds, a sweeping salt marsh,
and two miles of unspoiled ocean beach.

I enter a long, green tunnel formed by overarching oaks and hickories.
The spreading oak limbs support colonies of resurrection ferns, which are
green after a rain, brown during a dry spell. I park my pickup truck to walk

Botany Bay Plantation.

along a causeway across the salt marsh to the magnificent beach. Fiddler crabs scurry away into the marsh grass as I approach. A great blue heron flaps over a creek filling with water from the incoming tide. Soon I hear the roar of the ocean surf on the beach. A volunteer greets me and tells me that earlier this morning he saw the season's first signs of loggerhead sea turtles, which crawl up on the beach at night to lay their eggs.

On the sandy, shell-flecked beach, I am alone except for a young couple I spy in the distance wading in the surf. A gentle ocean breeze wafts in the clean iodine smell of the sea and rustles the palmettos standing in groves just in back of the dunes. Overhead, squadrons of brown pelicans glide back and forth as if it is their solemn duty to patrol this beautiful place. Behind me, songbirds sing in the tangled thickets of saw palmetto, yaupon holly, and other shrubs. I hear them even over the roar of the surf.

Back in my truck, I drive across another causeway straddling some old duck ponds and stop to peer at the red-brick ruins of the old plantation house. I drive through live oak–dominated maritime woods bordered by a placid salt marsh, and then through a stand of stately pines. As I exit this resplendent place, I utter a word of thanks that it has been set aside, declared off-limits forever to bulldozers and chainsaws.

And yet, I know that another, more powerful threat looms—an inexorable force that ultimately could ruin this magnificent place and others like it despite our best efforts to save them. One day, perhaps in our grandchildren's lifetimes, much of the ACE Basin and other huge portions of the Southeast coast could be underwater. As sea levels rise, vast stretches of salt marsh could disappear beneath the ocean. Estuaries could lose much of their vitality and productivity. Entire towns and cities could be forced to retreat to higher ground.

The Warming

An international legion of scientists is convinced that the sea will rise between seven and twenty-three inches by the end of this century. Some say it could be even more—as much as three to seven feet if the polar ice caps continue to melt.

The sea level has been rising, of course, since the peak of the last ice age some twenty thousand years ago, when the glaciers slowly began to melt and recede. For most of that time the rise was about one millimeter per year—a tiny fraction of an inch. Salt marshes were not damaged by the rise because sediments deposited by rivers and ocean currents kept pace with it. Since the Industrial Revolution began around 1750, however, fossil-fuel burning has boosted the amount of carbon dioxide and other gases in the atmosphere, trapping more of Earth's reflected heat—the greenhouse effect.

The melting is a double whammy: additional water goes into the oceans and the water expands as it warms. As a result, the global rate of sea level rise has tripled over the past century to an average of about three millimeters—about a tenth of an inch—per year. The Southeast coast's sea level rise reflects the global average. Scientists report that the sea level along Georgia's coast has risen about three millimeters a year for the past seventy years.[11] The current relative rate of sea level rise in Charleston is approximately three and a quarter millimeters per year, or approximately one foot per century.[12]

It was the prestigious Intergovernmental Panel on Climate Change that predicted the seven- to twenty-three-inch global sea level rise by 2100.[13] The assessment was a state-of-the-science report providing scenarios of how climate change will alter ecosystems, natural resources, and societies worldwide. But no sooner was the report released than some scientists were calling it much too conservative. More refined projections, they contended, put the increase at perhaps three to six feet by the end of the century. Famed coastal geologist Orrin Pilkey Jr. advised "governments, businesses, and homeowners [to] . . . assume that the world's oceans will rise by at least two meters—roughly seven feet—this century."[14] The disparities and the wide ranges were—and still are—the results of gaping unknowns: How much of the ice sheets in Greenland and Antarctica actually will melt? Will humans manage to significantly slow the rate of greenhouse gas emissions? Will ocean currents and chemistry change? Will the water rise be gradual or will it occur in bursts?

Other factors also need to be figured in. For instance, the amount of coastal land that will be covered by rising water may depend on the degree of naturally occurring land subsidence. Over the past several thousand years, large swaths of the Southeast coast have been slowly sinking as the sediments deposited there over millennia have compacted. As an example, scientists estimate that the Charleston area has sunk by roughly six inches during the past seventy years.

Scientists, government officials, community leaders, environmental groups, and others in the Southeast are not waiting for all the data to come in. They say they have enough evidence in hand to warrant taking action. Spurred by the knowledge that some 25 percent of the populations of Georgia, South Carolina, North Carolina, and northeast Florida live in the coastal areas most at risk from sea level rise, they already are studying and devising—and in some cases implementing—strategies to mitigate the impacts of sea level rise.

"The problems [of sea level rise] aren't insolvable," Ron Carroll, director of the University of Georgia's River Basin Center, told me. "But we have to be willing to say, 'Start planning now.'" His center is mapping areas of population growth and critical habitat in Georgia that are likely to be affected. Meanwhile, planners in the Savannah area are looking at wider mandatory setbacks from water bodies and stringent new storm-water management tools as a first-line defense not only for sea level rise but also for more powerful hurricanes and flooding.

Most of the predictions are based on climate-change models and computer-generated maps. For salt marshes, the models paint an especially gloomy picture. If the models are right, no amount of planning may be able to save many wide stretches of marsh from the predicted inunda-tion. One computer model suggests that 20–45 percent of Georgia's total salt marsh acreage will have converted to open water by 2100.[15] Similar scenarios are forecast for South Carolina and North Carolina. The U.S. Fish and Wildlife Service says the thirty thousand acres of salt marsh in South Carolina's Cape Romain National Wildlife Refuge—an important waterfowl sanctuary north of Charleston—could dwindle to about five thousand acres by the end of this century.[16] A three-foot sea level rise in North Carolina would inundate much of the coast for a mile inland.[17]

Despite their hardiness, salt marshes can't stay healthy when they are constantly flooded. Marsh grasses die from stress, the sediments disperse, and then the wetland sinks. If salt marshes are wiped out, nurseries for marine life, sinks for carbon dioxide and nitrogen, flood prevention, nutri-ent control, waste treatment, and bird and animal feeding areas will be lost as well.

The ability for salt marshes to keep pace with sea level rise depends on location, elevation, sediment supply, and the opportunity to migrate land-ward. Many salt marshes in the past have escaped constant inundation by naturally migrating inland over forest edges and other upland areas. Now, the pace of that migration may be accelerating. Both South Carolina and North Carolina are already facing dramatic losses of uplands as marshes and tidal creeks try to move inland.

Sooner or later, though, the migrating marshes will bump into concrete and asphalt. Many property owners likely will try to stave off the rising water by building bulkheads and revetments. The walls may work for a while, but the rising seas will eventually win—at the cost of the salt marsh. "If you build a bulkhead along a salt marsh and prevent it from migrating inland, then the marsh will eventually drown," warned James T. Morris, director of the University of South Carolina's Belle W. Baruch Institute.[18]

As if all of this weren't enough, many salt marshes are suffering from still another deficiency: lack of incoming sediment. Salt marshes have stayed a step ahead of rising seas by adding on new layers of soil from sedi-ments ferried in by tidal currents and rivers transporting eroded soil from uplands. Now, however, the supply of sediments is diminishing at a time when the marshes need them most. Dredging, dams, seawalls, and revet-ments are interfering with the movement of sediment into the salt marshes and other wetlands. John H. Tibbetts, editor of *Coastal Heritage* magazine, says that the really important question is: "For the next 50 to 100 years, will we be able to get enough sediment to maintain the wetlands' elevation above sea level?"[19] Sea level rise aside, climate change may spawn other adversities that would spell serious trouble for coastal ecosystems. New diseases and pests associated with a warmer climate might pose a menace to people and wildlife. More ferocious hurricanes might wreak massive damage on the coast. Disruptions in rainfall patterns could seriously hamper the seasonal flow of fresh water into estuaries and thus alter salinity patterns. Many marine animals would not be able to cope with the salinity changes. Decreased river flows could allow salt water to move up streams and rivers, taint groundwater drinking supplies, and transform freshwater swamps into "ghost forests" of dead trees. Encroaching salt water also could cause highly productive fresh and brackish marshes to convert to highly saline salt marshes.

A statement in the 2009 draft comprehensive management plan for the Hollings National Wildlife Refuge, deep in the ACE Basin, sums up the uncertainties surrounding climate change and suggests a practical approach for dealing with the possible calamities:

> No one can be certain exactly how climate change would affect the refuge's plants and animals; however, there is little doubt that the effects would be quite noticeable when comparing biological notations over a span of 30–80 years.
>
> At best, wildlife and plant species would adapt to the changed environment, but in a worse case situation the refuge could lose many species of plants and animals. Perhaps the first to adapt or be eradicated from the refuge would be reptiles, amphibians and fish. Because there are no clear cut answers to the total effects of climate change, perhaps it would be best to prepare for the worst and hope for the best.[20]

EPILOGUE

MOST OF THIS BOOK has been a portrayal of the ills facing the Southeast coast and the obstacles that groups and individuals face in trying to resolve them. There is no shortage of recommendations and guidelines for protecting the coast. In general, coastal experts agree on several approaches to ward off environmental degradation along the seashore. Some key recommendations include the following.

At the state and county level:

- Take a cue from the ACE Basin Project in South Carolina. Obtain conservation easements and purchase land development rights from landowners to permanently protect the land. To protect the water, you must protect the land.
- Encourage or require "smart-growth strategies" such as alternative and mixed-use developments that maximize pedestrian-friendly areas, protect open spaces, and minimize vehicle use. These designs will enhance the quality of life and protect the quality of tidal creeks.
- Place strict limits on clear-cutting of trees and other vegetation and draining of wetlands.
- Use alternatives to impervious surfaces such as porous concrete and pavers. Now available, for instance, is a semipervious substance that allows water to pass into the soil below yet provides enough structural support for automobiles.
- Require natural, scientifically certified vegetated buffers along streams, around parking lots, and elsewhere to limit storm-water runoff and filter out pollutants.
- Encourage or require new collection systems that can funnel storm-water runoff from parking lots to filters that use layers of absorbent minerals and organic material to cleanse the polluted water.

At neighborhood and subdivision levels:

- Minimize as much as possible the use of pavement and other impervious surfaces. Aim for a goal of no more than 10–15 percent impervious surface in a watershed.
- Design and build retention ponds, rain gardens, and constructed wetlands to provide added treatment of storm water.
- Direct surface water runoff into swales and vegetated buffers to trap pollutants and increase infiltration, thus slowing the movement of storm water into creeks.
- Prepare and publish guidelines and standards that developers must follow to prevent pollution from entering tidal creek and marsh habitats.

At the household level:

- Follow label directions when applying fertilizers and pesticides, and store and dispose of these hazardous household products properly.
- Dispose of trash properly; recycle when possible.
- Pick up and properly dispose of pet wastes (pooper scooper programs).

DANA BEACH POSED some important questions in his Pew Commission report. "Which development patterns can sustain aquatic ecosystems? If sprawl will not work, what will? How do we put the necessary land-use changes in practice throughout America's coastal regions?"[1]

One hopeful sign in tackling such issues on the Southeast coast is the South Atlantic Alliance Partnership Agreement signed in 2009 by the governors of North Carolina, South Carolina, Georgia, and Florida. The pact, which created the Governors' South Atlantic Alliance, is touted as a historic agreement among a quartet of states that have squabbled bitterly during the past over water, coastal pollution, and economic expansion. The alliance's mission is to "implement science-based policies and solutions that enhance and protect the value of coastal and ocean resources of the southeastern United States to support the region's culture and economy now and for future generations." To that end, movers and shakers in government, academics, private business, environmental activism, and other areas will

The *Anna*, a research vessel belonging to the Georgia Department
of Natural Resources, at its dock in Brunswick, Georgia.

be brought together to work out ways to better manage and protect coastal
resources while ensuring economic sustainability and resiliency.[2]

Among the alliance's stated goals are to "enable coastal managers and
decision-makers to predict, prevent, enforce, respond and mitigate ecosystem and health impacts" and to "improve ecosystem structure and function by developing and applying sound scientific data to support habitat
conservation, enhancement, and restoration."[3]

These are laudable goals. But even before the ink was dry on the governors' signatures, skeptics and critics were weighing in. For instance, they
rightly pointed out that we have long had laws on the books that could
achieve much of the alliance's stated goals if they were enforced. The laws
include the various states' marsh protection and shore protection acts, the
federal Clean Water Act, the Clean Air Act, the Endangered Species Act,
and the Magnuson-Stevens Fishery Conservation and Management
Act. Perhaps if those measures had been enforced and obeyed to the letter
and spirit of the law, and if the governors and state legislators had given

them full backing, many of the alliance's promised endeavors already would be nearing success. Instead, we continue to see assaults on environmental laws and blatant attempts to weaken them by those who consider them hindrances to money and power. Even more shameful, the attacks have often taken place with the apparent concurrence of governors and legislators, the very ones who should be pushing for stronger enforcement.

But maybe the new effort will work. Maybe the governors and their alliance will accomplish great things—as when powerful forces came together in 1970 to pass Georgia's monumental Coastal Marshlands Protection Act, and when enlightened South Carolina landowners in 1989 joined forces with the government, industry, and environmentalists to protect tens of thousands of acres of the ACE Basin.

We know the problems facing the coast. We need fortitude, commitment, and courage to resolve conflicts with the tools already available. Saluting the four governors for creating the new alliance, the Nature Conservancy laid out in a nutshell the challenges the alliance must grapple with:

> In the Southeast, our coasts and oceans are important to our livelihood and quality of life. People turn to the water for food, recreation, and transportation. At the same time, these waters support a vast array of natural resources—from coastal salt marshes and seagrasses to the birds, fish, and marine mammals that feed and live along our shores. But our coasts and oceans face increasing pressure and conflict. Coastal development impacts water quality and increases risk to human life during hurricanes and coastal storms. Increases in sea level and climate change also are altering natural and human communities. Commercial and recreational uses can crowd our waterways, causing conflicts between man and nature. At the same time, ecosystems and species do not recognize even well-intentioned political boundaries, making effective coastal and ocean management a challenge.[4]

Right now, policy to resolve the growing conflicts between resource protection and economic development is lacking. No one seems to have a good handle, for instance, on how to go about limiting the amount of impervious surfaces, which surely will increase and further degrade ecosystems. Good science is the backbone of good policy, but what is still unknown about salt marshes, estuaries, and other coastal resources will keep researchers busy for many years to come. The causes of marsh die-off are still poorly understood. We don't fully comprehend how estuaries

Creek bank in Georgia's marshes of Glynn.

function and the essential roles of fresh water in them. We don't know the impacts of groundwater on coastal ecosystems, although the effects may be substantial. We still lack knowledge about the vital roles of bacteria and other microorganisms in recycling nutrients and wastes in marsh and estuary. And no one knows with a high degree of certainty the full impacts of sea level rise.

BUT WE NEED more than scientists, politicians, and lawyers to comprehend and protect our coasts. We also need poets, artists, and composers to inspire us, as they have done through the ages.

Friends introduced Steven Darsey, an Atlanta composer and music director, to Sidney Lanier's poetry in 1986. "Through his passionate poems, I developed a great love of our wonderful, fertile salt marshes," Darsey told me. "I absorbed everything Sidney Lanier wrote and all that had been written about him." Darsey went to Brunswick and tried to retrace Lanier's footsteps to better understand the poet's fascination with the great marsh.

"I believe Lanier came to understand the salt marshes long before the scientists did," Darsey said.

Then Darsey had an idea—he would take Lanier's great work to a new height: he would set it to music. Sometime soon a symphony orchestra in concert with a choir of dozens of voices will imbue "The Marshes of Glynn" with new spirit. Lanier's immortal verse will be sung. And perhaps new generations will be uplifted and weary minds refreshed "by a world of marsh that borders a world of sea."

Chapter One. The Poetry of the Marsh

1. Mary Day Lanier, ed., with a memorial by William Hayes Ward, *The Poems of Sidney Lanier* (Athens: University of Georgia Press, 1967).

2. Ibid.

3. Ibid.

4. Ibid.

5. Edwin Mims, *A Biography of Sidney Lanier* (Champaign, Ill.: Project Gutenberg, 1998), http://www.gutenberg.org/ebooks/1224.

6. Ibid.

7. Pat Conroy, *The Prince of Tides* (Boston: Houghton Mifflin, 1986), 5.

8. John Teal and Mildred Teal, *Life and Death of the Salt Marsh* (New York: Ballantine Books, 1971), 2.

9. Daniel Parshley, "Comments from the Glynn Environmental Coalition on Environmental Protection Agency, 40 CFR part 52, EPA-R04-OAR-2005-GA-0005-0001; FRL-8003-4," December 29, 2005.

10. James M. Fallows, *The Water Lords* (New York: Bantam Books, 1971), 128.

11. Richard J. Lenz, *Longstreet Highroad Guide to the Georgia Coast & Okefenokee* (Lanham, Md.: Taylor Trade Publishing, 2001), 217.

12. Ibid.

13. U.S. Environmental Protection Agency, Region IV Superfund, "LCP Chemicals Site Summary Profile," EPA ID: GAD099303182.

14. Sherry Baker, "A Toxic Legacy," *Public Health* (fall 1997): 10–11.

15. Agency for Toxic Substances and Disease Registry, Atlanta, Ga., "ToxFAQs for Mercury," CAS 7439-97-6.

16. United States of America v. Christian A. Hansen, Alfred R. Taylor, et al., 262 F.3d 1217 (11th Cir. 2001), case no. 99-11638.

17. U.S. Environmental Protection Agency, Region IV Superfund, "Terry Creek Dredge Spoil Area/Hercules Outfall Site Summary Profile," EPA ID: GAD982112658.

18. "Grass Shrimp May Become a Leading Ecological Indicator," NOAA *Magazine*, August 15, 2006, http://www.noaanews.noaa.gov/stories2006/s2682.htm.

19. Georgia Department of Natural Resources, "Guidelines for Eating Fish from

Georgia Waters, 2010 Update," 51–55, http://www.gaepd.org/Files_PDF/gaenviron /GADNR_FishConsumptionGuidelines_Y2010.pdf.

20. Keith A. Maruya, Leo Francendese, and Randall O. Manning, "Residues of Toxaphene Decrease in Estuarine Fish after Removal of Contaminated Sediments," *Estuaries and Coasts* 28 (October 2005): 786–93.

21. U.S. Environmental Protection Agency, Region IV Superfund, "Hercules 009 Landfill Site Summary Profile," EPA ID: GAD980556906.

22. U.S. Environmental Protection Agency, Region IV Superfund, "Brunswick Wood Preserving Site Summary Profile," EPA ID: GAD981024466.

23. Center for Quality Growth and Regional Development at the Georgia Institute of Technology, *Georgia Coast 2030: Population Projections for the 10-County Coastal Region* (Atlanta: Coastal Georgia Regional Development Center, 2006), 4.

Chapter Two. A Walk across the Marsh

1. James G. Turek, Timothy E. Goodger, Thomas E. Bigford, et al., "Influence of Freshwater Flows on Estuarine Productivity," NOAA Technical Memorandum NMFS-F/NEC-46, May 1987, 7–8.

2. John M. Teal, "Distribution of Crabs in Georgia Salt Marshes," *Ecology* 39 (April 1958): 186–93.

3. USDA Natural Resources Conservation Service, "Plant Guide: Groundsel Tree, *Baccharis halimifolia*."

4. Dale Rosengarten, *Row upon Row: Sea Grass Baskets of the South Carolina Lowcountry* (Columbia: University of South Carolina Press, 1986).

5. Richard J. Wiegert and Byron J. Freeman, "Tidal Salt Marshes of the Southeastern Atlantic Coast: A Community Profile," *Biological Report* 85 (7.29), U.S. Fish and Wildlife Service, September 1990.

6. Teal, "Distribution of Crabs in Georgia Salt Marshes."

7. Wiegert and Freeman, "Tidal Salt Marshes of the Southeastern Atlantic Coast."

8. Ibid.

9. Charles M. Hudson, *Black Drink: A Native American Tea* (Athens: University of Georgia Press, 1979).

10. Timothy J. Wilt, Areef Ishani, Gerold Stark, et al., "Saw Palmetto Extracts for Treatment of Benign Prostatic Hyperplasia," *Journal of the American Medical Association* 280 (November 11, 1998): 1604–9.

11. "Little St. Simons Island," *New Georgia Encyclopedia*, http://www.georgia encyclopedia.org/nge/Article.jsp?id=h-647.

12. Center for Quality Growth and Regional Development, *Georgia Coast 2030: Population Projections for the 10-County Coastal Region* (Atlanta: Georgia Institute of Technology, September 2006), 4.

13. Scenic America, "Losing Our Landscapes: Top Ten At-Risk Areas," November 16, 2001, Washington, D.C.

Chapter Three. Tide Watching

1. Charles Peter Hoffer, *Cry Liberty: The Great Stono River Rebellion of 1793* (Oxford: Oxford University Press, 2010).

2. Richard J. Wiegert and Byron J. Freeman, "Tidal Salt Marshes of the Southeastern Atlantic Coast: A Community Profile," *Biological Report* 85 (7.29), U.S. Fish and Wildlife Service, September 1990, 4.

3. Ibid.

4. Ibid.

5. Lawrence Pomeroy and Richard Wiegert, eds., *The Ecology of a Salt Marsh* (New York: Springer-Verlag, 1981), 10.

6. Ibid.

7. Ibid.

8. Wiegert and Freeman, "Tidal Salt Marshes of the Southeastern Atlantic Coast."

9. John Teal and Mildred Teal, *Life and Death of the Salt Marsh* (New York: Ballantine Books, 1971), 86–94.

10. John W. Day Jr., Charles A. S. Hall, W. Michael Kemp, et al., eds., *Estuarine Ecology* (New York: John Wiley and Sons, 1989), 214.

11. Ibid.

12. Teal and Teal, *Life and Death of the Salt Marsh.*

13. H. E. Taylor Schottle, "Coastal Georgia's Natural History: Salt Marshes," University of Georgia Marine Extension Service, http://www.marex.uga.edu /aquarium/NatMarsh.html.

14. Ibid.

15. Ibid.

16. Ibid.

17. Wiegert and Freeman, "Tidal Salt Marshes of the Southeastern Atlantic Coast."

18. Ibid.

19. Richard Dame, Merryl Alber, Dennis Allen, et al., "Estuaries of the South Atlantic Coast of North America: Their Geographical Signatures," *Estuaries* 23 (December 2000): 793–819.

20. Ibid.

21. Ibid.

22. Wiegert and Freeman, "Tidal Salt Marshes of the Southeastern Atlantic Coast," 2.

23. Ibid.

24. Ibid.

25. Ibid.

26. Dame et al., "Estuaries of the South Atlantic Coast of North America."

27. Merryl Alber and Janice Flory, "Effects of Changing Freshwater Inflow to Estuaries: A Georgia Perspective," Georgia Coastal Research Council, November 2002.

28. John Teal, "Energy Flow in the Salt Marsh Ecosystem of Georgia," *Ecology* 43 (1962): 614–24.

29. Pamela Mason and Lyle Varnell, "Detritus: Mother Nature's Rice Cake," Technical Report 96-10, Virginia Institute of Marine Sciences, 1996.

30. Ibid.

31. Ibid.

32. Ibid.

33. Evelyn B. Haines, "The Origins of Detritus in a Georgia Salt Marsh," *Oikos* 29 (1977): 254–60.

34. Wiegert and Freeman, "Tidal Salt Marshes of the Southeastern Atlantic Coast," 16–21.

35. Ibid.

36. National Oceanic and Atmospheric Administration, "Sapelo Island National Research Reserve Management Plan 2008–2013," 2008, 3.

37. Teal and Teal, *Life and Death of the Salt Marsh*, 180.

38. Zhaohui Alec Wang and Wei-jun Cai, "Carbon Dioxide Degassing and Inorganic Carbon Export from a Marsh-Dominated Estuary (the Duplin River): A Marsh CO2 Pump," *Limnology and Oceanography* 49, no. 2 (2004): 341–54.

39. Georgia Department of Natural Resources, Coastal Resources Division, "Georgia's Salt Marshes," http://crd.dnr.state.ga.us/content/displaycontent.asp?txtDocument=22.

40. Wiegert and Freeman, "Tidal Salt Marshes of the Southeastern Atlantic Coast," 1.

Chapter Four. Too Big for Its Britches

1. Michael Norman and Beth Scott, *Haunted Heritage: A Definitive Collection of North American Ghost Stories* (New York: Forge Books–Macmillan, 2002), 245.

2. Official letter from Roy E. Crabtree, NIMS regional administrator, to Lt. Col. Jason Kirk, commander of Charleston District of the U.S. Army Corps of Engineers, October 28, 2010.

3. S. B. Bricker, B. Longstaff, W. Dennison, et al., *Effects of Enrichment in the Nation's Estuaries: A Decade of Change*, NOAA Coastal Ocean Program Decision Analysis, series no. 26 (Silver Spring, Md.: National Centers for Coastal Ocean Science, 2007).

4. Ibid.

5. Peter Verity, Merryl Alber, and Suzanne Bricker, "Development of Hypoxia in

Well-Mixed Subtropical Estuaries in the Southeastern USA," *Estuaries and Coasts* 29 (2006): 665–73.

6. Peter Verity and David Borkman, "A Decade of Change in the Skidaway River Estuary. III. Plankton," *Estuaries and Coasts* 33 (2009): 513–40.

7. Laura Birsa and Marc Frischer, "Are the Gelatinous Phytoplankton Increasing in the Skidaway River Estuary?" (paper presented at the ASLO Aquatic Sciences meeting, Puerto Rico, February 13–18, 2011).

8. Marc Frischer, Laura Birsa, and Peter Verity, "The Skidaway Estuary: The Continuing Saga of an Anthropogenic Eutrophication Process" (paper presented at the ASLO Aquatic Sciences Meeting, Puerto Rico, February 13–18, 2011).

9. Dana Beach, *Coastal Sprawl: The Effects of Urban Design on Aquatic Ecosystems in the United States* (Arlington, Va.: Pew Oceans Commission, 2002), 11.

10. Fred Holland, Denise Sanger, Dan Bearden, et al., *The Tidal Creeks Project: Understanding Coastal Waterways* (Columbia: South Carolina DNR, 2005).

11. Ibid.

12. Personal interview with Fred Holland, September 27, 2007.

13. Beach, *Coastal Sprawl*, 11.

14. Holland et al., *The Tidal Creeks Project.*

15. Ibid.

16. Fred Holland and Denise Sanger, *Tidal Creek Habitats: Sentinels of Coastal Health*, South Carolina Sea Grant Consortium, National Ocean Service agreement MOA-2006-025/7182, 2006.

17. South Carolina Department of Health and Environmental Control, Office of Ocean and Coastal Resource Management, "Charleston Harbor Special Area Management Plan," February 2000.

18. Bo Petersen, "Pollution from Stormwater Threatens Harbor," *Charleston Post and Courier*, August 27, 2007, sec. 1-A.

19. Ibid.

20. Ibid.

21. John H. Tibbetts, "Gullah's Radiant Light," *Coastal Heritage* 19 (South Carolina Sea Grant Consortium) (winter 2004–5): 3–13.

22. National Park Service, "Low Country Gullah Culture: Special Resource Study and Final Environmental Impact Statement," Southeast Regional Office, Atlanta, Ga., July 2005, 92.

23. Beach, *Coastal Sprawl*.

Chapter Five. Farms in the River

1. Buddy Sullivan, *Early Days on the Georgia Tidewater* (Darien, Ga.: McIntosh County Commission, 1990).

2. Richard J. Lenz, *Longstreet Highroad Guide to the Georgia Coast & Okefenokee* (Lanham, Md.: Taylor Trade Publishing, 2001).

3. Ibid.

4. Ibid.

5. Melissa Faye Greene, *Praying for Sheetrock* (New York: Da Capo Press, 2006).

6. Joseph H. Kelly, Orrin Pilkey, and J. A. G. Cooper, *America's Most Vulnerable Coastal Communities* (Boulder, Colo.: Geological Society of America, 2009), 85.

7. David A. Stallman, *Echoes of Topsail: Stories of the Island's Past* (Caribou, Maine: ECHOES Press, 2004), back cover.

8. Kathleen Angione, "Crowding Out Shellfish," *Coastwatch* (winter 2006): 7–9.

9. Ibid.

10. Wade Rawlins, "Tougher Rules Likely for Storm Runoff," *Raleigh News and Observer*, October 7, 2007, sec. 1-A.

11. Ibid.

12. Associated Press, "NC Stormwater Rules Receive Final Approval," July 15, 2008

13. Ibid.

14. Michael A. Mallin, "Wading in Waste," *Scientific American* 294 (June 2006): 52–59.

15. Ibid.

16. Dana Beach, *Coastal Sprawl: The Effects of Urban Design on Aquatic Ecosystems in the United States* (Arlington, Va.: Pew Oceans Commission, 2002), 11.

Chapter Six. Gone with the Flow

1. The Nature Conservancy and the Southeast Aquatics Resources Partnership, "Conserving the Altamaha River Watershed: Conservation Action Plan," November 2005.

2. Ibid.

3. Cathy J. Sakas, "Altamaha River Watershed Education Module," Gray's Reef National Marine Sanctuary.

4. "America's Most Endangered Rivers of 2002," http://www.americanrivers.org /assets/pdfs/mer-past-reports/Past%20MER/mer_2002.pdf, 26.

5. Georgia Department of Natural Resources, "Altamaha River Could Support Withdrawal by TSG, Says the Environmental Protection Division of the Georgia Department of Natural Resources," press release, December 4, 1997.

6. Merryl Alber, "A Conceptual Model of Estuarine Freshwater Inflow Management," *Estuaries and Coasts* 25 (2002): 1246–61.

7. R. E. Krause and J. S. Clarke, "Coastal Ground Water at Risk—Saltwater Contamination at Brunswick, Ga., and Hilton Head Island, S.C.," U.S. Geological Survey Water Resources Investigations Report 01-4107, 2001.

8. J. David Whitaker, "Sea Science—Blue Crabs," brochure 06MR5468, Marine Resources Division, South Carolina DNR.

9. Merryl Alber and Joan R. Shelton, "Trends in Salinities and Flushing Times

of Georgia Estuaries," in *Proceedings of the 1999 Georgia Water Conference*, March 30–31, 1999, University of Georgia, Athens, 528.

10. Steven Koppes, "A River Runs to It," *University of Georgia Research Magazine* (summer 1999): 7–12.

11. Alber and Sheldon, "Trends in Salinities and Flushing Times of Georgia Estuaries."

12. Koppes, "A River Runs to It."

13. "New Sponge Crab Regulations to Go into Effect," *Georgia Blue Crab Journal* (April 2002) (Coastal Resources Division, Georgia DNR).

14. C. H. Wharton, W. M. Kitchens, E. C. Pendleton, et al., "The Ecology of Bottomland Hardwood Swamps of the Southeast: A Community Profile," *Biological Report* FWS/OBS-81/37, U.S. Fish and Wildlife Service, Biological Services Program, Washington, D.C., 1982.

15. Christopher K. DeScherer, L. P. Fabrizio, William W. Sapp, et al., *At the Tipping Point* (Charlottesville, Va.: Southern Environmental Law Center, 2007).

16. Brad Haire, "Tiny Creatures Indicate River's Health," *University of Georgia Research Magazine* (fall 2007): 6.

17. Wharton et al., "The Ecology of Bottomland Hardwood Swamps of the Southeast."

18. Patrick J. Mulholland, "Formation of Particulate Organic Carbon in Water from a Southeastern Swamp-Stream," *Limnology and Oceanography* 26 (July 1981): 790–95.

Chapter Seven. A Tale of Two Rivers

1. Monica Simon Dodd, "Lower Savannah River Restoration Study," in *Proceedings of the Georgia Water Resources Conference*, April 20–21, 1993, University of Georgia, Athens.

2. Edwin M. EuDaly, "Reconnaissance and Planning Aid Report on Savannah River Basin Study," U.S. Fish and Wildlife Service, Southeast Region, Atlanta, Ga., July 1999.

3. Analysis of the 2009 Toxic Release Inventory released by the U.S. Environmental Protection Agency, December 16, 2010, http://www.epa.gov/tri/.

4. "Restoration of Flood Pulses to the Lower Savannah River: Responses of Floodplain Invertebrates and Fish," abstract for U.S. Geological Survey Project 2007GA142B.

5. Judy Meyer, Merryl Alber, Will Duncan, et al., "Summary Report Supporting the Development of Ecosystem Flow Recommendations for the Savannah River below Thurmond Dam," River Basin Center, Odum School of Ecology, University of Georgia, June 2003.

6. Amanda Wrona, Donna Wear, Jason Ward, et al., "Restoring Ecological Flows to the Lower Savannah River: A Collaborative Scientific Approach to Adaptive

Management," in *Proceedings of the 2007 Georgia Water Resources Conference*, March 27–29, 2007, University of Georgia, Athens.

7. Ibid.

8. Sandra Postel, "To Save a Sturgeon," Nature Conservancy, http://www.global waterpolicy.org/sturgeon.pdf.

9. National Marine Fisheries Service Shortnose Sturgeon Recovery Team, "Final Recovery Plan for the Shortnose Sturgeon (*Acipenser brevirostrum*)," December 1998.

10. Postel, "To Save a Sturgeon."

11. Tom Mackenzie, "U.S. Fish and Wildlife Service Withdraws from Savannah Harbor Deepening Stakeholder Group," U.S. Fish and Wildlife Service, press release R99-019, February 11, 1999.

12. Edwin M. EuDaly, "Plan Formulation Planning Aid Report on Savannah Harbor Expansion," U.S. Fish and Wildlife Service, Southeast Region, Atlanta, Ga., June 2008.

13. Ibid.

14. Wrona et al., "Restoring Ecological Flows to the Lower Savannah River."

15. Southern Environmental Law Center, "Corps Study Shows Deepening of Savannah Harbor Unneeded and Wasteful," press release, January 25, 2011.

16. EuDaly, "Plan Formulation Planning Aid Report on Savannah Harbor Expansion."

17. Letter dated June 18, 2008, from Timothy N. Hall, field supervisor, U.S. Fish and Wildlife Service, Charleston, S.C., to Col. Edward J. Kertis Jr., District Engineer, U.S. Army Corps of Engineers, Savannah, Ga.

18. Ibid.

19. Wrona et al., "Restoring Ecological Flows to the Lower Savannah River."

20. Jeffrey A. Garnett and Darold P. Batzer, "A Study of Fish Communities along a Floodplain Gradient in Two Georgia Watersheds," in *Proceedings of the 2009 Georgia Water Resources Conference*, 298–301.

21. William W. Duncan, Mary C. Freeman, Cecil A. Jennings, et al., "Considerations for Flow Alternatives that Sustain Savannah River Fish Populations," *Proceedings of the 2003 Georgia Water Resources Conference*, April 23–24, 2003, University of Georgia, Athens.

22. John Staed, "Hartwell Is Just One of Competing Lake, River Interests, Corps Commander Says," *Anderson Independent Mail*, May 14, 2009, 1-A.

23. Letter from Rep. J. Gresham Barrett to Mary Glackin, acting director of NOAA, February 10, 2009.

24. Rob Pavey, "Projects to Get $4 Billion," *Augusta Chronicle*, March 26, 2009.

Chapter Eight. An Endangered Culture

1. National Park Service, "Low Country Gullah Culture: Special Resource Study and Final Environmental Impact Statement," Southeast Regional Office, Atlanta, Ga., July 2005, 13.

2. Ibid.

3. Ibid.

4. Ibid., 14.

5. National Trust for Historic Preservation, "National Trust for Historic Preservation Announces 2004 List of America's 11 Most Endangered Historic Places," press release, May 24, 2004.

6. Patricia Guthrie, *Catching Sense: African American Communities on a South Carolina Sea Island* (Westport, Conn.: Praeger, 1996), 1.

7. Marquetta Goodwin, remarks at a briefing at the Foreign Press Center, Washington, D.C., January 31, 2004.

8. Dennis Adams and Hilary Barnwell, "The Gullah Language and Sea Island Culture," Beaufort County, S.C., Library, 2007.

9. Ibid.

10. Ibid.

11. National Park Service, "Low Country Gullah Culture."

12. David Lauderdale, "Riverman Honored by State for Preserving Seaside Traditions," *Island Packet*, Hilton Head, S.C., May 30, 2009.

13. Dahleen Glanton, "Gullah Culture in Danger of Fading Away," *Chicago Tribune*, June 8, 2001.

14. Pierre McGowan, *The Gullah Mailman* (Raleigh, N.C.: Pentland Press, 2000), 99.

15. Congressman James E. Clyburn, "Gullah Land Must Be Preserved on Historic St. Helena Island," press release, Washington, August 7, 2002.

16. Transcript of public hearing held by the National Park Service at Wesley United Methodist Church, John's Island, S.C., July 7, 2009, on the Gullah-Geechee Cultural Heritage Corridor: South Carolina Public Hearings.

17. Dale Rosengarten, *Row upon Row: Sea Grass Baskets of the South Carolina Lowcountry* (Columbia: University of South Carolina Press, 1986).

18. Ibid.

19. Zachary Hart, Angela Halfacre, and Marianne Burke, "Community Participation in Preservation of Lowcountry South Carolina Sweetgrass (*Muhlenbergia filipes*)," *Economic Botany* 58, no. 2 (2004): 161–71.

20. Ibid.

21. Ibid.

22. Clarence Thomas, *My Grandfather's Son: A Memoir* (New York: Harper, 2007).

23. Georgia Conservancy, "Pin Point: Blueprints for Successful Communities" (report prepared for the Pin Point Betterment Association, fall 2009), 11.

24. Ibid.

25. Michele Nicole Johnson, *Sapelo Island's Hog Hammock, GA* (Mount Pleasant, S.C.: Arcadia Publishing, 2009), 7.

26. Cornelia Walker Bailey and Christena Bledsoe, *God, Dr. Buzzard, and the Bolito Man: A Saltwater Geechee Talks about Life on Sapelo Island, Georgia* (New York: Anchor Books, 2001).

27. Ibid.

28. Ibid.

29. Buddy Sullivan, *Images of America: Sapelo Island* (Mount Pleasant, S.C.: Arcadia Publishing, 2000).

30. Ibid.

31. Ibid.

Chapter Nine. The Institute

1. Betty Jean Craige, *Eugene Odum: Ecosystem Ecologist and Environmentalist* (Athens: University of Georgia Press, 2002).

2. Gary W. Barrett and Theresa Lee Barrett, *Holistic Science: The Evolution of the Georgia Institute of Ecology (1940–2000)* (New York: Taylor and Francis, 2001).

3. Ibid.

4. Barbara Kinsey, *A Sapelo Island Handbook* (University of Georgia Marine Institute, 1982).

5. Lawrence Pomeroy, as quoted in Alex Krevar, "Sapelo's Golden Anniversary," *Georgia Magazine* 82 (June 2003): 7.

6. Ibid.

7. Jim Alberts, as quoted in Krevar, "Sapelo's Golden Anniversary," 8.

8. Buddy Sullivan, "Ecology as History in the Sapelo Island National Estuarine Research Reserve," *Occasional Papers of the Sapelo Island NERR* 1 (2008): 18.

9. Vernon J. Henry, "Geology of the Georgia Coast," in *The New Georgia Encyclopedia*, 2009, http://www.georgiaencyclopedia.org/nge/Article.jsp?id=h-2777.

10. Eugene Odum, "Living Marsh," in *Guale, the Golden Coast of Georgia*, ed. Robert Hanie (New York: Friends of the Earth/Seabury Press, 1977).

11. John M. Teal, "Energy Flow in the Salt Marsh System of Georgia," *Ecology* 43, no. 4 (1962): 614–24.

12. Eugene Odum, *Fundamentals of Ecology*, 3rd ed. (Philadelphia: W. B. Saunders, 1977).

13. Michael P. Weinstein and Daniel A. Kreeger, *Concepts and Controversies in Tidal Marsh Ecology* (New York: Springer, 2000), 393.

14. Eugene Odum, keynote address at the dedication of a new wing of the Narragansett, Rhode Island, Laboratory, June 1977, EPA 600/9-79-35.

15. Eugene Odum, "Tidal Marshes as Outwelling/Pulsing Systems," in *Concepts and Controversies in Tidal Marsh Ecology*, ed. Michael Weinstein and Daniel Kreeger, 3–7 (New York: Springer, 2000).

16. Ibid.

1. James E. Kundell and J. Alec Little, "Management of Georgia's Marshlands under the Coastal Marshlands Protection Act of 1970," in *Proceedings of the Fifteenth Annual Conference on Wetlands Restoration and Creation*, May 19–20, 1988 (Madison: University of Wisconsin Digital Collections), 157–71.

2. Ibid.

3. Personal interview with Fred Marland, March 16, 2009.

4. Ibid.

5. Richard J. Wiegert and Byron J. Freeman, "Tidal Salt Marshes of the Southeastern Atlantic Coast: A Community Profile," *Biological Report* 85 (7.29), U.S. Fish and Wildlife Service, September 1990, 45.

6. Videotaped interview with Reid Harris, February 8, 2010, by the University of Georgia Richard B. Russell Library for Political Research and Studies, http://www.libs.uga.edu/russell/collections/reflections.shtml.

7. Reid W. Harris, *And the Coastlands Wait* (Saint Simons, Ga.: self-published, 2008).

8. Gordon Jackson, "Marshes Had Friend in Harris," *Florida Times-Union*, July 2, 2008.

9. Betty Jean Craige, *Eugene Odum: Ecosystem Ecologist & Environmentalist* (Athens: University of Georgia Press, 2002), 101.

10. Ibid.

11. Preamble to the Coastal Marshlands Protection Act of 1970, OCGA, sec. 12-5-280.

12. Harris, "And the Coastlands Wait."

13. Bill Shipp, "Developers Set Their Sights on Coast," *Athens Banner-Herald*, December 10, 2006.

14. Eugene Odum, "Living Marsh," in *Guale, the Golden Coast of Georgia* (New York: Friends of the Earth and Seabury Press, 1977).

15. Ibid.

16. Tonya D. Clayton, Lewis A. Taylor, William J. Cleary, et al., *Living with the Georgia Shore* (Durham, N.C.: Duke University Press, 1992), 81.

17. James E. Kundell, "Status of Georgia's Wetlands Policies and Programs," in *Proceedings of the 2003 Georgia Water Resources Conference*, April 20–21, 2003, University of Georgia, Athens.

18. Shipp, "Developers Set Their Sights on Coast."

19. Mary Landers, "Georgia Supreme Court Declines to Hear Case of Marsh Development," *Savannah Morning News*, May 10, 2004.

20. Terry Dickson, "DNR Rule Goes Too Far, Marsh Act Author Says," *Florida Times-Union*, February 7, 2007.

21. Jim Stokes, "Georgia's Marshes Deserve a Strong Shield," guest editorial, *Atlanta Journal-Constitution*, December 5, 2006.

22. Ibid.

23. Center for a Sustainable Coast et al. v. Coastal Marshlands Protection Committee et al., Supreme Court of Georgia, no. S07G1745, November 17, 2008.

24. Christopher DeScherer, "Georgia Supreme Court Issues Decision in Cumberland Harbour Case That Fails to Fully Protect Coastal Marshlands," Southern Environmental Law Center, press release, November 17, 2008.

25. Vernon "Jim" Henry, personal communication, September 8, 2009.

26. James Charles Cobb, *The Selling of the South: The Southern Crusade for Industrial Development* (Champaign: University of Illinois Press, 1993).

27. Michael N. Danielson and Patricia R. F. Danielson, *Profits and Politics in Paradise: The Development of Hilton Head* (Columbia: University of South Carolina Press, 1995).

28. Ibid.

29. *Time*, January 26, 1970.

30. Danielson and Danielson, *Profits and Politics in Paradise*.

31. Werner Albelhauser, *German Industry and Global Enterprise, BASF: The History of a Company* (Cambridge: Cambridge University Press, 2003).

32. Robert E. McNair, Governor McNair Oral History Project, South Carolina Department of Archives and History, December 13, 1982.

33. "Coastal Management in South Carolina: Past, Present & Future," South Carolina *DHEC*, February 2003.

34. Ibid.

35. Jimmy Chandler, *Mountains & Marshes*, newsletter of the South Carolina Environmental Law Project, December 2003.

Chapter Eleven. Saving the Oyster

1. "Oyster Reef Habitats," Smithsonian Marine Station, Fort Pierce, Fla., 2002, http://www.sms.si.edu/irlspec/Oyster_reef.htm.

2. Roger I. E. Newell, "Ecological Changes in Chesapeake Bay, Are They the Result of Overharvesting the Eastern Oyster (*Crassostrea virginica*)?," in *Understanding the Estuary*, ed. M. P. Lynch and E. C. Krome, 536–46, Chesapeake Research Consortium Publication 129 (CBP/TRS 24/88), Gloucester Point, Va., 1988. For a contradictory opinion, see Lawrence R. Pomeroy, Christopher F. D'Elia, and Linda C. Schaffner, "Limits to Top-Down Control of Phytoplankton by Oysters in Chesapeake Bay," *Marine Ecology Progress Series* 325 (2006): 301–9.

3. Michael W. Beck, Robert D. Brumbaugh, Laura Airoldi, et al, *Shellfish Reefs at Risk: A Global Analysis of Risks and Solutions* (Arlington, Va.: The Nature Conservancy, 2009).

4. Ibid.

5. Newell, "Ecological Changes in Chesapeake Bay."

6. See the laboratory's website at http://www.shellfish.uga.edu.

7. L. M. Bahr and W. P. Lanier, *The Ecology of Intertidal Oyster Reefs of the South Atlantic Coast: A Community Profile*, FWS/OBS 81/15 (Washington, D.C.: U.S. Fish and Wildlife Service, Office of Biological Services, 1981).

8. Richard F. Dame and Bernard C. Patten, "Analysis of Energy Flow in an Intertidal Oyster Reef," *Marine Ecology Progress Series* 5 (1981): 115–24.

9. Ibid.

10. Ibid.

11. Ibid.

12. Eastern Oyster Biological Review Team, "Status Review of the Eastern Oyster (*Crassostrea virginica*)" (report to the National Marine Fisheries Service, Northeast Regional Office, February 16, 2007).

13. Ibid.

14. Beck et al., *Shellfish Reefs at Risk*.

15. Ibid.

16. Ibid.

17. South Carolina Oyster Restoration and Enhancement, http://score.dnr.sc.gov/deep.php?subject=2&topic=17.

18. Ibid.

19. "Notes from the Field. Indian River Lagoon: Oyster Reef Restoration Project," Nature Conservancy Indian River Lagoon Program, Melbourne, Fla., http://www.nature.org/media/florida/oyster restoration fact sheet.pdf.

20. Roger Mann and Eric Powell, "Why Oyster Restoration Goals in the Chesapeake Bay Are Not and Probably Cannot Be Achieved," *Journal of Shellfish Research* 26, no. 4 (2007): 905–17.

21. Ann Green, "Oyster Science on the Edge: Reef Design and Disease Resistance," *Coastwatch* (autumn 2004): 6–9.

22. Pat Conroy, *Pat Conroy Cookbook: Recipes of My Life* (New York: Bantam Books, 2004).

23. Collins Doughtie, "May Day for the May River: How Can We Save the County's Pristine Waters," *Island Packet*, Hilton Head, S.C., January 28, 2009.

24. Weston Newton, *Bluffton (S.C.) Today*, February 8, 2009, 7.

25. South Carolina Department of Health and Environmental Control, Shellfish Sanitation Section, "2009: Shellfish Growing Area Status Report," Columbia, March 2010.

26. "Bluffton Township Watershed Plan," South Carolina Coastal Conservation League, Charleston, http://coastalconservationleague.org/projects/bluffton-township-watershed-plan/.

27. Comprehensive Annual Financial Report for the Town of Bluffton, South Carolina, February 9, 2009.

28. Ibid.

29. Robert F. Van Dolah, Denise Sanger, and Amy Filipowicz, "A Baseline Assessment of Environmental and Biological Conditions in the May River, Beaufort County, South Carolina," S.C. DNR, 2004.

30. Coastal Conservation League, "Bluffton Township Watershed Plan: User Guide & Study Summary," August 2009, 1.

31. Town of Bluffton, "May River Shellfish Harvesting Area Reclassification," press release, August 20, 2010.

32. Ernest Ingersoll, *The Oyster Industry* (Washington, D.C.: Government Printing Office, 1881), 126.

33. Victor Burell, "Overview of the South Atlantic Oyster Industry," in *Proceedings of the North America Oyster Workshop,* World Mariculture Society special publication 1 (1982): 125–31.

34. Ibid.

35. Justin Manley, Alan Power, and Randal Walker, "Wild Eastern Oyster, *Crassostrea virginica,* Spat Collection for Commercial Grow-out in Georgia," University of Georgia Marine Extension Service, 2008.

36. E. P. Churchill Jr., *The Oyster and the Oyster Industry of the Atlantic and Gulf Coasts* (Washington, D.C.: Bureau of Fisheries, U.S. Department of Commerce, 1920), 7.

37. Fran Marscher, *Remembering the Way It Was at Hilton Head, Bluffton, and Daufuskie* (Charleston, S.C.: History Press, 2005).

38. Victor Burrell Jr., *South Carolina Oyster Industry: A History* (Columbia: South Carolina DNR, 2003).

39. Ibid.

40. Jeanne Moutoussamy-Ashe, *Daufuskie Island: 25th Anniversary Edition* (Columbia: University of South Carolina Press, 2007).

41. Marscher, *Remembering the Way It Was.*

Chapter Twelve. Saving the Marsh

1. Chandra Franklin, Marsh Dieback Research Laboratory, Savannah State University, Savannah, Ga., http://linux.savannahstate.edu/mdrl/contactus.htm.

2. Brian R. Silliman, Johan van de Koppl, Mark D. Bertness, et al., "Drought, Snails, and Large-Scale Die-off of Southern U.S. Salt Marshes," *Science* 310 (December 16, 2005): 1803–6.

3. Ibid.

4. Merryl Alber, "Update on Coastal Marsh Dieback Prepared for GA DNR—Coastal Resources Division," Georgia DNR, Coastal Resources Division, Brunswick, January 2008.

5. Steven Y. Newell, "Multiyear Patterns of Fungal Mass Dynamics and Produc-

tivity within Naturally Decaying Smooth Cordgrass Shoots," *Limnology and Ocean-ography* 46, no. 3 (2001): 573–83.

6. Brian R. Silliman and Steven Y. Newell, "Fungal Farming in a Snail," *Proceedings of the National Academy of Sciences* 100, no. 26 (2003): 15643–48.

7. Ibid.

8. Whitney M. Kiehn and James T. Morris, "Relationships between *Spartina alterniflora* and *Littoraria irrorata* in a South Carolina Salt Marsh," *Wetlands* 29, no. 3 (2009): 818–25.

9. Mark D. Bertness, "Ribbed Mussels and *Spartina alterniflora* Production in a New England Salt Marsh," *Ecology* 65 (December 1984): 1794–1807.

10. Barbara H. Grimes, Melvin T. Huish, J. Howard Kerby, et al., "Species Profile: Atlantic Marsh Fiddler," *Biological Report* 82 (11.114), TR-EL-82-4, U.S. Fish and Wildlife Service, September 1989.

11. Elizabeth Wenner, "Fiddler Crabs," South Carolina DNR, http://www.dnr.sc .gov/cwcs/pdf/FiddlerCrab.pdf.

12. Steven Y. Newell's website: http://newell.myweb.uga.edu/mussels.htm.

13. Gary Anderson, "Species Profile: Grass Shrimp," *Biological Report* 82 (11.35), TR-EL-82-4, U.S. Fish and Wildlife Service, 1985.

14. Barbara J. Abraham, "Species Profile: Mummichog and Killifish," *Biological Report* 82 (11.40), TR-EL-82-4, U.S. Fish and Wildlife Service, 1985.

15. Ronald T. Kneib, "The Role of *Fundulus heteroclitus* in Salt Marsh Trophic Dynamics," *American Zoology* 26, no. 1 (1986): 259–69.

Chapter Thirteen. Rice Fields and Causeways

1. Preamble to the Coastal Marshlands Protection Act of 1970, OCGA, sec. 12-5-280.

2. Richard G. Wiegert and Byron J. Freeman, "Tidal Marshes of the Southeast Atlantic Coast: A Community Profile," *Biological Report* 85 (7.29), U.S. Fish and Wildlife Service, September 1990.

3. Elizabeth Wenner, "Dynamics of the Salt Marsh," Marine Resources Division, South Carolina DNR, Columbia, 2010.

4. U.S. Army Corps of Engineers, "Savannah District Approves First Ga. Salt Marsh Bank," *Clean Water Act News* 1, no. 1 (October–December 2009).

5. Rebecca L. Kihslinger, "Success of Wetland Mitigation Projects," *National Wetlands Newsletter* 30, no. 2 (2008): 14–16.

6. Judith Weis, *Salt Marshes: A Natural and Unnatural History* (Piscataway, N.J.: Rutgers University Press, 2009), 12.

7. Wiegert and Freeman, "Tidal Marshes of the Southeast Atlantic Coast."

8. Position statement, Wetland Mitigation Banking, http://www.sws.org/wet land_concerns/banking.mgi.

9. M. J. James-Pirri, K. B. Raposa, J. G. Catena, et al., "Diet Composition of Mummichogs, *Fundulus heteroclitus*, from Restoring and Unrestricted Regions of a New England Salt Marsh," *Estuarine, Coastal and Shelf Science* 52, no. 3 (2001): 205–13.

10. Skidaway Institute of Oceanography, "Back to Nature: New Life for a Salt Marsh," press release 05-14, September 20, 2005.

11. Wiegert and Freeman, "Tidal Marshes of the Southeast Atlantic Coast."

12. Dan Rice, Susan Knudson, and Lisa Westberry, "Restoration of the Wormsloe Plantation Salt Marsh in Savannah, Georgia," in *Proceedings of the 2005 Georgia Water Resources Conference*, April 25–27, 2005, University of Georgia, Athens.

13. J. David Whitaker, "Feasibility Study to Examine Potential Hydrological and Biological Benefits from Restoring Flow of a Salt Marsh Creek at the Edisto Beach Causeway: Final Project Completion Report," South Carolina DNR, Columbia, July 26, 2007.

14. Rice et al., "Restoration of the Wormsloe Plantation Salt Marsh."

15. Whitaker, "Feasibility Study."

16. Ibid.

Chapter Fourteen. Bridging the Marsh

1. South Carolina Department of Natural Resources, "Coastal Zone and Ecoregion Terrestrial and Aquatic Habitats," http://www.dnr.sc.gov/cwcs/pdf/habitat/CoastalZoneHabitat.pdf.

2. Christine Hladik, Alana Lynes, Chester Jackson, et al., "Understanding Plant Distributions Surrounding Marsh Hammocks within the Georgia Coastal Ecosystems LTER," poster no. 320 (presented at 2009 LTER Scientists Meeting, September 14–16, 2009, Estes Park, Colorado).

3. Laura Fabrizio and Maria S. Calvi, *Georgia's Marsh Hammocks: A Biological Survey* (Charlottesville, Va.: Southern Environmental Law Center, 2003).

4. *Savannah Morning News*, "Ben Affleck and Jennifer Lopez among First to Buy Homes on Hampton Island," April 22, 2003.

5. Eugene Odum, quoted from interview in the film *Georgia's Marsh Hammocks: Circle of Life* (produced by the Georgia Conservancy, Atlanta, 2003).

6. J. David Whitaker, John W. McCord, Philip P. Maier, et al., "An Ecological Characterization of Coastal Hammock Islands in South Carolina," Marine Resources Division, South Carolina DNR, Charleston, 2004, 1.

7. Coastal Marsh Hammock Advisory Council, *Report of the Coastal Marsh Hammock Advisory Council*, Georgia Department of Natural Resources, March 2002, 7.

8. Jingle Davis and Stacy Shelton, "Coastal Controversy: Hammocks: Islands at Risk," *Atlanta Journal-Constitution*, September 22, 2002, F-1.

9. Center for a Sustainable Coast et al. v. Coastal Marshlands Protection Committee, 2002CV52219, Superior Court of Fulton County, Ga., October 24, 2002.

10. Ibid.

11. Gayle Albers and Merryl Alber, "A Vegetative Survey of Back-Barrier Islands Near Sapelo Island, Georgia," in *Proceedings of the 2003 Georgia Water Resources Conference*, April 23–24, 2003, University of Georgia, Athens.

12. Coastal Marsh Hammock Advisory Council, *Report*.

13. South Carolina Coastal Conservation League et al. v. South Carolina Department of Health and Environmental Control, South Carolina Administrative Law Court, Docket no. 99-ALJ-07-0082-CC, May 1, 2000.

14. Coastal Marsh Hammock Advisory Council, *Report*.

15. Ibid., 6.

16. Buddy Sullivan, "Ecology as History in the Sapelo Island National Estuarine Research Reserve," *Occasional Papers of the Sapelo Island NERR* 1 (2008).

17. Fabrizio and Calvi, *Georgia's Marsh Hammocks*.

18. Whitaker et al., "An Ecological Characterization of Coastal Hammock Islands in South Carolina."

19. Ibid.

20. Ibid.

21. Ibid.

22. Coastal Marsh Hammock Advisory Council, *Report*.

23. Stacy Shelton, "50-Foot Buffer to Protect Coastal Marshland Passes," *Atlanta Journal-Constitution*, March 1, 2007, B-8.

24. Nancy Vinson, "Evolution of Regulations for Bridges to Marsh Islands in South Carolina," *Southeastern Environmental Law Journal* 15 (fall 2006): 19.

25. Ibid.

26. *Post and Courier*, "Bridge across Marsh to Park Island Ruled OK," February 23, 2005, B-3.

27. Vinson, "Evolution of Regulations for Bridges to Marsh Islands in South Carolina."

28. Allison Castellan, "Management Tools to Minimize the Impacts of Residential Docks and Piers" (paper presented at a workshop in Durham, New Hampshire, by NOAA, Office of Coastal and Resource Management, November 2003).

29. Arthur Felts and Marijana Radic, *Survey of Coastal Residents' Perceptions of Docks* (Joseph P. Riley Institute for Urban Affairs and Policy Studies, College of Charleston, prepared for the South Carolina Department of Health and Environmental Control, 2001).

30. Denise Sanger, Fred Holland, and C. Gainey, "Cumulative Impacts of Dock Shading on *Spartina alterniflora* in South Carolina Estuaries," *Environmental Management* 33, no. 5 (2004): 741–48.

31. Merryl Alber, Janice Flory, and Karen Payne, *Assessment of Coastal Water Resources and Watershed Conditions at Cumberland Island National Seashore, Georgia*, Technical Report NPS/NRWRD/NRTR-2005/332, National Park Service, 2005.

32. Sanger et al., "Cumulative Impacts of Dock Shading on *Spartina alterniflora* in South Carolina Estuaries."

33. Clark R. Alexander and Michael H. Robinson, "GIS and Field-Based Analysis of the Impacts of Recreational Docks on the Saltmarshes of Georgia" (final report prepared for the Georgia Coastal Zone Management Program, July 2004).

34. Ibid.

35. Mary Landers, "Riverkeeper Questions Dock Rules," *Savannah Morning News*, January 2, 2010.

Chapter Fifteen. The Ultimate Price

1. U.S. Fish and Wildlife Service, "Species Profile: Dusky Seaside Sparrow (*Ammodramus maritimus nigrescens*)," http://ecos.fws.gov/speciesProfile/profile/speciesProfile.action?spcode=B00R.

2. Verlyn Klinkenborg, "Countdown to Extinction," *National Geographic* (January 2009): 82–93.

3. Mark Jerome Walters, *A Shadow and a Song: The Struggle to Save an Endangered Species* (White River Junction, Vt.: Chelsea Green Publishing, 2002).

4. John C. Avis and William S. Nelson, "Molecular Genetics Relationships of the Extinct Dusky Seaside Sparrow," *Science* 243 (February 3, 1989): 646–48.

5. Todd M. Schneider, Giff Beaton, Timothy S. Keyes, and Nathan A. Klaus, *The Breeding Bird Atlas of Georgia* (Athens: University of Georgia Press, 2010), 382–83.

6. Ibid.

7. Ibid.

8. Leigh Ann Harden, Nicholas A. Diluzio, J. Whitfield Gibbons, et al., "Spatial and Thermal Ecology of Diamondback Terrapins (*Malaclemys terrapin*) in a South Carolina Salt Marsh," *Journal of the North Carolina Academy of Sciences* 123, no. 3 (2007): 154–62.

9. William M. Palmer and Carroll L. Cordes, "Habitat Suitability Index Models: Diamondback Terrapin (Nesting)—Atlantic Coast," *Biological Report* 82 (10.151), U.S. Fish and Wildlife Service, 1988.

10. Whit Gibbons, "Diamondback Terrapins Join the List of Turtles Needing Protection," *Athens Banner-Herald*, June 23, 2003.

11. Matt J. Elliott, J. Whitfield Gibbons, Carlos D. Camp, et al., *Amphibians and Reptiles of Georgia* (Athens: University of Georgia Press, 2008), 485–87.

12. Whit Gibbons, "Diamondback Terrapin Is a Favorite Animal," *Athens Banner-Herald*, October 28, 1996.

13. Elliott et al., *Amphibians and Reptiles of Georgia*.

14. Brian R. Silliman and Mark D. Bertness, "A Trophic Cascade Regulates Salt Marsh Primary Production," *Proceedings of the National Academy of Sciences* 99 (2002): 10500–505.

15. J. Whitfield Gibbons, Jeffrey E. Lovich, Anton D. Tucker, et al., "Demographic and Ecological Factors Affecting Conservation and Management of the Diamondback Terrapin (*Malaclemys terrapin*) in South Carolina," *Chelonian Conservation and Biology* 4, no. 1 (2001): 66–74.

16. Andrew M. Grosse, J. Daniel van Dijk, Kerry L. Holcomb, et al., "Diamondback Terrapin Mortality in Crab Pots in a Georgia Tidal Marsh," *Chelonian Conservation and Biology* 8, no. 1 (2009): 98–100.

17. Vincent Guillory, Anne McMillen-Jackson, and Leslie Hartman, *Blue Crab Derelict Traps and Trap Removal Program*, Gulf States Marine Fisheries Commission Publication 88 (May 2001).

18. Helen Fosgate, "Terrapins in Trouble," *University of Georgia Research Magazine* (fall 2008): 7.

19. Michael E. Dorcas, John D. Willson, and J. Whitfield Gibbons, "Crab Trapping Causes Population Decline and Demographic Changes in Diamondback Terrapins over Two Decades," *Biological Conservation* 127 (2007): 334–40.

20. Ibid.

21. Ibid.

22. Ibid.

23. Megan A. Rook, Romuald N. Lipcius, Bret M. Brononer, et al., "Bycatch Reduction Device Conserves Diamondback Terrapin without Affecting Catch of Blue Crab," *Inter-Research Marine Ecology Progress Series* 409 (2010): 171–79.

24. Dorcas et al., "Crab Trapping Causes Population Decline and Demographic Changes in Diamondback Terrapins."

25. Linda Skinner, "Drum: A Culinary Fad Decimated Redfish Stocks, Leaving Black Drum and Imports to Fill the Gap," *Seafood Business* 25, no. 9 (2006).

26. President George W. Bush, "Protection of Striped Bass and Red Drum Fish Populations," Executive Order 13449, October 20, 2007.

27. Ibid.

28. President George W. Bush, remarks made October 20, 2007, at the Chesapeake Bay Maritime Museum, St. Michael's, Md., during signing ceremony of EO 13449.

Chapter Sixteen. Living on the Edge

1. Erin L. Pulster, Kelly L. Smalling, Eric Zolman, et al., "Persistent Organochlorine Pollutants and Toxaphene Congener Profiles in Bottlenose Dolphins (*Tursiops truncatus*) Frequenting the Turtle/Brunswick River Estuary, Georgia, USA," *Environmental Toxicology and Chemistry* 28 (July 2009): 1390–99.

2. National Ocean Service, NOAA, "Scientists Reveal 'Secret Pathologies of Dolphins,'" press release, February 23, 2010.

3. Lori Schwacke, "Ecosystems, Dolphins and Human Health: Understanding Linkages on the Georgia Coast," PowerPoint presentation, http://www.sapelonerr.org/symposium/Lori%20Schwacke%20Ecosystems,%20Dolphins%20and%20Human%20Health%20PPT.pdf.

4. National Ocean Service, NOAA, "Dolphins and PCBs," press release, February 18, 2010.

5. Erin L. Pulster and Keith A. Maruya, "Geographic Specificity of Aroclor 1268 in Bottlenose Dolphins (*Tursiops truncatus*) Frequenting the Turtle/Brunswick River Estuary, Georgia (USA)," *Science of the Total Environment* 393 (April 15, 2008): 367–75.

6. Pulster et al., "Persistent Organochlorine Pollutants and Toxaphene Congener Profiles in Bottlenose Dolphins."

7. Erin L. Pulster, Kelly Smalling, and Keith Maruya, "Predicted Dietary Exposure of POPs in Southeastern U.S. Bottlenose Dolphins" (paper presented at the 25th Annual Meeting of the Society of Environmental Toxicology and Chemistry, Portland, Ore., November 2004).

8. Georgia Department of Natural Resources, "Guidelines for Eating Fish from Georgia Waters, 2010 Update," 53.

9. U.S. Environmental Protection Agency, Region IV Superfund, "LCP Chemicals Site Summary Profile," EPA ID GAD099303182.

10. Ibid.

11. United States of America v. Christian A. Hansen, Alfred R. Taylor, et al., 262 F.3d 121 (11th Cir. 2001), case no. 99-11638, para. 3.

12. Ron R. Odom, "Mercury Contamination in Georgia Rails," Georgia DNR, 1975.

13. United States of America v. Christian A. Hansen et al., para. 4.

14. Ibid.

15. Ibid., para. 6.

16. Ibid.

17. Madilyn Fletcher, Peter Verity, Marc Frischer, et al., "Microbial Indicators and Phytoplankton and Bacterial Communities as Evidence of Contamination Caused by Changing Land Use Pattern" (Land Use–Coastal Ecosystem Study State of Knowledge Report, South Carolina Sea Grant Consortium), 36.

18. Kurunthachalam Kannan, Haruhiko Nakata, Rod Stafford, et al., "Bioaccumulation and Toxic Potential of Extremely Hydrophobic Polychlorinated Biphenyl Cogeners in Biota Collected at a Superfund Site Contaminated with Arochlor 1268," *Environmental Science Technology* 32 (March 13, 1998): 1214–21.

19. Agency for Toxic Substances and Disease Registry, "Toxicological Profile for Mercury," CAS 7439-97-6, March 1999.

20. Natural Resources Defense Council, "New EPA Rules Take Small Step Forward, Giant Leap Backward, on Mercury," press release, September 4, 2003.

21. National Oceanic and Atmospheric Administration, "LCP Chemical Site Monitoring Study," NOAA Technical Memorandum NOS OR&R 5, August 1998.

22. U.S. Environmental Protection Agency, "Mercury, Health Effects, Methylmercury Effects," http://www.epa.gov/mercury/exposure.htm.

23. "Georgia Case Secures Successful Endangered Species Prosecution," U.S. Fish and Wildlife Service, Fish & Wildlife News, July/August 1999, 16.

24. "LCP Abuses: Do Others Share Some Blame?" Chemical Week, August 26, 1998.

25. United States of America v. Christian A. Hansen et al., para. 7.

26. Merryl Alber, Janice Flory, and Karen Payne, "Assessment of Coastal Water Resources and Watershed Conditions at Cumberland Island National Seashore, Georgia," Technical Report NPS/NRWRD/NRTR-2005/332, National Park Service, 2005.

27. Agency for Toxic Substances and Disease Registry, "Public Health Assessment for LCP Chemicals Superfund Site," September 22, 2010, 4.

28. Georgia Coastal Ecosystem LTER site brochure, School of Marine Programs, University of Georgia, Athens, January 19, 2006.

29. Skidaway Institute of Oceanography, "1991 Tritium Release Prompts Current Salt Marsh Research," press release, April 4, 2010.

30. Elizabeth Wenner, "Fiddler Crabs," Comprehensive Wildlife Conservation Strategy Report, South Carolina DNR, 2005, 87.

31. Graeme M. Smith and Judith S. Weis, "Predator-Prey Relationship in Mummichogs (Fundulitis heteroclitus): Effects of Living in a Polluted Environment," Journal of Experimental Marine Biology and Ecology 209, nos. 1–2 (1997): 75–87.

32. James Pinckney, "The Effects of Sublethal Concentrations of Agricultural Herbicides on the Structure and Function of Estuarine Phytoplankton Communities," project no. R/ER-31, Ecosystems Dynamics—Archived FY06-08, 2009, South Carolina Sea Grant Consortium.

33. Maria del Carmen Alvarez and Lee A. Fuiman, "Environmental Levels of Atrazine and Its Degradation Products Impair Survival Skills and Growth of Red Drum Larvae," Aquatic Toxicology 74 (2005): 229–41.

34. Jennifer Beth Sass and Aaron Colangelo, "European Union Bans Atrazine, while the United States Negotiates Continued Use," International Journal of Occupational and Environment Health 12, no. 6 (2006): 260–67.

35. Richard F. Lee and Keith A. Maruya, "Chemical Contaminants Entering Estuaries in the South Atlantic Bight as a Result of Current and Past Land Use," in Changing Land Use Patterns in the Coastal Zone, ed. Gary S. Keppel et al., 205–27 (New York: Springer, 2005).

Chapter Seventeen. The Last Season

1. Derald Pacetti Jr., "Shrimping at Fernandina, Florida, before 1920: Industry Development, Fisheries Regulation, Maritime Maturation" (master's thesis, Florida State University, 1980).

2. Ibid.

3. Mary Alice Monroe, quoted in Marline Wolfe-Miller, "Shrimp Tales with Mary Alice Monroe—Highlight of Fleet Week!" Town of Mount Pleasant, South Carolina, news release, April 5, 2010.

4. John H. Tibbetts, "Our Changing Waterfronts," *Coastal Heritage* 22, no. 2 (fall 2007): 1.

5. Personal communication, Brett Witt, public information director, South Carolina DNR, February 15, 2010.

6. Georgia Department of Natural Resources, Coastal Resources Division, Brunswick, "Commercial Fishing License Data," 2010.

7. Georgia Department of Natural Resources, Coastal Resources Division, "Summary of Georgia Historical Landings," http://crd.dnr.state.ga.us/assets/documents/marfish/broadhis72+.pdf.

8. Stacy Webb and Ronald T. Kneib, "Individual Growth Rates and Movement of Juvenile White Shrimp in a Tidal Marsh Nursery," *Fishery Bulletin* 102, no. 2 (2004): 376–88.

9. National Marine Fisheries Service, "U.S. Seafood Consumption Declines Slightly in 2009," press release, September 9, 2010.

10. National Marine Fisheries Service, "FishWatch: U.S. Seafood Facts," 2010.

11. Mac V. Rawson, "Shrimp Industry," *New Georgia Encyclopedia*, 2003, http://www.georgiaencyclopedia.com/nge/Article.jsp?id=h-794.

12. J. David Whitaker, "Shrimp in S.C.," information brochure from the Sea Science program of the South Carolina DNR, Columbia.

13. Ibid.

Chapter Eighteen. The Beloved Land

1. Daniel L. Tufford, "State of Knowledge Report: South Carolina Coastal Wetland Impoundments," South Carolina Sea Grant Consortium, 2005.

2. "The ACE Basin Project," http://www.acebasin.net/history.html.

3. Ibid.

4. "ACE Basin Project Celebrates 20 Years of Land Conservation," press release, November 25, 2009, South Carolina DNR.

5. National Oceanic and Atmospheric Administration, "ACE Basin Project Elements," http://www.nerrs.noaa.gov/doc/siteprofile/acebasin/html/manage/mgproele.htm#nerr.

6. "Brosnan Forest Easement Largest in State History," *Current Events: Newsletter of Ashepoo, Combahee, Edisto Basin* 17, no. 1 (2009) (South Carolina DNR).

7. Martha Zierden, Suzanne Linder, Ronald Anthony, et al., "Willtown: An Archaeological and Historical Perspective," *Archaelogical Contributions* 27 (1999) (Charleston Museum, South Carolina Department of Archives and History).

8. Ibid.

9. Joey Holleman, "Ace Basin: Protected Forever," *Columbia (S.C.) State*, November 10, 2008, 1.

10. Ibid.

11. Anthony N. Foyle, Vernon J. Henry, and Clark R. Alexander, "Georgia-Coastal Erosion Study: Phase 2 Southern Study Region," South Carolina Sea Grant Consortium, Skidaway Institute of Oceanography, Georgia Southern University, et al., 2004, 8.

12. U.S. Environmental Protection Agency, "The Impact of Climate Change on the Mid-Atlantic Region," 2011, http://www.epa.gov/reg3artd/globclimate/ccimpact.html.

13. Susan Solomon, Dahe Qin, Martin Manning, et al., eds., *Climate Change 2007: The Physical Science Basis. Contribution of Working Group I to the Fourth Assessment Report of the Intergovernmental Panel on Climate Change* (New York: Cambridge University Press, 2007).

14. Orrin H. Pilkey and Rob Young, *The Rising Sea* (Washington, D.C.: Island Press, 2009).

15. Christopher Craft, Jonathan Clough, Jeff Ehman, et al., "Forecasting the Effects of Accelerated Sea-Level Rise on Marsh Ecosystem Services," *Frontiers in Ecology and the Environment* 7, no. 2 (2009): 73–78.

16. Kevin Godsea, "Cape Romain National Wildlife Refuge: Climate Change Impacts," U.S. Fish and Wildlife Service PowerPoint presentation, 2010, http://www.mpa.gov/pdf/fac/10mtg_apr20_22/cc_cape_romain_kevin_godsea.pdf.

17. Justin Gillis, "As Glaciers Melt, Scientists Seek Data on Rising Seas," *New York Times*, November 13, 2010, 1.

18. John H. Tibbets, "Sea-Level Rise: Adapting to a Changing Coast," *Coastal Heritage* 24, no. 1 (2009): 3–11.

19. John H. Tibbets, "Rising Tide: Will Climate Change Drown Coastal Wetlands," *Coastal Heritage* 21, no. 3 (2007): 3–8.

20. U.S. Fish and Wildlife Service, "Draft Comprehensive Conservation Plan and Environmental Assessment: Ernest F. Hollings ACE Basin National Wildlife Refuge," April 2009, 71.

Epilogue

1. Dana Beach, Coastal Sprawl: The Effects of Urban Design on Aquatic Ecosystems in the United States (Arlington, Va.: Pew Oceans Commission, 2002).

2. Governors' South Atlantic Alliance, "Action Plan," 2009, http://www.south atlanticalliance.org/docs/Action_Plan_Final.pdf.

3. Ibid.

4. The Nature Conservancy, "The Nature Conservancy Applauds Governors' Formation of South Atlantic Alliance," press release, November 2, 2009.

alterniflora); spartina (*Spartina cynosuroides*)

crabbing, 103, 104–8; impact of, on diamondback terrapin, 274, 275, 276, 278, 279

crabs, 20, 51, 54, 282; associated with oyster reefs, 206, 283; green porcelain, 206; hermit, 107; horseshoe, 303; marsh, 44, 54, 57; mud, 197, 198; pea, 198; stone, 198; wharf, 44, 54; white-clawed mud, 55. *See also* blue crabs (*Callinectes sapidus*); fiddler crabs (*Uca*)

Credle, Larry, 307–10

Cumberland Harbour case, 180, 182

cunjuh (voodoo), 3, 135

dam, 47, 120, 121, 123; Hartwell, 116, 117; J. Strom Thurmond, 126, 127, 128, 129; mitigation of damage from, 126, 127; Richard B. Russell, 117

Dame, Richard, 200

Darien, Ga., 84, 109

DDT, 68, 267, 268, 287, 295, 298

decomposition: of algae; 64; of spartina, 49, 59, 229, 234. *See also* detritus

denitrification, 195

detritus, 5, 45, 49–50, 161, 166, 265; consumers of, 52, 53, 199; exported from marsh, 166–68, 200; importance of, 49–50, 51. *See also* outwelling

development, 7, 19, 32–33, 60–61, 62, 213; in coastal Georgia, 32–33; in coastal North Carolina, 88–90, 91, 92, 93; in coastal South Carolina, 188, 209–11, 273, 314, 319; effect of, on estuary, 75, 78, 92, 163, 329; effect of, on salt marsh, 250–51, 257, 285, 329; impact of, on Gullah

culture, 131–33, 141, 145, 146; impact of, on shellfish, 203, 207, 216; impact of, on tidal creeks, 66–69, 273, 278; impervious, 96; in Savannah River basin, 123, 124; secondary, 94

diatoms, 50, 51, 57, 168, 200

dikes, 161, 237, 239; in mosquito control 268, 269; in rice growing, 241, 242, 243. *See also* impoundments

dinoflagellates, 50, 107, 168

disturbance, 256, 263

docks, 131, 176, 180, 181, 190, 212; benefits of, 261–62; impact of, on salt marsh, 263, 265, 266, 273; proliferation of, 261–64, 266; shading from, 263–64

dolphins, Atlantic bottled-nosed, 31, 296, 306, 308; PCBs in, 284–85, 286, 288, 295; sickness in, 286–87; studied in coastal Georgia, 284; toluene in, 287, 295

Dorcas, Michael, 277, 278

dredging: of marsh, 170, 174, 176, 237, 244, 245; of Port Royal Sound, 185, 187, 188; of Savannah River ship channel, 118, 121, 122, 125

drought, 99, 127; and blue crab decline, 107, 108, 109; and marsh dieback, 225–27, 228

Duplin River, Ga., 151, 163, 164

Eastern oyster (*Crassostrea virginica*). *See* oysters

Eastern red cedar, 27, 30, 31, 248, 254

ebb tide, 35, 45, 166, 167

Edisto Beach (S.C.), 246, 320

Edisto Island (S.C.), 144, 246, 315, 319, 320

Edisto River, 311, 315, 317, 318, 319. *See also* ACE (Ashepoo, Cumbahee, Edisto) Basin (S.C.)

Emerald Pointe case (Ga.), 178–79, 180, 251–52, 253, 255, 259

estuary, 6, 163; characteristics of, 44–47; eutrophication in, 63, 65, 195; flushing of, 102, 126; food web in, 48, 49, 161; hypoxia in, 64, 195; impact of growth on, 63, 64, 65, 66, 70, 78–79; importance of fresh water in, 100–103, 107, 109, 110, 115, 330; mixing in, 46–47; nutrient trapping in, 45, 98, 165; and outwelling, 167–68; and oysters, 192–94, 197; pollution in, 18, 62, 163, 299; productivity in, 48, 50, 51, 115, 172, 322; riverine swamp relation to, 112, 114; river relation to, 103–4, 114, 119; and salt marsh, 44, 166–67, 172, 175; tidal rhythms in, 57; value of, 175, 176. See also salinity

fiddler crabs (*Uca*), 23–25, 54, 231–32; as food source, 62, 273, 279; during high tide, 54; during low tide, 56; mud (*Uca pugnax*), 44, 54, 231; pollution in, 285, 287, 292, 297, 298; red-jointed (brackish water; *Uca minax*), 44, 242; sand (*Uca pugilator*), 44, 54, 231

fish consumption guidelines, 18, 67, 91, 292

Florida, 38; barrier islands, 164; growth, 32–33, 95; marsh dieback in, 225; phosphate mining in, 170, 174; red drum fishing in, 281; sea level rise in, 323; seaside sparrow in, 267–70; shrimping in, 394

Floridan aquifer, 101, 295

flounder, 5, 53, 62, 313

food web, 48, 49–50, 98, 268; fiddler crabs in, 232; fungi in, 229; grass shrimp in, 234; mummichog in, 236;

pollutants in, 268, 285, 286–87, 292, 295, 297, 299

forest, maritime, 6, 21, 27, 165, 244, 254

Franklin, Chandra, 225

Fraser, Charles, 184–85, 186

fresh water, 100–103, 111, 114; in estuary, 44, 46, 119, 330; impact of land-use changes on, 108–9, 114; influence of, on marsh plants, 21, 23; in rice cultivation, 242; and salinity, 46–47, 101, 107, 110, 305, 313

freshwater flow, 102, 107, 242, 325; and blue crab disease, 108; dam impediment of, 116, 119, 121; in nutrient transport, 115; riverine swamp relation to, 114–15; sturgeon need for, 120–21. See also river flow

freshwater marshes, 37, 116

Frischer, Marc, 66

fungi, 26, 231, 234; in marsh dieback, 227–28; snail relation to, 229–30; in spartina decomposition, 48–49, 227. See also periwinkle snail

Georgia, 48, 50, 96; coastal growth in, 19, 32–33, 81, 96, 178, 183; estuaries, 48, 65, 103–4; marsh dieback, 223–26; salt marsh, 38, 50–51, 86, 174, 270; tides in, 38

Georgia Blue Crab Management Program, 106

Georgia Coastal Marshlands Protection Act, 237, 250; and bridges, 251, 253; challenges to, 178–79, 183; effectiveness of, 177, 178; passage of, 171–76, 329

Georgia Conservancy, 181, 251

Georgia Department of Natural Resources (DNR), 11, 108, 183, 274; and dock permitting, 266; and

mercury, 17, 289, 291, 292, 293
Mims, Edwin, 9, 10
mink, 49, 55, 57, 196, 256, 292
Moody Forest (Ga.), 113
Mount Pleasant, S.C., 72, 146
Morris, James T., 324
mosquito control, 111, 131, 235, 236; and
    dusky seaside sparrow, 266, 268, 269
mud, marsh, 12, 24, 27, 42, 54;
    anaerobic, 40, 41; effects of drought
    on, 226; in low marsh, 42–43;
    odor of, 12, 13, 21, 34; pluff, 12, 26;
    pollution in, 68, 297; pore water in,
    39–40
mudflat, 34, 39
mud snail (*Ilynassa obsoleta*), 35, 51, 56,
    228
mullet, 31, 285, 288
mummichogs, 18, 53, 234–36, 242, 298

National Oceanic and Atmospheric
    Administration (NOAA): and dock
    studies, 262; and dolphin studies,
    286, 295; and estuarine reserve
    system, 163; and shortnose sturgeon,
    128, 129
National Park Service, 74, 142, 154, 263
Nature Conservancy, 98, 126; ACE
    Basin protection by, 311, 314, 315, 317,
    319; islands donated to, 177; oyster
    study of, 194, 203, 207
nematodes, 26, 43, 53, 115, 234. *See also*
    meiofauna
Newell, Roger, 193
Newell, Steve, 229, 230, 233
Newton, Weston, 208
North Carolina, 38; barrier islands, 164;
    coastal growth in, 90–93, 94–95;
    oyster decline in, 203, 204, 206;
    shellfish farming in, 88, 89
nutrients, 4, 98, 102, 165, 232; in

eutrophication, 63–65; in marsh
    zonation, 25, 42, 43; in outwelling,
    167, 168; from rivers, 115; as
    supporting marsh growth, 35, 41, 45,
    227, 234

Ocmulgee River, 7, 97
Odum, Eugene, 5; and BASF fight, 185;
    ecology concepts of, 162, 165; and
    marine institute founding, 156–59;
    and marsh hammock protection,
    249, 250, 253, 254; and marsh
    protection in Georgia, 175–77;
    outwelling hypothesis of, 167–68,
    172, 173, 236
Ogeechee River, 100, 243, 265
outwelling, 167, 168, 172, 173, 175, 236
overfishing: of diamondback terrapin,
    272; of oysters, 193, 194, 203, 215, 268;
    of red drum, 280, 281, 282, 283; of
    sturgeon, 120, 121
oxygen, 36, 49, 41, 107; dissolved, 51, 64,
    65, 69, 121, 201; injection of, 123, 126;
    lack of, 172, 195
oyster canning, 214, 216, 221, 299;
    decline of, 217
oyster consumption, history of, 213–14,
    215
oyster reefs, 31, 192–94; decline of, 194,
    203–4; formation of, 197, 200, 201–2;
    importance of, 195, 197, 199–200;
    intertidal, 200, 201; restoration of,
    204–6; subtidal, 200; used by other
    species, 197–99, 201
oysters, 191, 192–93, 194–95, 201; in
    Chesapeake Bay, 193; decline of, 194,
    203–4; diseases of, 203; evolution
    of, 202–3; filtering capacity of, 53,
    191, 195; in Georgia, 194; harvesting
    of, 196–97, 216, 219; and hypoxia,
    64; intertidal, 201, 215; in North

oysters (*continued*)
  Carolina, 87–90, 93; and pollution, 65, 69, 207, 209; reproduction of, 202; and salinity, 47, 103; in South Carolina, 206–7; subtidal, 201. *See also* oyster reefs

painted bunting, 31, 257, 261, 270
palmetto tree, 2, 29, 30–31,
Park Island case (S.C.), 252, 259, 260, 261
Parshley, Daniel, 18–19
PCBs (polychlorinated biphenyls), 285, 287; Arochlor 1268, 289; in dolphins, 284–87; source of, 288–90, 291, 294
Pee Dee River, 45
periwinkle snail, 26, 44, 228, 229, 273; farming by, 229–30; at high tide, 53–54; implicated in marsh dieback, 227–28; at low tide, 56
Petersen, Bo, 72
Phillips, Charlie, 76–78, 79–80, 85, 86–87
Phillips, Mike, 85
Phillips community (S.C.), 73, 74
phytoplankton, 50, 64; as food source, 51, 52, 168, 195, 233
Pilkey, Orrin, 323
Pinckney, James, 298
Pin Point community (Ga.), 147–50, 245
plankton, 36, 192, 199, 235, 304
pollution, 3, 19, 78, 163, 186, 236; from growth, 71, 94, 123, 283; nonpoint-source, 67, 93, 94, 296; and oyster decline, 193, 203, 215; point-source, 71, 296; of tidal creeks, 67, 327
polychaetes, 44, 199, 234
Pomeroy, Lawrence, 51, 161, 162, 168
Pope, David, 33
pore water, 39–40

Port Royal Sound, 183, 187
primary production, 48, 50, 168, 231, 234, 245–46
Pulster, Erin, 286

raccoons, 55, 78, 199, 233
red cedar, 27, 30, 31, 248, 254
red drum, 44; conservation of, 279–83; pollution's effect on, 299; reproduction of, 283–84; tailing of, 53, 279
red-winged blackbirds, 14, 34, 57, 124
Reynolds, Richard J., Jr.: death of, 163; and Hog Hammock, 155; and marine institute founding, 156–58, 159, 161; as Sapelo Island purchaser, 154
ribbed mussels, 26, 230, 232–33
rice cultivation, 36, 113, 243, 318; and impoundments, 46, 237, 238, 242, 243, 310, 315
river flow, 44, 97, 102, 127; dam interference of, 47; nutrient transport by, 112, 119; salinity influenced by, 46, 47, 109, 119; and sturgeon reproduction, 121; swamp regulation of, 114

Saint Helena Island (S.C.), 133–34, 135, 136, 140–41, 143
Saint Johns River, 45, 268
Saint Simons Island (Ga.), 16, 98, 293
salinity, 20–21, 46, 102, 227; adaptation to, 47, 101, 114, 125, 305; and dredging, 121; and fresh water, 46–47, 101, 103, 107, 119, 325; and spartina, 160; zones, 46, 69
salt marsh, 4, 6, 20, 34; conservation of, 6, 19, 171–73; destruction of, 6, 71, 80, 239, 244–45; dieback of, 223–26; and docks, 261–66; and estuaries, 44; freshwater marsh, 37, 116; in

Georgia, 19, 38, 170–83; as nursery, 5, 44, 47; odor of, 12, 13, 40; organisms in, 20; origins of, 40–41; polluting of, 296–97; productivity in, 4–5, 20, 38, 47–50, 52, 166–68; and sea level rise, 322–25; as shelter, 5, 51; in South Carolina, 38, 183–89, 363; as storm protector, 5, 44; value of, 175, 176; as water cleanser, 5, 44. *See also* brackish water marsh; marsh restoration

salt marsh zones. *See* high marsh; levees; low marsh; zonation

salt pan, 26

saltwort, 25

Sanger, Denise, 66, 69, 95

Sapelo Island (Ga.), 154; early scientific studies on, 168, 169, 172, 174, 177, 253; ecology of, 164–67; Gullah-Geechee culture on, 151–53, 154–55; marine institute on, 155, 156–61, 162, 163, 164, 166, 171; shell ring on, 213

Sapelo Island National Estuarine Research Reserve, 163–64

Sapelo River, 76, 80, 85, 164, 193

Satilla River, 104, 106, 107, 113

Savannah, Ga., 147, 215, 240, 245, 264; industrial pollution in, 125; Pin Point community near, 147–50, 245; and sea level rise, 323

Savannah Harbor. *See* Savannah ship channel

Savannah National Wildlife Refuge, 117, 122, 124–25

Savannah River, 115, 116–19, 123, 125, 297; dredging of, 121, 125; flow restoration in, 127–28; and shortnose sturgeon, 120–21, 126; tide gate, 121–22

Savannah River Site, 118, 297

Savannah ship channel, 118, 123–24, 125

saw palmetto, 28–29, 32

Schneider, Todd, 11, 12, 13, 14, 62

Schwacke, Lori, 285, 286, 287, 295

Seabrook, Carl, 58, 60, 62

Seabrook, Jim, 13

Seabrook, Mildred, 58–59, 60

Seabrook, Wilson, 34, 60

sea islands, 1, 3, 37, 70, 169, 172; growth on, 132, 139, 244; and Gullah-Geechee, 130–31, 132, 152

sea level rise, 322; in coastal South Carolina, 314; and seaside sparrow, 270; along Southeast Atlantic coast, 322–25, 329, 330; theory of, 40

sediment, 36, 45, 50, 98, 224, 231–32; compaction of, 323; lack of, 324, 325; pollution in, 95, 285, 294, 297; and spartina, 40, 43

sedimentation, 270, 278

sheepshead, 53, 199, 232, 261

shellfish, 64, 69, 292; pollution in, 67, 70, 89–90, 93–95, 102, 201

Shipp, Bill, 178

shorebirds, 99, 105, 164

shrimp, 5, 44, 56, 304–5; brown, 304–5; cooking of, 61; grass, 18, 233–34, 287; pink, 304; and pollution, 68–69; and salt marsh, 52; snapping, 56, 261; white, 50, 304–5

shrimping industry, 52, 306; decline of, 302–3, 306–10; history of, 301–2

Silliman, Brian, 226–27, 228, 229, 230

Skidaway Institute of Oceanography, 62, 224, 264–65, 284, 299

Skidaway Island (Ga.), 20, 62, 66, 147, 247

Skidaway Island State Park (Ga.), 32, 245

Skidaway River, 20, 63, 64, 65, 245

smooth cord grass. *See* spartina (*Spartina alterniflora*)

Thomas, Clarence, 147, 148
Thurmond, Lake, 127–28, 129
Tibbetts, John H., 324–25
tidal creeks, 2, 18, 34, 35, 37, 243; docks on, 262–63; as early sentinels of estuarine degradation, 66; and headwaters, 69, 72; homesites on, 69, 73; impairment of, by impervious surfaces, 67–68, 70, 71; as nurseries, 69; salinity in, 47
Tidal Creeks Project, 66–69, 70, 79
tidal cycle, 39
tidal marsh restoration. *See* marsh restoration.
tides, 4, 6, 34–35, 165, 175; compared with circulatory system, 36; explanation of, 37–38; as transporters, 40–41, 45, 49, 160, 297, 304; and water mixing, 47. *See also* ebb tide; high tide; low tide; spring tide
Timmons, Edgar "Sonny," Sr., 195–96, 197, 199
Toomer, Larry, 217, 219, 220, 221–22
Toomer, Tina, 217, 219, 221–22
Topsail Island (N.C.), 87, 88
toxaphene, 17–18, 287, 288, 295, 298
Turtle River, 284, 288

University of Georgia, 86, 119, 156, 163, 241; dock study, 263; shrimping improvements by, 302; sparrow genetic study, 269; support of marsh protection legislation, 175, 176
University of Georgia Marine Institute, 155–61, 162, 163, 164, 166, 171
University of North Carolina, Wilmington, 91, 94

University of South Carolina, 324
upland edge, 21–23, 27, 255
U.S. Environmental Protection Agency (EPA), 118, 186, 289; atrazine study, 299; LCP Chemicals investigation, 291, 292, 293, 294; Superfund, 18, 288
U.S. Fish and Wildlife Service, 268; global warming concern of, 324; investigation of LCP Chemicals, 292–93; opposition of, to Savannah ship channel deepening, 125–26
U.S. Geological Survey, 101

Van Dolah, Bob, 72
Verity, Peter, 62–65, 66
voodoo (cunjuh), 3, 135

Walker, Randal, 204
wax myrtle, 27, 28, 32, 165, 254
Weis, Judith, 241
wetlands: banking, 239; buffering effects of, 114; loss of, 110, 113, 243; and no-net-loss policy, 239; restoration of, 241, 242. *See also* marsh restoration
Wharton, Charles, 114
Whitaker, J. David, 225, 245, 246
Wiegert, Richard, 103
Woodward, Spud, 65
wrack, 55, 56, 264, 265, 270

yaupon holly (*Ilex vomitoria*), 28, 165, 321

zonation: salinity, 46; in salt marsh, 21, 42, 160. *See also* high marsh; levees; low marsh; upland edge
zooplankton, 48, 50, 52, 98